CORTINA/GROSSET

BASIC

SPANISH

DICTIONARY

ENGLISH-SPANISH / SPANISH-ENGLISH

by
**Luis M. Laita, Ph.D., Instructor of Spanish
St. Mary's College, Notre Dame, Indiana**
and
Carmen Gil de Montes, F.G.E.

•

SERIES GENERAL EDITORS
Dilaver Berberi, Ph.D.
Edel A. Winje, Ed.D.

•

Under the Editorial Direction of
R. D. Cortina Co., Inc., New York

A GD/Perigee Book

Perigee Books
are published by
The Putnam Publishing Group
200 Madison Avenue
New York, New York 10016

Library of Congress catalog card number: 73-18525
ISBN 0-399-50959-3

First Perigee printing, 1983
Five previous Grosset & Dunlap printings
Printed in the United States of America
        5   6   7   8   9

Contents

How to Use This Dictionary _____ v
Key to Spanish Pronunciation _____ vii
Abbreviations _____ xi
English to Spanish _____ 1
Spanish to English _____ 161
Phrases for Use Abroad _____ 309
Menu Reader _____ 327
A Concise Spanish Grammar _____ 336

How to Use This Dictionary

This handy Dictionary was created especially for your needs as a traveler planning to spend a day, a month, or a year in a Spanish-speaking country. It can be used equally well by beginners and by readers who already have a knowledge of Spanish.

The entries number over 10,000 (5000-plus in the English-Spanish section, 5000-plus in the Spanish-English section). In choosing English entries, the needs and concerns of a traveler have been carefully considered: what situations is he most likely to encounter, and what words and phrases is he most likely to need to be able to say? Spanish entries were selected from words that occur most frequently in the course of everyday life in Spanish-speaking countries. Thus, you will find here the words you are actually hearing and seeing most often during your stay.

Special Features of This Dictionary

In addition to the entries themselves, this Dictionary includes the following extra features to enable you to actually use the Spanish language during your travels.

Guide to Pronunciation. The pronunciation of each Spanish entry is given in simple English alphabet transcriptions. Thus, the user can pronounce a new word immediately, just by following the simple guide which appears with each entry. The "Key to Spanish Pronunciation," found on page vii, explains Spanish sounds and gives examples of each one, and shows how they compare with English.

Concise Spanish Grammar. For the user who wishes a quick overview of Spanish grammar, or who wants an explanation of how verbs are conjugated or noun plurals formed, this

Grammar Section is an invaluable aid. It is divided into sections treating nouns, verbs, adjectives, adverbs, sentence formation, etc., for easy reference and use.

Helpful Notes for the Reader

1. *All verbs* are marked *v.*, and irregular verbs are marked *irreg*. There are tables of irregular verbs showing their conjugation at the end of the Dictionary, and the "Concise Grammar" explains the conjugation of regular verbs.

2. *Reflexive verbs* are those that have the suffix *-se*. These are always used with the reflexive pronoun. See the "Concise Grammar" for an explanation of the use of these verbs.

3. *All Spanish nouns* have a designated gender, and adjectives must agree in gender with the nouns they modify. Regularly, Spanish nouns which end in *o* are masculine and those which end in *a* are feminine. Exceptions to this rule, and all other Spanish nouns, are marked *m* or *f* in the Dictionary. Adjectives regularly have four forms for masculine and feminine, singular and plural, ending in *o*, *a*, *os*, and *as*. Irregular adjectives are marked in the Dictionary.

4. *Parts of speech* of entries (except verbs) are marked only if the translation does not indicate the part of speech or if the word appears as different parts of speech.

5. *Many common or idiomatic expressions* are included in the Dictionary, along with their pronunciation, so that the reader can use them correctly.

6. *In the Pronunciation Guide*, the Castilian pronunciation (that most commonly used in Spain) has been used. The differences between Castilian and Latin-American pronunciation are explained in the "Key to Spanish Pronunciation." Use of this pronunciation will not cause misunderstanding by Latin-Americans, as the differences are actually quite minor and also familiar to all speakers of Spanish.

Using this Dictionary before and during your trip is sure to make your contact with the Spanish people and their language much more pleasurable and satisfying.

Key to Spanish Pronunciation

Vowels

There are five vowel sounds in Spanish: *i, e, u, o, a*. Unlike the English vowels, Spanish vowels are always pronounced the same, no matter where they occur in a word. They are transcribed in this dictionary according to their approximate English pronunciation, as follows:

Spanish spelling	Phonetic symbol	Sound description & examples
a	ah	always pronounced like *a* in f*a*ther, c*a*rbon. *Ex.*: **casa** [*kah'-sah*] house; **cama** [*kah'-mah*] bed
e	eh	always pronounced like *e* in n*e*ver, b*e*t, *e*lement. *Ex.*: **elemento** [*eh-leh-mehn'-toh*] element; **tela** [*teh'-lah*] cloth
i	ee	pronounced like *ee* in p*ee*l, or like *ea* in *ea*t. *Ex.*: **mina** [*mee'-nah*] mine; **idiota** [*ee-dee-oh'-tah*] idiot
o	oh	always pronounced like *o* in n*o*rth, c*o*operation, or like *au* in P*au*l. *Ex.*: **norte** [*nohr'-teh*] north; **cooperación** [*koh-oh-peh-rah-thee-ohn'*] cooperation
u	oo	always pronounced like *u* in p*u*t, or like *oo* in f*oo*t. *Ex.*: **sucursal** [*soo-koor-sahl'*] branch; **puro** [*poo-roh*] pure

In Spanish spelling the vowel *u* in *ue* and *ui* after *g* and *q* is not pronounced unless it has a dieresis (two dots over a vowel to show that it is pronounced). Note:

    guitarra [*ghee-tah'-rrah*] guitar

    queso [*keh'-soh*] cheese

but **cigüeña** [*thee-goo-eh'-nyah*] stork

Diphthongs

For diphthongs, or two adjacent vowels, each vowel is transcribed with its phonetic symbol and with the accent on the more prominent vowel.

nación [*nah-thee-ohn'*] nation
huevo [*oo-eh'-voh*] egg
cooperación [*koh-oh-peh-rah-thee-ohn'*] cooperation

Consonants

Spanish consonants p, b, t, d, k, g, x, f, v, and ch are pronounced approximately like their English counterparts. The differences in other Spanish consonants are explained below:

Spanish spelling	Phonetic symbol	Sound description & examples
c	k	before vowels *a*, *o*, *u* and before consonants (including itself), pronounced like *k* in *k*ing. *Ex*.: **casa** [*kah'-sah*] house; **acción** [*ahk-thee-ohn'*] action
c	th	in Castilian Spanish before vowels *i* and *e*, pronounced like *th* in *th*ousand. *Ex*.: **cena** [*theh'-nah*] supper; **ciclo** [*thee'-kloh*] cycle
c	s	in Latin American Spanish before vowels *i* and *e*, pronounced like *s* in *s*alt. *Ex*.: **cena** [*seh'-nah*] supper; **ciclo** [*see'-kloh*] cycle

NOTE: This pronunciation of *c* before *i* and *e* and the use of the second person of the plural form of verbs are the only important differences between Castilian and Latin American Spanish. In this dictionary we use the symbol *th* to transcribe *c* before *i* and *e* as in the Castilian pronunciation.

g	g	pronounced like *g* in *g*ap before vowels *a*, *o*, *u* and before consonants. *Ex*.: **gato** [*gah'-toh*] cat; **goma** [*goh'-mah*] rubber; **Inglaterra** [*een-glah-teh'-rrah*] England

g	h	pronounced *h* as in *h*ot before vowels *i*, *e*. *Ex.*: **gitano** [*hee-tah'-noh*] gypsy; **gente** [*hehn'-teh*] pcoplc
g	gh	pronounced like *gh* in *gh*etto before vowels *ue* and *ui* where *u* is not pronounced. *Ex.*: **guerra** [*gheh'-rrah*] war; **guía** [*ghee'-ah*] guide
h		is never pronounced. *Ex.*: **héroe** [*eh-roh'-eh*] hero
j	h	pronounced like *h* in *h*ot. *Ex.*: **jamón** [*hah-mohn'*] ham
l	l	is always pronounced like the first *l* in *l*ittle, never like the second one. *Ex.*: **local** [*loh-kahl'*] place
ll	y	generally pronounced like *y* in *y*es; but in Castilian is pronounced like *lli* in bi*lli*ard and in Argentina like *sh* in *sh*ip. *Ex.*: **calle** [*kah'-yeh*] street; **calle** [*kah'-lyeh*] street; **calle** [*kah'-sheh*] street
ñ	ny	pronounced like *ny* in ca*ny*on. *Ex.*: **año** [*ah'-nyoh*] year
r	r	at the beginning of a word, pronounced like an *rr* (see below); otherwise *r* is pronounced like a British *r* (tip of the tongue more forward than with the American *r*). *Ex.*: **rama** [*rah'-mah*] branch; **para** [*pah'-rah*] for
rr	rr	pronounced with the tip of the tongue vibrating behind the upper teeth. *Ex.*: **carro** [*kah'-rroh*] car; **perro** [*peh'-rroh*] dog
y	y	pronounced like *y* in *y*es before vowels. *Ex.*: **yo** [*yoh*] I; **ya** [*yah*] already
y	ee	after vowels, pronounced like *ee* in f*ee*t. *Ex.*: **hoy** [*oh'-ee*] today
z	th	in Castilian Spanish pronounced like *th* in *th*ousand. *Ex.*: **zanja** [*thahn'-hah*] ditch; **cerveza** [*thehr-veh'-thah*] beer

| z | s | in Latin American Spanish, pronounced like *s* in *sin*. *Ex.*: **zanja** [*san'-hah*] ditch; **cerveza** [*sehr-veh'-sah*] beer |

Stress

When the accent is marked in Spanish spelling, the stress then falls on the accented vowel:

jabón [*hah-bohn'*] soap
lástima [*lahs'-tee-mah*] pity, shame

For Spanish words which do not carry the accent in spelling and which end in a vowel or *n* or *s*, the stress falls on the next to the last syllable; otherwise the stress falls on the last syllable:

paso [*pah'-soh*] step, pass
peligro [*peh-lee'-groh*] danger
datos [*dah'-tohs*] information
hablan [*ah'-blahn*] they speak
realidad [*reh-ah-lee-dahd'*] reality
recuperar [*reh-koo-peh-rahr'*] recuperate

Abbreviations Used in This Dictionary

adj.	adjective	*irreg.*	irregular
adv.	adverb	*m.*	masculine
anat.	anatomy	*naut.*	nautical
arch.	architecture	*n.*	noun
art.	article	*obj.*	object
Aux.	auxiliary verb	*pers.*	person, personal
conj.	conjunction	*pl.*	plural
dem.	demonstrative	*prep.*	preposition
eccl.	ecclesiastic	*pron.*	pronoun
f.	feminine	*rel.*	relative
interj.	interjection	*sing.*	singular
interr.	interrogative	*subj.*	subject
invar.	invariable	*v.*	verb

English/Spanish

A

a, un, uno, una [*oon, oo'-noh, oo'-nah*]
abandon *v.,* abandonar [*ah-bahn-doh-nahr'*]
ability, capacidad (f) [*kah-pah-thee-dahd'*]
able, capaz [*kah-pahth'*]
  be able *v.,* poder (irreg) [*poh-dehr'*]
aboard, a bordo [*ah bohr'-doh*]
abolish *v.,* suprimir [*soo-pree-meer'*]
abound *v.,* abundar [*ah-boon-dahr'*]
about *adv.,* casi [*kah'-see*]
about *prep.,* acerca de [*ah-thehr'-kah deh*]
above, arriba [*ah-rree'-bah*]
above all, sobre todo [*soh'-breh toh'-doh*]
abroad, en el extranjero [*ehn ehl ehks-trahn-heh'-roh*]
absence, ausencia [*ah-oo-sehn'-thee-ah*]
absent, ausente [*ah-oo-sehn'-teh*]
absent-minded, distraído [*dees-trah-ee'-doh*]
absolute, absoluto [*ahb-soh-loo'-toh*]
absolutely, absolutamente [*ahb-soh-loo-tah-mehn'-teh*]
absorb *v.,* absorber [*ahb-sohr-behr'*]
absorbed, absorto [*ahb-sohr'-toh*]
abstract *adj.,* abstracto [*ahbs-trahk'-toh*]
abstract *n.,* resumen (m) [*reh-soo'-mehn*]
abstraction, abstracción (f) [*ahbs-trahk-thee-ohn'*]
absurd, absurdo [*ahb-soor'-doh*]
abundance, abundancia [*ahb-oon-dahn'-thee-ah*]
abundant, abundante [*ah-boon-dahn'-teh*]
abuse *v.,* abusar [*ah-boo-sahr'*]
academy, academia [*ah-kah-deh'-mee-ah*]
accelerator, acelerador (m) [*ah-theh-leh-rah-dohr'*]
accent *n.,* acento [*ah-thehn'-toh*]
accent *v.,* acentuar [*ah-thehn-too-ahr'*]
accept *v.,* aceptar [*ah-thehp-tahr'*]

1

acceptable, aceptable [*ah-thehp-tah'-bleh*]
acceptance, aceptación (f) [*ah-thehp-tah-thee-ohn'*]
access, acceso [*ahk-theh'-soh*]
accessible, accesible [*ahk-theh-see'-bleh*]
accident, accidente (m) [*ahk-thee-dehn'-teh*]
accidental, accidental [*ahk-thee-dehn-tahl'*]
accommodate *v.*, acomodar [*ah-koh-moh-dahr'*]
accommodation, acomodación (f) [*ah-koh-moh-dah-thee-ohn'*]
accompany *v.*, acompañar [*ah-kohm-pah-nyahr'*]
accomplish *v.*, realizar [*reh-ah-lee-thahr'*]
accomplishment, realización (f) [*reh-ah-lee-thah-thee-ohn'*]
accord, acuerdo [*ah-koo-ehr'-doh*]
accordingly, en conformidad [*ehn kohn-fohr-mee-dahd'*]
according to, según [*seh-goon'*]
account *n.*, cuenta [*koo-ehn'-tah*]
   bank account, cuenta corriente [*koo-ehn'-tah koh-rree-ehn'-teh*]
   pay an account, pagar una cuenta [*pah-gahr' oo'-nah koo-ehn'-tah*]
account for *v.*, explicar, responder de [*ehks-plee-kahr', rehs-pohn-dehr' deh*]
accuracy, precisión (f) [*preh-thee-see-ohn'*]
accurate, preciso [*preh-thee'-soh*]
accusation, acusación (f) [*ah-koo-sah-thee-ohn'*]
accuse *v.*, acusar [*ah-koo-sahr'*]
accused, acusado [*ah-koo-sah'-doh*]
accustom *v.*, acostumbrar [*ah-kohs-toom-brahr'*]
ache *n.*, dolor (m) [*doh-lohr'*]
   headache, dolor (m) de cabeza [*doh-lohr' deh kah-beh'-thah*]
ache *v.*, doler (irreg) [*doh-lehr'*]
achieve *v.*, llevar a cabo [*yeh-vahr' ah kah'-boh*]
acid, ácido [*ah'-thee-doh*]
acknowledge *v.*, reconocer (irreg), agradecer (irreg) [*reh-koh-noh-thehr', ah-grah-deh-thehr'*]
acquaint *v.*, familiarizar [*fah-mee-lee-ah-ree-thahr'*]
acquaintance, conocimiento [*koh-noh-thee-mee-ehn'-toh*]
acquire *v.*, adquirir [*ahd-kee-reer'*]
acquisition, adquisición (f) [*ahd-kee-see-thee-ohn'*]

acquit v., absolver (irreg) [ahb-sohl-vehr']
acre, acre (m) [ah'-kreh]
across, a través, al otro lado [ah trah-vehs', ahl oh'-troh lah'-doh]
act n., acto [ahk'-toh]
act v., actuar [ahk-too-ahr']
action, acción (f) [ahk-thee-ohn']
active, activo [ahk-tee'-voh]
activity, actividad (f) [ahk-tee-vee-dahd']
actor, actor (m) [ahk-tohr']
actress, actriz (f) [ahk-treeth']
actual, real [reh-ahl']
actually, realmente [reh-ahl'-mehn-teh]
adapt v., adaptar [ah-dahp-tahr']
add v., añadir [ah-nyah-deer']
addition, adición (f) [ah-dee-thee-ohn']
additional, adicional [ah-dee-thee-oh-nahl']
address [place], dirección (f) [dee-rehk-thee-ohn']
address [speech], discurso [dees-koor'-soh]
address [a letter] v., escribir la dirección [ehs-kree-beer' lah dee-rehk-thee-ohn']
address [speak to] v., dirigirse a [dee-ree-heer'-seh ah]
adept, adepto [ah-dehp'-toh]
adequate, adecuado [ah-deh-koo-ah'-doh]
adhesive tape, cinta adhesiva [theen'-tah ahd-eh-see'-vah]
adjacent, adyacente [ahd-yah-thehn'-teh]
adjective, adjetivo [ahd-heh-tee'-voh]
adjoining, colindante [koh-leen-dahn'-teh]
adjust v., ajustarse [ah-hoos-tahr'-seh]
adjustment, ajuste (m) [ah-hoos'-teh]
administer v., administrar [ahd-mee-nees-trahr']
administration, administración (f) [ahd-mee-nees-trah-thee-ohn']
admirable, admirable [ahd-mee-rah'-bleh]
admiral, almirante (m) [ahl-mee-rahn'-teh]
admiration, admiración (f) [ahd-mee-rah-thee-ohn']
admire v., admirar [ahd-mee-rahr']
admirer, admirador (m) [ahd-mee-rah-dohr']

admission, admisión (f) [*ahd-mee-see-ohn'*]
admit *v.,* admitir [*ahd-mee-teer'*]
admittance, admisión (f) [*ahd-mee-see-ohn'*]
  no admittance, se prohibe entrar [*seh proh-ee'-beh ehn-trahr'*]
admonish *v.,* amonestar [*ah-moh-nehs-tahr'*]
adopt *v.,* adoptar [*ah-dohp-tahr'*]
adoption, adopción (f) [*ah-dohp-thee-ohn'*]
adore *v.,* adorar [*ah-doh-rahr'*]
adorn *v.,* adornar [*ah-dohr-nahr'*]
adult, adulto [*ah-dool'-toh*]
advance *n.,* avance (m) [*ah-vahn'-theh*]
  in advance, por anticipado [*pohr ahn-tee-thee-pah'-doh*]
advance *v.,* avanzar [*ah-vahn-thahr'*]
advancement, avance (m), anticipo [*ah-vahn'-theh, ahn-tee-thee'-poh*]
advantage, ventaja [*vehn-tah'-hah*]
adventure, aventura [*ah-vehn-too'-rah*]
adverb, adverbio [*ahd-vehr'-bee-oh*]
adversary, adversario [*ahd-vèhr-sah'-ree-oh*]
adverse, adverso [*ahd-vehr'-soh*]
adversity, adversidad (f) [*ahd-vehr-see-dahd'*]
advertise *v.,* anunciar [*ah-noon-thee-ahr'*]
advertisement, anuncio [*ah-noon'-thee-oh*]
advice, consejo [*kohn-seh'-hoh*]
advise *v.,* aconsejar [*ah-kohn-seh-hahr'*]
affair, asunto, amorío [*ah-soon'-toh, ah-moh-ree'-oh*]
affect *v.,* afectar [*ah-fehk-tahr'*]
affected, afectado [*ah-fehk-tah'-doh*]
affection, afecto, cariño [*ah-fehk'-toh, kah-ree'-nyoh*]
affectionate, afectuoso, cariñoso [*ah-fehk-too-oh'-soh, kah-ree-nyoh'-soh*]
affirm *v.,* afirmar [*ah-feer-mahr'*]
affirmative, afirmativo [*ah-feer-mah-tee'-voh*]
afflict *v.,* afligir [*ah-flee-heer'*]
afford *v.,* proporcionar, poder, permitirse [*proh-pohr-thee-oh-nahr', poh-dehr', pehr-mee-teer'-seh*]
afloat, a flote, sin rumbo [*ah floh'-teh, seen room'-boh*]

afraid, asustado [*ah-soos-tah'-doh*]
  be afraid *v.*, tener miedo, estar asustado [*teh-nehr' mee-eh'-doh, ehs-tahr' ah-soos-tah'-doh*]
Africa, Africa [*ah'-free-kah*]
African, africano [*ah-free-kah'-noh*]
after, después [*dehs-poo-ehs'*]
  after all, después de todo, al fin y al cabo [*dehs-poo-ehs' deh toh'-doh, ahl feen' ee ahl kah'-boh*]
afternoon, tarde (f) [*tahr'-deh*]
afterwards, después [*dehs-poo-ehs'*]
again, otra vez [*oh'-trah vehth*]
  never again, nunca más [*noon'-kah mahs*]
  once again, una vez más [*oo'-nah vehth mahs*]
against, contra [*kohn'-trah*]
age *n.*, edad (f) [*eh-dahd'*]
age *v.*, envejecer (irreg) [*ehn-veh-heh-thehr'*]
agency, agencia [*ah-hehn'-thee-ah*]
  travel agency, agencia de viajes [*ah-hehn'-thee-ah deh vee-ah'-hehs*]
agent, agente (m) [*ah-hehn'-teh*]
aggravate *v.*, agravar [*ah-grah-vahr'*]
aggression, agresión (f) [*ah-greh-see-ohn'*]
aggressive, agresivo [*ah-greh-see'-voh*]
ago, hace [*ah'-theh*]
agony, agonía [*ah-goh-nee'-ah*]
agree *v.*, estar de acuerdo [*ehs-tahr' deh ah-koo-ehr'-doh*]
agreeable, agradable [*ah-grah-dah'-bleh*]
agreement, acuerdo [*ah-koo-ehr'-doh*]
agriculture, agricultura [*ah-gree-kool-too'-rah*]
ahead, delante [*deh-lahn'-teh*]
  Go ahead! ¡Adelante! [*ah-deh-lahn'-teh*]
aid *n.*, ayuda, auxilio [*ah-yoo'-dah, ah-oo-ksee'-lee-oh*]
  first aid, primeros auxilios [*pree-meh'-rohs ah-oo-ksee'-lee-ohs*]
aid *v.*, auxiliar [*ah-oo-ksee-lee-ahr'*]
aim *n.*, blanco, intento [*blahn'-koh, een-tehn'-toh*]
aim *v.*, apuntar, intentar [*ah-poon-tahr', een-tehn-tahr'*]
air, aire (m) [*ah'-ee-reh*]

air-conditioning, aire acondicionado [*ah'-ee-reh ah-kohn-dee-thee-oh-nah'-doh*]

airline, linea aérea [*lee'-neh-ah ah-eh'-reh-ah*]

air mail, correo aéreo, por avión [*koh-rreh'-oh ah-eh'-reh-oh, pohr ah-vee-ohn'*]

airplane, avión (m) [*ah-vee-ohn'*]

airport, aeropuerto [*ah-eh-roh-poo-ehr'-toh*]

aisle, pasillo, nave (f) [*pah-see'-yoh, nah'-veh*]

alarm *n.,* alarma [*ah-lahr'-mah*]

alarm *v.,* alarmar [*ah-lahr-mahr'*]

alarm clock, despertador (m) [*dehs-pehr-tah-dohr'*]

alcohol, alcohol (m) [*ahl-koh-ohl'*]

ale, cerveza [*thehr-veh'-thah*]

alert *adj.,* alerta [*ah-lehr'-tah*]

alert *v.,* alertar [*ah-lehr-tahr'*]

alike, semejantes [*seh-meh-hahn'-tehs*]

alive, vivo [*vee'-voh*]

all, todo [*toh'-doh*]

all right, está bién [*ehs-tah' bee-ehn'*]

alleged, alegado [*ah-leh-gah'-doh*]

alley, callejón (m) [*kah-yeh-hohn'*]

allied, aliado [*ah-lee-ah'-doh*]

allow *v.,* permitir [*pehr-mee-teer'*]

allowance, permiso, concesión (f) [*pehr-mee'-soh, kohn-theh-see-ohn'*]

almost, casi [*kah'-see*]

alone, solo [*soh'-loh*]

along, a lo largo de [*ah loh lahr'-goh deh*]

alongside of, al costado de [*ahl kohs-tah'-doh deh*]

aloud, en voz alta [*ehn vohth' ahl'-tah*]

already, ya [*yah*]

also, también [*tahm-bee-ehn'*]

altar, altar (m) [*ahl-tahr'*]

alter *v.,* alterar [*ahl-teh-rahr'*]

although, aunque [*ah-oon'-keh*]

altitude, altitud (f) [*ahl-tee-tood'*]

always, siempre [*see-ehm'-preh*]

am: I am, soy, estoy [*soh'-ee, ehs-toh'-ee*]

amaze v., asombrar [ah-sohm-brahr']
amazement, asombro [ah-sohm'-broh]
ambassador, embajador (m) [ehm-bah-hah-dohr']
amber, ámbar (m) [ahm'-bahr]
ambition, ambición (f) [ahm-bee-thee-ohn']
ambitious, ambicioso [ahm-bee-thee-oh'-soh]
ambulance, ambulancia [ahm-boo-lahn'-thee-ah]
amends pl., enmienda [ehn-mee-ehn'-dah]
America, América [ah-meh'-ree-kah]
  North America, Norte América [nohr'-teh ah-meh'-ree-kah]
  South America, Sudamérica [sood-ah-meh'-ree-kah]
American, americano [ah-meh-ree-kah'-noh]
ammunition, munición (f) [moo-nee-thee-ohn']
among, entre [ehn'-treh]
amount n., importe (m), cantidad (f) [eem-pohr'-teh, kahn-tee-dahd']
amount v., ascender a (irreg) [ahs-thehn-dehr' ah]
ample, amplio [ahm'-plee-oh]
amuse v., divertir (irreg) [dee-vehr-teer']
amusement, diversión (f) [dee-vehr-see-ohn']
an, un [oon]
analysis, análisis (m) [ah-nah'-lee-sees]
anarchy, anarquía [ah-nahr-kee'-ah]
ancestor, antepasado [ahn-teh-pah-sah'-doh]
anchor n., ancla [ahn'-klah]
anchor v., anclar, sujetar [ahn-klahr', soo-heh-tahr']
anchovy, anchoa [ahn-choh'-ah]
ancient, antiguo [ahn-tee'-goo-oh]
and, y [ee]
anecdote, anécdota [ah-nehk'-doh-tah]
angel, ángel (m) [ahn'-hehl]
anger, cólera [koh'-leh-rah]
angle, ángulo [ahn'-goo-loh]
angry, enojado [eh-noh-hah'-doh]
  get angry v., enojarse [eh-noh-hahr'-seh]
anguish, angustia [ahn-goos'-tee-ah]
animal, animal (m) [ah-nee-mahl']
animate adj., animado [ah-nee-mah'-doh]

animate v., animar [ah-nee-mahr']

ankle, tobillo [toh-bee'-yoh]

anniversary, aniversario [ah-nee-vehr-sah'-ree-oh]

announce v., anunciar [ah-noon-thee-ahr']

announcement, anuncio [ah-noon'-thee-oh]

annoy v., molestar [moh-lehs-tahr']

annoying, molesto [moh-lehs'-toh]

annual, anual [ah-noo-ahl']

anonymous, anónimo [ah-noh'-nee-moh]

another, otro [oh'-troh]

answer n., respuesta [rehs-poo-ehs'-tah]

answer v., responder [rehs-pohn-dehr']

ant, hormiga [ohr-mee'-gah]

anticipate v., anticipar, prever (irreg) [ahn-tee-thee-pahr', preh-vehr']

antidote, antídoto [ahn-tee'-doh-toh]

antique n., antigüedades (pl) [ahn-tee-goo-eh-dah'-dehs]
    antique dealer, anticuario [ahn-tee-koo-ah'-ree-oh]

antiquity, antigüedad (f) [ahn-tee-goo-eh-dahd']

anxious, ansioso, inquieto [ahn-see-oh'-soh, een-kee-eh'-toh]

any, algún [ahl-goon']

anybody, alguien [ahl'-ghee-ehn]

anyhow, de todos modos [deh toh'-dohs moh'-dohs]

anything, algo [ahl'-goh]

anyway, de cualquier modo [deh koo-ahl-kee-ehr' moh'-doh]

anywhere, en cualquier parte [ehn koo-ahl-kee-ehr' pahr'-teh]

apart, aparte [ah-pahr'-teh]

apartment, apartamento, piso [ah-pahr-tah-mehn'-toh, pee'-soh]

apartment house, casa de apartamentos [kah'-sah deh ah-pahr-tah-mehn'-tohs]

apiece, cada uno [kah'-dah oo'-noh]

apologize v., excusarse [ehks-koo-sahr'-seh]

apology, excusa [ehks-koo'-sah]

apparatus, aparato [ah-pah-rah'-toh]

apparent, aparente [ah-pah-rehn'-teh]

apparently, aparentemente [ah-pah-rehn-teh-mehn'-teh]

appeal *n*., atracción (f), apelación (f) [*ah-trahk-thee-ohn'*, *ah-peh-lah-thee-ohn'*]

appeal *v*., apelar, atraer (irreg) [*ah-peh-lahr'*, *ah-trah-ehr'*]

appear *v*., aparecer (irreg) [*ah-pah-reh-thehr'*]

appearance, apariencia [*ah-pah-ree-ehn'-thee-ah*]

appendicitis, apendicitis (m) [*ah-pehn-dee-thee'-tees*]

appetite, apetito [*ah-peh-tee'-toh*]

applaud *v*., aplaudir [*ah-plah-oo-deer'*]

applause, aplauso [*ah-plah-oo'-soh*]

apple, manzana [*mahn-thah'-nah*]

apple pie, pastel de manzana [*pahs-tehl' deh mahn-thah'-nah*]

apple tree, manzano [*mahn-thah'-noh*]

applicant, solicitante (m, f) [*soh-lee-thee-tahn'-teh*]

application, solicitud (f) [*soh-lee-thee-tood'*]

apply *v*., aplicar [*ah-plee-kahr'*]

appoint *v*., designar, emplear [*deh-seeg-nahr'*, *ehm-pleh-ahr'*]

appointment, cita, puesto [*thee'-tah, poo-ehs'-toh*]

appreciate *v*., apreciar [*ah-preh-thee-ahr'*]

apprehend *v*., prender [*prehn-dehr'*]

apprentice, aprendiz (m) [*ah-prehn-deeth'*]

approach *n*., acercamiento [*ah-thehr-kah-mee-ehn'-toh*]

approach *v*., acercar [*ah-thehr-kahr'*]

appropriate *adj*., apropiado [*ah-proh-pee-ah'-doh*]

appropriate *v*., apropiarse [*ah-proh-pee-ahr'-seh*]

approval, aprobación (f) [*ah-proh-bah-thee-ohn'*]

approve *v*., aprobar (irreg) [*ah-proh-bahr'*]

approximately, aproximadamente [*ah-proh-ksee-mah-dah-mehn'-teh*]

April, abril [*ah-breel'*]

apron, delantal (m) [*deh-lahn-tahl'*]

Arab, árabe [*ah'-rah-beh*]

arbitrary, arbitrario [*ahr-bee-trah'-ree-oh*]

arch, arco [*ahr'-koh*]

architect, arquitecto [*ahr-kee-tehk'-toh*]

architecture, arquitectura [*ahr-kee-tehk-too'-rah*]

area, área [*ah'-reh-ah*]

Argentina, Argentina [*ahr-hehn-tee'-nah*]

Argentine, argentino [*ahr-hehn-tee'-noh*]
argue *v.*, argüir (irreg) [*ahr-goo-eer'*]
argument, discusión (f) [*dees-koo-see-ohn'*]
arid, árido [*ah'-ree-doh*]
arise *v.*, levantarse [*leh-vahn-tahr'-seh*]
arisen, levantado [*leh-vahn-tah'-doh*]
aristocrat, aristócrata (m, f) [*ah-rees-toh'-krah-tah*]
aristocratic, aristocrático [*ah-rees-toh-krah'-tee-koh*]
arm *n.*, brazo, arma [*brah'-thoh, ahr'-mah*]
arm *v.*, armar [*ahr-mahr'*]
armchair, butaca [*boo-tah'-kah*]
army, ejército [*eh-hehr'-thee-toh*]
around, alrededor [*ahl-reh-deh-dohr'*]
arrange *v.*, disponer (irreg) [*dees-poh-nehr'*]
arrangement, disposición (f) [*dees-poh-see-thee-ohn'*]
arrest *n.*, arresto [*ah-rrehs'-toh*]
arrest *v.*, arrestar [*ah-rrehs-tahr'*]
arrival, llegada [*yeh-gah'-dah*]
arrive *v.*, llegar [*yeh-gahr'*]
arrogance, arrogancia [*ah-rroh-gahn'-thee-ah*]
art, arte (m), artes (f, pl) [*ahr'-teh, ahr'-tehs*]
artery, arteria [*ahr-teh'-ree-ah*]
article, artículo [*ahr-tee'-koo-loh*]
artificial, artificial [*ahr-tee-fee-thee-ahl'*]
artist, artista (m, f) [*ahr-tees'-tah*]
artistic, artístico [*ahr-tees'-tee-koh*]
as, como [*koh'-moh*]
  as much as, tanto como [*tahn'-toh koh'-moh*]
ascend *v.*, subir, ascender (irreg) [*soo-beer', ahs-thehn-dehr'*]
ascent, ascenso, subida [*ahs-thehn'-soh, soo-bee'-dah*]
ash, ceniza [*theh-nee'-thah*]
ashamed, avergonzado [*ah-vehr-gohn-thah'-doh*]
ashore, en tierra [*ehn tee-eh'-rrah*]
ashtray, cenicero [*theh-nee-theh'-roh*]
Asia, Asia [*ah'-see-ah*]
Asiatic, asiático [*ah-see-ah'-tee-koh*]
aside, a un lado [*ah oon lah'-doh*]
ask *v.*, preguntar [*preh-goon-tahr'*]

asleep, dormido [*dohr-mee'-doh*]
   fall asleep *v.*, dormirse (irreg) [*dohr-meer'-seh*]
asparagus, espárrago [*ehs-pah'-rrah-goh*]
aspiration, aspiración (f) [*ahs-pee-rah-thee-ohn'*]
aspire *v.*, aspirar [*ahs-pee-rahr'*]
aspirin, aspirina [*ahs-pee-ree'-nah*]
assault *v.*, asaltar [*ah-sahl-tahr'*]
assemble *v.*, montar [*mohn-tahr'*]
assembly, asamblea [*ah-sahm-bleh'-ah*]
assign *v.*, asignar [*ah-seeg-nahr'*]
assignment, asignación (f), lección (f) [*ah-seeg-nah-thee-ohn'*,
   lehk-thee-ohn']
assist *v.*, asistir [*ah-sees-teer'*]
assistance, asistencia [*ah-sees-tehn'-thee-ah*]
assistant, asistente (m), ayudante (m) [*ah-sees-tehn'-teh,
   ah-yoo-dahn'-teh*]
associate *n.*, asociado [*ah-soh-thee-ah'-doh*]
associate *v.*, asociar [*ah-soh-thee-ahr'*]
assorted, surtido [*soor-tee'-doh*]
assortment, surtido [*soor-tee'-doh*]
assume *v.*, asumir [*ah-soo-meer'*]
assumption, suposición (f) [*soo-poh-see-thee-ohn'*]
assurance, seguridad (f) [*seh-goo-ree-dahd'*]
assure *v.*, asegurar [*ah-seh-goo-rahr'*]
astonish *v.*, asombrar [*uh-sohm-brahr'*]
astonishing, asombroso [*ah-sohm-broh'-soh*]
astronomy, astronomía [*ahs-troh-noh-mee'-ah*]
at, en [*ehn*]
   at first, al principio [*ahl preen-thee'-pee-oh*]
   at once, enseguida [*ehn-seh-ghee'-dah*]
athletic, atlético [*aht-leh'-tee-koh*]
athletics, atletismo [*aht-leh-tees'-moh*]
Atlantic, Atlántico [*aht-lahn'-tee-koh*]
atmosphere, atmósfera [*aht-mohs'-feh-rah*]
atonement, reparación (f) [*reh-pah-rah-thee-ohn'*]
attach *v.*, pegar, juntar [*peh-gahr'*, *hoon-tahr'*]
attack *n.*, ataque (m) [*ah-tah'-keh*]
attack *v.*, atacar [*ah-tah-kahr'*]

attain *v.*, lograr [*loh-grahr'*]
attempt *v.*, intentar [*een-tehn-tahr'*]
attend *v.*, atender (irreg), asistir [*ah-tehn-dehr'*, *ah-sees-teer'*]
attendant, asistente (m) [*ah-sees-tehn'-teh*]
attention, atención (f) [*ah-tehn-thee-ohn'*]
attentive, atento [*ah-tehn'-toh*]
attic, ático [*ah'-tee-koh*]
attire, atavío [*ah-tah-vee'-oh*]
attitude, actitud (f) [*ahk-tee-tood'*]
attorney, abogado, procurador (m) [*ah-boh-gah'-doh*, *proh-koo-rah-dohr'*]
attract *v.*, atraer (irreg) [*ah-trah-ehr'*]
attraction, atracción (f) [*ah-trahk-thee-ohn'*]
attractive, atractivo [*ah-trahk-tee'-voh*]
auction, subasta [*soo-bahs'-tah*]
audience, audiencia [*ah-oo-dee-ehn'-thee-ah*]
August, agosto [*ah-gohs'-toh*]
aunt, tía [*tee'-ah*]
Australia, Australia [*ah-oos-trah'-lee-ah*]
Australian, australiano [*ah-oos-trah-lee-ah'-noh*]
Austria, Austria [*ah'-oos-tree-ah*]
Austrian, austríaco [*ah-oos-tree'-ah-koh*]
authentic, auténtico [*ah-oo-tehn'-tee-koh*]
author, autor (m) [*ah-oo-tohr'*]
authority, autoridad (f) [*ah-oo-toh-ree-dahd'*]
authorize *v.*, autorizar [*ah-oo-toh-ree-thahr'*]
automatic, automático [*ah-oo-toh-mah'-tee-koh*]
automobile, automóvil (m) [*ah-oo-toh-moh'-veel*]
autumn, otoño [*oh-toh'-nyoh*]
available, disponible [*dees-poh-nee'-bleh*]
avalanche, avalancha [*ah-vah-lahn'-chah*]
avenge *v.*, vengar [*vehn-gahr'*]
avenue, avenida [*ah-veh-nee'-dah*]
average *n.*, promedio [*proh-meh'-dee-oh*]
average *adj.*, medio [*meh'-dee-oh*]
avoid *v.*, evitar [*eh-vee-tahr'*]
awake *v.*, despertar (irreg) [*dehs-pehr-tahr'*]
awake *adj.*, despierto [*dehs-pee-ehr'-toh*]

award *n.*, premio [*preh'-mee-oh*]
award *v.*, adjudicar [*ahd-hoo-dee-kahr'*]
aware, enterado [*ehn-teh-rah'-doh*]
away, lejos [*leh'-hohs*]
  far away, muy lejos [*moo-ee' leh'-hohs*]
awful, horrible [*oh-rree'-bleh*]
awkward, torpe [*tohr'-peh*]
axe, hacha [*ah'-chah*]
axle, eje (m) [*eh'-heh*]

B

baby, nene (m), bebé (m) [*neh'-neh, beh-beh'*]
bachelor, soltero [*sohl-teh'-roh*]
back *n.*, espalda [*ehs-pahl'-dah*]
back *adv.*, atrás [*ah-trahs'*]
  be back, estar de vuelta (irreg) [*ehs-tahr' deh voo-ehl'-tah*]
back up *v.*, volverse atrás (irreg), echarse atrás [*vohl-vehr'-seh ah-trahs', eh-chahr'-seh ah-trahs'*]
backward, atrasado [*ah-trah-sah'-doh*]
bacon, tocino [*toh-thee'-noh*]
bad, malo [*mah'-loh*]
badge, insignia, placa [*een-seeg'-nee-ah, plah'-kah*]
badly, mal [*mahl*]
bad-tempered, de mal genio [*deh mahl heh'-nee-oh*]
baggage, equipaje (m) [*eh-kee-pah'-heh*]
bait, cebo [*theh'-boh*]
bake *v.*, cocinar al horno [*koh-thee-nahr' ahl ohr'-noh*]
bakery, panadería [*pah-nah-deh-ree'-ah*]
balance *n.*, balanza, balance (m), equilibrio [*bah-lahn'-thah, bah-lahn'-theh, eh-kee-lee'-bree-oh*]
balance *v.*, equilibrar [*eh-kee-lee-brahr'*]
balcony, balcón (m) [*bahl-kohn'*]
bald, calvo [*kahl'-voh*]
ball, pelota [*peh-loh'-tah*]

ballet, ballet [*bah'-leht*]
balloon, globo [*gloh'-boh*]
banana, plátano [*plah'-tah-noh*]
band, banda [*bahn'-dah*]
bandage *n.*, venda [*vehn'-dah*]
bandage *v.*, vendar [*vehn-dahr'*]
bandaid, esparadrapo [*ehs-pah-rah-drah'-poh*]
bank *n.*, banco [*bahn'-koh*]
bank *v.*, amontonar, depositar dinero [*ah-mohn-toh-nahr', deh-poh-see-tahr' dee-neh'-roh*]
bankruptcy, quiebra [*kee-eh'-brah*]
banquet, banquete (m) [*bahn-keh'-teh*]
baptism, bautismo [*bah-oo-tees'-moh*]
bar, bar (m), barra [*bahr, bah'-rrah*]
barber, barbero [*bahr-beh'-roh*]
bare *adj.*, desnudo [*dehs-noo'-doh*]
barefoot, descalzo [*dehs-kahl'-thoh*]
bargain *n.*, ganga, buen negocio [*gahn'-gah, boo-enh' neh-goh'-thee-oh*]
bargain *v.*, regatear, negociar [*reh-gah-teh-ahr', neh-goh-thee-ahr'*]
bark [of dog], ladrido [*lah-dree'-doh*]
barn, granero [*grah-neh'-roh*]
barracks, cuartel (m) [*koo-ahr-tehl'*]
barrel, barril (m) [*bah-rreel'*]
barricade *n.*, barricada [*bah-rree-kah'-dah*]
base *n.*, base (f) [*bah'-seh*]
basement, sótano [*soh'-tah-noh*]
basic, básico [*bah'-see-koh*]
basin, palangana [*pah-lahn-gah'-nah*]
basket, cesta [*thehs'-tah*]
bath, baño [*bah'-nyoh*]
   take a bath, tomar un baño [*toh-mahr' oon bah'-nyoh*]
bathe *v.*, bañar [*bah-nyahr'*]
bathing suit, traje (m) de baño [*trah'-heh deh bah'-nyoh*]
bathroom, cuarto de baño [*koo-ahr'-toh deh bah'-nyoh*]
bathtub, bañera, baño [*bah-nyeh'-rah, bah'-nyoh*]
battery, batería [*bah-teh-ree'-ah*]

battle, batalla [*bah-tah'-yah*]

bay, bahía [*bah-ee'-ah*]

be, ser (irreg), estar (irreg) [*sehr', ehs-tahr'*]

beach, playa [*plah'-yah*]

beads, cuentas (f, pl) [*koo-ehn'-tahs*]

beans, alubias, frijoles (m, pl) [*ah-loo'-bee-ahs, free-hoh'-lehs*]

bear [carry] *v.,* llevar [*yeh-vahr'*]

bear [endure] *v.,* sobrellevar [*soh-breh-yeh-vahr'*]

bear [give birth] *v.,* dar a luz (irreg) [*dahr ah looth*]

beard, barba [*bahr'-bah*]

beardless, imberbe [*eem-behr'-beh*]

beast, bestia [*behs'-tee-ah*]

beat [pulse] *n.,* latido [*lah-tee'-doh*]

beat [overcome] *v.,* batir [*bah-teer'*]

beat [pulsate] *v.,* latir [*lah-teer'*]

beautiful, bello [*beh'-yoh*]

beauty, belleza [*beh-yeh'-thah*]

beauty parlor, salón de belleza (m) [*sah-lohn' deh beh-yeh'-thah*]

because, porque [*pohr'-keh*]

because of, a causa de [*ah kah'-oo-sah deh*]

become *v.,* hacerse (irreg) [*ah-thehr'-seh*]

bed, cama [*kah'-mah*]

bedroom, dormitorio, alcoba [*dohr-mee-toh'-ree-oh, ahl-koh'-bah*]

bee, abeja [*ah-beh'-hah*]

beef, carne (f) de vaca o toro [*kahr'-neh deh vah'-kah oh toh'-roh*]

beefsteak, bistec (m) [*bees-tehk'*]

beer, cerveza [*thehr-veh'-thah*]

beet, remolacha [*reh-moh-lah'-chah*]

before [time], antes [*ahn'-tehs*]

before [place], delante de [*deh-lahn'-teh deh*]

beforehand, de antemano [*deh ahn-teh-mah'-noh*]

beg *v.,* rogar (irreg), solicitar [*roh-gahr', soh-lee-thee-tahr'*]

begin *v.,* empezar (irreg) [*ehm-peh-thahr'*]

beginning, comienzo [*koh-mee-ehn'-thoh*]

behave v., comportarse, conducirse (irreg) [*kohm-pohr-tahr'-seh, kohn-doo-theer'-seh*]

behavior, conducta, comportamiento [*kohn-dook'-tah, kohm-pohr-tah-mee-ehn'-toh*]

behind, detrás [*deh-trahs'*]

being, ser (m), ente (m) [*sehr, ehn'-teh*]

Belgian, belga [*behl'-gah*]

Belgium, Bélgica [*behl'-hee-kah*]

belief, creencia [*kreh-ehn'-thee-ah*]

believe v., creer [*kreh-ehr'*]

bell, campana, timbre (m) [*kahm-pah'-nah, teem'-breh*]

bellboy, botones (m, sing & pl) [*boh-toh'-nehs*]

belong v., pertenecer (irreg) [*pehr-teh-neh-thehr'*]

belongings, pertenencias (f, pl) [*pehr-teh-nehn'-thee-ahs*]

below adv., abajo [*ah-bah'-hoh*]

below prep., debajo (de) [*deh-bah'-hoh (deh)*]

belt, cinturón (m) [*theen-too-rohn'*]

beneath, debajo de [*deh-bah'-hoh deh*]

bench, banco [*bahn'-koh*]

bend v., doblar [*doh-blahr'*]

benefit, beneficio [*beh-neh-fee'-thee-oh*]

beside, al lado de, junto a [*ahl lah'-doh deh, hoon'-toh ah*]

besides, además [*ah-deh-mahs'*]

best adj., mejor [*meh-hohr'*]

best adv., óptimo, el mejor [*ohp'-tee-moh, ehl meh-hohr'*]

bet n., apuesta [*ah-poo-ehs'-tah*]

bet v., apostar (irreg) [*ah-pohs-tahr'*]

betray v., traicionar [*trah-ee-thee-oh-nahr'*]

better, mejor [*meh-hohr'*]

between, entre [*ehn'-treh*]

beware v., tener cuidado (irreg), guardarse de [*teh-nehr' koo-ee-dah'-doh, goo-ahr-dahr'-seh deh*]

beyond, más allá [*mahs' ah-yah'*]

Bible, Biblia [*bee'-blee-ah*]

bicycle, bicicleta [*bee-thee-kleh'-tah*]

bid n., oferta, declaración (f) [*oh-fehr'-tah, deh-klah-rah-thee-ohn'*]

bid v., ofrecer (irreg) [*oh-freh-thehr'*]

big, grande [*grahn'-deh*]
bill, cuenta, factura [*koo-ehn'-tah, fahk-too'-rah*]
bind *v.,* atar [*ah-tahr'*]
bird, pájaro [*pah'-hah-roh*]
birth, nacimiento [*nah-thee-mee-ehn'-toh*]
   give birth to *v.,* dar a luz (irreg) [*dahr ah looth*]
birthday, cumpleaños (m, sing & pl) [*koom-pleh-ah'-nyohs*]
   Happy birthday, Feliz cumpleaños [*feh-leeth' koom-pleh-ah'-nyohs*]
biscuit, bizcocho [*beeth-koh'-choh*]
bishop, obispo [*oh-bees'-poh*]
bit, poquito, pedazito [*poh-kee'-toh, peh-dah-thee'-toh*]
bite *v.,* morder (irreg) [*mohr-dehr'*]
bitter, amargo [*ah-mahr'-goh*]
black, negro [*neh'-groh*]
blade, hoja [*oh'-hah*]
blame *n.,* culpa [*kool'-pah*]
blame *v.,* culpar [*kool-pahr'*]
blank, en blanco [*ehn blahn'-koh*]
blanket, manta, frazada [*mahn'-tah, frah-thah'-dah*]
bleach *n.,* blanqueo [*blahn-keh'-oh*]
bleach *v.,* blanquear [*blahn-keh-ahr'*]
bleed *v.,* sangrar [*sahn-grahr'*]
bless *v.,* bendecir (irreg) [*behn-deh-theer'*]
blessing, bendición (f) [*behn-dee-thee-ohn'*]
blind, ciego [*thee-eh'-goh*]
blindness, ceguera [*theh-gheh'-rah*]
blister, ampolla [*ahm-poh'-yah*]
block *n.,* cuadras, manzana (Sp) [*koo-ah'-drahs, mahn-thah'-nah*]
blonde, rubio [*roo'-bee-oh*]
blood, sangre (f) [*sahn'-greh*]
blossom *n.,* brote (m) [*broh'-teh*]
blossom *v.,* florecer (irreg) [*floh-reh-thehr'*]
blouse, blusa [*bloo'-sah*]
blow *n.,* golpe (m), soplido [*gohl'-peh, soh-plee'-doh*]
blow *v.,* soplar, volar (irreg) [*soh-plahr', voh-lahr'*]
board *n.,* tablero, junta [*tah-bleh'-roh, hoon'-tah*]

board *v.*, subir a, embarcar(se) [*soo-beer' ah, ehm-bahr-kahr'-seh*]
boat, barco [*bahr'-koh*]
body, cuerpo [*koo-ehr'-poh*]
boil *v.*, hervir (irreg) [*ehr-veer'*]
bold, audaz, descarado [*ah-oo-dahth', dehs-kah-rah'-doh*]
Bolivia, Bolivia [*boh-lee'-vee-ah*]
Bolivian, boliviano [*boh-lee-vee-ah'-noh*]
bolt, cerrojo [*theh-rroh'-hoh*]
bond *n.*, vínculo [*veen'-koo-loh*]
bone, hueso [*oo-eh'-soh*]
  fishbone, espina [*ehs-pee'-nah*]
book, libro [*lee'-broh*]
bookcase, estante (m) [*ehs-tahn'-teh*]
bookstore, librería [*lee-breh-ree'-ah*]
boot, bota [*boh'-tah*]
border, borde (m), frontera [*bohr'-deh, frohn-teh'-rah*]
bore [drill] *n.*, taladro [*tah-lah'-droh*]
bore [a hole] *v.*, taladrar [*tah-lah-drahr'*]
boring, aburrido [*ah-boo-rree'-doh*]
born: to be born, nacer (irreg) [*nah-thehr'*]
borrow *v.*, pedir prestado (irreg) [*peh-deer' prehs-tah'-doh*]
boss, jefe (m) [*heh'-feh*]
both, ambos [*ahm'-bohs*]
bother *n.*, molestia [*moh-lehs'-tee-ah*]
bottle, botella [*boh-teh'-yah*]
  baby bottle, biberón (m) [*bee-beh-rohn'*]
bottom, fondo [*fohn'-doh*]
boundary, límite (m) [*lee'-mee-teh*]
bow *n.*, reverencia, arco [*reh-veh-rehn'-thee-ah, ahr'-koh*]
bow *v.*, reverenciar [*reh-veh-rehn-thee-ahr'*]
bow [of ship] *n.*, proa [*proh'-ah*]
box, caja [*kah'-hah*]
boxing, boxeo [*boh-kseh'-oh*]
box office, taquilla [*tah-kee'-yah*]
boy, muchacho [*moo-chah'-choh*]
bracelet, brazalete (m) [*brah-thah-leh'-teh*]
brag *v.*, jactarse [*hahk-tahr'-seh*]

braggart, fanfarrón (m) [*fahn-fah-rrohn'*]
braid *n.*, trenza [*trehn'-thah*]
braid *v.*, trenzar [*trehn-thahr'*]
brain, cerebro [*theh-reh'-broh*]
brake *n.*, freno [*freh'-noh*]
brake *v.*, frenar [*freh-nahr'*]
branch, rama, sucursal (f) [*rah'-mah, soo-koor-sahl'*]
brand *n.*, marca [*mahr'-kah*]
brand-new, flamante [*flah-mahn'-teh*]
brandy, coñac (m) [*koh-nyahk'*]
brass, latón (m) [*lah-tohn'*]
brassiere, ajustador (m) [*ah-hoos-tah-dohr'*]
brave, bravo [*brah'-voh*]
Brazil, Brasil [*brah-seel'*]
Brazilian, brasileño [*brah-see-leh'-nyoh*]
bread, pan (m) [*pahn*]
break *v.*, romper [*rohm-pehr'*]
breakdown, abatimiénto [*ah-bah-tee-mee-ehn'-toh*]
breakfast, desayuno [*deh-sah-yoo'-noh*]
   have breakfast, desayunar [*deh-sah-yoo-nahr'*]
breast, pecho [*peh'-choh*]
breath, respiración (f), aliento [*rehs-pee-rah-thee-ohn', ah-lee-ehn'-toh*]
breathe *v.*, respirar [*rehs-pee-rahr'*]
breeze, brisa [*bree'-sah*]
bribe *n.*, soborno [*soh-bohr'-noh*]
bribe *v.*, sobornar [*soh-bohr-nahr'*]
brick, ladrillo [*lah-dree'-yoh*]
bride, novia [*noh'-vee-ah*]
bridegroom, novio [*noh'-vee-oh*]
bridesmaid, dama de honor [*dah'-mah deh oh-nohr'*]
bridge *n.*, puente (m) [*poo-ehn'-teh*]
brief *adj.*, breve [*breh'-veh*]
bright, brillante [*bree-yahn'-teh*]
bring *v.*, traer (irreg) [*trah-ehr'*]
   bring me, tráigame [*trah'-ee-ghah-meh*]
   bring together, reunir [*reh-oo-neer'*]
   bring up, educar [*eh-doo-kahr'*]

brisk, animado [*ah-nee-mah'-doh*]
Britain, (gran) Bretaña [(*grahn*) *breh-tah'-nyah*]
British, británico [*bree-tah'-nee-koh*]
broad, amplio [*ahm'-plee-oh*]
broadcast *n.*, transmisión (f) [*trahns-mee-see-ohn'*]
broil *v.*, asar a la parrilla [*ah-sahr' ah lah pah-rree'-yah*]
broiled, a la parrilla [*ah lah pah-rree'-yah*]
broken, roto [*roh'-toh*]
bronze, bronce (m) [*brohn'-theh*]
brooch, broche (m) [*broh'-cheh*]
brook, arroyo [*ah-rroh'-yoh*]
broom, escoba [*ehs-koh'-bah*]
broth, caldo [*kahl'-doh*]
brother, hermano [*ehr-mah'-noh*]
brother-in-law, cuñado [*koo-nyah'-doh*]
brow, ceja [*theh'-hah*]
brown, castaño, moreno [*kahs-tah'-nyoh, moh-reh'-noh*]
bruise, contusión (f) [*kohn-too-see-ohn'*]
brunette, morena [*moh-reh'-nah*]
brush *n.*, cepillo, brocha [*theh-pee'-yoh, broh'-chah*]
brush *v.*, cepillar [*theh-pee-yahr'*]
bucket, cubo [*koo'-boh*]
buckle, hebilla [*eh-bee'-yah*]
budget, presupuesto [*preh-soo-poo-ehs'-toh*]
bug, bicho [*bee'-choh*]
build *v.*, construir (irreg) [*kohns-troo-eer'*]
building, edificio [*eh-dee-fee'-thee-oh*]
bulb [light], bombilla [*bohm-bee'-yah*]
bull, toro [*toh'-roh*]
bulletin, boletín (m) [*boh-leh-teen'*]
bullfight, corrida de toros [*koh-rree'-dah deh toh'-rohs*]
bullfighter, torero [*toh-reh'-roh*]
bumper [auto], parachoques (m, sing) [*pah-rah-choh'-kehs*]
bundle, fardo [*fahr'-doh*]
burden *n.*, carga [*kahr'-gah*]
bureau, escritorio, oficina [*ehs-kree-toh'-ree-oh, oh-fee-thee'-nah*]

burglar, ladrón (m) [*lah-drohn'*]
burial, entierro [*ehn-tee-eh'-rroh*]
burn *v.*, quemar [*keh-mahr'*]
burst *v.*, reventar (irreg) [*reh-vehn-tahr'*]
bury *v.*, enterrar (irreg) [*ehn-teh-rrahr'*]
bus, autobús, ómnibus (m) [*ah-oo-toh-boos', ohm'-nee-boos*]
bush, arbusto [*ahr-boos'-toh*]
business, negocio [*neh-goh'-thee-oh*]
businessman, hombre (m) de negocios [*ohm'-breh deh neh-goh'-thee-ohs*]
busy, ocupado [*oh-koo-pah'-doh*]
but, pero [*peh'-roh*]
butcher, carnicero [*kahr-nee-theh'-roh*]
butter, mantequilla [*mahn-teh-kee'-yah*]
butterfly, mariposa [*mah-ree-poh'-sah*]
button, botón (m) [*boh-tohn'*]
buy *v.*, comprar [*kohm-prahr'*]
buyer, comprador (m) [*kom-prah-dohr'*]
by, por, a, para [*pohr, ah, pah'-rah*]
   by chance, por casualidad [*pohr kah-soo-ah-lee-dahd'*]
   by the way, a propósito [*ah proh-poh'-see-toh*]
   by then, para entonces [*pah'-rah ehn-tohn'-thehs*]

C

cab, taxi (m) [*tah'-ksee*]
cabaret, cabaret (m) [*kah-bah-reht'*]
cabbage, repollo [*reh-poh'-yoh*]
cabin, cabaña, cabina [*kah-bah'-nyah, kah-bee'-nah*]
cable, cable (m) [*kah'-bleh*]
cafe, café (m) [*kah-feh'*]
cage, jaula [*hah'-oo-lah*]
cake, pastel (m), torta [*pahs-tehl', tohr'-tah*]
calendar, calendario [*kah-lehn-dah'-ree-oh*]
calf, ternero [*tehr-neh'-roh*]

call n., llamada [*yah-mah'-dah*]
  telephone call, llamada telefónica [*yah-mah'-dah teh-leh-foh'-nee-kah*]
call v., llamar [*yah-mahr'*]
  call on, visitar [*vee-see-tahr'*]
  call off, suspender [*soos-pehn-dehr'*]
calm n., calma [*kahl'-mah*]
calm adj., tranquilo [*trahn-kee'-loh*]
calm down v., calmarse [*kahl-mahr'-seh*]
camera, cámara [*kah'-mah-rah*]
camp n., campamento [*kahm-pah-mehn'-toh*]
camp v., acampar [*ah-kahm-pahr'*]
can n., lata, envase (m) [*lah'-tah, ehn-vah'-seh*]
can [to be able] v., poder (irreg) [*poh-dehr'*]
  I can run, Puedo correr [*poo-eh'-doh koh-rrehr'*]
  I can't run, No puedo correr [*noh poo-eh'-doh koh-rrehr'*]
Canada, Canadá [*kah-nah-dah'*]
Canadian, canadiense [*kah-nah-dee-ehn'-seh*]
canal, canal (m) [*kah-nahl'*]
cancel v., anular, cancelar [*ah-noo-lahr', kahn-theh-lahr'*]
candle, vela [*veh'-lah*]
candlestick, palmatoria [*pahl-mah-toh'-ree-ah*]
candy, dulce (m) [*dool'-theh*]
cane, bastón (m), caña [*bahs-tohn', kah'-nyah*]
  sugarcane, caña de azúcar [*kah'-nyah deh ah-thoo'-kahr*]
can opener, abrelatas (m) [*ah-breh-lah'-tahs*]
cap [headgear], gorra [*goh'-rrah*]
capable, capaz [*kah-pahth'*]
capacity, capacidad (f) [*kah-pah-thee-dahd'*]
cape [garment], capa [*kah'-pah*]
cape [point of land], cabo [*kah'-boh*]
capital [city], capital (f) [*kah-pee-tahl'*]
capital [money], capital (m) [*kah-pee-tahl'*]
captain, capitán (m) [*kah-pee-tahn'*]
car, automóvil (m) [*ah-oo-toh-moh'-veel*]
  streetcar, tranvía (m) [*trahn-vee'-ah*]
card, tarjeta [*tahr-heh'-tah*]
  calling card, tarjeta de visita [*tahr-heh'-ta deh vee-see'-tah*]

playing cards, naipes (m, pl) [*nah'-ee-pehs*]
cardboard, cartón (m) [*kahr-tohn'*]
care v., cuidar [*koo-ee-dahr'*]
  care about, preocuparse de [*preh-oh-koo-pahr'-seh deh*]
  care for [to like], gustar [*goos-tahr'*]
  take care of, cuidar de [*koo-ee-dahr' deh*]
career, carrera [*kah-rreh'-rah*]
careful, cuidadoso [*koo-ee-dah-doh'-soh*]
carefully, cuidadosamente [*koo-ee-dah-doh-sah-mehn'-teh*]
careless, descuidado [*dehs-koo-ee-dah'-doh*]
caress n., caricia [*kah-ree'-thee-ah*]
cargo, carga [*kahr'-gah*]
Caribbean Sea, Mar Caribe [*mahr kah-ree'-beh*]
carnival, carnaval (m) [*kahr-nah-vahl'*]
carpenter, carpintero [*kahr-peen-teh'-roh*]
carpet, alfombra [*ahl-fohm'-brah*]
carriage, carruaje (m) [*kah-rroo-ah'-heh*]
carry v., llevar [*yeh-vahr'*]
case [matter], caso [*kah'-soh*]
  in any case, en todo caso [*ehn toh'-doh kah'-soh*]
  in that case, en ese caso [*ehn eh'-seh kah'-soh*]
case [box], caja [*kah'-hah*]
cash n., dinero efectivo [*dee-neh'-roh eh-fehk-tee'-voh*]
cash v., cobrar [*koh-brahr'*]
cashier, cajero [*kah-heh'-roh*]
castanets, castañuelas (f, pl) [*kahs-tah-nyoo-eh'-lahs*]
Castilian, castellano [*kahs-teh-yah'-noh*]
castle, castillo [*kahs-tee'-yoh*]
casually, casualmente [*kah-soo-ahl-mehn'-teh*]
cat, gato [*gah'-toh*]
catalog, catálogo [*kah-tah'-loh-goh*]
Catalonian, catalán, catalana [*kah-tah-lahn', kah-tah-lah'-nah*]
catch v., coger [*koh-hehr'*]
cathedral, catedral (f) [*kah-teh-drahl'*]
Catholic, católico [*kah-toh'-lee-koh*]
cattle, ganado [*gah-nah'-doh*]
cauliflower, coliflor (f) [*koh-lee-flohr'*]

cause *n.*, causa [*kah'-oo-sah*]
cause *v.*, causar [*kah-oo-sahr'*]
caution *n.*, precaución (f) [*preh-kah-oo-thee-ohn'*]
cave, cueva [*koo-eh'-vah*]
cavity, cavidad (f) [*kah-vee-dahd'*]
cease *v.*, cesar [*theh-sahr'*]
ceiling, techo [*teh'-choh*]
celebrate *v.*, celebrar [*theh-leh-brahr'*]
celebration, celebración (f) [*theh-leh-brah-thee-ohn'*]
celery, apio [*ah'-pee-oh*]
cell, celda [*thehl'-dah*]
cellar, bodega [*boh-deh'-gah*]
cement *n.*, cemento [*theh-mehn'-toh*]
cement *v.*, cementar [*theh-mehn-tahr'*]
cemetery, cementerio [*theh-mehn-teh'-ree-oh*]
censorship, censura [*thehn-soo'-rah*]
cent, centavo [*thehn-tah'-voh*]
center, centro [*thehn'-troh*]
central heating, calefacción central (f) [*kah-leh-fahk-thee-ohn' thehn-trahl'*]
century, siglo [*see'-gloh*]
cereal, cereal (m) [*theh-reh-ahl'*]
ceremony, ceremonia [*theh-reh-moh'-nee-ah*]
certain, cierto [*thee-ehr'-toh*]
certainly, ciertamente [*thee-ehr-tah-mehn'-teh*]
certificate, certificado [*thehr-tee-fee-kah'-doh*]
certify *v.*, certificar [*thehr-tee-fee-kahr'*]
chain, cadena [*kah-deh'-nah*]
chair, silla [*see'-yah*]
challenge *n.*, desafío [*deh-sah-fee'-oh*]
challenge *v.*, desafiar [*deh-sah-fee-ahr'*]
champagne, champaña [*chahm-pah'-nyah*]
champion, campeón (m) [*kahm-peh-ohn'*]
chance, casualidad (f), oportunidad (f) [*kah-soo-ah-lee-dahd', oh-pohr-too-nee-dahd'*]
  by chance, por casualidad [*pohr kah-soo-ah-lee-dahd'*]
  take a chance, correr un albur [*koh-rrehr' oon ahl-boor'*]
change *n.*, cambio [*kahm'-bee-oh*]

change *v.*, cambiar [*kahm-bee-ahr'*]
channel, canal (m) [*kah-nahl'*]
chapel, capilla [*kah-pee'-yah*]
chapter, capítulo [*kah-pee'-too-loh*]
character, carácter (m) [*kah-rahk'-tehr*]
characteristic, característico [*kah-rahk-teh-rees'-tee-koh*]
charge [price] *n.*, precio [*preh'-thee-oh*]
charge [battery] *n.*, carga [*kahr'-gah*]
charge [a battery] *v.*, cargar [*kahr-gahr'*]
charm, encanto [*ehn-kahn'-toh*]
charming, encantador [*ehn-kahn-tah-dohr'*]
chart, mapa (m) [*mah'-pah*]
charter *v.*, alquilar [*ahl-kee-lahr'*]
chase *v.*, perseguir (irreg), cazar [*pehr-seh-gheer', kah-thahr'*]
chat *v.*, charlar [*chahr-lahr'*]
chauffeur, chofer (m) [*choh'-fehr*]
cheap, barato [*bah-rah'-toh*]
cheat *v.*, engañar, timar [*ehn-gah-nyahr', tee-mahr'*]
check [bank] *n.*, cheque (m) [*cheh'-keh*]
 baggage check, contraseña de equipaje [*koh-trah-seh'-nyah dch ch-kee-pah'-heh*]
 checking account, cuenta corriente [*koo-ehn'-tah koh-rree-ehn'-teh*]
check *v.*, comprobar (irreg), verificar [*kohm-proh-bahr', veh-ree-fee-kahr'*]
cheek, mejilla [*meh-hee'-yah*]
cheer *n.*, alegría, ánimo [*ah-leh-gree'-ah, ah'-nee-moh*]
cheer *v.*, alegrar, animar [*ah-leh-grahr', ah-nee-mahr'*]
cheerful, alegre [*ah-leh'-greh*]
cheese, queso [*keh'-soh*]
cherry, cereza [*theh-reh'-thah*]
chest [anat.], pecho [*peh'-choh*]
chest of drawers, cómoda [*koh'-moh-dah*]
chew *v.*, masticar [*mahs-tee-kahr'*]
chicken, pollo [*poh'-yoh*]
chief *n.*, jefe (m) [*heh'-feh*]
chief *adj.*, principal [*preen-thee-pahl'*]
child, niño [*nee'-nyoh*]

childbirth, parto [*pahr'-toh*]
childhood, niñez (f) [*nee-nyehth'*]
Chile, Chile [*chee'-leh*]
Chilean, chileno [*chee-leh'-noh*]
chilly, frío [*free'-oh*]
chime *n.,* repique (m) [*reh-pee'-keh*]
chimney, chimenea [*chee-meh-neh'-ah*]
chin, mentón (m) [*mehn-tohn'*]
China, China [*chee'-nah*]
chinaware, vajilla de porcelana [*vah-hee'-yah deh pohr-theh-lah'-nah*]
Chinese, chino [*chee'-noh*]
chocolate *n.,* chocolate (m) [*choh-koh-lah'-teh*]
choice, elección (f) [*eh-lehk-thee-ohn'*]
choke [auto], obturador (m) [*ohb-too-rah-dohr'*]
choose *v.,* escoger [*ehs-koh-hehr'*]
chop [cut of meat] *n.,* chuleta [*choo-leh'-tah*]
chosen, elegido, escogido [*eh-leh-hee'-doh, ehs-koh-hee'-doh*]
Christian, cristiano [*krees-tee-ah'-noh*]
Christmas, Navidad (f) [*nah-vee-dahd'*]
   Merry Christmas, ¡Felices Pascuas! [*feh-lee'-thehs pahs'-koo-ahs*]
church, iglesia [*ee-gleh'-see-ah*]
cider, sidra [*see'-drah*]
cigar, tabaco [*tah-bah'-koh*]
cigarette, cigarrillo [*thee-gah-rree'-yoh*]
circle *n.,* círculo [*theer'-koo-loh*]
circle *v.,* cercar [*thehr-kahr'*]
circulation, circulación (f) [*theer-koo-lah-thee-ohn'*]
circumstance, circunstancia [*theer-koon-stahn'-thee-ah*]
circus, circo [*theer'-koh*]
citizen, ciudadano [*thee-oo-dah-dah'-noh*]
citizenship, ciudadanía [*thee-oo-dah-dah-nee'-ah*]
city, ciudad (f) [*thee-oo-dahd'*]
city hall, ayuntamiento [*ah-yoon-tah-mee-ehn'-toh*]
civil engineer, ingeniero civil [*een-heh-nee-eh'-roh thee-veel'*]
civilization, civilización (f) [*thee-vee-lee-thah-thee-ohn'*]
claim *n.,* reclamo [*reh-klah'-moh*]

claim *v.*, reclamar [*reh-klah-mahr'*]
clam, almeja [*ahl-meh'-hah*]
clasp *v.*, abrochar [*ah-broh-chahr'*]
class, clase (f) [*klah'-seh*]
  first class, primera clase (f) [*pree-meh'-rah klah'-seh*]
  second class, segunda clase (f) [*seh-goon'-dah klah'-seh*]
classic *n. & adj.*, clásico [*klah'-see-koh*]
classmate, compañero de clase [*kohm-pah-nyeh'-roh deh klah'-seh*]
classroom, aula [*ah-oo'-lah*]
clean *v.*, limpiar [*leem-pee-ahr'*]
clean *adj.*, limpio [*leem'-pee-oh*]
clean-cut, de buen parecer [*deh boo-ehn' pah-reh-thehr'*]
cleaner's shop, tintorería [*teen-toh-reh-ree'-ah*]
cleaning woman, limpiadora [*leem-pee-ah-doh'-rah*]
cleanliness, aseo, limpieza [*ah-seh'-oh, leem-pee-eh'-thah*]
clear *adj.*, claro [*klah'-roh*]
clearance [sale], venta (de liquidación) [*vehn'-tah (deh lee-kee-dah-thee-ohn'*)]
clergy, clero [*kleh'-roh*]
clerk, dependiente (m, f) [*deh-pehn-dee-ehn'-teh*]
clever, inteligente [*een-teh-lee-hehn'-teh*]
client, cliente (m, f) [*klee-ehn'-teh*]
climate, clima (m) [*klee'-mah*]
climb *v.*, trepar, escalar [*treh-pahr', ehs-kah-lahr'*]
cloakroom, guardarropa (m) [*goo-ahr-dah-rroh'-pah*]
clock, reloj (m) [*reh-lohh'*]
close [near], cerca [*thehr'-kah*]
close *v.*, cerrar (irreg) [*theh-rrahr'*]
closet, guardarropa (m) [*goo-ahr-dah-rroh'-pah*]
cloth, tela [*teh'-lah*]
clothes, ropa [*roh'-pah*]
cloud, nube (f) [*noo'-beh*]
cloudy, nublado [*noo-blah'-doh*]
club, club (m) [*kloob*]
coach, entrenador (m) [*ehn-treh-nah-dohr'*]
coal, carbón (m) [*kahr-bohn'*]
coal mine, mina de carbón [*mee'-nah deh kahr-bohn'*]

coarse, grosero [*groh-seh'-roh*].
coast, costa [*kohs'-tah*]
coat [apparel], abrigo [*ah-bree'-goh*]
cocoa, cacao [*kah-kah'-oh*]
coconut, coco [*koh'-koh*]
coffee, café (m) [*kah-feh'*]
  iced coffee, granizada de café [*grah-nee-thah'-dah deh kah-feh'*]
coffin, ataúd (m) [*ah-tah-ood'*]
coin, moneda [*moh-neh'-dah*]
coincidence, coincidencia [*koh-een-thee-dehn'-thee-ah*]
cold *adj.*, frío, resfriado [*free'-oh, rehs-free-ah'-doh*]
  be cold *v.*, tener frío [*teh-nehr' free'-oh*]
  catch a cold *v.*, resfriar(se) [*rehs-free-ahr'-seh*]
coldness, frialdad (f) [*free-ahl-dahd'*]
collapse *v.*, desplomarse [*dehs-ploh-mahr'-seh*]
collar, cuello [*koo-eh'-yoh*]
colleague, colega (m, f) [*koh-leh'-gah*]
collect *v.*, coleccionar [*koh-lehk-thee-oh-nahr'*]
collection, colección (f) [*koh-lehk-thee-ohn'*]
college, universidad (f) [*oo-nee-vehr-see-dahd'*]
collide *v.*, chocar [*choh-kahr'*]
colloquial, familiar [*fah-mee-lee-ahr'*]
Colombia, Colombia [*koh-lohm'-bee-ah*]
Colombian, colombiano [*koh-lohm-bee-ah'-noh*]
colony, colonia [*koh-loh'-nee-ah*]
color *n.*, color (m) [*koh-lohr'*]
color *v.*, colorear [*koh-loh-reh-ahr'*]
column, columna [*koh-loom'-nah*]
comb *n.*, peine (m) [*peh'-ee-neh*]
comb *v.*, peinar(se) [*peh-ee-nahr'-seh*]
combination, combinación (f) [*kohm-bee-nah-thee-ohn'*]
combustible, combustible [*kohm-boos-tee'-bleh*]
come *v.*, venir (irreg) [*veh-neer'*]
  come across, atravesar (irreg) [*ah-trah-veh-sahr'*]
  come back, volver (irreg) [*vohl-vehr'*]
  come down, bajar [*bah-hahr'*]

come for, venir por [*veh-neer' pohr*]
come forward, avanzar [*ah-vahn-thahr'*]
Come here, Venga aquí [*vehn'-gah ah-kee'*]
Come in, Adelante [*ah-deh-lahn'-teh*]
come out, salir (irreg) [*sah-leer'*]
comedian, comediante (m) [*koh-meh-dee-ahn'-teh*]
comedy, comedia [*koh-meh'-dee-ah*]
comfort *n.,* comodidad (f) [*koh-moh-dee-dahd'*]
comfort *v.,* consolar (irreg) [*kohn-soh-lahr'*]
comfortable, cómodo [*koh'-moh-doh*]
command *n.,* orden (f) [*ohr'-dehn*]
command *v.,* mandar [*mahn-dahr'*]
comment *n.,* comentario [*koh-mehn-tah'-ree-oh*]
comment *v.,* comentar [*koh-mehn-tahr'*]
commercial, comercial [*koh-mehr-thee-ahl'*]
commission, comisión (f) [*koh-mee-see-ohn'*]
commit *v.,* comprometerse [*kohm-proh-meh-tehr'-seh*]
committee, comité (m) [*koh-mee-teh'*]
common, común [*koh-moon'*]
commotion, conmoción (f) [*kohn-moh-thee-ohn'*]
communicate *v.,* comunicar [*koh-moo-nee-kahr'*]
communication, comunicación (f) [*koh-moo-nee-kah-thee-ohn'*]
communist, comunista (m, f) [*koh-moo-nees'-tah*]
community, comunidad (f) [*koh-moo-nee-dahd'*]
companion, compañero [*kohm-puh-nyeh'-roh*]
company, compañía [*kohm-pah-nyee'-ah*]
compare *v.,* comparar [*kohm-pah-rahr'*]
compartment, compartimiento [*kohm-pahr-tee-mee-ehn'-toh*]
compass [directional], brújula [*broo'-hoo-lah*]
compel *v.,* obligar [*oh-blee-gahr'*]
compensation, compensación (f) [*kohm-pehn-sah-thee-ohn'*]
competent, competente [*kohm-peh-tehn'-teh*]
competition, competición (f) [*kohm-peh-tee-thee-ohn'*]
complain *v.,* quejarse [*keh-hahr'-seh*]
complaint, queja [*keh'-hah*]
complete *adj.,* completo [*kohm-pleh'-toh*]
complete *v.,* completar [*kohm-pleh-tahr'*]
completely, completamente [*kohm-pleh-tah-mehn'-teh*]

complexion, cutis (m) [*koo'-tees*]
complicate v., complicar [*kohm-plee-kahr'*]
complicated, complicado [*kohm-plee-kah'-doh*]
compliment, cumplido [*koom-plee'-doh*]
  pay a compliment, hacer un cumplido [*ah-thehr' oon koom-plee'-doh*]
compose v., componer (irreg) [*kohm-poh-nehr'*]
composer, compositor (m) [*kohm-poh-see-tohr'*]
composure, compostura [*kohm-pohs-too'-rah*]
compound adj., compuesto [*kohm-poo-ehs'-toh*]
comprehend v., comprender, abarcar (irreg) [*kohm-prehn-dehr', ah-bahr-kahr'*]
compromise v., transigir [*trahn-see-heer'*]
compulsion, compulsión (f) [*kohm-pool-see-ohn'*]
conceal v., ocultar [*oh-kool-tahr'*]
conceit, presunción (f) [*preh-soon-thee-ohn'*]
conceited, vanidoso [*vah-nee-doh'-soh*]
conceive v., concebir (irreg) [*kohn-theh-beer'*]
concentrate v., concentrar [*kohn-thehn-trahr'*]
concept, concepto, idea [*kohn-thehp'-toh, ee-deh'-ah*]
concerning, sobre [*soh'-breh*]
concert, concierto [*kohn-thee-ehr'-toh*]
concise, conciso [*kohn-thee'-soh*]
conclusion, conclusión (f) [*kohn-kloo-see-ohn'*]
condemn v., condenar [*kohn-deh-nahr'*]
condemnation, condenación (f) [*kohn-deh-nah-thee-ohn'*]
condense v., condensar [*kohn-dehn-sahr'*]
condition, condición (f) [*kohn-dee-thee-ohn'*]
  in good condition, en buen estado [*ehn boo-ehn' ehs-tah'-doh*]
conditional, condicional [*kohn-dee-thee-oh-nahl'*]
conduct n., conducta [*kohn-dook'-tah*]
conduct v., conducir (irreg), dirigir [*kohn-doo-theer', dee-ree-heer'*]
conductor, conductor (m), director (m) [*kohn-dook-tohr', dee-rehk-tohr'*]
confer v., conferir (irreg) [*kohn-feh-reer'*]
conference, conferencia [*kohn-feh-rehn'-thee-ah*]

confess v., confesar (irreg) [*kohn-feh-sahr'*]
confession, confesión (f) [*kohn-feh-see-ohn'*]
confident, confiado [*kohn-fee-ah'-doh*]
confidential, confidencial [*kohn-fee-dehn-thee-ahl'*]
confirm v., confirmar [*kohn-feer-mahr'*]
conflict, conflicto [*kohn-fleek'-toh*]
confusion, confusión (f) [*kohn-foo-see-ohn'*]
congratulate v., felicitar [*feh-lee-thee-tahr'*]
congratulations, felicitaciones [*feh-lee-thee-tah-thee-oh'-nehs*]
congress, congreso [*kohn-greh'-soh*]
connection, conexión (f) [*koh-nehk-see-ohn'*]
conquer v., conquistar [*kohn-kees-tahr'*]
conscience, conciencia [*kohn-thee-ehn'-thee-ah*]
conscientious, concienzudo [*kohn-thee-ehn-thoo'-doh*]
conscious, consciente [*kohns-thee-ehn'-teh*]
consent n., consentimiento [*kohn-sehn-tee-mee-ehn'-toh*]
consent v., consentir (irreg) [*kohn-sehn-teer'*]
consequence, consecuencia [*kohn-seh-koo-ehn'-thee-ah*]
consequent, consecuente [*kohn-seh-koo-ehn'-teh*]
conservative, conservador [*kohn-sehr-vah-dohr'*]
consider v., considerar [*kohn-see-deh-rahr'*]
considerable, considerable [*kohn-see-deh-rah'-bleh*]
consist of v., consistir en [*kohn-sees-teer' ehn*]
consistent, consistente [*kohn-sees-tehn'-teh*]
console v., consolar (irreg) [*kohn-soh-lahr'*]
constant, constante [*kohns-tahn'-teh*]
constitute v., constituir [*kohns-tee-too-eer'*]
construct v., construir (irreg) [*kohns-troo-eer'*]
construction, construcción (f) [*kohns-trook-thee-ohn'*]
consul, cónsul (m) [*kohn'-sool*]
consulate, consulado [*kohn-soo-lah'-doh*]
consult v., consultar [*kohn-sool-tahr'*]
consume v., consumir [*kohn-soo-meer'*]
consumer, consumidor (m) [*kohn-soo-mee-dohr'*]
contact n., contacto [*kohn-tahk'-toh*]
contact v., ponerse (irreg) en contacto [*poh-nehr'-seh ehn kohn-tahk'-toh*]

contagious, contagioso [*kohn-tah-hee-oh'-soh*]
contain *v.*, contener (irreg) [*kohn-teh-nehr'*]
container, recipiente (m) [*reh-thee-pee-ehn'-teh*]
contemporary, contemporáneo [*kohn-tehm-poh-rah'-neh-oh*]
contempt, desprecio [*dehs-preh'-thee-oh*]
contents, contenido [*kohn-teh-nee'-doh*]
contest *n.*, concurso [*kohn-koor'-soh*]
continent, continente (m) [*kohn-tee-nehn'-teh*]
continuation, continuación (f) [*kohn-tee-noo-ah-thee-ohn'*]
continue *v.*, continuar [*kohn-tee-noo-ahr'*]
contract, contrato [*kohn-trah'-toh*]
contradiction, contradicción (f) [*kohn-trah-deek-thee-ohn'*]
contrary, contrario [*kohn-trah'-ree-oh*]
  on the contrary, al contrario [*ahl kohn-trah'-ree-oh*]
contrast, contraste (m) [*kohn-trahs'-teh*]
contribute *v.*, contribuir (irreg) [*kohn-tree-boo-eer'*]
control *n.*, control (m) [*kohn-trohl'*]
control *v.*, controlar [*kohn-troh-lahr'*]
controversy, controversia [*kohn-troh-vehr'-see-ah*]
convenient, conveniente [*kohn-veh-nee-ehn'-teh*]
convent, convento [*kohn-vehn'-toh*]
conversation, conversación (f) [*kohn-vehr-sah-thee-ohn'*]
convert *n.*, converso [*kohn-vehr'-soh*]
convert *v.*, convertir (irreg) [*kohn-vehr-teer'*]
convict *n.*, presidiario [*preh-see-dee-ah'-ree-oh*]
convict *v.*, declarar culpable [*deh-klah-rahr' kool-pah'-bleh*]
convince *v.*, convencer [*kohn-vehn-thehr'*]
cook *n.*, cocinero [*koh-thee-neh'-roh*]
cook *v.*, cocinar [*koh-thee-nahr'*]
cool *adj.*, fresco [*frehs'-koh*]
cool *v.*, enfriar [*ehn-free-ahr'*]
cooperation, cooperación (f) [*koh-oh-peh-rah-thee-ohn'*]
copper, cobre (m) [*koh'-breh*]
copy *n.*, copia [*koh'-pee-ah*]
copy *v.*, copiar [*koh-pee-ahr'*]
cord, cuerda [*koo-ehr'-dah*]
cordial *adj.*, cordial [*kohr-dee-ahl'*]
cork, corcho [*kohr'-choh*]

corkscrew, sacacorchos (m, sing) [*sah-kah-kohr'-chohs*]
corn, maíz (m) [*mah-eeth'*]
corner, esquina [*ehs-kee'-nah*]
corporation, corporación (f) [*kohr-poh-rah-thee-ohn'*]
correct *adj.,* correcto [*koh-rrehk'-toh*]
correct *v.,* corregir (irreg) [*koh-rreh-heer'*]
correction, corrección (f) [*koh-rrehk-thee-ohn'*]
correspondence, correspondencia [*koh-rrehs-pohn-dehn'-thee-ah*]
corridor, corredor (m), pasillo [*koh-rreh-dohr', pah-see'-yoh*]
corrupt, corrompido [*koh-rrohm-pee'-doh*]
corruption, corrupción (f) [*koh-rroop-thee-ohn'*]
cosmetics, cosméticos [*kohs-meh'-tee-kohs*]
cost *n.,* costo [*kohs'-toh*]
  cost of living, coste de vida [*kohs'-teh deh vee'-dah*]
cost *v.,* costar (irreg) [*kohs-tahr'*]
  How much does this cost?, ¿Cuánto cuesta esto? [*koo-ahn'-toh koo-ehs'-tah ehs'-toh*]
Costa Rica, Costa Rica [*kohs'-tah ree'-kah*]
Costa Rican, costarricense [*kohs-tah-rree-then'-seh*]
costly, costoso [*kohs-toh'-soh*]
cot, catre (m) [*kah'-treh*]
cottage, casa de campo [*kah'-sah deh kahm'-poh*]
cotton, algodón (m) [*ahl-goh-dohn'*]
couch, sofá (m) [*soh-fah'*]
cough *n.,* tos (f) [*tohs*]
cough *v.,* toser [*toh-sehr'*]
council, consejo [*kohn-seh'-hoh*]
count [title], conde (m) [*kohn'-deh*]
count *v.,* contar (irreg) [*kohn-tahr'*]
  count on, confiar en [*kohn-fee-ahr' ehn*]
country [nation], país (m) [*pah-ees'*]
country [land; rural region], campo [*kahm'-poh*]
countryman, compatriota (m, f) [*kohm-pah-tree-oh'-tah*]
couple, pareja [*pah-reh'-hah*]
courage, valor (m) [*vah-lohr'*]
courageous, valiente [*vah-lee-ehn'-teh*]
course, curso [*koor'-soh*]

of course, por supuesto [*pohr soo-poo-ehs'-toh*]
court [law] *n.*, corte (m), tribunal (m) [*kohr'-teh, tree-boo-nahl'*]
court [tennis] *n.*, pista [*pees'-tah*]
court *v.*, cortejar [*kohr-teh-hahr'*]
courtyard, patio [*pah'-tee-oh*]
cousin, primo [*pree'-moh*]
cover *n.*, cubierta [*koo-bee-ehr'-tah*]
cover *v.*, cubrir [*koo-breer'*]
cow, vaca [*vah'-kah*]
coward, cobarde (m, f) [*koh-bahr'-deh*]
crab, cangrejo [*kahn-greh'-hoh*]
crack *n.*, crujido [*kroo-hee'-doh*]
cradle, cuna [*koo'-nah*]
craftsman, artesano [*ahr-teh-sah'-noh*]
crank [mech.], manubrio [*mah-noo'-bree-oh*]
crash *v.*, chocar, estrellarse [*choh-kahr', ehs-treh-yahr'-seh*]
crawfish, langostino [*lahn-gohs-tee'-no*]
crawl *v.*, arrastrarse [*ah-rrahs-trahr'-seh*]
crazy, loco [*loh'-koh*]
cream, crema [*kreh'-mah*]
create *v.*, crear [*kreh-ahr'*]
creation, creación (f) [*kreh-ah-thee-ohn'*]
creature, criatura [*kree-ah-too'-rah*]
credit *n.*, crédito [*kreh'-dee-toh*]
creditor, acreedor (m) [*ah-kreh-eh-dohr'*]
crew, tripulación (f) [*tree-poo-lah-thee-ohn'*]
crib, camita de niño [*kah-mee'-tah deh nee'-nyoh*]
crime, crimen (m) [*kree'-mehn*]
criminal, criminal [*kree-mee-nahl'*]
crisis, crisis (f) [*kree'-sees*]
critical, crítico [*kree'-tee-koh*]
criticize *v.*, criticar [*kree-tee-kahr'*]
crook, estafador (m, f) [*ehs-tah-fah-dohr'*]
crooked, torcido [*tohr-thee'-doh*]
crop, cosecha [*koh-seh'-chah*]
cross *n.*, cruz (f), cruce (m) [*krooth, kroo'-theh*]

cross *v.*, cruzar [*kroo-thahr'*]

crossing, cruce (m) [*kroo'-theh*]

crossroads, encrucijada [*ehn-kroo-thee-hah'-dah*]

crowd, gentío [*hehn-tee'-oh*]

crowded, atestado, lleno [*ah-tehs-tah'-doh, yeh'-noh*]

crown, corona [*koh-roh'-nah*]

cruel, cruel [*kroo-ehl'*]

cruelty, crueldad (f) [*kroo-ehl-dahd'*]

cruise, travesía [*trah-veh-see'-ah*]

crumb, miga [*mee'-gah*]

crush *v.*, aplastar [*ah-plahs-tahr'*]

cry [shout] *n.*, grito [*gree'-toh*]

cry [weep] *v.*, llorar [*yoh-rahr'*]

crystal, cristal (m) [*krees-tahl'*]

Cuba, Cuba [*koo'-bah*]

Cuban, cubano [*koo-bah'-noh*]

cube, cubo [*koo'-boh*]

cucumber, pepino [*peh-pee'-noh*]

culture, cultura [*kool-too'-rah*]

cunning *adj.*, astuto [*ahs-too'-toh*]

cup, taza [*tah'-thah*]

cupboard, aparador (m) [*ah-pah-rah-dohr'*]

cure *n.*, cura [*koo'-rah*]

cure *v.*, curar [*koo-rahr'*]

curiosity, curiosidad (f) [*koo-ree-oh-see-dahd'*]

curious, curioso [*koo-ree-oh'-soh*]

curl *n.*, rizo [*ree'-thoh*]

curl *v.*, rizar (irreg) [*ree-thahr'*]

currency, moneda corriente [*moh-neh'-dah koh-rree-ehn'-teh*]

current, corriente (m) [*koh-rree-ehn'-teh*]

curse *n.*, maleficio [*mah-leh-fee'-thee-oh*]

curse *v.*, maldecir (irreg) [*mahl-deh-theer'*]

curtain, cortina [*kohr-tee'-nah*]

curve, curva [*koor'-vah*]

   dangerous curve, curva peligrosa [*koor'-vah peh-lee-groh'-sah*]

cushion, cojín (m) [*koh-heen'*]

custom, costumbre (f) [*kohs-toom'-breh*]
customary, habitual [*ah-bee-too-ahl'*]
customer, cliente (m, f) [*klee-ehn'-teh*]
customs, aduana [*ah-doo-ah'-nah*]
   customs duties, derechos de aduana [*deh-reh'-chohs deh ah-doo-ah'-nah*]
   customs officer, aduanero [*ah-doo-ah-neh'-roh*]
cut *n.*, corte (m) [*kohr'-teh*]
cut *v.*, cortar [*kohr-tahr'*]

D

daily, diario [*dee-ah'-ree-oh*]
dainty, delicado, exquisito [*deh-lee-kah'-doh, ehks-kee-see'-toh*]
dairy, lechería [*leh-cheh-ree'-ah*]
dam, presa, dique (m) [*preh'-sah, dee'-keh*]
damage *n.*, daño [*dah'-nyoh*]
damaged, dañado [*dah-nyah'-doh*]
damp, húmedo [*oo'-meh-doh*]
dance *n.*, baile (m) [*bah'-ee-leh*]
dance *v.*, bailar [*bah-ee-lahr'*]
dancer, bailarín (m), bailarina (f) [*bah-ee-lah-reen', bah-ee-lah-ree'-nah*]
danger, peligro [*peh-lee'-groh*]
dangerous, peligroso [*peh-lee-groh'-soh*]
Danish, danés [*dah-nehs'*]
dare *n.*, reto, provocación (f) [*reh'-toh, proh-voh-kah-thee-ohn'*]
dare *v.*, atrever [*ah-treh-vehr'*]
daring, atrevido [*ah-treh-vee'-doh*]
dark, oscuro [*ohs-koo'-roh*]
darkness, oscuridad (f) [*ohs-koo-ree-dahd'*]
dash *v.*, estrellar [*ehs-treh-yahr'*]

date [appointment], fecha, compromiso [*feh'-chah, kohm-proh-mee'-soh*]

daughter, hija [*ee'-hah*]

daughter-in-law, nuera [*noo-eh'-rah*]

dawn, amanecer (m) [*ah-mah-neh-thehr'*]

day, día (m) [*dee'-ah*]

  day after tomorrow, pasado mañana [*pah-sah-doh mah-nyah'-nah*]

  day before yesterday, anteayer [*ahn-teh-ah-yehr'*]

dead, muerto [*moo-ehr'-toh*]

deadly, mortal [*mohr-tahl'*]

deaf, sordo [*sohr'-doh*]

deal *n.,* trato [*trah'-toh*]

  a great deal of, mucho [*moo'-choh*]

deal *v.,* tratar [*trah-tahr'*]

  deal with, tratar con/de [*trah-tahr' kohn/deh*]

dealer, negociante (m) [*neh-ghoh-thee-ahn'-teh*]

dear, querido [*keh-ree'-doh*]

dearly, cariñosamente [*kah-ree-nyoh-sah-mehn'-teh*]

death, muerte (f) [*moo-ehr'-teh*]

debt, deuda [*deh-oo'-dah*]

decade, década [*deh'-kah-dah*]

decay *n.,* decaimiento [*deh-kah-ee-mee-ehn'-toh*]

decay *v.,* decaer (irreg) [*deh-kah-ehr'*]

deceased, difunto [*dee-foon'-toh*]

deceit, engaño [*ehn-gah'-nyoh*]

deceive *v.,* engañar [*ehn-gah-nyahr'*]

December, diciembre [*dee-thee-ehm'-breh*]

decency, decencia [*deh-thehn'-thee-ah*]

decent, decente [*deh-thehn'-teh*]

decide *v.,* decidir [*deh-thee-deer'*]

decision, decisión (f) [*deh-thee-see-ohn'*]

deck [naut.], cubierta [*koo-bee-ehr'-tah*]

declaration, declaración (f) [*deh-klah-rah-thee-ohn'*]

declare *v.,* declarar [*deh-klah-rahr'*]

decline *v.,* declinar [*deh-klee-nahr'*]

decorate *v.,* decorar [*deh-koh-rahr'*]

decoration, decoración (f) [*deh-koh-rah-thee-ohn'*]

decrease v., disminuir [*dees-mee-noo-eer'*]
decree n., decreto [*deh-kreh'-toh*]
dedicate v., dedicar [*deh-dee-kahr'*]
deed, hecho, acto [*eh'-choh, ahk'-toh*]
deep, profundo [*proh-foon'-doh*]
defeat n., derrota [*deh-rroh'-tah*]
defeat v., derrotar [*deh-rroh-tahr'*]
defect n., defecto [*deh-fehk'-toh*]
defective, defectuoso [*deh-fehk-too-oh'-soh*]
defend v., defender (irreg) [*deh-fehn-dehr'*]
defense, defensa [*deh-fehn'-sah*]
deficient, deficiente [*deh-fee-thee-ehn'-teh*]
define v., definir [*deh-fee-neer'*]
definite, definido [*deh-fee-nee'-doh*]
definition, definición (f) [*deh-fee-nee-thee-ohn'*]
degree, grado [*grah'-doh*]
delay v., demorar [*deh-moh-rahr'*]
delegate, delegado [*deh-leh-gah'-doh*]
deliberate adj., deliberado [*deh-lee-beh-rah'-doh*]
delicate, delicado [*deh-lee-kah'-doh*]
delicious, delicioso [*deh-lee-thee-oh'-soh*]
delight n., deleite (m) [*deh-leh'-ee-teh*]
delight v., deleitar [*deh-leh-ee-tahr'*]
deliver v., entregar [*ehn-treh-gahr'*]
delivery, entrega [*ehn-treh'-gah*]
demand n., demanda, exigencia [*deh-mahn'-dah, ehk-see-hehn'-thee-ah*]
demand v., reclamar [*reh-klah-mahr'*]
democracy, democracia [*deh-moh-krah'-thee-ah*]
demonstrate v., demostrar (irreg) [*deh-mohs-trahr'*]
demonstration, demostración (f), manifestación (f) [*deh-mohs-trah-thee-ohn', mah-nee-fehs-tah-thee-ohn'*]
denial, negativa [*neh-gah-tee'-vah*]
Denmark, Dinamarca [*dee-nah-mahr'-kah*]
dense, denso [*dehn'-soh*]
density, densidad (f) [*dehn-see-dahd'*]
dentist, dentista (m, f) [*dehn-tees'-tah*]
deny v., negar (irreg) [*neh-gahr'*]

depart *v.*, partir [*pahr-teer'*]

department, departamento [*deh-pahr-tah-mehn'-toh*]

departure, partida [*pahr-tee'-dah*]

depend *v.*, depender [*deh-pehn-dehr'*]

  depend on, contar con [*kohn-tahr' kohn*]

  that depends, eso depende [*eh'-soh deh-pehn'-deh*]

dependent, dependiente (m) [*deh-pehn-dee-ehn'-teh*]

deposit *n.*, depósito [*deh-poh'-see-toh*]

deposit *v.*, depositar [*deh-poh-see-tahr'*]

depot, depósito, almacén (m) [*deh-poh'-see-toh, ahl-mah-thehn'*]

deprive *v.*, privar [*pree-vahr'*]

depth, profundidad (f) [*proh-foon-dee-dahd'*]

deputy, diputado [*dee-poo-tah'-doh*]

descend *v.*, descender (irreg) [*dehs-thehn-dehr'*]

describe *v.*, describir [*dehs-kree-beer'*]

description, descripción (f) [*dehs-kreep-thee-ohn'*]

desert *n.*, desierto [*deh-see-ehr'-toh*]

desert *v.*, desertar [*deh-sehr-tahr'*]

deserve *v.*, merecer (irreg) [*meh-reh-thehr'*]

desirable, deseable [*deh-seh-ah'-bleh*]

desire *n.*, deseo [*deh-seh'-oh*]

desire *v.*, desear [*deh-seh-ahr'*]

desk, escritorio [*ehs-kree-toh'-ree-oh*]

despair *n.*, desesperación (f) [*deh-sehs-peh-rah-thee-ohn'*]

despair *v.*, desesperar [*deh-sehs-peh-rahr'*]

desperate, desesperado [*deh-sehs-peh-rah'-doh*]

dessert, postre (m) [*pohs'-treh*]

destiny, destino [*dehs-tee'-noh*]

destitute, destituido [*dehs-tee-too-ee'-doh*]

destroy *v.*, destruir (irreg) [*dehs-troo-eer'*]

destruction, destrucción (f) [*dehs-trook-thee-ohn'*]

detail, detalle (m) [*deh-tah'-yeh*]

detain *v.*, detener (irreg) [*deh-teh-nehr'*]

detained, detenido [*deh-teh-nee'-doh*]

determine *v.*, determinar [*deh-tehr-mee-nahr'*]

detour, desviación (f) [*dehs-vee-ah-thee-ohn'*]

develop *v.*, desarrollar [*deh-sah-rroh-yahr'*]

development, desarrollo [*deh-sah-rroh'-yoh*]

device, ardid (m), instrumento [*ahr-deed'*, *eens-troo-mehn'-toh*]

devil, diablo [*dee-ah'-bloh*]

devoted, dedicado [*deh-dee-kah'-doh*]

` **otion,** devoción (f) [*deh-voh-thee-ohn'*]

 w, rocío [*roh-thee'-oh*]

 agram, diagrama (m) [*dee-ah-grah'-mah*]

dial *n.*, esfera, cuadrante (m) [*ehs-feh'-rah*, *koo-ah-drahn'-teh*]

dial [a telephone] *v.*, marcar (las cifras) [*mahr-kahr' (lahs thee'-frahs)*]

dialect, dialecto [*dee-ah-lehk'-toh*]

dialogue, diálogo [*dee-ah'-loh-goh*]

diamond, diamante (m) [*dee-ah-mahn'-teh*]

diarrhea, diarrea [*dee-ah-rreh'-ah*]

dice, dados (m, pl) [*dah'-dohs*]

dictate *v.*, dictar [*deek-tahr'*]

dictation, dictado [*deek-tah'-doh*]

dictionary, diccionario [*deek-thee-oh-nah'-ree-oh*]

die *v.*, morir (irreg) [*moh-reer'*]

diet, dieta [*dee-eh'-tah*]

difference, diferencia [*dee-feh-rehn'-thee-ah*]

  It does not make any difference, No importa [*noh eem-pohr'-tah*]

different, diferente [*dee-feh-rehn'-teh*]

difficult, difícil [*dee-fee'-theel*]

difficulty, dificultad (f) [*dee-fee-kool-tahd'*]

dig *v.*, cavar [*kah-vahr'*]

digestion, digestión (f) [*dee-hehs-tee-ohn'*]

dignity, dignidad (f) [*deeg-nee-dahd'*]

dim, obscuro [*ohbs-koo'-roh*]

dimension, dimensión (f) [*dee-mehn-see-ohn'*]

diminish *v.*, disminuir (irreg) [*dees-mee-noo-eer'*]

dine, *v.*, comer [*koh-mehr'*]

dining car, coche (m) restaurante [*koh'-che rehs-tah-oo-rahn'-teh*]

dining room, comedor (m) [*koh-meh-dohr'*]

dinner, comida [*koh-mee'-dah*]
diploma, diploma (m) [*dee-ploh'-mah*]
diplomat, diplomático [*dee-ploh-mah'-tee-koh*]
diplomatic, diplomático [*dee-ploh-mah'-tee-koh*]
direct *adj.*, directo [*dee-rehk'-toh*]
direct *v.*, dirigir [*dee-ree-heer'*]
direction, dirección (f) [*dee-rehk-thi-ohn'*]
directly, directamente [*dee-rehk-tah-mehn'-teh*]
director, director (m) [*dee-rehk-tohr'*]
dirt, suciedad (f) [*soo-thee-eh-dahd'*]
dirty, sucio [*soo'-thee-oh*]
disability, incapacidad (f) [*een-kah-pah-thee-dahd'*]
disabled, incapacitado [*een-kah-pah-thee-tah'-doh*]
disadvantage, desventaja [*dehs-vehn-tah'-hah*]
disagree *v.*, no estar de acuerdo [*noh ehs-tahr' deh ah-koo-ehr'-doh*]
disagreeable, desagradable [*deh-sah-grah-dah'-bleh*]
disagreement, desacuerdo [*deh-sah-koo-ehr'-doh*]
disappear *v.*, desaparecer (irreg) [*deh-sah-pah-reh-thehr'*]
disappoint *v.*, decepcionar [*deh-thehp-thee-oh-nahr'*]
disappointed, decepcionado [*deh-thehp-thee-oh-nah'-doh*]
disapprove *v.*, desaprovar (irreg) [*deh-sah-proh-vahr'*]
disaster, desastre (m) [*deh-sahs'-treh*]
discharge *n.*, descarga, descargo [*dehs-kahr'-gah, dehs-kahr'-goh*]
discipline *n.*, disciplina [*dees-thee-plee'-nah*]
disclose *v.*, revelar, divulgar [*reh-veh-lahr', dee-vool-gahr'*]
discomfort, incomodidad (f) [*een-koh-moh-dee-dahd'*]
discontinue *v.*, discontinuar [*dees-kohn-tee-noo-ahr'*]
discourage *v.*, desalentar (irreg) [*deh-sah-lehn-tahr'*]
discouraged, desalentado [*deh-sah-lehn-tah'-doh*]
discover *v.*, descubrir [*dehs-koo-breer'*]
discovery, descubrimiento [*dehs-koo-bree-mee-ehn'-toh*]
discuss *v.*, discutir [*dees-koo-teer'*]
discussion, discusión (f) [*dees-koo-see-ohn'*]
disease, enfermedad (f) [*ehn-fehr-meh-dahd'*]
disgrace *n.*, desgracia [*dehs-grah'-thee-ah*]
disgrace *v.*, desacreditar [*deh-sah-kreh-dee-tahr'*]

disguise *n.*, disfraz (m) [*dees-frahth'*]
disgusted, disgustado [*dees-goos-tah'-doh*]
dish, plato [*plah'-toh*]
dishonest, deshonesto [*dehs-oh-nehs'-toh*]
dislike *v.*, no gustar [*noh goos-tahr'*]
dismal, lúgubre [*loo'-goo-breh*]
dismay, desmayo [*dehs-mah'-yoh*]
dismiss *v.*, despedir [*dehs-peh-deer'*]
disobey *v.*, desobedecer (irreg) [*deh-soh-beh-deh-thehr'*]
disorder, desorden (m) [*dehs-ohr'-dehn*]
display *n.*, exhibición (f) [*ehk-see-bee-thee-ohn'*]
display *v.*, exhibir [*ehk-see-beer'*]
dispose *v.*, disponer (irreg) [*dees-poh-nehr'*]
   dispose of, deshacerse de [*dehs-ah-thehr'-seh deh*]
dispute *n.*, disputa [*dees-poo'-tah*]
dissolve *v.*, disolver (irreg) [*dee-sohl-vehr'*]
distance, distancia [*dees-tahn'-thee-ah*]
distant, distante [*dees-tahn'-teh*]
distinct, único [*oo'-nee-koh*]
distinguish *v.*, distinguir [*dees-teen-gheer'*]
distinguished, distinguido [*dees-teen-ghee'-doh*]
distress *v.*, afligir [*ah-flee-heer'*]
distribute *v.*, distribuir (irreg) [*dees-tree-boo-eer'*]
distribution, distribución (f) [*dees-tree-boo-thee-ohn'*]
district, distrito [*dees-tree'-toh*]
distrust *n.*, desconfianza [*dehs-kohn-fee-ahn'-thah*]
distrust *v.*, desconfiar [*dehs-kohn-fee-ahr'*]
disturb *v.*, molestar [*moh-lehs-tahr'*]
disturbance, disturbio [*dees-toor'-bee-oh*]
ditch, zanja [*thahn'-hah*]
dive *v.*, sumergirse [*soo-mehr-heer'-seh*]
divide *v.*, dividir [*dee-vee-deer'*]
divine, divino [*dee-vee'-noh*]
division, división (f) [*dee-vee-see-ohn'*]
divorce *n.*, divorcio [*dee-vohr'-thee-oh*]
divorce *v.*, divorciarse [*dee-vohr-thee-ahr'-seh*]
dizzy, mareado [*mah-reh-ah'-doh*]
do *v.*, hacer (irreg) [*ah-thehr'*]

Do me a favor, Hágame el favor de . . . [*ah'-gah-meh ehl fah-vohr' deh*]

How do you do? ¿Como está usted? [*koh'-moh ehs-tah' oos-tehd'*]

What can I do for you? ¿En qué puedo servirle? [*ehn keh' poo-eh'-doh, sehr-veer'-leh*]

dock *n.,* muelle (m) [*moo-eh'-yeh*]

dock *v.,* atracar [*ah-trah-kahr'*]

doctor, doctor (m) [*dohk-tohr'*]

document, documento [*doh-koo-mehn'-toh*]

dog, perro [*peh'-rroh*]

doll, muñeca [*moo-nyeh'-kah*]

dollar, dólar (m) [*doh'-lahr*]

dome, cúpula [*koo'-poo-lah*]

domestic *n. & adj.,* doméstico [*doh-mehs'-tee-koh*]

Dominican, dominicano [*doh-mee-nee-kah'-noh*]

Dominican Republic, República Dominicana [*reh-poo'-blee-kah doh-mee-nee-kah'-nah*]

done, hecho [*eh'-choh*]

donkey, burro [*boo'-rroh*]

door, puerta [*poo-ehr'-tah*]

dormitory, dormitorio [*dohr-mee-toh'-ree-oh*]

dose, dósis (f) [*doh'-sees*]

double, doble [*doh'-bleh*]

doubt *n.,* duda [*doo'-dah*]

  no doubt, sin duda [*seen doo'-dah*]

doubt *v.,* dudar [*doo-dahr'*]

doubtful, dudoso [*doo-doh'-soh*]

doubtless, sin duda [*seen doo'-dah*]

down, abajo [*ah-bah'-hoh*]

  Down with . . . !, ¡Abajo con . . . ! [*ah-bah'-hoh kohn*]

  fall down *v.,* caerse [*kah-ehr'-seh*]

downfall, ruina [*roo-ee'-nah*]

downstairs, abajo [*ah-bah'-hoh*]

doze *v.,* dormitar [*dohr-mee-tahr'*]

dozen, docena [*doh-theh'-nah*]

draft [money order], giro [*hee'-roh*]

drag *v.,* arrastrar [*ah-rrahs-trahr'*]

drain *n*., desagüe (m) [*deh-sah'-goo-eh*]
drain *v*., secar [*seh-kahr'*]
drama, drama (m) [*drah'-mah*]
dramatic, dramático [*drah-mah'-tee-koh*]
draw [sketch] *v*., dibujar [*dee-boo-hahr'*]
drawer, cajón (m), gaveta [*kah-hohn', gah-veh'-tah*]
dread *n*., temor (m) [*teh-mohr'*]
dreadful, espantoso [*ehs-pahn-toh'-soh*]
dream *n*., sueño [*soo-eh'-nyoh*]
dream *v*., soñar (irreg) [*soh-nyahr'*]
dress *n*., vestido [*vehs-tee'-doh*]
  evening dress, vestido de noche [*vehs-tee'-doh deh noh'-cheh*]
  get dressed *v*., vestirse [*vehs-teer'-seh*]
dressing table, tocador (m) [*toh-kah-dohr'*]
dressmaker, modista [*moh-dees'-tah*]
drink *n*., bebida [*beh-bee'-dah*]
drink *v*., beber [*beh-behr'*]
drip *v*., gotear [*goh-teh-ahr'*]
drive *v*., conducir (irreg), manejar [*kohn-doo-theer', mah-neh-hahr'*]
driver, chófer (m) [*choh'-fehr*]
driving license, licencia para conducir [*lee-thehn'-thee-ah pah'-rah kohn-doo-theer'*]
drop *v*., gotear [*goh-teh-ahr'*]
drown *v*., ahogarse [*ah-oh-gahr'-seh*]
drug, droga [*droh'-gah*]
drugstore, farmacia [*fahr-mah'-thee-ah*]
drum, tambor (m) [*tahm-bohr'*]
drunk, borracho [*boh-rrah'-choh*]
dry *adj*., seco [*seh'-koh*]
dry *v*., secar [*seh-kahr'*]
duchess, duquesa [*doo-keh'-sah*]
due, debido [*deh-bee'-doh*]
  fall due *v*., vencer [*vehn-thehr'*]
duke, duque (m) [*doo'-keh*]
dull, insulso [*een-sool'-soh*]
dumb [mute], mudo [*moo'-doh*]

dungeon, calabozo [*kah-lah-boh'-thoh*]
durable, duradero [*doo-rah-deh'-roh*]
during, durante [*doo-rahn'-teh*]
dusk, caída de la tarde [*kah-ee'-dah deh lah tahr'-deh*]
dust, polvo [*pohl'-voh*]
Dutch, holandés [*oh-lahn-dehs'*]
duty, deber (m) [*deh-behr'*]
  duty-free, libre de derechos [*lee'-breh deh deh-reh'-chohs*]
  be on duty, estar de servicio [*ehs-tahr' deh sehr-vee'-thee-oh*]
dwell *v.,* residir [*reh-see-deer'*]
dye *n.,* tinte (m) [*teen'-teh*]
dye *v.,* teñir (irreg) [*teh-nyeer'*]
dysentery, disentería [*dee-sehn-teh-ree'-ah*]

E

each, cada [*kah'-dah*]
  each one, cada uno [*kah'-dah oo'-noh*]
  each other, el uno al otro [*ehl oo'-noh ahl oh'-troh*]
eager, ansioso [*ahn-see-oh'-soh*]
ear, oreja [*oh-reh'-hah*]
early, temprano [*tehm-prah'-noh*]
earn *v.,* ganar [*gah-nahr'*]
earring, pendiente (m), arete (m) [*pehn-dee-ehn'-teh, ah-reh'-teh*]
earth, tierra [*tee-eh'-rrah*]
earthquake, terremoto [*teh-rreh-moh'-toh*]
ease, facilidad (f) [*fah-thee-lee-dahd'*]
easily, fácilmente [*fah-theel-mehn'-teh*]
east, este (m) [*ehs'-teh*]
Easter, Pascua Florida [*pahs'-koo-ah floh-ree'-dah*]
easy, fácil [*fah'-theel*]
  Take it easy! ¡Tenga calma! [*tehn'-gah kahl'-mah*]

eat v., comer [*koh-mehr'*]
echo, eco [*eh'-koh*]
economical, económico [*eh-koh-noh'-mee-koh*]
Ecuador, Ecuador (m) [*eh-koo-ah-dohr'*]
Ecuadorian, ecuatoriano [*eh-koo-ah-toh-ree-ah'-noh*]
edge, orilla [*oh-ree'-yah*]
edible, comestible [*koh-mehs-tee'-bleh*]
edition, edición (f) [*eh-dee-thee-ohn'*]
editor, editor (m) [*eh-dee-tohr'*]
education, educación (f) [*eh-doo-kah-thee-ohn'*]
effect n., efecto [*eh-fehk'-toh*]
effective, eficaz [*eh-fee-kahth'*]
efficient, eficiente [*eh-fee-thee-ehn'-teh*]
effort, esfuerzo [*ehs-foo-ehr'-thoh*]
egg, huevo [*oo-eh'-voh*]
  fried eggs, huevos fritos [*oo-eh'-vohs free'-tohs*]
  hard-boiled eggs, huevos duros [*oo-eh'-vohs doo'-rohs*]
  scrambled eggs, huevos revueltos [*oo-eh'-vohs reh-voo-ehl'-tohs*]
  soft-boiled eggs, huevos pasados por agua [*oo-eh'-vohs pah-sah'-dohs pohr ah'-goo-ah*]
Egypt, Egipto [*eh-heep'-toh*]
Egyptian, egipcio [*eh-heep'-thee-oh*]
eight, ocho [*oh'-choh*]
eighteen, dieciocho [*dee-eh-thee-oh'-choh*]
eighth, octavo [*ohk-tah'-voh*]
eighty, ochenta [*oh-chehn'-tah*]
either, uno u otro [*oo'-noh oo oh'-troh*]
either [one], cualquiera [*koo-ahl-kee-eh'-rah*]
elaborate adj., elaborado [*eh-lah-boh-rah'-doh*]
elastic adj. & n., elástico [*eh-lahs'-tee-koh*]
elated, gozoso, alborozado [*goh-thoh'-soh, ahl-boh-roh-thah'-doh*]
elbow, codo [*koh'-doh*]
elder, mayor [*mah-yohr'*]
elderly, de edad [*deh eh-dahd'*]
elect v., elegir (irreg) [*eh-leh-heer'*]
election, elección (f) [*eh-lehk-thee-ohn'*]

electric, eléctrico [*eh-lehk'-tree-koh*]
electricity, electricidad (f) [*eh-lehk-tree-thee-dahd'*]
elegant, elegante [*eh-leh-gahn'-teh*]
element, elemento [*eh-leh-mehn'-toh*]
elementary, elemental [*eh-leh-mehn-tahl'*]
elephant, elefante (m) [*eh-leh-fahn'-teh*]
elevator, ascensor (m) [*ahs-thehn-sohr'*]
eleven, once [*ohn'-theh*]
eliminate v., eliminar [*eh-lee-mee-nahr'*]
else, otro, más [*oh'-troh, mahs'*]
   anything else, algo más [*ahl'-goh mahs'*]
   nothing else, nada más [*nah'-dah mahs'*]
   someone else, alguna otra persona [*ahl-goo'-nah oh'-trah pehr-soh'-nah*]
   somewhere else, en alguna otra parte [*ehn ahl-goo'-nah oh'-trah pahr'-teh*]
embargo, embargo [*ehm-bahr'-goh*]
embark v., embarcar [*ehm-bahr-kahr'*]
embarrass v., desconcertar (irreg) [*dehs-kohn-thehr-tahr'*]
embarrassed, abochornado [*ah-boh-chohr-nah'-doh*]
embassy, embajada [*ehm-bah-hah'-dah*]
embrace n., abrazo [*ah-brah'-thoh*]
embrace v., abrazar [*ah-brah-thahr'*]
embroidery, bordado [*bohr-dah'-doh*]
emerald, esmeralda [*ehs-meh-rahl'-dah*]
emergency, emergencia [*eh-mehr-hehn'-thee-ah*]
   in case of emergency, en caso de urgencia [*ehn kah'-soh deh oor-hehn'-thee-ah*]
emigrant, emigrante (m, f) [*eh-mee-grahn'-teh*]
emigration, emigración (f) [*eh-mee-grah-thee-ohn'*]
emotion, emoción (f) [*eh-moh-thee-ohn'*]
emperor, emperador [*ehm-peh-rah-dohr'*]
emphasis, énfasis (m) [*ehn'-fah-sees*]
emphasize v., dar énfasis [*dahr ehn'-fah-sees*]
employer, patrón (m) [*pah-trohn'*]
employment, empleo [*ehm-pleh'-oh*]
employment agency, agencia de empleos [*ah-hehn'-thee-ah deh ehm-pleh'-ohs*]

empty, vacío [*vah-thee'-oh*]
enclose *v.*, incluir (irreg) [*een-kloo-eer'*]
encounter *n.*, encuentro [*ehn-koo-ehn'-troh*]
encounter *v.*, encontrarse con [*ehn-kohn-trahr'-seh kohn*]
encourage *v.*, animar [*ah-nee-mahr'*]
encouragement, estímulo [*ehs-tee'-moo-loh*]
end *n.*, fin (m) [*feen'*]
end *v.*, terminar [*tehr-mee-nahr'*]
endeavor *v.*, intentar [*een-tehn-tahr'*]
endless, sin fin [*seen feen'*]
endure *v.*, durar [*doo-rahr'*]
enemy, enemigo [*eh-neh-mee'-goh*]
energy, energía [*eh-nehr-hee'-ah*]
engage *v.*, comprometerse [*kohm-proh-meh-tehr'-seh*]
engaged, comprometido [*kohm-proh-meh-tee'-doh*]
engagement, compromiso [*kohm-proh-mee'-soh*]
engine, motor (m) [*moh-tohr'*]
engineer, ingeniero [*een-heh-nee-eh'-roh*]
England, Inglaterra [*een-glah-teh'-rrah*]
English, inglés [*een-glehs'*]
enjoy *v.*, gozar [*goh-thahr'*]
  Enjoy yourself! ¡Diviértase! [*dee-vee-ehr'-tah-seh*]
enjoyment, gozo [*goh'-thoh*]
enormous, enorme [*eh-nohr'-meh*]
enough, bastante [*bahs-tahn'-teh*]
  That's enough, Basta [*bahs'-tah*]
enroll *v.*, alistar [*ah-lees-tahr'*]
enter *v.*, entrar [*ehn-trahr'*]
  do not enter, prohibido pasar [*proh-ee-bee'-doh pah-sahr'*]
enterprise, empresa [*ehm-preh'-sah*]
entertain *v.*, divertir (irreg), entretener (irreg) [*dee-vehr-teer', ehn-treh-teh-nehr'*]
entertaining, entretenido [*ehn-treh-teh-nee'-doh*]
entertainment, espectáculo [*ehs-pehk-tah'-koo-loh*]
enthusiasm, entusiasmo [*ehn-too-see-ahs'-moh*]
entire, entero [*ehn-teh'-roh*]
entirely, enteramente [*ehn-teh-rah-mehn'-teh*]
entrance, entrada [*ehn-trah'-dah*]

envelope, sobre (m) [*soh'-breh*]
environment, medio ambiente [*meh'-dee-oh ahm-bee-ehn'-teh*]
envy *v.,* envidiar [*ehn-vee-dee-ahr'*]
epoch, época [*eh'-poh-kah*]
equal, igual [*ee-goo-ahl'*]
equality, igualdad (f) [*ee-goo-ahl-dahd'*]
equator, ecuador (m) [*eh-koo-ah-dohr'*]
equipment, equipo [*eh-kee'-poh*]
equivalent, equivalente [*eh-kee-vah-lehn'-teh*]
erase *v.,* borrar [*boh-rrahr'*]
eraser, borrador (m) [*boh-rrah-dohr'*]
err *v.,* errar [*eh-rrahr'*]
errand, recado [*reh-kah'-doh*]
error, error (m) [*eh-rrohr'*]
escape *n.,* fuga [*foo'-gah*]
escape *v.,* escapar [*ehs-kah-pahr'*]
especially, especialmente [*ehs-peh-thee-ahl-mehn'-teh*]
essential, esencial [*eh-sehn-thee-ahl'*]
establish *v.,* establecer (irreg) [*ehs-tah-bleh-thehr'*]
establishment, establecimiento [*ehs-tah-bleh-thee-mee-ehn'-toh*]
estate, bienes (m, pl), propiedad (f) [*bee-eh'-nehs, proh-pee-eh-dahd'*]
esteem *v.,* estimar [*ehs-tee-mahr'*]
estimate [of price], cálculo [*kahl'-koo-loh*]
estimate *v.,* estimar [*ehs-tee-mahr'*]
eternal, eterno [*eh-tehr'-noh*]
Europe, Europa [*eh-oo-roh'-pah*]
European, europeo [*eh-oo-roh-peh'-oh*]
evacuate *v.,* evacuar [*eh-vah-koo-ahr'*]
eve, víspera [*vees'-peh-rah*]
  Christmas Eve, Nochebuena [*noh-cheh-boo-eh'-nah*]
even *adv.,* aun [*ah-oon'*]
  even so, aun así [*ah-oon' ah-see'*]
  even though, aun cuando [*ah-oon' koo-ahn'-doh*]
even *adj.,* justo [*hoos'-toh*]
  even number, número par [*noo'-meh-roh pahr*]

evening, tarde (f), noche (f) [*tahr'-deh, noh'-cheh*]
  good evening, buenas noches [*boo-eh'-nahs noh'-chehs*]
  tomorrow evening, mañana por la noche [*mah-nyah'-nah pohr lah noh'-cheh*]
  yesterday evening, anoche [*ah-noh'-cheh*]
event, suceso [*soo-theh'-soh*]
  in the event of, en caso de [*ehn kah'-soh deh*]
eventually, eventualmente [*eh-vehn-too-ahl-mehn'-teh*]
ever, alguna vez [*ahl-goo'-nah veth*]
  as ever, como siempre [*koh'-moh see-ehm'-preh*]
  forever, para siempre [*pah'-rah see-ehm'-preh*]
every, cada, todo [*kah'-dah, toh'-doh*]
  every day, todos los días [*toh'-dohs lohs dee'-ahs*]
  every time, cada vez [*kah'-dah vehth*]
everybody, todo el mundo [*toh'-doh ehl moon'-doh*]
everything, todo [*toh'-doh*]
everywhere, por todas partes [*pohr toh'-dahs pahr'-tehs*]
evidence, evidencia [*eh-vee-dehn'-thee-ah*]
evident, evidente [*eh-vee-dehn'-teh*]
evidently, evidentemente [*eh-vee-dehn-teh-mehn'-teh*]
evil *n.*, mal (m) [*mahl*]
evil *adj.*, malo [*mah'-loh*]
exact, exacto [*ehk-sahk'-toh*]
exactly, exactamente [*ehk-sahk-tah-mehn'-teh*]
exaggerate *v.*, exagerar [*ehk-sah-heh-rahr'*]
exaggeration, exageración (f) [*ehk-sah-heh-rah-thee-ohn'*]
examination, examen (m) [*ehk-sah'-mehn*]
examine *v.*, examinar [*ehk-sah-mee-nahr'*]
example, ejemplo [*eh-hehm'-ploh*]
for example, por ejemplo [*pohr eh-hehm'-ploh*]
exceed *v.*, exceder [*ehks-theh-dehr'*]
excellent, excelente [*ehks-theh-lehn'-teh*]
except, excepto [*ehks-thehp'-toh*]
exception, excepción (f) [*ehks-thehp-thee-ohn'*]
exceptional, excepcional [*ehks-thehp-thee-oh-nahl'*]
excess, exceso [*ehks-theh'-soh*]
exchange *v.*, cambiar [*kahm-bee-ahr'*]
  in exchange for, a cambio de [*ah kahm'-bee-oh deh*]

excited, excitado [*ehks-thee-tah'-doh*]

   Don't get excited, No se excite [*noh seh ehks-thee'-teh*]

exclusive, exclusivo [*ehks-kloo-see'-voh*]

excursion, excursión (f) [*ehks-koor-see-ohn'*]

excuse v., excusar, dispensar [*ehks-koo-sahr', dees-pehn-sahr'*]

   Excuse me, Dispénseme [*dees-pehn'-seh-meh*]

exercise, ejercicio [*eh-hehr-thee'-thee-oh*]

exhausted, agotado [*ah-goh-tah'-doh*]

exhibit v., exhibir [*ehk-see-beer'*]

exhibition, exhibición (f) [*ehk-see-bee-thee-ohn'*]

exist v., existir [*ehk-sees-teer'*]

existence, existencia [*ehk-sees-tehn'-thee-ah*]

exit, salida [*sah-lee'-dah*]

expect v., esperar [*ehs-peh-rahr'*]

expedition, expedición (f) [*ehks-peh-dee-thee-ohn'*]

expense, gasto [*gahs'-toh*]

expensive, costoso, caro [*kohs-toh'-soh, kah'-roh*]

experience, experiencia [*ehks-peh-ree-ehn'-thee-ah*]

experiment n., experimento [*ehks-peh-ree-mehn'-toh*]

expert, experto [*ehks-pehr'-toh*]

explain v., explicar (irreg) [*ehks-plee-kahr'*]

explanation, explicación (f) [*ehks-plee-kah-thee-ohn'*]

explore v., explorar [*ehks-ploh-rahr'*]

explosion, explosión (f) [*ehks-ploh-see-ohn'*]

export v., exportar [*ehks-pohr-tahr'*]

express n., expreso [*ehks-preh'-soh*]

express v., expresar [*ehks-preh-sahr'*]

exquisite, exquisito [*ehks-kee-see'-toh*]

extend v., extender (irreg) [*ehks-tehn-dehr'*]

extension, extensión (f) [*ehks-tehn-see-ohn'*]

exterior n., exterior (m) [*ehks-teh-ree-ohr'*]

external, externo [*ehks-tehr'-noh*]

extinguish v., extinguir [*ehks-teen-gheer'*]

extra, extra [*ehks'-trah*]

extract v., extraer (irreg) [*ehks-trah-ehr'*]

extraordinary, extraordinario [*ehks-trah-ohr-dee-nah'-ree-oh*]

extravagant, extravagante [*ehks-trah-vah-gahn'-teh*]

extreme, extremo [*ehks-treh'-moh*]
extremely, extremadamente [*ehks-treh-mah-dah-mehn'-teh*]
eye, ojo [*oh'-hoh*]
eyeball, globo del ojo [*gloh'-boh dehl oh'-hoh*]
eyebrow, ceja [*theh'-hah*]
eye doctor, oculista (m) [*oh-koo-lees'-tah*]
eyeglasses, gafas (pl) [*gah'-fahs*]
eyelashes, pestañas [*pehs-tah'-nyahs*]
eyelid, párpado [*pahr'-pah-doh*]
eyesight, vista [*vees'-tah*]
eyewitness, testigo ocular [*tehs-tee'-goh oh-koo-lahr'*]

F

fabric, tela [*teh'-lah*]
face *n.*, cara [*kah'-rah*]
face *v.*, afrontar [*ah-frohn-tahr'*]
fact, hecho [*eh'-choh*]
  in fact, en realidad [*ehn reh-ah-lee-dahd'*]
factory, fábrica [*fah'-bree-kah*]
faculty, facultad (f) [*fah-kool-tahd'*]
fad, manía [*mah-nee'-ah*]
fade *v.*, descolorarse [*dehs-koh-loh-rahr'-seh*]
fail *v.*, fracasar [*frah-kah-sahr'*]
failure, fracaso [*frah-kah'-soh*]
faint [weak], débil [*deh'-beel*]
faint *v.*, desmayarse [*dehs-may-yahr'-seh*]
fair [exposition] *n.*, feria [*feh'-ree-ah*]
fair *adj.*, justo [*hoos'-toh*]
fairness, justicia [*hoos-tee'-thee-ah*]
faith, fe (f) [*feh*]
faithful, fiel [*fee-ehl'*]
fall [season], otoño [*oh-toh'-nyoh*]
fall [descent] *n.*, caída [*kah-ee'-dah*]
fall *v.*, caer (irreg) [*kah-ehr'*]

fall back, retroceder [*reh-troh-theh-dehr'*]
fall in love, enamorarse [*eh-nah-moh-rahr'-seh*]
false, falso [*fahl'-soh*]
falsehood, falsedad (f) [*fahl-seh-dahd'*]
fame, fama [*fah'-mah*]
familiar, familiar [*fah-mee-lee-ahr'*]
family, familia [*fah-mee'-lee-ah*]
famous, famoso [*fah-moh'-soh*]
fan, ventilador (m), abanico [*vehn-tee-lah-dohr', ah-bah-nee'-koh*]
fancy *n.,* fantasía [*fahn-tah-see'-ah*]
fantastic, fantástico [*fahn-tahs'-tee-koh*]
far, lejos [*leh'-hohs*]
  far away, muy lejos [*moo-ee' leh'-hohs*]
  How far? ¿A qué distancia? [*ah keh' dees-tahn'-thee-ah*]
fare, tarifa [*tah-ree'-fah*]
farewell *n.,* despedida [*dehs-peh-dee'-dah*]
farm, granja [*grahn'-hah*]
farmer, granjero [*grahn-heh'-roh*]
farmyard, corral (m) [*koh-rrahl'*]
farther, más lejos [*mahs' leh'-hohs*]
fascinate *v.,* fascinar [*fahs-thee-nahr'*]
fascinating, fascinante [*fahs-thee-nahn'-teh*]
fashion, moda [*moh'-dah*]
fashionable, de moda [*deh moh'-dah*]
fast *adj.,* rápido [*rah'-pee-doh*]
fast *v.,* ayunar [*ah-yoo-nahr'*]
fasten *v.,* fijar [*fee-hahr'*]
fat *n.,* grasa, manteca [*grah'-sah, mahn-teh-kah*]
fat *adj.,* gordo [*gohr'-doh*]
fate, destino [*dehs-tee'-noh*]
father, padre (m) [*pah'-dreh*]
father-in-law, suegro [*soo-eh'-groh*]
fatigue, fatiga [*fah-tee'-gah*]
faucet, grifo [*gree'-foh*]
fault, falta, culpa [*fahl'-tah, kool'-pah*]
favor *n.,* favor (m) [*fah-vohr'*]
favor *v.,* favorecer (irreg) [*fah-voh-reh-thehr'*]

favorite, favorito [*fah-voh-ree'-toh*]
fear n., miedo [*mee-eh'-doh*]
fear v., tener miedo [*teh-nehr' mee-eh'-doh*]
fearful, temeroso [*teh-meh-roh'-soh*]
fearless, sin miedo [*seen mee-eh'-doh*]
feast, fiesta [*fee-ehs'-tah*]
feather, pluma [*ploo'-mah*]
feature [trait], rasgo [*rahs'-goh*]
February, febrero [*feh-breh'-roh*]
federal, federal [*feh-deh-rahl'*]
fee, honorarios (pl) [*oh-noh-rah'-ree-ohs*]
feed v., dar (irreg) de comer, alimentar [*dahr de koh-mehr', ah-lee-mehn-tahr'*]
feel v., sentir (irreg) [*sehn-teer'*]
feeling, sentimiento [*sehn-tee-mee-ehn'-toh*]
feet, pies (m, pl) [*pee-ehs'*]
fellow, tipo, compañero [*tee'-poh, kohm-pah-nyeh'-roh*]
female, hembra [*ehm'-brah*]
feminine, femenino [*feh-meh-nee'-noh*]
fence n., cerca [*thehr'-kah*]
fencing, esgrima [*ehs-gree'-mah*]
fender, guardafango [*goo-ahr-dah-fahn'-goh*]
ferryboat, barca de pasaje [*bahr'-kah deh pah-sah'-heh*]
festival, festival (m) [*fehs-tee-vahl'*]
fetch v., ir a buscar [*eer ah boos-kahr'*]
fever, fiebre (f) [*fee-eh'-breh*]
feverish, febril [*feh-breel'*]
few, pocos (m, pl) [*poh'-kohs*]
  a few, unos pocos [*oo'-nohs poh'-kohs*]
fewer, menos [*meh'-nohs*]
fiancé, novio [*noh'-vee-oh*]
fiancée, novia [*noh'-vee-ah*]
fiction, ficción (f) [*feek-thee-ohn'*]
fidget v., agitar [*ah-hee-tahr'*]
field, campo [*kahm'-poh*]
field glasses, anteojos de larga vista [*ahn-teh-oh'-hohs deh lahr'-gah vees'-tah*]
fierce, fiero [*fee-eh'-roh*]

fifteen, quince [*keen'-theh*]
fifth, quinto [*keen'-toh*]
fifty, cincuenta [*theen-koo-ehn'-tah*]
fig, higo [*ee'-goh*]
fight *n.*, pelea [*peh-leh'-ah*]
fight *v.*, pelear [*peh-leh-ahr'*]
figure [form] *n.*, figura [*fee-goo'-rah*]
figure [number] *n.*, cifra [*thee'-frah*]
file [tool], lima [*lee'-mah*]
file [record], archivo [*ahr-chee'-voh*]
fill *v.*, llenar [*yeh-nahr'*]
filling [tooth] *n.*, empaste [*ehm-pahs'-teh*]
film, película [*peh-lee'-koo-lah*]
filter, filtro [*feel'-troh*]
filthy, sucio, mugriento [*soo'-thee-oh, moo-gree-ehn'-toh*]
final, final [*fee-nahl'*]
finally, finalmente [*fee-nahl-mehn'-teh*]
financial, financiero [*fee-nahn-thee-eh'-roh*]
find *v.*, encontrar (irreg) [*ehn-kohn-trahr'*]
fine *n.*, multa [*mool'-tah*]
fine [excellent] *adj.*, bueno, excelente [*boo-eh'-noh, ehks-theh-lehn'-teh*]
fine [small] *adj.*, fino [*fee'-noh*]
finger, dedo [*deh'-doh*]
fingerprint, huella digital [*oo-eh'-yah dee-hee-tahl'*]
finish *v.*, terminar, acabar [*tehr-mee-nahr', ah-kah-bahr'*]
fire, fuego [*foo-eh'-goh*]
fireman, bombero [*bohm-beh'-roh*]
fireplace, chimenea [*chee-meh-neh'-ah*]
fireproof, incombustible [*een-kohm-boos-tee'-bleh*]
firm *n.*, firma [*feer'-mah*]
firm *adj.*, firme [*feer'-meh*]
first, primero [*pree-meh'-roh*]
   at first, al principio [*ahl preen-thee'-pee-oh*]
first aid, primeros auxilios [*pree-meh'-rohs ah-oo-ksee'-lee-ohs*]
first name, nombre de pila [*nohm'-breh deh pee'-lah*]
fish *n.*, pez (m), pescado [*pehth, pehs-kah'-doh*]

fish v., pescar [*pehs-kahr'*]

fisherman, pescador (m) [*pehs-kah-dohr'*]

fishing, pesca [*pehs'-kah*]

fishing boat, barco de pesca [*bahr'-koh deh pehs'-kah*]

fist, puño [*poo'-nyoh*]

fit [of clothing] n., ajuste (m) [*ah-hoos'-teh*]

   fit for, apropiado para [*ah-proh-pee-ah'-doh pah'-rah*]

fit v., ajustar, cuadrar [*ah-hoos-tahr'*, *koo-ah-drahr'*]

fitting n., ajuste (m) [*ah-hoos'-teh*]

five, cinco [*theen'-koh*]

fix [repair] v., arreglar, reparar [*ah-rreh-glahr'*, *reh-pah-rahr'*]

fix [attach] v., adherir (irreg) [*ah-deh-reer'*]

fixed, fijo [*fee'-hoh*]

fixed price, precio fijo [*preh'-thee-oh fee'-hoh*]

flag, bandera [*bahn-deh'-rah*]

flame, llama, flama [*yah'-mah, flah'-mah*]

flannel, franela [*frah-neh'-lah*]

flare, llamarada, destello [*yah-mah-rah'-dah, dehs-teh'-yoh*]

flash, relámpago [*reh-lahm'-pah-goh*]

flask, frasco [*frahs'-koh*]

flat, llano [*yah'-noh*]

flatterer, lisonjero [*lee-sohn-heh'-roh*]

flattery, lisonja [*lee-sohn'-hah*]

flavor n., sabor (m) [*sah-bohr'*]

flavor v., condimentar [*kohn-dee-mehn-tahr'*]

flea, pulga [*pool'-gah*]

flee v., huir (irreg) [*oo-eer'*]

fleece, vellón (m) [*veh-yohn'*]

fleet n., flota [*floh'-tah*]

flesh, carne (f) [*kahr'-neh*]

flexible, flexible [*flehk-see'-bleh*]

flight, vuelo [*voo-eh'-loh*]

fling v., arrojar [*ah-rroh-hahr'*]

flirt v., coquetear [*koh-keh-teh-ahr'*]

float v., flotar [*floh-tahr'*]

flood, inundación (f) [*ee-noon-dah-thee-ohn'*]

floor, piso, planta [*pee'-soh, plahn'-tah*]

flour, harina [*ah-ree'-nah*]

flow *v.*, fluir (irreg) [*floo-eer'*]
flower, flor (f) [*flohr'*]
flower shop, florería [*floh-reh-ree'-ah*]
fluent, fluente [*floo-ehn'-teh*]
fluently, corrientemente [*koh-rree-ehn-teh-mehn'-teh*]
fluid, flúido [*floo'-ee-doh*]
flush [blush] *v.*, ruborizarse [*roo-boh-ree-thahr'-seh*]
flute, flauta [*flah'-oo-tah*]
fly *n.*, mosca [*mohs'-kah*]
fly *v.*, volar (irreg) [*voh-lahr'*]
foam, espuma [*ehs-poo'-mah*]
focus, foco [*foh'-koh*]
foe, enemigo [*eh-neh-mee'-goh*]
fog, neblina [*neh-blee'-nah*]
foggy, brumoso [*broo-moh'-soh*]
fold *v.*, doblar [*doh-blahr'*]
follow *v.*, seguir (irreg) [*seh-gheer'*]
following, siguiente [*see-ghee-ehn'-teh*]
fond, cariñoso [*kah-ree-nyoh'-soh*]
food, comida [*koh-mee'-dah*]
fool, tonto [*tohn'-toh*]
foolish, necio [*neh'-thee-oh*]
foot, pie (m) [*pee-eh'*]
football, fútbol (m) [*foot'-bohl*]
for, para, por [*pah'-rah, pohr'*]
  for example, por ejemplo [*pohr eh-hehm'-ploh*]
  for instance, por ejemplo [*pohr eh-hehm'-ploh*]
  What for? ¿Para qué? [*pah'-rah keh*]
forbid *v.*, prohibir [*proh-ee-beer'*]
force *n.*, fuerza [*foo-ehr'-thah*]
force *v.*, forzar (irreg), obligar [*fohr-thahr', oh-blee-gahr'*]
forehead, frente (f) [*frehn'-teh*]
foreign, extranjero [*ehks-trahn-heh'-roh*]
foreigner, extranjero [*ehks-trahn-heh'-roh*]
foreign minister, ministro de relaciones exteriores [*mee-nees'-troh deh reh-lah-thee-oh'-nehs ehks-teh-ree-oh'-rehs*]

foreign office, ministerio de negocios extranjeros [*mee-nees-teh'-ree-oh deh neh-goh'-thee-ohs ehks-trahn-heh'-rohs*]

foreign policy, política exterior [*poh-lee'-tee-kah ehks-teh-ree-ohr'*]

forest, selva [*sehl'-vah*]

forever, para siempre [*pah'-rah see-ehm'-preh*]

forget *v.*, olvidar [*ohl-vee-dahr'*]

forget-me-not, no me olvides [*noh meh ohl-vee'-dehs*]

forgive *v.*, perdonar [*pehr-doh-nahr'*]

forgotten, olvidado [*ohl-vee-dah'-doh*]

fork, tenedor (m) [*teh-neh-dohr'*]

form *n.*, forma [*fohr'-mah*]

form *v.*, formar [*fohr-mahr'*]

formal, formal [*fohr-mahl'*]

formality, formalidad (f) [*fohr-mah-lee-dahd'*]

former, anterior [*ahn-teh-ree-ohr'*]

formula, fórmula [*fohr'-moo-lah*]

fort, fortaleza [*fohr-tah-leh'-thah*]

forth, hacia adelante [*ah'-thee-ah ah-deh-lahn'-teh*]

  back and forth, hacia atrás y hacia adelante [*ah'-thee-ah ah-trahs' ee ah'-thee-ah ah-deh-lahn'-teh*]

fortunate, afortunado [*ah-fohr-too-nah'-doh*]

fortunately, afortunadamente [*ah-fohr-too-nah-dah-mehn'-teh*]

fortune, fortuna [*fohr-too'-nah*]

forty, cuarenta [*koo-ah-rehn'-tah*]

forum, tribunal (m) [*tree-boo-nahl'*]

forward, adelante [*ah-deh-lahn'-teh*]

foundation, fundación (f) [*foon-dah-thee-ohn'*]

fountain, fuente (f) [*foo-ehn'-teh*]

fountain pen, pluma estilográfica [*ploo'-mah ehs-tee-loh-grah'-fee-kah*]

four, cuatro [*koo-ah'-troh*]

fourteen, catorce [*kah-tohr'-theh*]

fourth, cuarto [*koo-ahr'-toh*]

fracture, fractura [*frahk-too'-rah*]

fragile, frágil [*frah'-heel*]

fragrance, fragancia [*frah-gahn'-thee-ah*]

frame, marco, armazón (m) [*mahr'-koh, ahr-mah-thohn'*]

France, Francia [*frahn'-thee-ah*]

frank, franco [*frahn'-koh*]

frantic, frenético [*freh-neh'-tee-koh*]

fraternity, fraternidad (f) [*frah-tehr-nee-dahd'*]

fraud, fraude (m) [*frah'-oo-deh*]

free *adj.,* libre [*lee'-breh*]

free *v.,* libertar [*lee-behr-tahr'*]

freedom, libertad (f) [*lee-behr-tahd'*]

freeze *v.,* congelar [*kohn-heh-lahr'*]

freight, flete (m), carga [*fleh'-teh, kahr'-gah*]

French, francés [*frahn-thehs'*]

Frenchman, francés [*frahn-thehs'*]

frequent, frecuente [*freh-koo-ehn'-teh*]

frequently, frecuentemente [*freh-koo-ehn-teh-mehn'-teh*]

fresh, fresco [*frehs'-koh*]

fret *v.,* apurarse [*ah-poo-rahr'-seh*]

Friday, viernes (m) [*vee-ehr'-nehs*]

fried, frito [*free'-toh*]

friend, amigo [*ah-mee'-goh*]

friendship, amistad (f) [*ah-mees-tahd'*]

frighten *v.,* asustar [*ah-soos-tahr'*]

frog, rana [*rah'-nah*]

from, de, desde [*deh, dehs'-deh*]

   come from *v.,* provenir (irreg) [*proh-veh-neer'*]

   from far, desde lejos [*dehs'-deh leh'-hohs*]

   from now on, desde ahora en adelante [*dehs'-deh ah-oh'-rah ehn ah-deh-lahn'-teh*]

front, frente (m) [*frehn'-teh*]

frost, escarcha [*ehs-kahr'-chah*]

frown *n.,* entrecejo [*ehn-treh-theh'-hoh*]

frown *v.,* fruncir el ceño [*froon-theer' ehl theh'-nyoh*]

frozen, congelado [*kohn-heh-lah'-doh*]

fruit, fruta [*froo'-tah*]

fruit salad, ensalada de frutas [*ehn-sah-lah'-dah deh froo'-tahs*]

fruit store, frutería [*froo-teh-ree'-ah*]

fry *v.*, freír (irreg) [*freh-eer'*]
frying pan, sartén (f) [*sahr-tehn'*]
fuel *n.*, combustible (m) [*kohm-boos-tee'-bleh*]
full, lleno [*yeh'-noh*]
fumble *v.*, buscar a tientas [*boos-kahr' ah tee-ehn'-tahs*]
fun, diversión (f) [*dee-vehr-see-ohn'*]
function, función (f) [*foon-thee-ohn'*]
funds, fondos (m, pl) [*fohn'-dohs*]
funeral, funeral (m) [*foo-neh-rahl'*]
funny, cómico [*koh'-mee-koh*]
fur, piel (f) [*pee-ehl'*]
fur coat, abrigo de pieles [*ah-bree'-goh deh pee-eh'-lehs*
furious, furioso [*foo-ree-oh'-soh*]
furnish [provide] *v.*, suministrar [*soo-mee-nee-strahr'*]
furnish [put furniture into] *v.*, amueblar [*ah-moo-eh-blahr'*]
furnished room, habitación (f) amueblada [*ah-bee-tah-thee-ohn' ah-moo-eh-blah'-dah*]
furniture, muebles (m, pl) [*moo-eh'-blehs*]
further, más, más lejos [*mahs', mahs' leh'-hohs*]
furthermore, además [*ah-deh-mahs'*]
future, futuro [*foo-too'-roh*]
  in the future, en el futuro [*ehn ehl foo-too'-roh*]

G

gadget, artefacto [*ahr-teh-fahk'-toh*]
gaiety, alborozo [*ahl-boh-roh'-thoh*]
gain *n.*, ganancia [*gah-nahn'-thee-ah*]
gain *v.*, ganar [*gah-nahr'*]
gallon, galón (m) [*gah-lohn'*]
gamble *v.*, jugar (irreg) [*hoo-gahr'*]
game, juego, partido [*hoo-eh'-goh, pahr-tee'-doh*]
gangplank, pasarela [*pah-sah-reh'-lah*]
garage, garage (m) [*gah-rah'-heh*]
garbage, basura [*bah-soo'-rah*]

garden, jardín (m) [*hahr-deen'*]

gardener, jardinero [*hahr-dee-neh'-roh*]

garlic, ajo [*ah'-hoh*]

garment, prenda [*prehn'-dah*]

garret, desván (m) [*dehs-vahn'*]

garter, liga [*lee'-gah*]

gasoline, gasolina [*gah-soh-lee'-nah*]

gasoline station, gasolinera [*gah-soh-lee-neh'-rah*]

gas tank, depósito de gasolina [*deh-poh'-see-toh deh gah-soh-lee'-nah*]

gate, puerta [*poo-ehr'-tah*]

gather *v.,* recoger, reunir [*reh-koh-hehr', reh-oo-neer'*]

gaudy, vistoso [*vees-toh'-soh*]

gauge *n.,* indicador (m) [*een-dee-kah-dohr'*]

gay, alegre [*ah-leh'-greh*]

gear, engranaje (m) [*ehn-grah-nah'-heh*]

gem, egma [*heh'-mah*]

gender, género [*heh'-neh-roh*]

general *n. & adj.,* general [*heh-neh-rahl'*]

   in general, por lo general [*pohr loh heh-neh-rahl'*]

generally, generalmente [*heh-neh-rahl-mehn'-teh*]

generation, generación (f) [*heh-neh-rah-thee-ohn'*]

generous, generoso [*heh-neh-roh'-soh*]

genius, genio [*heh'-nee-oh*]

gentle, suave [*soo-ah'-veh*]

gentleman, caballero [*kah-bah-yeh'-roh*]

genuine, genuino [*heh-noo-ee'-noh*]

geography, geografía [*heh-oh-grah-fee'-ah*]

germ, germen (m) [*hehr'-mehn*]

German, alemán [*ah-leh-mahn'*]

Germany, Alemania [*ah-leh-mah'-nee-ah*]

get [become] *v.,* llegar a ser [*yeh-gahr' ah sehr'*]

get [obtain] *v.,* conseguir (irreg) [*kohn-seh-gheer'*]

get [receive] *v.,* recibir [*reh-thee-beer'*]

   get back, volver (irreg), regresar [*vohl-vehr', reh-greh-sahr'*]

   get down, bajar [*bah-hahr'*]

   get in, entrar [*ehn-trahr'*]

get married, casarse [*kah-sahr'-seh*]
get off, bajarse [*bah-hahr'-seh*]
get to, llegar a [*yeh-gahr' ah*]
get up, levantarse [*leh-vahn-tahr'-seh*]
ghost, fantasma (m) [*fahn-tahs'-mah*]
gift, regalo [*reh-gah'-loh*]
gin, ginebra [*hee-neh'-brah*]
girdle, faja [*fah'-hah*]
girl, niña, muchacha [*nee'-nyah, moo-chah'-chah*]
give v., dar (irreg) [*dahr*]
  give back, devolver (irreg) [*deh-vohl-vehr'*]
  give in, ceder [*theh-dehr'*]
  give up, darse por vencido [*dahr'-seh pohr vehn-thee'-doh*]
glad, contento [*kohn-tehn'-toh*]
glamour, encanto [*ehn-kahn'-toh*]
glance n., golpe (m) de vista [*gohl'-peh deh vees'-tah*]
glance v., vislumbrar [*vees-loom-brahr'*]
gland, glándula [*glahn'-doo-lah*]
glare n., resplandor (m) [*rehs-plahn-dohr'*]
glass [container] n., vaso [*vah'-soh*]
glass [material] n., vidrio [*vee'-dree-oh*]
glasses pl., gafas, anteojos [*gah'-fahs, ahn-teh-oh'-hohs*]
glimpse v., vislumbrar [*vees-loom-brahr'*]
globe, globo [*gloh'-boh*]
gloomy, abatido [*ah-bah-tee'-doh*]
glory, gloria [*gloh'-ree-ah*]
glove, guante (m) [*goo-ahn'-teh*]
glow n., resplandor (m) [*rehs-plahn-dohr'*]
glue n., engrudo [*ehn-groo'-doh*]
go v., ir (irreg) [*eer*]
  Go away! ¡Váyase! [*vah'-yah-seh*]
  go back, regresar [*reh-greh-sahr'*]
  go down, bajar [*bah-hahr'*]
  go in, entrar [*ehn-trahr'*]
  go on, continuar [*kohn-tee-noo-ahr'*]
  go out, salir (irreg) [*sah-leer'*]
  go over, pasar por encima de [*pah-sahr' pohr ehn-thee'-mah deh*]

go to bed, acostarse [*ah-kohs-tahr'-seh*]
go up, subir [*soo-beer'*]
goal, meta [*meh'-tah*]
God, Dios (m) [*dee-ohs'*]
godfather, padrino [*pah-dree'-noh*]
godmother, madrina [*mah-dree'-nah*]
gold, oro [*oh'-roh*]
golden, dorado [*doh-rah'-doh*]
golf, golf (m) [*gohlf'*]
good, bueno [*boo-eh'-noh*]
   good afternoon, buenas tardes [*boo-eh'-nahs tahr'-dehs*]
   good-bye, adiós [*ah-dee-ohs'*]
   good evening, buenas tardes/noches [*boo-eh'-nahs tahr'-dehs/noh'-chehs*]
   good luck, buena suerte [*boo-eh'-nah soo-ehr'-teh*]
   good morning, buenos días [*boo-eh'-nohs dee'-ahs*]
   good night, buenas noches [*boo-eh'-nahs noh'-chehs*]
good-looking, guapo [*ghoo-ah'-poh*]
goodness, bondad (f) [*bohn-dahd'*]
goods, mercancía [*mehr-kahn-thee'-ah*]
gorgeous, suntuoso, magnífico [*soon-too-oh'-soh, mahg-nee'-fee-koh*]
gossip *n.,* chisme (m) [*chees'-meh*]
gossip *v.,* chismorrear [*chees-moh-rreh-ahr'*]
Gothic, gótico [*goh'-tee-koh*]
government, gobierno [*goh-bee-ehr'-noh*]
governor, gobernador (m) [*goh-behr-nah-dohr'*]
grace, gracia [*grah'-thee-ah*]
graceful, gracioso, agraciado [*grah-thee-oh'-soh, ah-grah-thee-ah'-doh*]
grade [degree, class] *n.,* grado [*grah'-doh*]
gradually, gradualmente [*grah-doo-ahl-mehn'-teh*]
graduate *n.,* graduado [*grah-doo-ah'-doh*]
graduate *v.,* graduarse [*grah-doo-ahr'-seh*]
graduation, graduación (f) [*grah-doo-ah-thee-ohn'*]
grain, grano [*grah'-noh*]
grammar, gramática [*grah-mah'-tee-kah*]
grandchild, nieto [*nee-eh'-toh*]

granddaughter, nieta [*nee-eh'-tah*]
grandfather, abuelo [*ah-boo-eh'-loh*]
grandmother, abuela [*ah-boo-eh'-lah*]
grandson, nieto [*nee-eh'-toh*]
grant *v.,* otorgar [*oh-tohr-gahr'*]
grape, uva [*oo'-vah*]
grapefruit, toronja [*toh-rohn'-hah*]
grass, hierba [*ee-ehr'-bah*]
grateful, agradecido [*ah-grah-deh-thee'-doh*]
gratitude, gratitud (f) [*grah-tee-tood'*]
grave *n.,* sepultura [*seh-pool-too'-rah*]
gravity, gravedad (f) [*grah-veh-dahd'*]
gravy, salsa [*sahl'-sah*]
gray, gris [*grees*]
grease, grasa [*grah'-sah*]
great, grande, gran [*grahn'-deh, grahn*]
  a great deal, mucho [*moo'-choh*]
  a great many, muchos [*moo'-chohs*]
Great Britain, Gran Bretaña [*grahn breh-tah'-nyah*]
greatness, grandeza [*grahn-deh'-thah*]
Greece, Grecia [*greh'-thee-ah*]
greedy, codicioso [*koh-dee-thee-oh'-soh*]
Greek, griego [*gree-eh'-goh*]
green, verde [*vehr'-deh*]
greet *v.,* saludar [*sah-loo-dahr'*]
greetings, saludos [*sah-loo'-dohs*]
grief, aflicción (f) [*ah-fleek-thee-ohn'*]
grieve *v.,* lamentarse [*lah-mehn-tahr'-seh*]
grin *n.,* sonrisa maliciosa [*sohn-ree'-sah mah-lee-thee-oh'-sah*]
grind *v.,* moler (irreg) [*moh-lehr'*]
grip *v.,* asir [*ah-seer'*]
groan *n.,* gemido [*heh-mee'-doh*]
groan *v.,* gemir (irreg) [*heh-meer'*]
grocery store, tienda de comestibles [*tee-ehn'-dah deh koh-mehs-tee'-blehs*]
ground [earth] *n.,* tierra, suelo [*tee-eh'-rrah, soo-eh'-loh*]
ground floor, piso bajo [*pee'-soh bah'-hoh*]

group, grupo [*groo'-poh*]
grow [increase] *v.,* crecer (irreg) [*kreh-thehr'*]
   grow crops, cultivar [*kool-tee-vahr'*]
   grow old, envejecer (irreg) [*ehn-veh-heh-thehr'*]
grumble *n.,* queja [*keh'-hah*]
guarantee *n.,* garantía [*gah-rahn-tee'-ah*]
guarantee *v.,* garantizar [*gah-rahn-tee-thahr'*]
guard *n.,* guardia [*goo-ahr'-dee-ah*]
guard *v.,* guardar [*goo-ahr-dahr'*]
Guatemala, Guatemala [*goo-ah-teh-mah'-lah*]
Guatemalan, guatemalteco [*goo-ah-teh-mahl-teh'-koh*]
guess *n.,* suposición (f) [*soo-poh-see-thee-ohn'*]
guess *v.,* adivinar [*ah-dee-vee-nahr'*]
guest, invitado [*een-vee-tah'-doh*]
guide *n.,* guía (m, f) [*guee'-ah*]
guilty, culpable [*kool-pah'-bleh*]
guitar, guitarra [*ghee-tah'-rrah*]
gum [anat.], encía [*ehn-thee'-ah*]
gum [chewing gum], chicle (m) [*chee'-kleh*]
gun, fusil (m) [*foo-seel'*]
gutter [street], arroyo [*ah-rroh'-yoh*]
gutter [roof], gotera [*goh-teh'-rah*]
gymnasium, gimnasio [*heem-nah'-see-oh*]
gypsy, gitano [*hee-tah'-noh*]

H

habit, hábito (m), costumbre (f) [*ah'-bee-toh, kohs-toom'-breh*]
hair, cabello, pelo [*kah-beh'-yoh, peh'-loh*]
haircut, corte (m) de pelo [*kohr'-teh deh peh'-loh*]
hairdresser, peluquero [*peh-loo-keh'-roh*]
hair tonic, tónico para el cabello [*toh'-nee-koh pah'-rah ehl kah-beh'-yoh*]
half *adj.,* medio [*meh'-dee-oh*]

half *n.*, mitad (f) [*mee-tahd'*]
  half open, entreabierto [*ehn-treh-ah-bee-ehr'-toh*]
  half past two, las dos y media [*lahs dohs' ee meh'-dee-ah*]
halfway, medio camino [*meh'-dee-oh kah-mee'-noh*]
hall, vestíbulo [*vehs-tee'-boo-loh*]
Halt! ¡Alto! [*ahl'-toh*]
ham, jamón (m) [*hah-mohn'*]
hammer, martillo [*mahr-tee'-yoh*]
hand, mano (f) [*mah'-noh*]
  on the other hand, por otra parte [*pohr oh'-trah pahr'-teh*]
handbag, bolsa de mano [*bohl'-sah deh mah'-noh*]
handicap, desventaja [*dehs-vehn-tah'-hah*]
handkerchief, pañuelo [*pah-nyoo-eh'-loh*]
handle *v.*, manejar [*mah-neh-hahr'*]
handmade, hecho a mano [*eh'-choh ah mah'-noh*]
handsome, buen mozo [*boo-ehn'moh'-thoh*]
handy [accessible], a la mano [*ah lah mah'-noh*]
hang *v.*, colgar (irreg) [*kohl-gahr'*]
hanger, percha [*pehr'-chah*]
happen *v.*, pasar, suceder [*pah-sahr', soo-theh-dehr'*]
happiness, felicidad (f) [*feh-lee-thee-dahd'*]
happy, feliz [*feh-leeth'*]
Happy birthday, Feliz cumpleaños [*feh-leeth' koom-pleh-ah'-nyohs*]
Happy New Year, Feliz Año Nuevo [*feh-leeth' ah'-nyoh noo-eh'-voh*]
harbor, puerto [*poo-ehr'-toh*]
hard, duro [*doo'-roh*]
hardly, apenas [*ah-peh'-nahs*]
harm *v.*, hacer (irreg) daño [*ah-thehr' dah'-nyoh*]
harmful, dañino [*dah-nyee'-noh*]
harp, arpa [*ahr'-pah*]
harsh, áspero [*ahs'-peh-roh*]
harvest *n.*, cosecha [*koh-seh'-chah*]
haste, prisa [*pree'-sah*]
hat, sombrero [*sohm-breh'-roh*]
hate *n.*, odio [*oh'-dee-oh*]
hate *v.*, odiar [*oh-dee-ahr'*]

have *v.*, tener (irreg) [*teh-nehr'*]
  have to, tener que [*teh-nehr' keh*]
he, él [*ehl'*]
head, cabeza [*kah-beh'-thah*]
headache, dolor (m) de cabeza [*doh-lohr' deh kah-beh'-thah*]
headlight, faro delantero [*fah'-roh deh-lahn-teh'-roh*]
headquarters [army], estado mayor [*ehs-tah'-doh mah-yohr'*]
headquarters [business], oficina principal [*oh-fee-thee'-nah preen-thee-pahl'*]
health, salud (f) [*sah-lood'*]
  to your health, a su salud [*ah soo sah-lood'*]
healthy, sano [*sah'-noh*]
hear *v.*, oir (irreg) [*oh-eer'*]
heart, corazón (m) [*koh-rah-thohn'*]
  by heart, de memoria [*deh meh-moh'-ree-ah*]
heart disease, enfermedad del corazón [*ehn-fehr-meh-dahd' dehl ko-rah-thohn'*]
heat *n.*, calor (m) [*kah-lohr'*]
heat *v.*, calentar (irreg) [*kah-lehn-tahr'*]
heating, calefacción (f) [*kah-leh-fahk-thee-ohn'*]
heaven, cielo [*thee-eh'-loh*]
heavy, pesado [*peh-sah'-doh*]
Hebrew, hebreo [*eh-breh'-oh*]
heel, talón (m) [*tah-lohn'*]
height, altura [*ahl-too'-rah*]
heir, heredero [*eh-reh-deh'-roh*]
heiress, heredera [*eh-reh-deh'-rah*]
hell, infierno [*een-fee-ehr'-noh*]
hello, hola [*oh'-lah*]
help *n.*, ayuda [*ah-yoo'-dah*]
help *v.*, ayudar [*ah-yoo-dahr'*]
her *pron.*, la, ella [*lah, eh'-yah*]
her *adj.*, su, suyo, suya, de ella [*soo, soo'-yoh, soo'-yah, deh eh'-yah*]
here, aquí [*ah-kee'*]
  Come here, Venga aquí [*vehn'-gah ah-kee'*]
  Here it is, Aquí está [*ah-kee' ehs-tah'*]
hero, héroe (m) [*eh'-roh-eh*]

hers, suyo, el suyo (de ella) [*soo'-yoh, ehl soo'-yoh (deh eh'-yoh)*]

herself, ella misma [*eh'-yah mees'-mah*]

hesitate *v.,* vacilar [*vah-thee-lahr'*]

hide *v.,* esconder [*ehs-kohn-dehr'*]

hideous, horripilante [*oh-rree-pee-lahn'-teh*]

high, alto [*ahl'-toh*]

high school, escuela secundaria [*ehs-koo-eh'-lah seh-koon-dah'-ree-ah*]

highway, carretera [*kah-rreh-teh'-rah*]

hill, colina [*koh-lee'-nah*]

him, él [*ehl'*]

himself, él mismo [*ehl' mees'-moh*]

hint *v.,* insinuar [*een-see-noo-ahr'*]

hip, cadera [*kah-deh'-rah*]

hire *v.,* alquilar, contratar [*ahl-kee-lahr', kohn-trah-tahr'*]

his, su, de él, suyo, suya [*soo, deh ehl', soo'-yoh, soo'-yah*]

history, historia [*ees-toh'-ree-ah*]

hit *v.,* pegar, golpear [*peh-gahr', gohl-peh-ahr'*]

hitchhike *v.,* hacer auto-stop [*ah-thehr' ah-oo'-toh-stop*]

hold *v.,* sostener (irreg) [*sohs-teh-nehr'*]

hole, agujero [*ah-goo-heh'-roh*]

holiday, día de fiesta (m) [*dee'-ah deh fee-ehs'-tah*]

Holland, Holanda [*oh-lahn'-dah*]

holy, santo [*sahn'-toh*]

home, casa, hogar (m) [*kah'-sah, oh-gahr'*]
   at home, en casa [*ehn kah'-sah*]
   Make yourself at home, Está en su casa [*ehs-tah' ehn soo kah'-sah*]

Honduras, Honduras [*ohn-doo'-rahs*]

Honduran, hondureño [*ohn-doo-reh'-nyoh*]

honest, honrado [*ohn-rah'-doh*]

honey, miel (f) [*mee-ehl'*]

honeymoon, luna de miel [*loo'-nah deh mee-ehl'*]

honor *n.,* honor (m) [*oh-nohr'*]

honor *v.,* honrar [*ohn-rahr'*]

hook, gancho [*gahn'-choh*]

hope *n.,* esperanza [*ehs-peh-rahn'-thah*]

hope *v.*, esperar [*ehs-peh-rahr'*]
hopeful, esperanzado [*ehs-peh-rahn-thah'-doh*]
hopeless, sin esperanza [*seen ehs-peh-rahn'-thah*]
horizon, horizonte (m) [*oh-ree-thohn'-teh*]
horn [animal or shape], cuerno [*koo-ehr'-noh*]
horn [trumpet or auto], bocina [*boh-thee'-nah*]
horrible, horrible [*oh-rree'-bleh*]
horse, caballo [*kah-bah'-yoh*]
hospital, hospital (m) [*ohs-pee-tahl'*]
hospitality, hospitalidad (f) [*ohs-pee-tah-lee-dahd'*]
host, anfitrión (m) [*ahn-ʃee-tree-ohn'*]
hostess, anfitriona [*ahn-fee-tree-oh'-nah*]
hostile, hostil [*ohs-teel'*]
hot, caliente [*kah-lee-ehn'-teh*]
   hot water, agua caliente [*ah'-goo-ah kah-lee-ehn'-teh*]
hotel, hotel (m) [*oh-tehl'*]
hotel room, habitación (f) de hotel [*ah-bee-tah-thee-ohn' deh oh-tehl'*]
hour, hora [*oh'-rah*]
hourly, por hora [*pohr oh'-rah*]
house, casa [*kah'-sah*]
housekeeper, casera [*kah-seh'-rah*]
housewife, mujer de su casa [*moo-hehr' deh soo kah'-sah*]
how? ¿cómo? [*koh'-moh*]
   How do you do? ¿Cómo está usted? [*koh'-moh ehs-tah' oos-tehd'*]
   how far? ¿a qué distancia? [*ah keh' dees-tahn'-thee-ah*]
   how long? ¿cuánto tiempo? [*koo-ahn'-toh tee-ehm'-poh*]
   how much? ¿cuánto? [*koo-ahn'-toh*]
however, sin embargo [*seen ehm-bahr'-goh*]
hug *n.*, abrazo [*ah-brah'-thoh*]
hug *v.*, abrazar [*ah-brah-thahr'*]
huge, enorme [*eh-nohr'-meh*]
human, humano [*oo-mah'-noh*]
humanity, humanidad (f) [*oo-mah-nee-dahd'*]
humble, humilde [*oo-meel'-deh*]
humid, húmedo [*oo'-meh-doh*]
humidity, humedad (f) [*oo-meh-dahd'*]

humorous, humorístico [*oo-moh-rees'-tee-koh*]
hundred, cien, ciento [*thee-ehn', thee-ehn'-toh*]
Hungarian, húngaro [*oon'-gah-roh*]
Hungary, Hungría [*oon-gree'-ah*]
hunger, hambre (m) [*ahm'-breh*]
  be hungry, tener hambre [*teh-nehr' ahm'-breh*]
hunt *v.*, cazar [*kah-thahr'*]
hunter, cazador (m) [*kah-thah-dohr'*]
hunting, caza [*kah'-thah*]
hurricane, huracán (m) [*oo-rah-kahn'*]
hurry *n.*, prisa [*pree'-sah*]
  be in a hurry *v.*, tener prisa [*teh-nehr' pree'-sah*]
hurry *v.*, apresurar(se) [*ah-preh-soo-rahr'-seh*]
  Hurry up, Dese prisa [*deh'-seh pree'-sah*]
hurt *v.*, dañar, doler (irreg) [*dah-nyahr', doh-lehr'*]
husband, esposo, marido [*ehs-poh'-soh, mah-ree'-doh*]
hypocrite, hipócrita (m, f) [*ee-poh'-kree-tah*]

I

I, yo [*yoh*]
ice, hielo [*ee-eh'-loh*]
ice cream, helado [*eh-lah'-doh*]
idea, idea [*ee-deh'-ah*]
ideal, ideal [*ee-deh-ahl'*]
identical, idéntico [*ee-dehn'-tee-koh*]
identification, identificación (f) [*ee-dehn-tee-fee-kah-thee-ohn'*]
identification card, tarjeta de identidad [*tahr-heh'-tah deh ee-dehn-tee-dahd'*]
identify *v.*, identificar [*ee-dehn-tee-fee-kahr'*]
idiot, idiota (m, f) [*ee-dee-oh'-tah*]
if, si [*see*]
  even if, aun si [*ah-oon' see*]
ignition [engine], encendido [*ehn-thehn-dee'-doh*]
ignorant, ignorante [*eeg-noh-rahn'-teh*]

ill, enfermo [*ehn-fehr'-moh*]
illegal, ilegal [*ee-leh-gahl'*]
illicit, ilícito [*ee-lee'-thee-toh*]
illiterate, analfabeto [*ah-nahl-fah-beh'-toh*]
illness, enfermedad (f) [*ehn-fehr-meh-dahd'*]
illustration, ilustración (f) [*ee-loos-trah-thee-ohn'*]
image, imagen (f) [*ee-mah'-hehn*]
imagination, imaginación (f) [*ee-mah-hee-nah-thee-ohn'*]
imagine *v.,* imaginar [*ee-mah-hee-nahr'*]
  Just imagine! ¡Imagínese! [*ee-mah-hee'-neh-seh*]
imitate *v.,* imitar [*ee-mee-tahr'*]
imitation, imitación (f) [*ee-mee-tah-thee-ohn'*]
immature, inmaduro [*een-mah-doo'-roh*]
immediate, inmediato [*een-meh-dee-ah'-toh*]
immediately, inmediatamente [*een-meh-dee-ah-tah-mehn'-teh*]
immense, inmenso [*een-mehn'-soh*]
immigration, inmigración (f) [*een-mee-grah-thee-ohn'*]
immoral, inmoral [*een-moh-rahl'*]
immunity, inmunidad (f) [*een-moo-nee-dahd'*]
impartial, imparcial [*eem-pahr-thee-ahl'*]
impatient, impaciente [*eem-pah-thee-ehn'-teh*]
impending, inminente [*een-mee-nehn'-teh*]
imperfect, imperfecto [*eem-pehr-fehk'-toh*]
imperialism, imperialismo [*eem-peh-ree-ah-lees'-moh*]
implement, instrumento [*eens-troo-mehn'-toh*]
impolite, descortés [*dehs-kohr-tehs'*]
import *v.,* importar [*eem-pohr-tahr'*]
importance, importancia [*eem-pohr-tahn'-thee-ah*]
important, importante [*eem-pohr-tahn'-teh*]
imported, importado [*eem-pohr-tah'-doh*]
impossible, imposible [*eem-poh-see'-bleh*]
impression, impresión (f) [*eem-preh-see-ohn'*]
impressive, imponente [*eem-poh-nehn'-teh*]
improve *v.,* mejorar [*meh-hoh-rahr'*]
improvement, mejora [*meh-hoh'-rah*]
impulse, impulso [*eem-pool'-soh*]
in, en, dentro de [*ehn, dehn'-troh deh*]

in back of, detrás de [*deh-trahs' deh*]
in front of, enfrente de [*ehn-frehn'-teh deh*]
in no way, de ninguna manera [*deh neen-goo'-nah mah-neh'-rah*]
in spite of, a pesar de [*ah peh-sahr' deh*]
inability, incapacidad (f) [*een-kah-pah-thee-dahd'*]
inaccurate, inexacto [*ee-nehk-sahk'-toh*]
inch, pulgada [*pool-gah'-dah*]
incident, incidente (m) [*een-thee-dehn'-teh*]
incidentally, incidentalmente [*een-thee-dehn-tahl-mehn'-teh*]
inclination, inclinación (f) [*een-klee-nah-thee-ohn'*]
include *v.,* incluir (irreg) [*een-kloo-eer'*]
included, incluido [*een-kloo-ee'-doh*]
income, ingresos (pl) [*een-greh'-sohs*]
income tax, impuesto sobre ingresos [*eem-poo-ehs'-toh soh'-breh een-greh'-sohs*]
incomplete, incompleto [*een-kohm-pleh'-toh*]
inconvenience, molestia [*moh-lehs'-tee-ah*]
incorrect, incorrecto [*een-koh-rrehk'-toh*]
increase *n.,* aumento [*ah-oo-mehn'-toh*]
increase *v.,* aumentar [*ah-oo-mehn-tahr'*]
incredible, increíble [*een-kreh-ee'-bleh*]
indecent, indecente [*een-deh-thehn'-teh*]
indeed, verdaderamente [*vehr-dah-deh-rah-mehn'-teh*]
    Yes, indeed!, ¡Claro que sí! [*klah'-roh keh see'*]
indefinite, indefinido [*een-deh-fee-nee'-doh*]
independence, independencia [*een-deh-pehn-dehn'-thee-ah*]
independent, independiente [*een-deh-pehn-dee-ehn'-teh*]
index, índice (m) [*een'-dee-theh*]
India, India [*een'-dee-ah*]
Indian, indio [*een'-dee-oh*]
indicate *v.,* indicar [*een-dee-kahr'*]
indifferent, indiferente [*een-dee-feh-rehn'-teh*]
indigestion, indigestión (f) [*een-dee-hehs-tee-ohn'*]
indignant, indignado [*een-deeg-nah'-doh*]
indirect, indirecto [*een-dee-rehk'-toh*]
indiscreet, indiscreto [*een-dees-kreh'-toh*]
individual *adj.,* individual [*een-dee-vee-doo-ahl'*]

indoors, adentro [*ah-dehn'-troh*]
industrial, industrial [*een-doos-tree-ahl'*]
industry, industria [*een-doos'-tree-ah*]
inefficient, ineficaz [*ee-neh-fee-kath'*]
inexpensive, económico [*eh-koh-noh'-mee-koh*]
infant, bebé [*beh-beh'*]
infection, infección (f) [*een-fehk-thee-ohn'*]
inferior, inferior [*een-feh-ree-ohr'*]
infinite, infinito [*een-fee-nee'-toh*]
infinitive, infinitivo [*een-fee-nee-tee'-voh*]
influence *n.,* influencia [*een-floo-ehn'-thee-ah*]
influence *v.,* influir en (irreg) [*een-floo-eer' ehn*]
inform *v.,* informar [*een-fohr-mahr'*]
informal, informal [*een-fohr-mahl'*]
information, información (f) [*een-fohr-mah-thee-ohn'*]
infrequent, pocofrecuente [*poh'-koh freh-koo-ehn'-teh*]
inhabitant, habitante (m) [*ah-bee-tahn'-teh*]
inherit *v.,* heredar [*eh-reh-dahr'*]
inheritance, herencia [*eh-rehn'-thee-ah*]
initial, inicial [*ee-nee-thee-ahl'*]
injection, inyección (f) [*een-yehk-thee-ohn'*]
injure *v.,* lesionar [*leh-see-oh-nahr'*]
injury, lesión (f) [*leh-see-ohn'*]
injustice, injusticia [*een-hoos-tee'-thee-ah*]
ink, tinta [*teen'-tah*]
inland, tierra adentro [*tee-eh'-rrah ah-dehn'-troh*]
inmate, presidiario [*preh-see-dee-ah'-ree-oh*]
inner, interior [*een-teh-ree-ohr'*]
innkeeper, mesonero [*meh-soh-neh'-roh*]
innocent *adj.,* inocente [*ee-noh-thehn'-teh*]
innumerable, innumerable [*een-noo-meh-rah'-bleh*]
inquire *v.,* preguntar [*preh-goon-tahr'*]
insane, loco [*loh'-koh*]
inside *adv.,* dentro [*dehn'-troh*]
  inside out, al revés [*ahl reh-vehs'*]
inside *n. & adj.,* interior [*een-tee-ree-ohr'*]
insight, discernimiento [*dees-thehr-nee-mee-ehn'-toh*]

insist *v.*, insistir [*een-sees-teer'*]
inspect *v.*, inspeccionar [*eens-pehk-thee-oh-nahr'*]
inspection, inspección (f) [*eens-pehk-thee-ohn'*]
inspector, inspector (m) [*eens-pehk-tohr'*]
inspiration, inspiración (f) [*eens-pee-rah-thee-ohn'*]
install *v.*, instalar [*eens-tah-lahr'*]
instead of, en lugar de [*ehn loo-gahr' deh*]
instinct, instinto [*eens-teen'-toh*]
institution, institución (f) [*eens-tee-too-thee-ohn'*]
instruct *v.*, instruir (irreg) [*eens-troo-eer'*]
instruction, instrucción (f) [*eens-trook-thee-ohn'*]
instructor, instructor (m) [*eens-trook-tohr'*]
instrument, instrumento [*eens-troo-mehn'-toh*]
insufficient, insuficiente [*een-soo-fee-thee-ehn'-teh*]
insult *n.*, insulto [*een-sool'-toh*]
insult *v.*, insultar [*een-sool-tahr'*]
insurance, seguro [*seh-goo'-roh*]
insure *v.*, asegurar [*ah-seh-goo-rahr'*]
intact, intacto [*een-tahk'-toh*]
intellectual, intelectual [*een-teh-lehk-too-ahl'*]
intelligent, inteligente [*een-teh-lee-hehn'-teh*]
intend *v.*, intentar [*een-tehn-táhr*
intense, intenso [*een-tehn'-soh*]
intent *adj.*, intento [*een-tehn'-toh*]
intention, intención (f) [*een-tehn-thee-ohn'*]
interest *n.*, interés (m) [*een-teh-rehs'*]
interest *v.*, interesar [*een-teh-reh-sahr'*]
   interested in, interesado en [*een-teh-reh-sah'-doh ehn*]
interesting, interesante [*een-teh-reh-sahn'-teh*]
interfere *v.*, interferir (irreg) [*een-tehr-feh-reer'*]
interior, interior (m) [*een-teh-ree-ohr'*]
intermission, entreacto [*ehn-treh-ahk'-toh*]
internal, interno [*een-tehr'-noh*]
international, internacional [*een-tehr-nah-thee-oh-nahl'*]
interpreter, intérprete (m & f) [*een-tehr'-preh-teh*]
intersection, intersección (f) [*een-tehr-sehk-thee-ohn'*]
interval, intervalo [*een-tehr-vah'-loh*]
interview, entrevista [*ehn-treh-vees'-tah*]

intimate, íntimo [*een'-tee-moh*]
into, dentro, en [*dehn'-troh, ehn*]
introduce *v.*, presentar [*preh-sehn-tahr'*]
introduction, introducción (f) [*een-troh-dook-thee-ohn'*]
intrude *v.*, entrometerse [*ehn-troh-meh-tehr'-seh*]
intuition, intuición (f) [*een-too-ee-thee-ohn'*]
invalid *adj.*, inválido [*een-vah'-lee-doh*]
invaluable, de gran valor [*deh grahn vah-lohr'*]
invasion, invasión (f) [*een-vah-see-ohn'*]
invention, invención (f) [*een-vehn-thee-ohn'*]
inventor, inventor (m) [*een-vehn-tohr*]
invest *v.*, invertir (irreg) [*een-vehr-teer'*]
investigate *v.*, investigar [*een-vehs-tee-gahr'*]
invisible, invisible [*een-vee-see'-bleh*]
invitation, invitación (f) [*een-vee-tah-thee-ohn'*]
invite *v.*, invitar [*een-vee-tahr'*]
invoice, factura [*fahk-too'-rah*]
involuntary, involuntario [*een-voh-loon-tah'-ree-oh*]
Ireland, Irlanda [*eer-lahn'-dah*]
Irish, irlandés [*eer-lahn-dehs'*]
iron [metal] *n.*, hierro [*ee-eh'-rroh*]
iron [flatiron] *n.*, plancha [*plahn'-chah*]
iron [clothes] *v.*, planchar [*plahn-chahr'*]
irregular, irregular [*ee-rreh-goo-lahr'*]
irresistible, irresistible [*ee-rreh-sees-tee'-bleh*]
irritate *v.*, irritar [*ee-rree-tahr'*]
is: he, she, it is, es, está [*ehs, ehs-tah'*]
island, isla [*ees'-lah*]
issue [magazine], número [*noo'-meh-roh*]
it, ello [*eh'-yoh*]
Italian, italiano [*ee-tah-lee-ah'-noh*]
Italy, Italia [*ee-tah'-lee-ah*]
itch *v.*, picar [*pee-kahr'*]
item, artículo [*ahr-tee'-koo-loh*]
itinerary, itinerario [*ee-tee-neh-rah'-ree-oh*]
its, su, sus (pl) [*soo', soos'*]
ivory, marfil (m) [*mahr-feel'*]

J

jacket, chaqueta [*chah-keh'-tah*]
jail, cárcel (f) [*kahr'-thehl*]
jam *v.*, estrujar [*ehs-troo-hahr'*]
jam [food] *n.*, conserva, compota [*kohn-sehr'-vah, kohm-poh'-tah*]
jam [traffic] *n.*, atascamiento [*ah-tahs-kah-mee-ehn'-toh*]
janitor, conserje (m) [*kohn-sehr'-heh*]
January, enero [*eh-neh'-roh*]
Japan, Japón (m) [*hah-pohn'*]
Japanese, japonés [*hah-poh-nehs'*]
jar, jarra [*hah'-rrah*]
jaw, quijada, mandíbula [*kee-hah'-dah, mahn-dee'-boo-lah*]
jazz, jazz (m) [*yahth*]
jealous, celoso [*theh-loh'-soh*]
jeer *v.*, mofar [*moh-fahr'*]
jelly, gelatina [*heh-lah-tee'-nah*]
jest *n.*, broma [*broh'-mah*]
Jew, Jewish, judío [*hoo-dee'-oh*]
jewel, joya [*hoh'-yah*]
jewelry store, joyería [*hoh-yeh-ree'-ah*]
jiffy, instante (m) [*eens-tahn'-teh*]
job, trabajo [*trah-bah'-hoh*]
join *v.*, juntar(se), unirse a [*hoon-tahr'-seh, oo-neer'-seh ah*]
joke *n.*, broma, chiste (m) [*broh'-mah, chees'-teh*]
joke *v.*, bromear [*broh-meh-ahr'*]
journal, periódico [*peh-ree-oh'-dee-koh*]
journalist, periodista (m, f) [*peh-ree-oh-dees'-tah*]
journey, jornada, viaje (m) [*hohr-nah'-dah, vee-ah'-heh*]
joy, alegría [*ah-leh-gree'-ah*]
joyful, alegre [*ah-leh'-greh*]
judge *n.*, juez (m) [*hoo-ehth'*]

judge *v.*, juzgar [*hooth-gahr'*]
judgment, juicio [*hoo-ee'-thee-oh*]
juice, jugo [*hoo'-goh*]
July, julio [*hoo'-lee-oh*]
jump *n.*, salto [*sahl'-toh*]
jump *v.*, saltar [*sahl-tahr'*]
June, junio [*hoo'-nee-oh*]
jungle, jungla [*hoon'-glah*]
junior, más joven [*mahs hoh'-vehn*]
jury, jurado [*hoo-rah'-doh*]
just *adj.*, justo [*hoos'-toh*]
just *adv.*, acabar de [*ah-kah-bahr' deh*]
  just now, ahora mismo [*ah-oh'-rah mees'-moh*]
justice, justicia [*hoos-tee'-thee-ah*]
justify *v.*, justificar [*hoos-tee-fee-kahr'*]

K

keep *v.*, guardar [*goo-ahr-dahr'*]
  Keep out! ¡No entre! [*noh ehn'-treh*]
  Keep quiet, please! ¡Cállese, por favor! [*kah'-yeh-seh, pohr fah-vohr'*]
key, llave (f) [*yah'-veh*]
kick *v.*, patear [*pah-teh-ahr'*]
kid [tease] *v.*, bromear [*broh-meh-ahr'*]
kid [child] *n.*, niño [*nee'-nyoh*]
kid [goat] *n.*, cabrito [*kah-bree'-toh*]
kidnap *v.*, secuestrar [*seh-koo-ehs-trahr'*]
kidney, riñón (m) [*ree-nyohn'*]
kill *v.*, matar [*mah-tahr'*]
kilogram, kilogramo [*kee-loh-grah'-moh*]
kilometer, kilómetro [*kee-loh'-meh-troh*]
kind *n.*, clase (f) [*klah'-seh*]
kind *adj.*, amable [*ah-mah'-bleh*]
kindness, amabilidad (f) [*ah-mah-bee-lee-dahd'*]

king, rey (m) [*reh'-ee*]
kingdom, reino [*reh'-ee-noh*]
kiss *n.,* beso [*beh'-soh*]
kiss *v.,* besar [*beh-sahr'*]
kitchen, cocina [*koh-thee'-nah*]
kite, cometa [*koh-meh'-tah*]
knee, rodilla [*roh-dee'-yah*]
kneel *v.,* arrodillarse [*ah-rroh-dee-yahr'-seh*]
knife, cuchillo [*koo-chee'-yoh*]
knight, caballero andante [*kah-bah-yeh'-roh ahn-dahn'-teh*]
knock *n.,* golpe (m) [*gohl'-peh*]
knock *v.,* golpear, llamar a la puerta [*gohl-peh-ahr', yah-mahr' ah lah poo-ehr'-tah*]
knot, nudo [*noo'-doh*]
know [someone] *v.,* conocer (irreg) [*koh-noh-thehr'*]
know [something] *v.,* saber (irreg) [*sah-behr'*]
  Do you know? ¿Sabe usted? [*sah'-beh oos-tehd'*]
  Who knows? ¿Quién sabe? [*kee-ehn' sah'-beh*]
knowledge, conocimiento [*koh-noh-thee-mee-ehn'-toh*]
known, conocido [*koh-noh-thee'-doh*]

L

label, etiqueta [*eh-tee-keh'-tah*]
labor, trabajo [*trah-bah'-hoh*]
  be in labor [give birth], estar de parto [*ehs-tahr' deh pahr'-toh*]
laboratory, laboratorio [*lah-boh-rah-toh'-ree-oh*]
laborer, trabajador (m) [*trah-bah-hah-dohr'*]
lace, encaje (m) [*ehn-kah'-heh*]
lack *v.,* carecer de (irreg) [*kah-reh-thehr' deh*]
lacking, falto, carente [*fahl'-toh, kah-rehn'-teh*]
ladder, escalera [*ehs-kah-leh'-rah*]
ladies' room, servicios (señoras) [*sehr-vee'-thee-ohs (seh-nyoh'-rahs)*]

lady, dama, señora [*dah'-mah, seh-nyoh'-rah*]

lake, lago [*lah'-goh*]

lamb, cordero [*kohr-deh'-roh*]

lame *adj.*, cojo [*koh'-hoh*]

lamp, lámpara [*lahm'-pah-rah*]

land *n.*, tierra [*tee-eh'-rrah*]

land [plane] *v.*, aterrizar [*ah-teh-rree-thahr'*]

land [ship] *v.*, atracar [*ah-trah-kahr'*]

landing, aterrizaje (m) [*ah-teh-rree-thah'-heh*]

landlady, dueña [*doo-eh'-nyah*]

landlord, dueño [*doo-eh'-nyoh*]

landmark, mojón (m) [*moh-hohn'*]

landowner, terrateniente (m) [*teh-rrah-teh-nee-ehn'-teh*]

landscape, paisaje (m) [*pah-ee-sah'-heh*]

language, idioma (m) [*ee-dee-oh'-mah*]

lantern, linterna [*leen-tehr'-nah*]

large, grande [*grahn'-deh*]

last *adj.*, último [*ool'-tee-moh*]

   at last, al fin [*ahl feen*]

   last night, anoche [*ah-noh'-cheh*]

   last week, la semana pasada [*lah seh-mah'-nah pah-sah'-dah*]

last *v.*, durar [*doo-rahr'*]

late, tarde [*tahr'-deh*]

   arrive late, llegar tarde [*yeh-gahr' tahr'-deh*]

   be late, estar retrasado [*ehs tahr' reh-trah-sah'-doh*]

lately, últimamente [*ool-tee-mah-mehn'-teh*]

later, más tarde [*mahs tahr'-deh*]

latest, último [*ool'-tee-moh*]

Latin, latín (m) [*lah-teen'*]

Latin *adj.*, latino [*lah-tee'-noh*]

laugh *n.*, risa [*ree'-sah*]

laugh *v.*, reir (irreg) [*reh-eer'*]

laundry, lavandería [*lah-vahn-deh-ree'-ah*]

law, ley (f) [*leh'-ee*]

lawful, legal [*leh-gahl'*]

lawn, césped (m) [*thehs'-pehd*]

lawyer, abogado [*ah-boh-gah'-doh*]

lax, relajado [*reh-lah-hah'-doh*]

lay *v.*, poner (irreg), colocar [*poh-nehr'*, *koh-loh-kahr'*]

lazy, perezoso [*peh-reh-thoh'-soh*]

lead [metal] *n.*, plomo [*ploh'-moh*]

lead *v.*, conducir (irreg) [*kohn-doo-theer'*]

leader, líder (m) [*lee'-dehr*]

leading, delantero [*deh-lahn-teh'-roh*]

leaf, hoja [*oh'-hah*]

league, liga [*lee'-gah*]

leak, gotera [*goh-teh'-rah*]

lean *v.*, inclinar, apoyarse [*een-klee-nahr'*, *ah-poh-yahr'-seh*]

leap *v.*, saltar [*sahl-tahr'*]

learn *v.*, aprender [*ah-prehn-dehr'*]

learning, aprendizaje (m), erudición (f) [*ah-prehn-dee-thah'-heh*, *eh-roo-dee-thee-ohn'*]

lease *n.*, arriendo [*ah-rree-ehn'-doh*]

least, mínimo [*mee'-nee-moh*]

   at least, al menos [*ahl meh'-nohs*]

   not in the least, de ningún modo [*deh neen-goon' moh'-doh*]

leather, cuero [*koo-eh'-roh*]

leave [abandon] *v.*, dejar [*deh-hahr'*]

leave [depart] *v.*, salir (irreg) [*sah-leer'*]

lecture *n.*, conferencia [*kohn-feh-rehn'-thee-ah*]

lecture *v.*, dar una conferencia, dar clase [*dahr oo'-nah kohn-feh-rehn'-thee-ah, dahr klah'-seh*]

left [direction], izquierdo [*eeth-kee-ehr'-doh*]

   to the left, a la izquierda [*ah lah eeth-kee-ehr'-dah*]

leg, pierna, pata [*pee-ehr'-nah, pah'-tah*]

legal, legal [*leh-gahl'*]

legitimate, legítimo [*leh-hee'-tee-moh*]

leisure, ocio [*oh'-thee-oh*]

lemon, limón (m) [*lee-mohn'*]

lemonade, limonada [*lee-moh-nah'-dah*]

lend *v.*, prestar [*prehs-tahr'*]

length, longitud (f) [*lohn-hee-tood'*]

lens, lente (f) [*lehn'-teh*]

less, menos [*meh'-nohs*]
  more or less, más o menos [*mahs oh meh'-nohs*]
lesson, lección (f) [*lehk-thee-ohn'*]
let [allow] *v.,* permitir [*pehr-mee-teer'*]
  Let's see, Vamos a ver [*vah'-mohs ah vehr*]
let [rent] *v.,* alquilar [*ahl-kee-lahr'*]
  room to let, se alquila un cuarto [*seh ahl-kee'-lah oon koo-ahr'-toh*]
letter [written character], letra [*leh'-trah*]
letter [missive], carta [*kahr'-tah*]
  letter of introduction, carta de presentación [*kahr'-tah deh preh-sehn-tah-thee-ohn'*]
  letter box, buzón (m) [*boo-thohn'*]
lettuce, lechuga [*leh-choo'-gah*]
level *adj.,* nivelado [*nee-veh-lah'-doh*]
level *n.,* nivel (m) [*nee-vehl'*]
liability, responsabilidad (f) [*rehs-pohn-sah-bee-lee-dahd'*]
liar, mentiroso [*mehn-tee-roh'-soh*]
liberal, liberal [*lee-beh-rahl'*]
liberty, libertad (f) [*lee-behr-tahd'*]
library, biblioteca [*bee-blee-oh-teh'-kah*]
license *n.,* licencia [*lee-thehn'-thee-ah*]
license plate, matrícula, placa [*mah-tree'-koo-lah, plah'-kah*]
lie [untruth] *n.,* mentira [*mehn-tee'-rah*]
lie [prevaricate] *v.,* mentir (irreg) [*mehn-teer'*]
lie down *v.,* tenderse, echarse [*tehn-dehr'-seh, eh-chahr'-seh*]
life, vida [*vee'-dah*]
lifeboat, salvavidas (m) [*sahl-vah-vee'-dahs*]
life insurance, seguro de vida [*seh-goo'-roh deh vee'-dah*]
life jacket, chaleco salvavidas [*chah-leh'-koh sahl-vah-vee'-dahs*]
lift *v.,* levantar, elevar [*leh-vahn-tahr', eh-leh-vahr'*]
light *n.,* luz (f) [*looth'*]
light *v.,* encender (irreg) [*ehn-thehn-dehr'*]
light [color] *adj.,* claro [*klah'-roh*]
light [weight] *adj.,* ligero [*lee-heh'-roh*]
lighter *n.,* encendedor (m) [*ehn-thehn-deh-dohr'*]
lighthouse, faro [*fah'-roh*]

lightning, relámpago [*reh-lahm'-pah-goh*]
likable, simpático [*seem-pah'-tee-koh*]
like *v.,* gustar [*goos-tahr'*]
  I would like . . . , Me gustaria . . . [*meh goos-tah-ree'-ah*]
  Would you like . . .? ¿Le gustaría . . . ? [*leh goos-tah-ree'-ah*]
like *adv., prep., conj.,* como [*koh'-moh*]
likely, probable [*proh-bah'-bleh*]
likewise, igualmente [*ee-goo-ahl-mehn'-teh*]
liking, simpatía, preferencia [*seem-pah-tee'-ah, preh-feh-rehn'-thee-ah*]
limb, rama, miembro [*rah'-mah, mee-ehm'-broh*]
limit, límite (m) [*lee'-mee-teh*]
line, línea [*lee'-neh-ah*]
linen, hilo, ropa blanca [*ee'-loh, roh'-pah blahn'-kah*]
lingerie, ropa interior [*roh'-pah een-teh-ree-ohr'*]
lining, forro [*foh'-rroh*]
lion, león (m) [*leh-ohn'*]
lip, labio [*lah'-bee-oh*]
lipstick, lápiz (m) de labios [*lah'-peeth deh lah'-bee-ohs*]
liquid *n. & adj.,* líquido [*lee'-kee-doh*]
liquor, licor (m) [*lee-kohr'*]
list, lista [*lees'-tah*]
listen *v.,* escuchar [*ehs-koo-chahr'*]
literally, literalmente [*lee-teh-rahl-mehn'-teh*]
literature, literatura [*lee-teh-rah-too'-rah*]
little *adj.,* pequeño [*peh-keh'-nyoh*]
  a little bit, un poquito [*oon poh-kee'-toh*]
little *adv.,* poco [*poh'-koh*]
  little by little, poco a poco [*poh'-koh ah poh'-koh*]
  very little, muy poco [*moo-ee' poh'-koh*]
live [be alive] *v.,* vivir [*vee-veer'*]
live [reside] *v.,* vivir, residir [*vee-veer', reh-see-deer'*]
lively, vivaz [*vee-vahth'*]
liver, hígado [*ee'-gah-doh*]
living room, sala [*sah'-lah*]
load *v.,* cargar [*kahr-gahr'*]
loaf [of bread], hogaza de pan [*oh-gah'-thah deh pahn*]

loan, préstamo [*prehs'-tah-moh*]
lobby, vestíbulo [*vehs-tee'-boo-loh*]
lobster, langosta [*lahn-gohs'-tah*]
local, local [*loh-kahl'*]
locate *v.,* situar [*see-too-ahr'*]
located, ubicado [*oo-bee-kah'-doh*]
location, sitio, lugar (m) [*see'-tee-oh, loo-gahr'*]
lock *n.,* cerradura [*theh-rrah-doo'-rah*]
lock *v.,* cerrar (irreg) [*theh-rrahr'*]
locomotive, locomotora [*loh-koh-moh-toh'-rah*]
lodging, alojamiento [*ah-loh-hah-mee-ehn'-toh*]
logical, lógico [*loh'-hee-koh*]
lonely, solitario [*soh-lee-tah'-ree-oh*]
long, largo [*lahr'-goh*]
  a long time, mucho tiempo [*moo'-choh tee-ehm'-poh*]
  how long? ¿cuánto tiempo? [*koo-ahn'-toh tee-ehm'-poh*]
  long ago, hace mucho tiempo [*ah'-theh moo'-choh tee-ehm'-poh*]
long-distance call, conferencia telefónica [*kohn-feh-rehn'-thee-ah teh-leh-foh' nee-kah*]
longer [time], más tiempo [*mahs tee-ehm'-poh*]
  no longer, ya no [*yah noh*]
longing, anhelo [*ahn-eh'-loh*]
look *v.,* mirar [*mee-rahr'*]
  Look! ¡Mire! [*mee'-reh*]
  look for, buscar [*boos-kahr'*]
  Look out! ¡Cuidado! [*koo-ee-dah'-doh*]
looks, apariencia [*ah-pah-ree-ehn'-thee-ah*]
loose, flojo [*floh'-hoh*]
loosen *v.,* aflojar [*ah-floh-hahr'*]
lord, señor (m) [*seh-nyohr'*]
lose *v.,* perder (irreg) [*pehr-dehr'*]
loss, pérdida [*pehr'-dee-dah*]
lost, perdido [*pehr-dee'-doh*]
  lost and found, perdido y hallado [*pehr-dee'-doh ee ah-yah'-doh*]
lot [real estate], terreno [*teh-rreh'-noh*]
lot [quantity], mucho [*moo'-choh*]

a lot of, una gran cantidad (f) de [*oo-nah grahn kahn-tee-dahd' deh*]
loud, ruidoso [*roo-ee-doh'-soh*]
loudspeaker, altavoz (m) [*ahl-tah-vohth'*]
love *n.*, amor (m) [*ah-mohr'*]
love *v.*, amar [*ah-mahr'*]
lovely, bello, encantador [*beh'-yoh, ehn-kahn-tah-dohr'*]
lover, amante (m, f) [*ah-mahn'-teh*]
low, bajo [*bah'-hoh*]
loyal, leal [*leh-ahl'*]
lubricate *v.*, lubricar [*loo-bree-kahr'*]
lubrication [auto], engrase (m), lubricación (f) [*ehn-grah'-seh, loo-bree-kah-thee-ohn'*]
luck, suerte (f) [*soo-ehr'-teh*]
 good luck, buena suerte (f) [*boo-eh'-nah soo-ehr'-teh*]
lucky, afortunado [*ah-fohr-too-nah'-doh*]
 be lucky *v.*, tener suerte [*teh-nehr' soo-ehr'-teh*]
luggage, equipaje (m) [*eh-kee-pah'-heh*]
lunch, almuerzo [*ahl-moo-ehr'-thoh*]
lung, pulmón (m) [*pool-mohn'*]
luxurious, lujoso [*loo-hoh'-soh*]
luxury, lujo [*loo'-hoh*]

M

machine, máquina [*mah'-kee-nah*]
machinery, maquinaria [*mah-kee-nah'-ree-ah*]
mad [angry], enfadado, enojado [*ehn-fah-dah'-doh, eh-noh-hah'-doh*]
mad [crazy], loco [*loh'-koh*]
madam, señora [*seh-nyoh'-rah*]
made, hecho [*eh'-choh*]
 man-made, hecho por el hombre [*eh'-choh pohr ehl ohm'-breh*]
magazine, revista [*reh-vees'-tah*]

magic *adj.*, mágico [*mah'-hee-koh*]
magnificent, magnífico [*mahg-nee'-fee-koh*]
mahogany, caoba [*kah-oh'-bah*]
maid, criada [*kree-ah'-dah*]
mail *n.*, correo [*koh-rreh'-oh*]
mail *v.*, enviar por correo [*ehn-vee-ahr' pohr koh-rreh'-oh*]
mailbox, buzón (m) [*boo-thohn'*]
mailman, cartero [*kahr-teh'-roh*]
main, principal [*preen-thee-pahl'*]
main office, oficina principal [*oh-fee-thee'-nah preen-thee-pahl'*]
main street, calle (f) principal [*kah'-yeh preen-thee-pahl'*]
mainly, principalmente [*preen-thee-pahl-mehn'-teh*]
maintain *v.*, mantener (irreg) [*mahn-teh-nehr'*]
major, mayor [*mah-yohr'*]
majority, mayoría [*mah-yoh-ree'-ah*]
make *v.*, hacer (irreg) [*ah-thehr'*]
  make a mistake, equivocarse [*eh-kee-voh-kahr'-seh*]
  make fun of, burlar(se) de [*boor-lahr'-seh deh*]
  make sure, asegurar [*ah-seh-goo-rahr'*]
  make up one's mind, decidir(se) [*deh-thee-deer'-seh*]
male, macho [*mah'-choh*]
malicious, malicioso [*mah-lee-thee-oh'-soh*]
man, hombre (m) [*ohm'-breh*]
manage *v.*, administrar [*ahd-mee-nees-trahr'*]
manager, administrador (m) [*ahd-mee-nees-trah-dohr'*]
manicure, manicura [*mah-nee-koo'-rah*]
manner, manera [*mah-neh'-rah*]
manners, modales (m, pl) [*moh-dah'-lehs*]
manual *n.*, manual (m) [*mah-noo-ahl'*]
manufacture *v.*, fabricar [*fah-bree-cahr'*]
manufacturer, fabricante (m) [*fah-bree-kahn'-teh*]
manuscript, manuscrito [*mah-noos-kree'-toh*]
many, muchos [*moo'-chohs*]
  how many? ¿cuántos? [*koo-ahn'-tohs*]
  too many, demasiados [*deh-mah-see-ah'-dohs*]
map, mapa (m) [*mah'-pah*]
marble, mármol (m) [*mahr'-mohl*]

March, marzo [*mahr'-thoh*]

march *v.,* marchar [*mahr-chahr'*]

mark *n.,* marca [*mahr'-kah*]

mark *v.,* marcar [*mahr-kahr'*]

market, mercado [*mehr-kah'-doh*]

marriage, matrimonio [*mah-tree-moh'-nee-oh*]

married, casado [*kah-sah'-doh*]

  get married, casarse [*kah-sahr'-seh*]

marvelous, maravilloso [*mah-rah-vee-yoh'-soh*]

mask, máscara [*mahs'-kah-rah*]

Mass [eccles.], Misa [*mee'-sah*]

mass [quantity], masa [*mah'-sah*]

massage *n.,* masaje (m) [*mah-sah'-heh*]

master *n.,* maestro [*mah-ehs'-troh*]

master *v.,* dominar [*doh-mee-nahr'*]

masterpiece, obra maestra [*oh'-brah mah-ehs'-trah*]

match [for igniting] *n.,* fósforo [*fohs'-foh-roh*]

match [contest] *n.,* partido [*pahr-tee'-doh*]

match [go together with] *v.,* hacer juego con [*ah-thehr' hoo-eh'-goh kohn*]

material, material (m) [*mah-teh-ree-ahl'*]

maternal, maternal [*mah-tehr-nahl'*]

maternity, maternidad (f) [*mah-tehr-nee-dahd'*]

mathematics, matemáticas (f, pl) [*mah-teh-mah'-tee-kahs*]

matter, materia [*mah-teh'-ree-ah*]

  What's the matter? ¿Qué pasa? [*keh' pah'-sah*]

  It doesn't matter, No importa [*noh eem-pohr'-tah*]

mattress, colchón (m) [*kohl-chohn'*]

mature, maduro [*mah-doo'-roh*]

May, mayo [*mah'-yoh*]

may *v.,* poder (irreg) [*poh-dehr'*]

  It may be, Puede ser [*poo-eh'-deh sehr'*]

  May I . . .? ¿Puedo . . .? [*poo-eh'-doh . . .*]

maybe, quizás [*kee-thahs'*]

mayor, alcalde (m) [*ahl-kahl'-deh*]

me, me [*meh*]

  with me, conmigo [*kohn-mee'-goh*]

meal, comida [*koh-mee'-dah*]

mean [base] *adj.*, ruin [*roo-een'*]

mean *v.*, significar [*seeg-nee-fee-kahr'*]
  What does that mean?¿Qué significa eso? [*keh seeg-nee-fee'-kah eh'-soh*]
  What do you mean? ¿Qué quiere usted decir? [*keh' kee-eh'-reh oos-tehd'-deh-theer'*]

means, medio [*meh'-dee-oh*]
  by means of, por medio de [*pohr meh'-dee-oh deh*]
  by all means, de todos modos [*deh toh'-dohs moh'-dohs*]
  by no means, de ningún modo [*deh neen-goon' moh'-doh*]

meanwhile, mientras tanto [*mee-ehn'-trahs tahn'-toh*]

measles, sarampión (m) [*sah-rahm-pee-ohn'*]

measure *n.*, medida [*meh-dee'-dah*]

measure *v.*, medir (irreg) [*meh-deer'*]

meat, carne (f) [*kahr'-neh*]

mechanic, mecánico [*meh-kah'-nee-koh*]

mechanical, mecánico [*meh-kah'-nee-koh*]

medal, medalla [*meh-dah'-yah*]

medical, médico [*meh'-dee-koh*]

medical school, escuela de medicina [*chs-koo-eh'-lah deh meh-dee-thee'-nah*]

medicine, medicina [*meh-dee-thee'-nah*]

Mediterranean, mediterráneo [*meh-dee-teh-rrah'-neh-oh*]

medium *adj.*, medio [*meh'-dee-oh*]

meek, manso [*mahn'-soh*]

meet *v.*, conocer (irreg), encontrar (irreg) [*koh-noh-thehr', ehn-kohn-trahr'*]
  Glad to meet you! ¡Encantado de conocerle! [*ehn-kahn-tah'-doh deh koh-noh-thehr'-leh*]

meeting, reunión (f) [*reh-oo-nee-ohn'*]

melody, melodía [*meh-loh-dee'-ah*]

melon, melón (m) [*meh-lohn'*]

melt *v.*, derretir(se) (irreg) [*deh-rreh-teer'-seh*]

member, miembro [*mee-ehm'-broh*]

memory, memoria [*meh-moh'-ree-ah*]

mend *v.*, remendar (irreg) [*reh-mehn-dahr'*]

mental, mental [*mehn-tahl'*]

mention *v.*, mencionar [*mehn-thee-oh-nahr'*]

menu, menú (m) [*meh-noo'*]

merchandise, mercancía [*mehr-kahn-thee'-ah*]

merchant, comerciante (m) [*koh-mehr-thee-ahn'-teh*]

mercy, misericordia [*mee-seh-ree-kohr'-dee-ah*]

merely, meramente [*meh-rah-mehn'-teh*]

merit *n.*, mérito [*meh'-ree-toh*]

merit *v.*, merecer (irreg) [*meh-reh-thehr'*]

merry, alegre [*ah-leh'-greh*]

message, mensaje (m) [*mehn-sah'-heh*]

messenger, mensajero [*mehn-sah-heh'-roh*]

metal, metal (m) [*meh-tahl'*]

meter [counter], contador (m) [*kohn-tah-dohr'*]

meter [measure], metro [*meh'-troh*]

method, método [*meh'-toh-doh*]

Mexican, mejicano [*meh-hee-kah'-noh*]

Mexico, Méjico [*meh'-hee-koh*]

middle, medio [*meh'-dee-oh*]

midnight, medianoche (f) [*meh-dee-ah-noh'-cheh*]

midway, a medio camino [*ah meh'-dee-oh kah-mee'-noh*]

might [past of MAY], podría [*poh-dree'-ah*]

mild, suave [*soo-ah'-veh*]

mile, milla [*mee'-yah*]

military, militar [*mee-lee-tahr'*]

military service, servicio militar [*sehr-vee'-thee-oh mee-lee-tahr'*]

milk, leche (f) [*leh'-cheh*]

million, millón (m) [*mee-yohn'*]

millionaire, millonario [*mee-yoh-nah'-ree-oh*]

mind *n.*, mente (f) [*mehn'-teh*]

mind [attend to] *v.*, atender a (irreg) [*ah-tehn-dehr' ah*]

mine *pron.*, mío, mía, míos, mías [*mee'-oh, mee'-ah, mee'-ohs, mee'-ahs*]

   Which is mine? ¿Cuál es mío? [*koo-ahl' ehs mee'-oh*]

mine *n.*, mina [*mee'-nah*]

miner, minero [*mee-neh'-roh*]

mineral, mineral (m) [*mee-neh-rahl'*]

minimum *n. & adj.*, mínimo [*mee'-nee-moh*]

minister [government], ministro [*mee-nees'-troh*]

minister [religious], oficiante [*oh-fee-thee-ahn'-teh*]
minor [age], menor (m, f) de edad [*meh-nohr'-deh eh-dahd'*]
minority, minoría [*mee-noh-ree'-ah*]
minus, menos [*meh'-nohs*]
minute, minuto [*mee-noo'-toh*]
mirror, espejo [*ehs-peh'-hoh*]
mischief, travesura [*trah-veh-soo'-rah*]
miserable, miserable [*mee-seh-rah'-bleh*]
misery, miseria [*mee-seh'-ree-ah*]
misfortune, infortunio [*een-fohr-too'-nee-oh*]
mislead *v.*, descarriar [*dehs-kah-rree-ahr'*]
Miss, señorita [*seh-nyoh-ree'-tah*]
miss [feel absence of] *v.*, echar de menos (irreg) [*eh-chahr'
    deh meh'-nohs*]
miss [lose] *v.*, perder (irreg) [*pehr-dehr'*]
missing, ausente [*ah-oo-sehn'-teh*]
mission, misión (f) [*mee-see-ohn'*]
missionary, misionero [*mee-see-oh-neh'-roh*]
mistake *n.*, equivocación (f), error (m) [*eh-kee-voh-kah-
    thee-ohn', eh-rrohr'*]
mistake *v.*, equivocar [*eh-kee-voh-kahr'*]
  be mistaken, estar equivocado [*ehs-tahr' eh-kee-voh-
    kah'-doh*]
  make a mistake, equivocarse [*eh-kee-voh-kahr'-seh*]
mistrust *v.*, desconfiar [*dehs-kohn-fee-ahr'*]
misunderstanding, malentendido [*mahl-ehn-tehn-dee'-doh*]
mix *v.*, mezclar [*mehth-klahr'*]
mixed, mezclado [*mehth-klah'-doh*]
mixture, mezcla [*mehth'-klah*]
model *n. & adj.*, modelo [*moh-deh'-loh*]
modern, moderno [*moh-dehr'-noh*]
modest, modesto [*moh-dehs'-toh*]
modesty, modestia [*moh-dehs'-tee-ah*]
modify *v.*, modificar [*moh-dee-fee-kahr'*]
moisture, humedad (f) [*oo-meh-dahd'*]
moment, momento [*moh-mehn'-toh*]
monarchy, monarquía [*moh-nahr-kee'-ah*]
monastery, monasterio [*moh-nahs-teh'-ree-oh*]

Monday, lunes (m) [*loo'-nehs*]
money, dinero [*dee-neh'-roh*]
monkey, mono [*moh'-noh*]
monotonous, monótono [*moh-noh'-toh-noh*]
monstrous, monstruoso [*mohns-troo-oh'-soh*]
month, mes (m) [*mehs'*]
monthly, mensual [*mehn-soo-ahl'*]
monument, monumento [*moh-noo-mehn'-toh*]
mood, humor (m) [*oo-mohr'*]
   in a bad mood, de mal humor [*deh mahl oo-mohr'*]
   in a good mood, de buen humor [*deh boo-ehn' oo-mohr'*]
moon, luna [*loo'-nah*]
moonlight, luz (f) de la luna [*looth deh lah loo'-nah*]
moral, moral [*moh-rahl'*]
morality, moralidad (f) [*moh-rah-lee-dahd'*]
morbid, morboso [*mohr-boh'-soh*]
more, más [*mahs*]
   more or less, más o menos [*mahs o meh'-nohs*]
   moreover, además [*ah-deh-mahs'*]
   once more, una vez más [*oo'-nah vehth mahs*]
morning, mañana [*mah-nyah'-nah*]
   good morning, buenos días [*boo-eh'-nohs dee'-ahs*]
   in the morning, por la mañana [*pohr lah mah-nyah'-nah*]
mortality, mortalidad (f) [*mohr-tah-lee-dahd'*]
mortgage, hipoteca [*ee-poh-teh'-kah*]
mosaic, mosaico [*moh-sah'-ee-koh*]
mosquito, mosquito [*mohs-kee'-toh*]
most *adj.*, más [*mahs*]
   most of, la mayor parte de [*lah mah-yohr' pahr'-teh deh*]
   the most, la más, el más [*lah mahs, ehl mahs*]
mother, madre (f) [*mah'-dreh*]
motherhood, maternidad (f) [*mah-tehr-nee-dahd'*]
mother-in-law, suegra [*soo-eh'-grah*]
motion, moción (f) [*moh-thee-ohn'*]
motionless, inmóvil [*een-moh'-veel*]
motive, motivo [*moh-tee'-voh*]
motor, motor (m) [*moh-tohr'*]
motorcycle, motocicleta [*moh-toh-thee-kleh'-tah*]

mount *v.*, montar [*mohn-tahr'*]
mountain, montaña [*mohn-tah'-nyah*]
mountain range, sierra [*see-eh'-rrah*]
mourning, luto [*loo'-toh*]
  in mourning, de luto [*deh loo'-toh*]
mouse, ratón (m) [*rah-tohn'*]
mouth, boca [*boh'-kah*]
move [change position of] *v.*, mover (irreg) [*moh-vehr'*]
move [change residence] *v.*, mudarse [*moo-dahr'-seh*]
move [touch the feelings of] *v.*, conmover (irreg) [*kohn-moh-vehr'*]
movies, movie theater, cine (m) [*thee'-neh*]
Mr., Señor [*seh-nyohr'*]
Mrs., Señora [*seh-nyoh'-rah*]
much, mucho [*moo'-choh*]
  as much as, tanto como [*tahn'-toh koh'-moh*]
  how much? ¿cuanto? [*koo-ahn'-toh*]
  too much, de masiado [*deh mah-see-ah'-doh*]
  very much, mucho, muchísimo [*moo'-choh, moo-chee'-see-moh*]
mud, fango [*fahn'-goh*]
muddy, fangoso [*fahn-goh'-soh*]
muffler [auto], silenciador (m) [*see-lehn-thee-ah-dohr'*]
muffler [scarf], bufanda [*boo-fahn'-dah*]
murder *v.*, asesinar [*ah-seh-see-nahr'*]
murderer, asesino [*ah-seh-see'-noh*]
muscle, músculo [*moos'-koo-loh*]
museum, museo [*moo-seh'-oh*]
mushroom, seta [*seh'-tah*]
music, música [*moo'-see-kah*]
musical, musical [*moo-see-kahl'*]
musician, músico [*moo-see-koh*]
must, deber, tener que (irreg) [*deh-behr', teh-nehr' keh*]
  I must go, Tengo que ir [*tehn'-goh keh eer*]
mustache, bigote (m) [*bee-goh'-teh*]
mustard, mostaza [*mohs-tah'-thah*]
mutual, mutuo [*moo'-too-oh*]
my, mi, mis (pl) [*mee, mees*]

myself, yo mismo [*yoh mees'-moh*]
mysterious, misterioso [*mees-teh-ree-oh'-soh*]
mystery, misterio [*mees-teh'-ree-oh*]
mystic, místico [*mees'-tee-koh*]

N

nail [fingernail] *n.,* uña [*oo'-nyah*]
nail [carpentry] *n.,* clavo [*klah'-voh*]
nail *v.,* clavar [*klah-vahr'*]
naive, ingenuo [*een-heh'-noo-oh*]
naked, desnudo [*dehs-noo'-doh*]
name *n.,* nombre (m) [*nohm'-breh*]
  first name, nombre de pila [*nohm'-breh deh pee'-lah*]
  last name, apellido [*ah-peh-yee'-doh*]
  What is your name? ¿Cómo se llama? [*koh'-moh seh yah'-mah*]
name *v.,* nombrar [*nohm-brahr'*]
namely, a saber [*ah sah-behr'*]
nap, siesta [*see-ehs'-tah*]
napkin, servilleta [*sehr-vee-yeh'-tah*]
  sanitary napkin, compresa [*kohm-preh'-sah*]
narrate *v.,* narrar [*nah-rrahr'*]
narrow *adj.,* estrecho [*ehs-treh'-choh*]
nasty, sucio, desagradable [*soo'-thee-oh, deh-sah-grah-dah'-bleh*]
nation, nación (f) [*nah-thee-ohn'*]
national, nacional [*nah-thee-oh-nahl'*]
nationality, nacionalidad (f) [*nah-thee-oh-nah-lee-dahd'*]
native *adj.,* nativo [*nah-tee'-voh*]
natural, natural [*nah-too-rahl'*]
naturally, naturalmente [*nah-too-rahl-mehn'-teh*]
nature, naturaleza [*nah-too-rah-leh'-thah*]
naughty, travieso [*trah-vee-eh'-soh*]
naval, naval [*nah-vahl'*]

navy, marina [*mah-ree'-nah*]
near, cerca [*thehr'-kah*]
nearby, cercano [*thehr-kah'-noh*]
nearly, casi [*kah'-see*]
neat, pulcro [*pool'-kroh*]
necessary, necesario [*neh-theh-sah'-ree-oh*]
neck, cuello [*koo-eh'-yoh*]
necklace, collar (m) [*koh-yahr'*]
necktie, corbata [*kohr-bah'-tah*]
need *v.,* necesitar [*neh-theh-see-tahr'*]
needle, aguja [*ah-goo'-hah*]
negative, negativo [*neh-gah-tee'-voh*]
neglect *v.,* descuidar [*dehs-koo-ee-dahr'*]
Negro *n. & adj.,* negro [*neh'-groh*]
neighbor, vecino [*veh-thee'-noh*]
neighborhood, vecindario [*veh-theen-dah'-ree-oh*]
neither, ninguno [*neen-goo'-noh*]
  neither . . . nor, ni . . . ni [*nee . . . nee*]
  neither one, ninguno de los dos [*neen-goo'-noh deh lohs dohs*]
nephew, sobrino [*soh-bree'-noh*]
nerve, nervio [*nehr'-vee-oh*]
nervous, nervioso [*nehr-vee-oh'-soh*]
nest, nido [*nee'-doh*]
net, red (f) [*rehd*]
  hairnet, redecilla [*reh-deh-thee'-yah*]
neutral, neutral [*neh-oo-trahl'*]
never, nunca [*noon'-kah*]
never mind, no importa [*noh eem-pohr'-tah*]
nevertheless, sin embargo [*seen ehm-bahr'-goh*]
new, nuevo [*noo-eh'-voh*]
news, noticias [*noh-tee'-thee-ahs*]
newspaper, periódico [*peh-ree-oh'-dee-koh*]
newsstand, puesto de periódicos [*poo-ehs'-toh deh peh-ree-oh'-dee-kohs*]
next, próximo [*prohk'-see-moh*]
  next month, el mes (m) próximo [*ehl mehs prohk'-see-moh*]
  next time, la próxima vez [*lah prohk'-see-mah vehth*]

next to, al lado de [*ahl lah'-doh deh*]
Nicaragua, Nicaragua [*nee-kah-rah'-goo-ah*]
Nicaraguan, nicaragüense [*nee-kah-rah-goo-ehn'-seh*]
nice, simpático [*seem-pah'-tee-koh*]
nickname, apodo [*ah-poh'-doh*]
niece, sobrina [*soh-bree'-nah*]
night, noche (f) [*noh'-cheh*]
  good night, buenas noches [*boo-eh'-nahs noh'-chehs*]
nightclub, cabaret (m) [*kah-bah-reht'*]
nightgown, camisa de dormir [*kah-mee'-sah deh dohr-meer'*]
nightmare, pesadilla [*peh-sah-dee'-yah*]
nine, nueve [*noo-eh'-veh*]
nineteen, diecinueve [*dee-eh-thee-noo-eh'-veh*]
ninety, noventa [*noh-vehn'-tah*]
ninth, noveno [*noh-veh'-noh*]
nipple, pezón (m) [*peh-thohn'*]
no, no [*noh*]
noble, noble [*noh'-bleh*]
nobody, nadie [*nah'-dee-eh*]
noise, ruido [*roo-ee'-doh*]
noisy, ruidoso [*roo-ee-doh'-soh*]
none, ninguno(s), nada [*neen-goo'-noh(s), nah'-dah*]
nonetheless, no menos [*noh meh'-nohs*]
nonsense, tontería, disparate (m) [*tohn-teh-ree'-ah, dees-pah-rah'-teh*]
noodles, pasta [*pahs'-tah*]
noon, mediodía (m) [*meh-dee-oh-dee'-ah*]
nor, ni [*nee*]
normal, normal [*nohr-mahl'*]
north, norte (m) [*nohr'-teh*]
North America, América del Norte [*ah-meh'-re-kah dehl nohr'-teh*]
northeast, nordeste (m) [*nohrd-ehs'-teh*]
northern, norteño [*nohr-teh'-nyoh*]
northwest, noroeste (m) [*nohr-oh-ehs'-teh*]
Norway, Noruega [*noh-roo-eh'-gah*]
nose, nariz (f) [*nah-reeth'*]
not, no [*noh*]

not at all, de ningún modo [*de neen-goon' moh'-doh*]
not even, ni siquiera [*nee see-kee-eh'-rah*]
not one, ni uno [*nee oo'-noh*]
note *n.,* nota [*noh'-tah*]
note *v.,* notar [*noh-tahr'*]
notebook, cuaderno [*koo-ah-dehr'-noh*]
nothing, nada [*nah'-dah*]
notice *n.,* aviso [*ah-vee'-soh*]
notice *v.,* notar [*noh-tahr'*]
notify *v.,* notificar [*noh-tee-fee-kahr'*]
notion, noción (f) [*noh-thee-ohn'*]
noun, substantivo [*soobs-tahn-tee'-voh*]
nourishment, alimento [*ah-lee-mehn'-toh*]
novel *n.,* novela [*noh-veh'-lah*]
novelty, novedad (f) [*noh-veh-dahd'*]
November, noviembre [*noh-vee-ehm'-breh*]
now, ahora [*ah-oh'-rah*]
  now and then, de vez en cuando [*deh vehth' ehn koo-ahn'-doh*]
nowadays, hoy día [*oh'-ee dee'-ah*]
nowhere, en ninguna parte [*ehn neen-goo'-nah pahr'-teh*]
number, número [*noo'-meh-roh*]
numerous, numeroso [*noo-meh-roh'-soh*]
nun, monja [*mohn'-hah*]
nurse, enfermera [*ehn-fehr-meh'-rah*]
nursery, lugar (m) donde se cuidan niños [*loo-gahr' dohn'-deh seh koo-ee'-dahn nee'-nyohs*]
nut [food], nuez (f) [*noo-ehth'*]
nut [for a bolt], tuerca [*too-ehr'-kah*]
nylon, nilón (m) [*nee-lohn'*]

O

oak, roble (m) [*roh'-bleh*]
oar, remo [*reh'-moh*]

oath, juramento [*hoo-rah-mehn'-toh*]
obedient, obediente [*oh-beh-dee-ehn'-teh*]
obey *v.,* obedecer (irreg) [*oh-beh-deh-thehr'*]
object *n.,* objeto [*ohb-heh'-toh*]
object *v.,* objetar [*ohb-heh-tahr'*]
objection, objeción (f) [*ohb-heh-thee-ohn'*]
oblige *v.,* obligar [*oh-blee-gahr'*]
obscene, obsceno [*ohbs-theh'-noh*]
observation, observación (f) [*ohb-sehr-vah-thee-ohn'*]
observe *v.,* observar [*ohb-sehr-váhr*]
obstacle, obstáculo [*ohbs-táh-koo-loh*]
obtain *v.,* obtener (irreg) [*ohb-teh-nehr'*]
obvious, obvio [*ohb'-vee-oh*]
occasion, ocasión (f) [*oh-kah-see-ohn'*]
occasionally, ocasionalmente [*oh-kah-see-oh-nahl-mehn'-teh*]
occupation, ocupación (f) [*oh-koo-pah-thee-ohn'*]
occupied, ocupado [*oh-koo-pah'-doh*]
occupy *v.,* ocupar [*oh-koo-pahr'*]
occur *v.,* ocurrir [*oh-koo-rreer'*]
occurrence, suceso [*soo-theh'-soh*]
ocean, océano [*oh-theh'-ah-noh*]
o'clock, en punto [*ehn poon'-toh*]
October, octubre (m) [*ohk-too'-breh*]
odd [unusual], raro [*rah'-roh*]
odd [not even], impar [*eem-pahr'*]
odds, diferencia, ventaja [*dee-feh-rehn'-thee-ah, vehn-tah'-hah*]
odor, olor (m) [*oh-lohr'*]
of, de, del [*deh, dehl*]
   of course, por supuesto [*pohr soo-poo-ehs'-toh*]
off, fuera [*foo-eh'-rah*]
offend *v.,* ofender [*oh-fehn-dehr'*]
offensive, ofensivo [*oh-fehn-see'-voh*]
offer *v.,* ofrecer (irreg) [*oh-freh-thehr'*]
office, oficina [*oh-fee-thee'-nah*]
officer, oficial (m) [*oh-fee-thee-ahl'*]
often, a menudo [*ah meh-noo'-doh*]
oil [lubricant] *n.,* aceite (m) [*ah-theh'-ee-teh*]

oil change, cambio de aceite [*kahm'-bee-oh-deh ah-theh'-ee-teh*]

oil [fuel] *n.,* petroleo [*peh-troh'-leh-oh*]

oil *v.,* engrasar [*ehn-grah-sahr'*]

old, viejo, antiguo [*vee-eh'-hoh, ahn-tee'-goo-oh*]

   How old are you? ¿Cuántos años tiene? [*koo-ahn'-tohs ah'-nyohs tee-eh'-neh*]

olive, aceituna, oliva [*ah-theh-ee-too'-nah, oh-lee'-vah*]

olive oil, aceite (m) de oliva [*ah-theh'-ee-teh deh oh-lee'-vah*]

omelet, tortilla de huevos [*tohr-tee'-yah deh oo-eh'-vohs*]

omission, omisión (f) [*oh-mee-see-ohn'*]

omit *v.,* omitir [*oh-mee-teer'*]

on, en, encima de [*ehn, ehn-thee'-mah deh*]

once, una vez [*oo'-nah vehth*]

   at once, enseguida [*ehn-seh-ghee'-dah*]

   once more, una vez más [*oo'-nah vehth mahs*]

one, un, uno, una [*oon, oo'-noh, oo'-nah*]

one-way street, calle de una sola dirección [*kah'-yeh deh oo'-nah sol'-lah dee-rehk-thee-ohn'*]

one-way ticket, billete de ida [*bee-yeh'-teh deh ee'-dah*]

onion, cebolla [*theh-boh'-yah*]

onlooker, espectador (m), mirón (m) [*ehs-pehk-tah-dohr', mee-rohn'*]

only *adv.,* solamente [*soh-lah-mehn'-teh*]

only *adj.,* único [*oo'-nee-koh*]

open *adj.,* abierto [*ah-bee-ehr'-toh*]

open *v.,* abrir [*ah-breer'*]

opening, apertura [*ah-pehr-too'-rah*]

opera, ópera [*oh'-peh-rah*]

operate *v.,* operar, manejar [*oh-peh-rahr', mah-neh-hahr'*]

operation, operación (f) [*oh-peh-rah-thee-ohn'*]

opinion, opinión (f) [*oh-pee-nee-ohn'*]

opportunity, oportunidad (f) [*oh-pohr-too-nee-dahd'*]

oppose *v.,* oponer (irreg) [*oh-poh-nehr'*]

opposite, opuesto [*oh-poo-ehs'-toh*]

optimist, optimista (m, f) [*ohp-tee-mees'-tah*]

or, o [*oh*]

oral, oral [*oh-rahl'*]

orange, naranja [*nah-rahn'-hah*]

orange juice, jugo de naranja [*hoo'-goh deh nah-rahn'-hah*]

orchard, huerto [*oo-ehr'-toh*]

orchestra, orquesta [*ohr-kehs'-tah*]

order *n.*, orden (m) [*ohr'-dehn*]

order *v.*, ordenar, pedir (irreg) [*ohr-deh-nahr'*, *peh-deer'*]

orderly *adj.*, ordenado [*ohr-deh-nah'-doh*]

ordinarily, ordinariamente [*ohr-dee-nah-ree-ah-mehn'-teh*]

ordinary, ordinario [*ohr-dee-nah'-ree-oh*]

organ, órgano [*ohr'-gah-noh*]

organic, orgánico [*ohr-gah'-nee-koh*]

organization, organización (f) [*ohr-gah-nee-thah-thee-ohn'*]

oriental, oriental [*oh-ree-ehn-tahl'*]

original, original [*oh-ree-hee-nahl'*]

originally, originalmente [*oh-ree-hee-nahl-mehn'-teh*]

ornament, ornamento [*ohr-nah-mehn'-toh*]

orphan, huérfano [*oo-ehr'-fah-noh*]

other, otro [*oh'-troh*]

  on the other hand, por otra parte [*pohr oh'-trah pahr'-teh*]

otherwise, de otro modo [*deh oh'-troh moh'-doh*]

ought to *v.*, deber de [*deh-behr' deh*]

ounce, onza [*ohn'-thah*]

our, nuestro, nuestros [*noo-ehs'-troh, noo-ehs'-trohs*]

ours, el nuestro, los nuestros [*ehl noo-ehs'-troh, lohs noo-ehs'-trohs*]

ourselves, nosotros mismos [*nohs-oh'-trohs mees'-mohs*]

out, fuera [*foo-eh'-rah*]

  out of order, fuera de servicio [*foo-eh'-rah deh sehr-vee'-thee-oh*]

outdo *v.*, excederse [*ehks-theh-dehr'-seh*]

outdoors, al aire (m) libre [*ahl ah-ee'-reh lee'-breh*]

outrageous, afrentoso [*ah-frehn-toh'-soh*]

outside, afuera [*ah-foo-eh'-rah*]

outstanding, sobresaliente [*soh-breh-sah-lee-ehn'-teh*]

outward, hacia fuera [*ah'-thee-ah foo-eh'-rah*]

oval, ovalado [*oh-vah-lah'-doh*]

oven, horno [*ohr'-noh*]

over [above], sobre [*soh'-breh*]

over [finished], acabado [*ah-kah-bah'-doh*]
overboard, al agua [*ahl ah'-goo-ah*]
overcoat, sobretodo, abrigo [*soh-breh-toh'-doh, ah-bree'-goh*]
overcome *v.,* vencer [*vehn-thehr'*]
overdo *v.,* excederse (refl) [*ehks-theh-dehr'-seh*]
overhead, arriba [*ah-rree'-bah*]
overload, sobrecarga [*soh-breh-kahr'-gah*]
overnight, durante la noche [*doo-rahn'-teh lah noh'-cheh*]
overseas, ultramar [*ool-trah-mahr'*]
oversight, descuido [*dehs-koo-ee'-doh*]
overtime, horas extra(ordinarias) (pl) [*oh'-rahs-ehks-trah(-ohr-dee-nah'-ree-ahs)*]
overturn *v.,* volcar (irreg) [*vohl-kahr'*]
owe *v.,* deber [*deh-behr'*]
  How much do I owe you? ¿Cuánto le debo? [*koo-ahn'-toh leh deh'-boh*]
owing to, debido a [*deh-bee'-doh ah*]
own *adj.,* propio [*proh'-pee-oh*]
own *v.,* poseer [*poh-seh-ehr'*]
owner, dueño [*doo-eh'-nyoh*]
oxygen, oxígeno [*ohk-see'-heh-noh*]
oyster, ostra [*ohs'-trah*]

P

pace, paso [*pah'-soh*]
Pacific [ocean], Pacífico [*pah-thee'-fee-koh*]
pack *v.,* empaquetar [*ehm-pah-keh-tahr'*]
pack of cards, juego de naipes [*hoo-eh'-goh deh nah'-ee-pehs*]
pack of cigarettes, caja de cigarrillos [*kah'-hah deh thee-gah-rree'-yohs*]
package, paquete (m) [*pah-keh'-teh*]
packing, embalaje (m) [*ehm-bah-lah'-heh*]
page, página [*pah'-hee-nah*]

paid, pagado [*pah-gah'-doh*]
pail, cubo [*koo'-boh*]
pain, dolor (m) [*doh-lohr'*]
painful, doloroso [*doh-loh-roh'-soh*]
paint *n.*, pintura [*peen-too'-rah*]
paint *v.*, pintar [*peen-tahr'*]
painter, pintor (m) [*peen-tohr'*]
painting, pintura [*peen-too'-rah*]
  oil painting, óleo [*oh'-leh-oh*]
pair, par (m) [*pahr*]
pajamas, pijama (m) [*pee-hah'-mah*]
palace, palacio [*pah-lah'-thee-oh*]
pale, pálido [*pah'-lee-doh*]
palm, palma [*pahl'-mah*]
palm tree, palmera [*pahl-meh'-rah*]
pan, cazuela [*kah-thoo-eh'-lah*]
Panama, Panamá [*pah-nah-mah'*]
Panamanian, panameño [*pah-nah-meh'-nyoh*]
pancake, tortita de harina [*tohr-tee'-tah deh ah-ree'-nah*]
panic, pánico [*pah'-nee-koh*]
pants [trousers], pantalones (m, pl) [*pahn-tah-loh'-nehs*]
pants [underpants], calzoncillos (m, pl), braga (*kahl-thohn-thee'-yohs, brah'-gah*]
paper, papel (m) [*pah-pehl'*]
  toilet paper, papel higiénico [*pah-pehl' ee-hee-eh'-nee-koh*]
  writing paper, papel de escribir [*pah-pehl' deh ehs-kree-beer'*]
parachute, paracaídas (m) [*pah-rah-kah-ee'-dahs*]
parade, desfile (m) [*dehs-fee'-leh*]
paradise, paraíso [*pah-rah-ee'-soh*]
paragraph, párrafo [*pah'-rrah-foh*]
Paraguay, Paraguay [*pah-rah-goo-ah'-ee*]
Paraguayan, paraguayo [*pah-rah-goo-ah'-yoh*]
parallel, paralelo [*pah-rah-leh'-loh*]
paralyze *v.*, paralizar [*pah-rah-lee-thahr'*]
parcel, paquete (m) [*pah-keh'-teh*]
pardon *n.*, perdón (m) [*pehr-dohn'*]
pardon *v.*, perdonar [*pehr-doh-nahr'*]

Pardon me, Perdóneme [*pehr-doh'-neh-meh*]
parents, padres (m, pl) [*pah'-drehs*]
parish, parroquia [*pah-rroh'-kee-ah*]
park *n.*, parque (m) [*pahr'-keh*]
park *v.*, estacionar [*ehs-tah-thee-oh-nahr'*]
parking, aparcamiento, estacionamiento [*ah-pahr-kah-mee-ehn'-toh, ehs-tah-thee-oh-nah-mee-ehn'-toh*]
  no parking, se prohibe estacionar [*seh proh-ee'-beh ehs-tah-thee-oh-nahr'*]
parliament, parlamento [*pahr-lah-mehn'-toh*]
parlor, sala [*sah'-lah*]
parsley, perejil (m) [*peh-reh-heel'*]
part *n.*, pieza, parte (f) [*pee-eh'-thah, pahr'-teh*]
part *v.*, partir [*pahr-teer'*]
partially, parcialmente [*pahr-thee-ahl-mehn'-teh*]
participate *v.*, participar [*pahr-tee-thee-pahr'*]
particular, particular [*pahr-tee-koo-lahr'*]
particularly, particularmente [*pahr-tee-koo-lahr-mehn'-teh*]
partly, en parte [*ehn pahr'-teh*]
partner, socio [*soh'-thee-oh*]
party [social event], fiesta [*fee-ehs'-tah*]
party [political], partido [*pahr-tee'-doh*]
pass *n.*, paso [*pah'-soh*]
pass *v.*, pasar [*pah-sahr'*]
passage [fare] pasaje (m) [*pah-sah'-heh*]
passenger, pasajero [*pah-sah-heh'-roh*]
passing, paso [*pah'-soh*]
passion, pasión (f) [*pah-see-ohn'*]
passionate, apasionado [*ah-pah-see-oh-nah'-doh*]
passive, pasivo [*pah-see'-voh*]
passport, pasaporte (m) [*pah-sah-pohr'-teh*]
past, pasado [*pah-sah'-doh*]
paste, pasta [*pahs'-tah*]
pastry, pastelería [*pahs-teh-leh-ree'-ah*]
patch *n.*, remiendo [*reh-mee-ehn'-doh*]
patch *v.*, componer (irreg), remendar (irreg) [*kohm-poh-nehr', reh-mehn-dahr'*]
path, sendero [*sehn-deh'-roh*]

patience, paciencia [*pah-thee-ehn'-thee-ah*]
patient, paciente [*pah-thee-ehn'-teh*]
patriotic, patriótico [*pah-tree-oh'-tee-koh*]
patrol, patrulla [*pah-troo'-yah*]
pattern, patrón (m) [*pah-trohn'*]
pavement, pavimento [*pah-vee-mehn'-toh*]
pawn *v.,* empeñar [*ehm-peh-nyahr'*]
pawnshop, casa de empeños [*kah'-sah deh ehm-peh'-nyohs*]
pay *v.,* pagar [*pah-gahr'*]
    pay a fine, pagar una multa [*pah-gahr' oo'-nah mool'-tah*]
    pay attention, poner/prestar atención [*poh-nehr'/prehs-tahr ah-tehn-thee-ohn'*]
    pay a visit, visitar [*vee-see-tahr'*]
    pay by installments, pagar a plazos [*pah-gahr' ah plah'-thohs*]
    pay cash, pagar al contado [*pah-gahr' ahl kohn-tah'-doh*]
payment, pago [*pah'-goh*]
pea, guisante (m) [*ghee-sahn'-teh*]
peace, paz (f) [*pahth*]
peaceful, pacífico [*pah-thee'-fee-koh*]
peach, melocotón (m) [*meh-loh-koh-tohn'*]
peak, cima [*thee'-mah*]
peanut, cacahuete (m) [*kah-kah-oo-eh'-teh*]
pear, pera [*peh'-rah*]
pearl, perla [*pehr'-lah*]
peculiar, peculiar [*peh-koo-lee-ahr'*]
peddler, vendedor (m) ambulante [*vehn-deh-dohr' ahm-boo-lahn'-teh*]
pedestrian, transeunte (m) [*trahn-seh-oon'-teh*]
peel [foods] *v.,* pelar [*peh-lahr'*]
pen [writing], pluma [*ploo'-mah*]
penalty, pena [*peh'-nah*]
pencil, lápiz (m) [*lah'-peeth*]
pendant, pendiente (m) [*pehn-dee-ehn'-teh*]
peninsula, península [*peh-neen'-soo-lah*]
penny, centavo [*thehn-tah'-voh*]
people, gente (f) [*hehn'-teh*]
pepper [fruit], pimiento [*pee-mee-ehn'-toh*]

pepper [spice], pimienta [*pee-mee-ehn'-tah*]
perceive *v.*, percibir [*pehr-thee-beer'*]
per cent, por ciento [*pohr thee-ehn'-toh*]
percentage, porcentaje (m) [*pohr-thehn-tah'-heh*]
perfect *adj.*, perfecto [*pehr-fehk'-toh*]
perfection, perfección (f) [*pehr-fehk-thee-ohn'*]
performance, función (f), funcionamiento [*foon-thee-ohn', foon-thee-oh-nah-mee-ehn'-toh*]
perfume, perfume (m) [*pehr-foo'-meh*]
perhaps, quizás [*kee-thahs'*]
period [*peh-ree'-oh-doh*]
  menstrual period, menstruación [*mehns-troo-ah-thee-ohn'*]
permanent, permanente [*pehr-mah-nehn'-teh*]
permanent wave, ondulación (f) permanente [*ohn-doo-lah-thee-ohn' pehr-mah-nehn'-teh*]
permanently, permanentemente [*pehr-mah-nehn-teh-mehn'-teh*]
permission, permiso [*pehr-mee'-soh*]
permit *n.*, autorización (f) [*ah-oo-toh-ree-thah-thee-ohn'*]
permit *v.*, permitir [*pehr-mee-teer'*]
Persian, persa [*pehr'-sah*]
persist *v.*, persistir [*pehr-sees-teer'*]
person, persona [*pehr-soh'-nah*]
personal, personal [*pehr-soh-nahl'*]
personality, personalidad (f) [*pehr-soh-nah-lee-dahd'*]
personally, personalmente [*pehr-soh-nahl-mehn'-teh*]
personnel, personal (m) [*pehr-soh-nahl'*]
perspiration, transpiración (f) [*trahns-pee-rah-thee-ohn'*]
perspire *v.*, sudar [*soo-dahr'*]
persuade *v.*, persuadir [*pehr-soo-ah-deer'*]
persuasive, persuasivo [*pehr-soo-ah-see'-voh*]
pertaining to, relativo a [*reh-lah-tee'-voh ah*]
Peru, Perú (m) [*peh-roo'*]
Peruvian, peruano [*peh-roo-ah'-noh*]
pessimist, pesimista (m, f) [*peh-see-mees'-tah*]
pessimistic, pesimista [*peh-see-mees'-tah*]
petition, petición (f) [*peh-tee-thee-ohn'*]
petroleum, petróleo [*peh-troh'-leh-oh*]

pharmacy, farmacia [*fahr-mah'-thee-ah*]
phase, fase (f) [*fah'-seh*]
Philippine Islands, Islas Filipinas [*ees'-lahs fee-lee-pee'-nahs*]
philosopher, filósofo [*fee-loh'-soh-foh*]
philosophy, filosofía [*fee-loh-soh-fee'-ah*]
phone *n.,* teléfono [*teh-leh'-foh-noh*]
  by phone, por teléfono [*pohr teh-leh'-foh-noh*]
phone *v.,* telefonear [*teh-leh-foh-neh-ahr'*]
phonograph, fonógrafo [*foh-noh'-grah-foh*]
photograph, fotografía [*foh-toh-grah-fee'-ah*]
photographer, fotógrafo [*foh-toh'-grah-foh*]
physical, físico [*fee'-see-koh*]
physician, médico [*meh'-dee-koh*]
physics, física [*fee'-see-kah*]
pianist, pianista (m, f) [*pee-ah-nees'-tah*]
piano, piano [*pee-ah'-noh*]
pick *v.,* escoger [*ehs-koh-hehr'*]
  pick up, recoger [*reh-koh-hehr'*]
pickpocket, carterista [*kahr-teh-rees'-tah*]
picture, cuadro [*koo-ah'-droh*]
picturesque, pintoresco [*peen-toh-rehs'-koh*]
pie, pastel (m) [*pahs-tehl'*]
piece, pedazo [*peh-dah'-thoh*]
pier, muelle (m) [*moo-eh'-yeh*]
pig, cerdo [*ther'-doh*]
pile [mass], pila [*pee'-lah*]
pill, píldora [*peel'-doh-rah*]
pillow, almohada [*ahl-moh-ah'-dah*]
pilot, piloto [*pee-loh'-toh*]
pin, alfiler (m) [*ahl-fee-lehr'*]
pinch *v.,* pellizcar [*peh-yeeth-kahr'*]
pineapple, piña [*pee'-nyah*]
pink, rosa [*roh'-sah*]
pipe [smoking], pipa [*pee'-pah*]
pipe [plumbing], tubería [*too-beh-ree'-ah*]
pistol, pistola [*pees-toh'-lah*]
pitcher, jarra [*hah'-rrah*]
pity, lástima [*lahs'-tee-mah*]

What a pity! ¡Qué lástima! [*keh lahs'-tee-mah*]
place *n.*, lugar (m) [*loo-gahr'*]
  in place of, en lugar de [*ehn loo-gahr' deh*]
  take place, tener lugar [*teh-nehr' loo-gahr'*]
place *v.*, colocar [*koh-loh-kahr'*]
plain *adj.*, sencillo [*sehn-thee'-yoh*]
plan *n.*, plan (m), plano [*plahn', plah'-noh*]
plan *v.*, planear [*plah-neh-ahr'*]
planet, planeta (m) [*plah-neh'-tah*]
plant *n.*, planta [*plahn'-tah*]
plant *v.*, plantar [*plahn-tahr'*]
plaster, yeso [*yeh'-soh*]
plastic, plástico [*plahs'-tee-koh*]
plate, plato [*plah'-toh*]
platform, plataforma [*plah-tah-fohr'-mah*]
play [drama] *n.*, obra de teatro [*oh'-brah deh teh-ah'-troh*]
play [a game] *v.*, jugar (irreg) [*hoo-gahr'*]
play [an instrument] *v.*, tocar [*toh-kahr'*]
playmate, compañero de juegos [*kohm-pah-nyeh'-roh deh hoo-eh'-gohs*]
plead *v.*, abogar [*ah-boh-gahr'*]
pleasant, agradable [*ah-grah-dah'-bleh*]
please *v.*, agradar [*ah-grah-dahr'*]
  Please! ¡Por favor! [*pohr fah-vohr'*]
pleasure, placer (m) [*plah-thehr'*]
  pleasure trip, viaje (m) de placer [*vee-ah'-heh deh plah-thehr'*]
plenty, mucho [*moo'-choh*]
plot [scheme], complot (m) [*kohm-ploht'*]
plow *v.*, arar [*ah-rahr'*]
plug, enchufe (m) [*ehn-choo'-feh*]
plum, ciruela [*thee-roo-eh'-lah*]
plumber, plomero, fontanero [*ploh-meh'-roh, fohn-tah-neh'-roh*]
plural, plural [*ploo-rahl'*]
plus, más [*mahs'*]
pneumonia, pulmonía [*pool-moh-nee'-ah*]
pocket, bolsillo [*bohl-see'-yoh*]

pocketbook, cartera [*kahr-teh'-rah*]
poem, poema (m) [*poh-eh'-mah*]
poet, poeta (m, f) [*poh-eh'-tah*]
poetry, poesía [*poh-eh-see'-ah*]
point [in time or space] *n*., punto [*poon'-toh*]
   point of view, punto de vista [*poon'-toh deh vees'-tah*]
point [tip] *n*., punta [*poon'-tah*]
point out *v*., indicar [*een-dee-kahr'*]
poison, veneno [*veh-neh'-noh*]
poisonous, venenoso [*veh-neh-noh'-soh*]
Poland, Polonia [*poh-loh'-nee-ah*]
Polish, polaco [*poh-lah'-koh*]
pole [piece of wood], poste (m) [*pohs'-teh*]
police, policía [*poh-lee-thee'-ah*]
policeman, policía (m) [*poh-lee-thee'-ah*]
police station, comisaría [*koh-mee-sah-ree'-ah*]
policy, política, póliza [*poh-lee'-tee-kah, poh'-lee-thah*]
polish *v*., pulir, lustrar [*poo-leer', loos-trahr'*]
polite, cortés [*kohr-tehs'*]
political, político [*poh-lee'-tee-koh*]
politics, política [*poh-lee'-tee-kah*]
pool [swimming], piscina [*pees-thee'-nah*]
poor, pobre [*poh'-breh*]
popular, popular [*poh-poo-lahr'*]
popularity, popularidad (f) [*poh-poo-lah-ree-dahd'*]
population, población (f) [*poh-blah-thee-ohn'*]
porch, pórtico, porche (m) [*pohr'-tee-koh, pohr'-cheh*]
pork, puerco [*poo-ehr'-koh*]
port [harbor], puerto [*poo-ehr'-toh*]
portable, portátil [*pohr-tah'-teel*]
porter, maletero [*mah-leh-teh'-roh*]
portrait, retrato [*reh-trah'-toh*]
Portugal, Portugal [*pohr-too-gahl'*]
Portuguese, portugués [*pohr-too-ghehs'*]
pose, postura, afectación (f) [*pohs-too'-rah, ah-fehk-tah-thee-ohn'*]
position, posición (f) [*poh-see-thee-ohn'*]
positive, positivo [*poh-see-tee'-voh*]

possess v., poseer [*poh-seh-ehr'*]
possession, posesión (f) [*poh-seh-see-ohn'*]
possibility, posibilidad (f) [*poh-see-bee-lee-dahd'*]
possible, posible [*poh-see'-bleh*]
  as soon as possible, tan pronto como sea posible [*tahn prohn'-toh koh'-moh seh'-ah poh-see'-bleh*]
possibly, posiblemente [*poh-see-bleh-mehn'-teh*]
post, poste (m) [*pohs'-teh*]
postage, franqueo [*frahn-keh'-oh*]
postage stamp, sello [*seh'-yoh*]
postcard, tarjeta postal [*tahr-heh'-tah pohs-tahl'*]
post office, correos (pl) [*koh-rreh'-ohs*]
  post office box, apartado de correos [*ah-pahr-tah'-doh deh koh-rreh'-ohs*]
postpone v., aplazar [*ah-plah-thahr'*]
pot, olla [*oh'-yah*]
potato, patata, papa [*pah-tah'-tah, pah'-pah*]
pottery, cerámica [*theh-rah'-mee-kah*]
pound n., libra [*lee'-brah*]
pour v., verter (irreg) [*vehr-tehr'*]
poverty, pobreza [*poh-breh'-thah*]
powder, polvo [*pohl'-voh*]
power, fuerza, poder (m) [*foo-ehr'-thah, poh-dehr'*]
powerful, poderoso [*poh-deh-roh'-soh*]
practical, práctico [*prahk'-tee-koh*]
practice v., practicar [*prahk-tee-kahr'*]
praise v., elogiar [*eh-loh-hee-ahr'*]
pray v., rezar [*reh-thahr'*]
prayer, oración (f) [*oh-rah-thee-ohn'*]
precaution, precaución (f) [*preh-kah-oo-thee-ohn'*]
precede v., preceder [*preh-theh-dehr'*]
precious, precioso [*preh-thee-oh'-soh*]
precise, preciso [*preh-thee'-soh*]
precisely, precisamente [*preh-thee-sah-mehn'-teh*]
prefer v., preferir (irreg) [*preh-feh-reer'*]
preferable, preferible [*preh-feh-ree'-bleh*]
preference, preferencia [*preh-feh-rehn'-thee-ah*]
pregnant, encinta [*ehn-theen'-tah*]

prejudice, prejuicio [*preh-hoo-ee'-thee-oh*]
premature, prematuro [*preh-mah-too'-roh*]
premonition, presentimiento [*preh-sehn-tee-mee-ehn'-toh*]
preparation, preparación (f) [*preh-pah-rah-thee-ohn'*]
prepare v., preparar [*preh-pah-rahr'*]
prescription, receta [*reh-theh'-tah*]
presence, presencia [*preh-sehn'-thee-ah*]
present [time] n., presente (m) [*preh-sehn'-teh*]
  at present, por el momento [*pohr ehl moh-mehn'-toh*]
present [gift] n., regalo [*reh-gah'-loh*]
present v., presentar [*preh-sehn-tahr'*]
presently, dentro de poco [*dehn'-troh deh poh'-koh*]
preserve v., preservar [*preh-sehr-vahr'*]
president, presidente (m) [*preh-see-dehn'-teh*]
press n., prensa [*prehn'-sah*]
press v., presionar [*preh-see-oh-nahr'*]
pressure, presión (f) [*preh-see-ohn'*]
prestige, prestigio [*prehs-tee'-hee-oh*]
pretend v., fingir, pretender [*feen-heer', preh-tehn-dehr'*]
pretty, bonito, lindo [*boh-nee'-toh, leen'-doh*]
prevent v., prevenir (irreg) [*preh-veh-neer'*]
prevention, prevención (f) [*preh-vehn-thee-ohn'*]
previous, previo [*preh'-vee-oh*]
price, precio [*preh'-thee-oh*]
price list, lista de precios [*lees'-tah deh preh'-thee-ohs*]
pride, orgullo [*ohr-goo'-yoh*]
priest, sacerdote (m) [*sah-thehr-doh'-teh*]
prince, príncipe (m) [*preen'-thee-peh*]
princess, princesa [*preen-theh'-sah*]
principal, principal [*preen-thee-pahl'*]
principally, principalmente [*preen-thee-pahl-mehn'-teh*]
principle, principio [*preen-thee'-pee-oh*]
print v., imprimir [*eem-pree-meer'*]
printed matter, impresos (pl) [*eem-preh'-sohs*]
printer, impresor (m) [*eem-preh-sohr'*]
prior, anterior [*ahn-teh-ree-ohr'*]
prison, prisión (f) [*pree-see-ohn'*]
prisoner, prisionero [*pree-see-oh-neh'-roh*]

privacy, privacidad (f) [*pree-vah-thee-dahd'*]
private *adj.*, privado [*pree-vah'-doh*]
privilege, privilegio [*pree-vee-leh'-hee-oh*]
prize, premio [*preh'-mee-oh*]
probable, probable [*proh-bah'-bleh*]
probably, probablemente [*proh-bah-bleh-mehn'-teh*]
problem, problema (m) [*proh-bleh'-mah*]
procedure, procedimiento [*proh-theh-dee-mee-ehn'-toh*]
proceed *v.*, proceder [*proh-theh-dehr'*]
process *n.*, proceso [*proh-theh'-soh*]
produce *v.*, producir (irreg) [*proh-doo-theer'*]
product, producto [*proh-dook'-toh*]
production, producción (f) [*proh-dook-thee-ohn'*]
profession, profesión (f) [*proh-feh-see-ohn'*]
professor, profesor (m) [*proh-feh-sohr'*]
profile, perfil (m) [*pehr-feel'*]
profit *n.*, beneficio [*beh-neh-fee'-thee-oh*]
program *n.*, programa (m) [*proh-grah'-mah*]
progress *n.*, progreso [*proh-greh'-soh*]
progress *v.*, progresar [*proh-greh-sahr'*]
progressive, progresista (m, f) [*proh-greh-sees'-tah*]
prohibit *v.*, prohibir [*proh-ee-beer'*]
prohibited, prohibido [*proh-ee-bee'-doh*]
project *n.*, proyecto [*proh-yehk'-toh*]
prominent, prominente [*proh-mee-nehn'-teh*]
promise *n.*, promesa [*proh-meh'-sah*]
promise *v.*, prometer [*proh-meh-tehr'*]
promotion, promoción (f) [*proh-moh-thee-ohn'*]
prompt, pronto [*prohn'-toh*]
pronoun, pronombre (m) [*proh-nohm'-breh*]
pronounce *v.*, pronunciar [*proh-noon-thee-ahr'*]
   How do you pronounce . . . ? ¿Cómo se pronuncia . . . ?
   [*koh'-moh seh proh-noon'-thee-ah*]
pronunciation, pronunciación (f) [*proh-noon-thee-ah-thee-ohn'*]
proof, prueba [*proo-eh'-bah*]
propaganda, propaganda [*proh-pah-gahn'-dah*]
propeller, hélice (f) [*eh'-lee-theh*]

proper, propio [*proh'-pee-oh*]
property, propiedad (f) [*proh-pee-eh-dahd'*]
proportion, proporción (f) [*proh-pohr-thee-ohn'*]
proposal, propuesta [*proh-poo-ehs'-tah*]
propose *v.,* proponer (irreg) [*proh-poh-nehr'*]
proposition, proposición (f) [*proh-poh-see-thee-ohn'*]
prosperity, prosperidad (f) [*prohs-peh-ree-dahd'*]
prosperous, próspero [*prohs'-peh-roh*]
protect *v.,* proteger [*proh-teh-hehr'*]
protection, protección (f) [*proh-tehk-thee-ohn'*]
protest *n.,* protesta [*proh-tehs'-tah*]
protest *v.,* protestar [*proh-tehs-tahr'*]
Protestant, protestante (m) [*proh-tehs-tahn'-teh*]
proud, orgulloso [*ohr-goo-yoh'-soh*]
prove *v.,* probar (irreg) [*proh-bahr'*]
proverb, proverbio [*proh-vehr'-bee-oh*]
provide *v.,* proveer (irreg) [*proh-veh-ehr'*]
provided that, con tal que [*kohn tahl keh*]
province, provincia [*proh-veen'-thee-ah*]
provincial, provincial, provinciano [*proh-veen-thee-ahl'*,
    proh-vin-thee-ah'-noh]
provisions, provisiones (f, pl) [*proh-vee-see-oh'-nehs*]
prune, ciruela [*thee-roo-eh'-lah*]
psychiatrist, psiquiatra (m, f) [*see-kee-ah'-trah*]
psychoanalysis, psicoanálisis (m) [*see-koh-ah-nah'-lee-sees*]
psychological, psicológico [*see-koh-loh'-hee-koh*]
public *n. & adj.,* público [*poo'-blee-koh*]
publication, publicación (f) [*poo-blee-kah-thee-ohn'*]
publicity, publicidad (f) [*poo-blee-thee-dahd'*]
publish *v.,* publicar [*poo-blee-kahr'*]
Puerto Rico, Puerto Rico [*poo-ehr'-toh ree'-koh*]
Puerto Rican, puertorriqueño [*poo-ehr-toh-rree-keh'-nyoh*]
pull *v.,* tirar de [*tee-rahr' deh*]
pull out *v.,* sacar [*sah-kahr'*]
pulse, pulso [*pool'-soh*]
pump *n.,* bomba [*bohm'-bah*]
pumpkin, calabaza [*kah-lah-bah'-thah*]
punctual, puntual [*poon-too-ahl'*]

punish *v.*, castigar [*kahs-tee-gahr'*]
punishment, castigo [*kahs-tee'-goh*]
pupil, alumno, discípulo [*ah-loom'-noh, dees-thee'-poo-loh*]
puppet, títere (m) [*tee'-teh-reh*]
purchase *n.*, compra [*kohm'-prah*]
purchase *v.*, comprar [*kohm-prahr'*]
pure, puro [*poo'-roh*]
purple, morado [*moh-rah'-doh*]
purpose, propósito [*proh-poh'-see-toh*]
   on purpose, adrede [*ah-dreh'-deh*]
purse, bolso [*bohl'-soh*]
pursue *v.*, perseguir (irreg) [*pehr-seh-gheer'*]
push *v.*, empujar [*ehm-poo-hahr'*]
put *v.*, poner (irreg) [*poh-nehr'*]
   put off, aplazar [*ah-plah-thahr'*]
   put on [clothes], ponerse (irreg) [*poh nehr'-seh*]
   put out [a light], apagar [*ah-pah-ghahr'*]
puzzle, rompecabezas (m) [*rohm-peh-kah-beh'-thahs*]
puzzled, perplejo [*pehr-pleh'-hoh*]
pyramid, pirámide (f) [*pee-ràh'-mee-deh*]

Q

qualification, calificación (f) [*kah-lee-fee-kah-thee-ohn'*]
quality, cualidad (f), calidad (f) [*koo-ah-lee-dahd', kah-lee-dahd'*]
quantity, cantidad (f) [*kahn-tee-dahd'*]
quarrel *n.*, riña [*ree'-nyah*]
quart, cuarto [*koo-ahr'-toh*]
quarter [one fourth], cuarto [*koo-ahr'-toh*]
quarter hour, cuarto de hora [*koo-ahr'-toh deh oh'-rah*]
queen, reina [*reh'-ee-nah*]
queer [odd], raro [*rah'-roh*]
question *n.*, pregunta [*preh-goon'-tah*]
question *v.*, preguntar [*preh-goon-tahr'*]

question mark, signo de interrogación [*seeg'-noh deh een-teh-rroh-gah-thee-ohn'*]

questionnaire, cuestionario [*koo-ehs-tee-oh-nah'-ree-oh*]

quick, rápido [*rah'-pee-doh*]

quickly, rápidamente [*rah-pee-dah-mehn'-teh*]

quicksand, arena movediza [*ah-reh'-nah moh-veh-dee'-thah*]

quiet, tranquilo, callado [*trahn-kee'-loh, kah-yah'-doh*]

   Be quiet!, ¡Cállese! [*kah'-yeh-seh*]

quit *v.,* abandonar, irse (irreg) [*ah-bahn-doh-nahr', eer'-seh*]

quite, bastante [*bahs-tahn'-teh*]

quotation, cita [*thee'-tah*]

quotation marks, comillas [*koh-mee'-yahs*]

quote *v.,* citar [*thee-tahr'*]

R

rabbit, conejo [*koh-neh'-hoh*]

race [ethnic group], raza [*rah'-thah*]

race [contest], carrera [*kah-rreh'-rah*]

   horse race, carrera de caballos [*kah-rreh'-rah deh kah-bah'-yohs*]

race-track, pista de carreras [*pees'-tah deh kah-rreh'-rahs*]

radiator, radiador (m) [*rah-dee-ah-dohr'*]

radio, radio (f) [*rah'-dee-oh*]

radio station, emisora de radio [*eh-mee-soh'-rah deh rah'-dee-oh*]

radish, rábano [*rah'-bah-noh*]

rag, trapo [*trah'-poh*]

rage *n.,* rabia [*rah'-bee-ah*]

raid *n.,* incursión (f) [*een-koor-see-ohn'*]

railroad, ferrocarril (m) [*feh-rroh-kah-rreel'*]

railroad car, vagón (m) [*vah-gohn'*]

railway crossing, paso a nivel [*pah'-soh ah nee-vehl'*]

rain *n.,* lluvia [*yoo'-vee-ah*]

rain v., llover (irreg) [*yoh-vehr'*]
rainbow, arco iris (m) [*ahr'-koh ee'-rees*]
raincoat, impermeable (m) [*eem-pehr-meh-ah'-bleh*]
raise [lift] v., levantar [*leh-vahn-tahr'*]
raise [increase] v., aumentar [*ah-oo-mehn-tahr'*]
raise [rear] v., criar [*kree-ahr'*]
raisin, pasa [*pah'-sah*]
random, azar (m) [*ah-thahr'*]
range n., alcance (m) [*ahl-kahn'-theh*]
rapid, rápido [*rah'-pee-doh*]
rapidly, rápidamente [*rah-pee-dah-mehn'-teh*]
rare [undercooked], poco asado [*poh'-koh ah-sah'-doh*]
rare [unusual], raro [*rah'-roh*]
rarely, raramente [*rah-rah-mehn'-teh*]
rash adj., atrevidó [*ah-treh-vee'-doh*]
rash [skin] n., crupción (f) [*eh-roop-thee-ohn'*]
rat, rata [*rah'-tah*]
rate [price], tarifa [*tah-ree'-fah*]
rate [speed], velocidad (f) [*veh-loh'-thee-dahd*]
rather, más bien [*mahs bee-ehn'*]
   I would rather . . . , Me gustaría más . . . [*meh ghoos-tah-ree'-ah mahs*]
raw, crudo [*kroo'-doh*]
raw material, materia prima [*mah-teh'-ree-ah pree'-mah*]
ray, rayo [*rah'-yoh*]
razor, navaja de afeitar [*nah-vah'-hah deh ah-feh-ee-tahr'*]
   electric razor, maquinilla de afeitar [*mah-kee-nee'-yah deh ah-feh-ee-tahr'*]
razor blade, hoja de afeitar [*oh'-hah deh ah-feh-ee-tahr'*]
reach v., alcanzar [*ahl-kahn-thahr'*]
reaction, reacción (f) [*reh-ahk-thee-ohn'*]
read v., leer [*leh-ehr'*]
reading, lectura [*lehk-too'-rah*]
ready, listo [*lees'-toh*]
ready-to-wear n., listo para ser usado [*lees'-toh pah'-rah sehr oo-sah'-doh*]
real, verdadero [*vehr-dah-deh'-roh*]

real estate, bienes inmuebles (m, pl) [*bee-eh'-nehs een-moo-eh'-blehs*]

realize *v.*, darse cuenta [*dahr'-seh koo-ehn'-tah*]

really, verdaderamente [*vehr-dah-deh-rah-mehn'-teh*]

rear *adj.*, trasero [*trah-seh'-roh*]

reason *n.*, razón (f) [*rah-thohn'*]

reason *v.*, razonar [*rah-thoh-nahr'*]

reasonable, razonable [*rah-thoh-nah'-bleh*]

rebel *n.*, rebelde [*reh-behl'-deh*]

recall [call back], volver a llamar [*vohl-vehr' ah yah-mahr'*]

recall [remember] *v.*, recordar (irreg) [*reh-kohr-dahr'*]

receipt, recibo [*reh-thee'-boh*]

receive *v.*, recibir [*reh-thee-beer'*]

recent, reciente [*reh-thee-ehn'-teh*]

recently, recientemente [*reh-thee-ehn-teh-mehn'-teh*]

reception, recepción (f) [*reh-thehp-thee-ohn'*]

recession, retroceso [*reh-troh-theh'-soh*]

recipe, receta [*reh-theh'-tah*]

reciprocate *v.*, corresponder [*koh-rrehs-pohn-dehr'*]

recognize *v.*, reconocer (irreg) [*reh-koh-noh-thehr'*]

recommend *v.*, recomendar (irreg) [*reh-koh-mehn-dahr'*]

recommendation, recomendación (f) [*reh-koh-mehn-dah-thee-ohn'*]

record [archive] *n.*, registro, archivo [*reh-hees'-troh, ahr-chee'-voh*]

record [phonograph], disco [*dees'-koh*]

recover *v.*, recuperar [*reh-koo-peh-rahr'*]

recovery, restablecimiento [*rehs-tah-bleh-thee-mee-ehn'-toh*]

recreation, recreo [*reh-kreh'-oh*]

red, rojo [*roh'-hoh*]

Red Cross, Cruz Roja [*krooth roh'-hah*]

reduce *v.*, reducir (irreg) [*reh-doo-theer'*]

reduction, reducción (f) [*reh-dook-thee-ohn'*]

red wine, vino tinto [*vee'-noh teen'-toh*]

reef, arrecife (m) [*ah-rreh-thee'-feh*]

refer *v.*, referir (irreg) [*reh-feh-reer'*]

referee, árbitro [*ahr'-bee-troh*]

reference, referencia [*reh-feh-rehn'-thee-ah*]

refined, refinado [*reh-fee-nah'-doh*]
reflect *v.*, reflejar [*reh-fleh-hahr'*]
reflection, reflexión (f), reflejo [*reh-flehk-see-ohn', reh-fleh'-hoh*]
reform *v.*, reformar [*reh-fohr-mahr'*]
refrain *v.*, abstenerse (irreg) [*ahbs-teh-nehr'-seh*]
refresh *v.*, refrescar [*reh-frehs-kahr'*]
refreshing, refrescante [*reh-frehs-kahn'-teh*]
refreshments, refrescos [*reh-frehs'-kohs*]
refrigerator, refrigerador (m) [*reh-free-heh-rah-dohr'*]
refuge, refugio [*reh-foo'-hee-oh*]
refugee, refugiado [*reh-foo-hee-ah'-doh*]
refund *n.*, reembolso [*reh-ehm-bohl'-soh*]
refund *v.*, reembolsar [*reh-ehm-bohl-sahr'*]
refusal, negativa [*neh-gah-tee'-vah*]
refuse *v.*, rehusar [*reh-oo-sahr'*]
regain *v.*, recobrar [*reh-koh-brahr'*]
regardless, a pesar de [*ah peh-sahr' deh*]
regards, recuerdos [*reh-koo-ehr'-dohs*]
regime, régimen (m) [*reh'-hee-mehn*]
regiment, regimiento [*reh-hee-mee-ehn'-toh*]
region, región (f) [*reh-hee-ohn'*]
register *n.*, registro [*reh-hees'-troh*]
register *v.*, inscribir [*eens-kree-beer'*]
registered letter, carta certificada [*kahr'-tah thehr-tee-fee-kah'-dah*]
regret *v.*, lamentar [*lah-mehn-tahr'*]
regular, regular [*reh-goo-lahr'*]
regular gas, gasolina ordinaria [*gah-soh-lee'-nah ohr-dee--nah'-ree-ah*]
regulate *v.*, regular [*reh-goo-lahr'*]
regulation, regulación (f) [*reh-goo-lah-thee-ohn'*]
rehearsal, ensayo [*ehn-sah'-yoh*]
rejoin *v.*, reunirse [*reh-oo-neer'-seh*]
related, relacionado [*reh-lah-thee-oh-nah'-doh*]
relationship, parentesco, relación (f) [*pah-rehn-tehs'-koh, reh-lah-thee-ohn'*]
relative *adj.*, relativo [*reh-lah-tee'-voh*]

relatively, relativamente [*reh-lah-tee-vah-mehn'-teh*]
relatives, parientes (m) [*pah-ree-ehn'-tehs*]
relax *v.*, relajar, descansar [*reh-la-hahr'*, *dehs-kahn-sahr'*]
relaxation, aflojamiento [*ah-floh-hah-mee-ehn'-toh*]
release *v.*, soltar (irreg) [*sohl-tahr'*]
reliable, de confianza [*deh kohn-fee-ahn'-thah*]
relief, alivio [*ah-lee'-vee-oh*]
relieve *v.*, librar, aliviar [*lee-brahr'*, *ah-lee-vee-ahr'*]
religion, religión (f) [*reh-lee-hee-ohn'*]
religious, religioso [*reh-lee-hee-oh'-soh*]
rely [on] *v.*, contar (irreg) con, fiarse de [*kohn-tahr' kohn*, *fee-ahr'-seh deh*]
remain *v.*, quedarse, permanecer (irreg) [*keh-dahr'-seh*, *pehr-mah-neh-thehr'*]
remainder, resto [*rehs'-toh*]
remark *n.*, observación (f) [*ohb-sehr-vah-thee-ohn'*]
remark *v.*, observar [*ohb-sehr-vahr'*]
remarkable, notable [*noh-tah'-bleh*]
remedy *n.*, remedio [*reh-meh'-dee-oh*]
remember *v.*, recordar (irreg) [*reh-kohr-dahr'*]
remind *v.*, recordar (irreg) [*reh-kohr-dahr'*]
remit *v.*, remitir [*reh-mee-teer'*]
remittance, envío [*ehn-vee'-oh*]
remove *v.*, quitar [*kee-tahr'*]
renew *v.*, renovar (irreg) [*reh-noh-vahr'*]
rent *n.*, alquiler (m), arriendo [*ahl-kee-lehr'*, *ah-rree-ehn'-doh*]
rent *v.*, alquilar, arrendar (irreg) [*ahl-kee-lahr'*, *ah-rrehn-dahr'*]
  for rent, se alquila [*seh ahl-kee'-lah*]
repair *n.*, reparación (f) [*reh-pah-rah-thee-ohn'*]
repair *v.*, reparar [*reh-pah-rahr'*]
repay *v.*, reembolsar [*reh-ehm-bohl-sahr'*]
repeat *v.*, repetir (irreg) [*reh-peh-teer'*]
  Please repeat, Repita, por favor [*reh-pee'-tah, pohr fah-vohr'*]
repel *v.*, repeler [*reh-peh-lehr'*]
replace *v.*, reemplazar [*reh-ehm-plah-thahr'*]

reply *n.*, respuesta [*rehs-poo-ehs'-tah*]
reply *v.*, contestar [*kohn-tehs-tahr'*]
report *v.*, reportar [*reh-pohr-tahr'*]
reporter, reportero [*reh-pohr-teh'-roh*]
represent *v.*, representar [*reh-preh-sehn-tahr'*]
representative, representante (m) [*reh-preh-sehn-tahn'-teh*]
reproduction, reproducción (f) [*reh-proh-dook-thee-ohn'*]
republic, república [*reh-poo'-blee-kah*]
reputation, reputación (f) [*reh-poo-tah-thee-ohn'*]
request *v.*, solicitar [*soh-lee-thee-tahr'*]
require *v.*, requerir (irreg) [*reh-keh-reer'*]
requirement, requisito [*reh-kee-see'-toh*]
rescue *v.*, rescatar [*rehs-kah-tahr'*]
research *n.*, investigación (f) [*een-vehs-tee-gah-thee-ohn'*]
resemblance, parecido [*pah-reh-thee'-doh*]
resemble *v.*, parecerse a (irreg) [*pah-reh-thehr'-seh ah*]
resentment, resentimiento [*reh-sehn-tee-mee-ehn'-toh*]
reservation, reserva [*reh-sehr'-vah*]
reserve *v.*, reservar [*reh-sehr-vahr'*]
residence, residencia [*reh-see-dehn'-thee-ah*]
resident, residente (m, f) [*reh-see-dehn'-teh*]
resign *v.*, renunciar [*reh-noon-thee-ahr'*]
resignation, dimisión (f) [*dee-mee-see-ohn'*]
resist *v.*, resistir [*reh-sees-teer'*]
resolution, resolución (f) [*reh-soh-loo-thee-ohn'*]
resolve *v.*, resolver (irreg) [*reh-sohl-vehr'*]
resort *v.*, recurrir [*reh-koo-rreer'*]
respect *n.*, respeto [*rehs-peh'-toh*]
  in respect to, con respecto a [*kohn rehs-pehk'-toh ah*]
respectable, respetable [*rehs-peh-tah'-bleh*]
responsibility, responsabilidad (f) [*rehs-pohn-sah-bee-lee-dahd'*]
responsible, responsable [*rehs-pohn-sah'-bleh*]
rest [repose] *n.*, descanso [*dehs-kahn'-soh*]
rest *v.*, descansar [*dehs-kahn-sahr'*]
restaurant, restaurante (m) [*rehs-tah-oo-rahn'-teh*]
restless, inquieto [*een-kee-eh'-toh*]
restore *v.*, restaurar [*rehs-tah-oo-rahr'*]

restraint, restricción (f) [*rehs-treek-thee-ohn'*]
result *n.*, resultado [*reh-sool-tah'-doh*]
resume *v.*, reanudar [*reh-ah-noo-dahr'*]
retail, al por menor [*ahl pohr meh-nohr'*]
retain *v.*, retener (irreg) [*reh-teh-nehr'*]
retire [be pensioned off] *v.*, jubilarse [*hoo-bee-lahr'-seh*]
retire [withdraw] *v.*, retirarse [*reh-tee-rahr'-seh*]
return [of persons] *n.*, regresso [*reh-greh'-soh*]
return [of goods] *n.*, restitución (f), retorno [*rehs-tee-too-thee-ohn'*, *reh-tohr'-noh*]
return *v.*, volver (irreg) [*vohl-vehr'*]
revenge, venganza [*vehn-gahn'-thah*]
reverse, revés (m) [*reh-vehs'*]
reverse [auto], marcha atrás [*mahr'-chah ah-trahs'*]
review *v.*, revisar [*reh-vee-sahr'*]
revolution, revolución (f) [*reh-voh-loo-thee-ohn'*]
revolve *v.*, girar [*hee-rahr'*]
revolver, revólver (m) [*reh-vohl'-vehr*]
reward *n.*, recompensa [*reh-kohm-pehn'-sah*]
reward *v.*, recompensar [*reh-kohm-pehn-sahr'*]
rheumatism, reumatismo [*reh-oo-mah-tees'-moh*]
rhythm, ritmo [*reet'-moh*]
rib, costilla [*kohs-tee'-yah*]
ribbon, cinta [*theen'-tah*]
rice, arroz (m) [*ah-rrohth'*]
rich, rico [*ree'-koh*]
rid, get rid of, deshacerse de (irreg) [*dehs-ah-thehr'-seh deh*]
ride *n.*, paseo [*pah-seh'-oh*]
ride *v.*, pasear, montar [*pah-seh-ahr'*, *mohn-tahr'*]
ridicule *n.*, ridículo [*ree-dee'-koo-loh*]
ridiculous, ridículo [*ree-dee'-koo-loh*]
right [direction], derecho [*deh-reh'-choh*]
  on the right, a la derecha [*ah lah deh-reh'-chah*]
  to the right, a la derecha [*ah lah deh-reh'-chah*]
right [correct], correcto [*koh-rrehk'-toh*]
  all right, está bien [*ehs-tah' bee-ehn'*]
  be right, tener (irreg) razón [*teh-nehr' rah-thohn'*]
  right away, ahora mismo [*ah-oh'-rah mees'-moh*]

ring [circular band] *n.*, anillo [*ah-nee'-yoh*]
ring *v.*, sonar (irreg) [*soh-nahr'*]
rinse *v.*, enjuagar [*ehn-hoo-ah-gahr'*]
riot *n.*, motín (m), desorden (m) [*moh-teen', deh-sohr'-dehn*]
rip *v.*, rasgar [*rahs-gahr'*]
ripe, maduro [*mah-doo'-roh*]
ripen *v.*, madurar [*mah-doo-rahr'*]
rise *v.*, ascender (irreg) [*ahs-thehn-dehr'*]
risk *n.*, riesgo [*ree-ehs'-goh*]
ritual *n.*, ritual (m) [*ree-too-ahl'*]
rival *n.*, rival (m, f) [*ree-vahl'*]
river, río [*ree'-oh*]
road, camino, carretera [*kah-mee'-noh, kah-rreh-teh'-rah*]
roar *v.*, rugir [*roo-heer'*]
roast *n.*, asado [*ah-sah'-doh*]
roast *v.*, asar [*ah-sahr'*]
roasted, asado [*ah-sah'-doh*]
rob *v.*, robar [*roh-bahr'*]
robber, ladrón (m) [*lah-drohn'*]
robbery, robo [*roh'-boh*]
rock *n.*, roca [*roh'-kah*]
rocking chair, mecedora [*meh-theh-doh'-rah*]
roll [bread] *n.*, panecillo [*pah-neh-thee'-yoh*]
roll *v.*, rodar (irreg) [*roh-dahr'*]
Roman, romano [*roh-mah'-noh*]
romantic, romántico [*roh-mahn'-tee-koh*]
Rome, Roma [*roh'-mah*]
roof, tejado [*teh-hah'-doh*]
room [apartment], habitación (f) [*ah-bee-tah-thee-ohn'*]
  double room, habitacíon doble [*ah-bee-tah-thee-ohn' doh'-bleh*]
  single room, habitación sencilla [*ah-bee-tah-thee-ohn' sehn-thee'-yah*]
room [space], espacio [*ehs-pah'-thee-oh*]
rope, soga [*soh'-gah*]
rose *n.*, rosa [*roh'-sah*]
rotten, podridó [*poh-dree'-doh*]
rouge, colorete (m) [*koh-loh-reh'-teh*]

rough, áspero, brusco [*ahs'-peh-roh, broos'-koh*]
round [circular], redondo [*reh-dohn'-doh*]
round trip, viaje (m) de ida y vuelta [*vee-ah'-heh deh ee'-dah ee voo-ehl'-tah*]
route, ruta [*roo'-tah*]
routine, rutina [*roo-tee'-nah*]
row [line] *n.,* fila [*fee'-lah*]
row [a boat] *v.,* remar [*reh-mahr'*]
royal, real [*reh-ahl'*]
rub *v.,* frotar [*froh-tahr'*]
rubber, goma [*goh'-mah*]
ruby, rubí (m) [*roo-bee'*]
rude, grosero [*groh-seh'-roh*]
rudeness, grosería [*groh-seh-ree'-ah*]
rug, alfombra [*ahl-fohm'-brah*]
ruin *n.,* ruina [*roo-ee'-nah*]
rule *v.,* gobernar (irreg) [*goh-behr-nahr'*]
ruler [measure], regla [*reh'-glah*]
rumor, rumor (m) [*roo-mohr'*]
run *v.,* correr [*koh-rrehr'*]
   run away, fugarse [*foo-gahr'-seh*]
   run into, chocar con [*choh-kahr' kohn*]
   run over, atropellar [*ah-troh-peh-yahr'*]
runaway, fugitivo [*foo-hee-tee'-voh*]
rural, rural [*roo-rahl'*]
rush *v.,* apresurar [*ah-preh-soo-rahr'*]
Russia, Rusia [*roo'-see-ah*]
Russian, ruso [*roo'-soh*]
rust *n.,* herrumbre (f) [*eh-rroom'-breh*]
rustic *n. & adj.,* rústico [*roos'-tee-koh*]

S

sabotage, sabotaje (m) [*sah-boh-tah'-heh*]
sack, saco [*sah'-koh*]

sacred, sagrado [*sah-grah'-doh*]
sad, triste [*trees'-teh*]
saddle, montura [*mohn-too'-rah*]
sadness, tristeza [*trees-teh'-thah*]
safe *adj.*, salvo, seguro [*sahl'-voh, seh-goo'-roh*]
safety, seguridad (f) [*seh-goo-ree-dahd'*]
safety pin, imperdible (m) [*eem-pehr-dee'-bleh*]
said, dicho [*dee'-choh*]
sail *n.*, vela [*veh'-lah*]
sail *v.*, navegar [*nah-veh-gahr'*]
sailboat, barco de vela [*bahr'-koh deh veh'-lah*]
sailor, marinero [*mah-ree-neh'-roh*]
saint *adj. & n.*, santo [*sahn'-toh*]
salad, ensalada [*ehn-sah-lah'-dah*]
salary, sueldo [*soo-ehl'-doh*]
sale, venta [*vehn'-tah*]
  for sale, en venta [*ehn vehn'-tah*]
salesclerk, dependiente (m) [*deh-pehn-dee-ehn'-teh*]
salmon, salmón (m) [*sahl-mohn'*]
salt, sal (f) [*sahl*]
salty, salado [*sah-lah'-doh*]
salute *v.*, saludar [*sah-loo-dahr'*]
Salvador, El Salvador (m) [*ehl sahl-vah-dohr'*]
Salvadorian, salvadoreño [*sahl-vah-doh-reh'-nyoh*]
same, mismo [*mees'-moh*]
  It's all the same to me, Lo mismo me da [*loh mees'-moh meh dah*]
sample *n.*, muestra [*moo-ehs'-trah*]
sanction *v.*, sancionar [*sahn-thee-oh-nahr'*]
sand, arena [*ah-reh'-nah*]
sandal, sandalia [*sahn-dah'-lee-ah*]
sandwich, emparedado [*ehm-pah-reh-dah'-doh*]
sane, cuerdo [*koo-ehr'-doh*]
sanitary, sanitario [*sah-nee-tah'-ree-oh*]
sanitary napkin, compresa [*kohm-preh'-sah*]
sapphire, zafiro [*thah-fee'-roh*]
sarcastic, sarcástico [*sahr-kahs'-tee-koh*]
satin, raso [*rah'-soh*]

satirical, satírico [*sah-tee'-ree-koh*]
satisfaction, satisfacción (f) [*sah-tees-fahk-thee-ohn'*]
satisfactory, satisfactorio [*sah-tees-fahk-toh'-ree-oh*]
satisfied, satisfecho [*sah-tees-feh'-choh*]
satisfy *v.,* satisfacer (irreg) [*sah-tees-fah-thehr'*]
Saturday, sábado [*sah'-bah-doh*]
sauce, salsa [*sahl'-sah*]
saucer, platillo [*plah-tee'-yoh*]
sausage, salchicha [*sahl-chee'-chah*]
savage, salvaje [*sahl-vah'-heh*]
save [preserve] *v.,* salvar [*sahl-vahr'*]
save [put aside] *v.,* ahorrar [*ah-oh-rrahr'*]
savings, ahorros [*ah-oh'-rrohs*]
savings account, cuenta de ahorros [*koo-ehn'-tah deh
    ah-oh'-rrohs*]
say *v.,* decir (irreg) [*deh-theer'*]
scale, escala [*ehs-kah'-lah*]
scandal, escándalo [*ehs-kahn'-dah-loh*]
scar, cicatriz (f) [*thee-kah-treeth'*]
scarce, escaso [*ehs-kah'-soh*]
scarcely, apenas [*ah-peh'-nahs*]
scare *v.,* asustar [*ah-soos-tahr'*]
scarf, bufanda, pañuelo [*boo-fahn'-dah, pah-nyoo-eh'-loh*]
scene, escena [*ehs-theh'-nah*]
scenery, paisaje (m) [*pah-ee-sah'-heh*]
schedule *n.,* horario [*oh-rah'-ree-oh*]
scheme *n.,* esquema (m) [*ehs-keh'-mah*]
school, escuela [*ehs-koo-eh'-lah*]
schoolteacher, maestro de escuela [*mah-ehs'-troh deh ehs-
    koo-eh'-lah*]
science, ciencia [*thee-ehn'-thee-ah*]
scientist, científico [*thee-ehn-tee'-fee-koh*]
scissors, tijeras [*tee-heh'-rahs*]
scold *v.,* regañar [*reh-gah-nyahr'*]
score *n.,* calificación (f) numérica [*kah-lee-fee-kah-thee-ohn'
    noo-meh'-ree-kah*]
Scotch, escocés (m) [*ehs-koh-thehs'*]
Scotland, Escocia [*ehs-koh'-thee-ah*]

scratch *v.*, rascar [*rahs-kahr'*]

scream *v.*, gritar [*gree-tahr'*]

screen, pantalla [*pahn-tah'-yah*]

screw *n.*, tornillo [*tohr-nee'-yoh*]

screwdriver, destornillador (m) [*dehs-tohr-nee-yah-dohr'*]

sculpture, escultura [*ehs-kool-too'-rah*]

sea, mar (m, f) [*mahr*]

seal [animal] *n.*, foca [*foh'-kah*]

seal [stamp, mark] *n.*, sello [*seh'-yoh*]

seal *v.*, sellar [*seh-yahr'*]

seam, costura [*kohs-too'-rah*]

seaport, puerto de mar [*poo-ehr'-toh deh mahr*]

search *n.*, búsqueda [*boos'-keh-dah*]

search *v.*, buscar, registrar [*boos-kahr', reh-hees-trahr'*]

seaside, costa [*kohs'-tah*]

season *n.*, estación (f) [*ehs-tah-thee-ohn'*]

season *v.*, sazonar [*sah-thoh-nahr'*]

seat *n.*, asiento [*ah-see-ehn'-toh*]

   Have a seat, Tome asiento [*toh'-meh ah-see-ehn'-toh*]

seat belt, centurón de seguridad [*theen-too-rohn' deh-seh-goo-ree-dahd'*]

seated, sentado [*sehn-tah'-doh*]

second *n. & adj.*, segundo [*seh-goon'-doh*]

secondary education, segunda enseñanza [*seh-goon'-dah ehn-seh-nyahn'-thah*]

secret *n. & adj.*, secreto [*seh-kreh'-toh*]

secretary, secretario [*seh-kreh-tah'-ree-oh*]

section, sección (f) [*sehk-thee-ohn'*]

secure *adj.*, seguro [*seh-goo'-roh*]

secure *v.*, asegurar [*ah-seh-goo-rahr'*]

security, seguridad (f) [*seh-goo-ree-dahd'*]

seduce *v.*, seducir (irreg) [*seh-doo-theer'*]

see *v.*, ver (irreg) [*vehr*]

   Let's see, Vamos a ver [*vah'-mohs ah vehr*]

seed, semilla [*seh-mee'-yah*]

seek *v.*, buscar [*boos-kahr'*]

seem *v.*, parecer (irreg) [*pah-reh-thehr'*]

seen, visto [*vees'-toh*]

seize v., agarrar [ah-gah-rrahr']

seldom, raramente [rah-rah-mehn'-teh]

select v., seleccionar [seh-lehk-thee-oh-nahr']

self, mismo [mees'-moh]

self-conscious, consciente (m, f) de sí mismo [kohns-thee-ehn'-teh deh see mees'- moh]

selfish, egoísta [eh-goh-ees'-tah]

sell v., vender [vehn-dehr']

senate, senado [seh-nah'-doh]

senator, senador (m) [seh-nah-dohr']

send v., enviar [ehn-vee-ahr']
  send for, mandar a buscar [mahn-dahr' ah boos-kahr']

senior, mayor [mah-yohr']

sense n., sentido [sehn-tee'-doh]
  common sense, sentido común [sehn-tee'-doh koh-moon']

sensible, sensato [sehn-sah'-toh]

sensitive, sensible [sehn-see'-bleh]

sensual, sensual [sehn-soo-ahl']

sentence, frase (f) [frah'-seh]

sentimental, sentimental [sehn-tee-mehn-tahl']

separate adj., separado [seh-pah-rah'-doh]

separate v., separar [seh-pah-rahr']

separately, por separado [pohr seh-pah-rah'-doh]

separation, separación (f) [seh-pah-rah-thee-ohn']

September, septiembre (m) [sehp-tee-ehm'-breh]

serene, sereno [seh-reh'-noh]

sergeant, sargento [sahr-hehn'-toh]

series, serie (f) [seh'-ree-eh]

serious, serio [seh'-ree-oh]

seriously, seriamente [seh-ree-ah-mehn'-teh]

servant, sirviente (m) [seer-vee-ehn'-teh]

serve v., servir (irreg) [sehr-veer']

service, servicio [sehr-vee'-thee-oh]

session, sesión (f) [seh-see-ohn']

set n., juego, conjunto [hoo-eh'-goh, kohn-hoon'-toh]

set v., poner (irreg), colocar [poh-nehr', koh-loh-kahr']
  set a watch, poner un reloj en hora [poh-nehr' oon reh-lohh' ehn oh'-rah]

set up, fijar [*fee-hahr'*]

settle *v.*, establecerse (irreg), arreglar [*ehs-tah-bleh-thehr'-seh, ah-rreh-glahr'*]

seven, siete [*see-eh'-teh*]

seventeen, diecisiete [*dee-eh-thee-see-eh'-teh*]

seventh, séptimo [*sehp'-tee-moh*]

seventy, setenta [*seh-tehn'-tah*]

several, varios [*vah'-ree-ohs*]

severe, severo [*seh-veh'-roh*]

sew *v.*, coser [*koh-sehr'*]

sewing machine, máquina de coser [*mah'-kee-nah deh koh-sehr'*]

sex, sexo [*sehk'-soh*]

shade [dark area] *n.*, sombra [*sohm'-brah*]

shade [trace] *n.*, matiz (m) [*mah-teeth'*]

shady, sombreado [*sohm-breh-ah'-doh*]

shake *v.*, sacudir [*sah-koo-deer'*]

  shake hands, dar la mano [*dahr lah mah'-noh*]

shame, vergüenza [*vehr-ghoo-ehn'-thah*]

shameful, vergonzoso [*vehr-gohn-thoh'-soh*]

shameless, sinvergüenza [*seen-vehr-ghoo-ehn'-thah*]

shampoo *n.*, champú (m) [*chahm-poo'*]

shape *n.*, forma [*fohr'-mah*]

shape *v.*, formar [*fohr-mahr'*]

share *n.*, parte (f) [*pahr'-teh*]

share *v.*, compartir [*kohm-pahr-teer'*]

shark, tiburón (m) [*tee-boo-rohn'*]

sharp, agudo [*ah goo'-doh*]

shave *n.*, afeitado [*ah-feh-ee-tah'-doh*]

shave *v.*, afeitar(se) [*ah-feh-ee-tahr'-seh*]

shaving brush, brocha de afeitas [*broh'-cha deh-ah-feh-ee-tahr'*]

shaving cream, crema de afeitar [*kreh'-mah deh-ah-feh-ee-tar'*]

shawl, mantón (m) [*mahn-tohn'*]

she, ella [*eh'-yah*]

sheet [bedding], sábana [*sah'-bah-nah*]

sheet [leaf], hoja [*oh'-hah*]

sheet [thin piece], hoja [*oh'-hah*]

shelf, estante (m) [*ehs-tahn'-teh*]

shell [seashell], concha [*kohn'-chah*]

shell [nutshell, eggshell], cáscara [*kahs'-kah-rah*]

shelter *n.*, refugio [*reh-foo'-hee-oh*]

shepherd, pastor (m) [*pahs-tohr'*]

sherry, vino de jerez [*vee'-noh deh heh-rehth'*]

shield *n.*, escudo [*ehs-koo'-doh*]

shift *v.*, cambiar [*kahm-bee-ahr'*]

shine *v.*, brillar [*bree-yahr'*]

ship *n.*, barco [*bahr'-koh*]

ship *v.*, despachar [*dehs-pah-chahr'*]

shipment, envío [*ehn-vee'-oh*]

shipwreck, naufragio [*nah-oo-frah'-hee-oh*]

shirt, camisa [*kah-mee'-sah*]

shiver *v.*, tiritar [*tee-ree-tahr'*]

shock *n.*, choque (m) [*choh'-keh*]

shoe, zapato [*thah-pah'-toh*]

shoe laces, cordones (m) de zapatos [*kohr-doh'-nehs de thah-pah'-tohs*]

shoemaker, zapatero [*thah-pah-teh'-roh*]

shoeshine boy, limpiabotas (m) [*leem-pee-ah-boh'-tahs*]

shoe store, zapatería [*thah-pah-teh-ree'-ah*]

shoot *v.*, disparar, fusilar [*dees-pah-rahr'*, *foo-see-lahr'*]

shop *n.*, tienda [*tee-ehn'-dah*]

shop *v.*, ir (irreg) de compras [*eer deh kohm'-prahs*]

shop window, escaparate (m) [*ehs-kah-pah-rah'-teh*]

shore, orilla [*oh-ree'-yah*]

short, corto, bajo [*kohr'-toh, bah'-hoh*]

  in a short time, en poco tiempo [*ehn poh'-koh tee-ehm'-poh*]

shorts, pantalón corto, shorts [*pahn-tah-lohn' kohr'-toh, sorts*]

shortsighted, corto de vista [*kohr'-toh deh vees'-tah*]

shot *n.*, disparo [*dees-pah'-roh*]

shoulder, hombro [*ohm'-broh*]

shout *n.*, grito [*gree'-toh*]

shout *v.*, gritar [*gree-tahr'*]

shovel, pala [*pah'-lah*]

show *n.*, función (f), exposición (f) [*foon-thee-ohn', ehks-poh-see-thee-ohn'*]

show *v.*, mostrar (irreg) [*mohs-trahr'*]

   Show me, Muéstreme [*moo-ehs'-treh-meh*]

shower [bath], ducha [*doo'-chan*]

shower [rain], aguacero [*ah-goo-ah-theh'-roh*]

shrimp, camarón (m) [*kah-mah-rohn'*]

shrink *v.*, encoger [*ehn-koh-hehr'*]

shut *v.*, cerrar (irreg) [*theh-rruhr'*]

shut *adj.*, cerrado [*theh-rrah'-doh*]

shutter, persiana [*pehr-see-ah'-nah*]

shy, tímido [*tee'-mee-doh*]

sick, enfermo [*ehn-fehr'-moh*]

sickness, enfermedad (f) [*ehn-fehr-meh-dahd'*]

side, lado [*lah'-doh*]

sidewalk, acera [*ah-theh'-rah*]

sigh *n.*, suspiro [*soos-pee'-roh*]

sight, vista [*vees'-tah*]

sightseeing, turismo [*too-rees'-moh*]

sign [mark or symbol] *n.*, signo [*seeg'-noh*]

sign [display] *n.*, letrero [*leh-treh'-roh*]

sign *v.*, firmar [*feer-mahr'*]

signal, señal (f) [*seh-nyahl'*]

signature, firma [*feer'-mah*]

silence *n.*, silencio [*see-lehn'-thee-oh*]

silent, silencioso [*see-lehn-thee-oh'-soh*]

silently, silenciosamente [*see-lehn-thee-oh-sah-mehn'-teh*]

silk, seda [*seh'-dah*]

silly, tonto [*tohn'-toh*]

silver, plata [*plah'-tah*]

   sterling silver, plata de ley [*plah'-tah deh leh'-ee*]

similar, similar [*see-mee-lahr'*]

simple, simple [*seem'-pleh*]

simply, simplemente [*seem-pleh-mehn'-teh*]

sin *n.*, pecado [*peh-kah'-doh*]

since *prep.*, desde [*dehs'-deh*]

since *conj.*, puesto que [*poo-ehs'-toh keh*]

sincere, sincero [*seen-theh'-roh*]

sincerely, sinceramente [*seen-theh-rah-mehn'-teh*]

sing *v.,* cantar [*kahn-tahr'*]

singer, cantante (m, f) [*kahn-tahn'-teh*]

single [sole], solo [*soh'-loh*]

   not a single one, ni uno solo [*nee oo'-noh soh'-loh*]

single [unmarried], soltero [*sohl-teh'-roh*]

sink *v.,* hundir [*oon-deer'*]

sir, señor, caballero [*seh-nyohr', kah-bah-yeh'-roh*]

sister, hermana [*ehr-mah'-nah*]

sister-in-law, cuñada [*koo-nyah'-dah*]

sit *v.,* sentar (irreg) [*sehn-tahr'*]

   sit down, sentarse [*sehn-tahr'-seh*]

situated, situado [*see-too-ah'-doh*]

situation, situación (f) [*see-too-ah-thee-ohn'*]

six, seis [*seh'-ees*]

sixteen, dieciséis [*dee-eh-thee-seh'-ees*]

sixth, sexto (m) [*sehks'-toh*]

sixty, sesenta [*seh-sehn'-tah*]

size, tamaño, talla [*tah-mah'-nyoh, tah'-yah*]

skate *v.,* patinar [*pah-tee-nahr'*]

skeleton, esqueleto [*ehs-keh-leh'-toh*]

sketch, boceto [*boh-theh'-toh*]

ski *v.,* esquiar [*ehs-kee-ahr'*]

skill, destreza, conocimiento [*dehs-treh'-thah, koh-noh-thee-mee-ehn'-toh*]

skillful, diestro [*dee-ehs'-troh*]

skin, piel (f) [*pee-ehl'*]

skinny, flaco [*flah'-koh*]

skirt, falda [*fahl'-dah*]

skull, calavera [*kah-lah-veh'-rah*]

sky, cielo [*thee-eh'-loh*]

skyscraper, rascacielos (m) [*rahs-kah-thee-eh'-lohs*]

slander *n.,* calumnia [*kah-loom'-nee-ah*]

slang, jerga [*hehr'-gah*]

slap *n.,* bofetada [*boh-feh-tah'-dah*]

slave, esclavo [*ehs-klah'-voh*]

slavery, esclavitud (f) [*ehs-klah-vee-tood'*]

sleep *n.*, sueño [*soo-eh'-nyoh*]
sleep *v.*, dormir (irreg) [*dohr-meer'*]
  be asleep, estar dormido [*ehs-tahr' dohr-mee'-doh*]
  be sleepy, tener sueño [*teh-nehr' soo-eh'-nyoh*]
sleeping car, coche (m) dormitorio [*koh'-cheh dohr-mee-toh'-ree-oh*]
sleeve, manga [*mahn'-gah*]
slender, esbelto [*ehs-behl'-toh*]
slice *n.*, tajada [*tah-hah'-dah*]
slide *v.*, resbalar, deslizar [*rehs-bah-lahr', dehs-lee-thahr'*]
slight [of little importance] *adj.*, ligero [*lee-heh'-roh*]
slip [act of slipping] *n.*, resbalón (m) [*rehs-bah-lohn'*]
slip [woman's undergarment] *n.*, combinación (f) [*kohm-bee-nah-thee-ohn'*]
slip *v.*, resbalar [*rehs-bah-lahr'*]
slippers, zapatillas [*thah-pah-tee'-yahs*]
slippery, resbaloso, resbaladizo [*rehs-bah-loh'-soh, rehs-bah-lah-dee'-thoh*]
sloppy, mal hecho [*mahl eh'-choh*]
slow, lento [*lehn'-toh*]
slowly, despacio [*dehs-pah'-thee-oh*]
small, pequeño [*peh-keh'-nyoh*]
small change, dinero suelto [*dee-neh'-roh soo-ehl'-toh*]
smaller, más pequeño [*mahs peh-keh'-nyoh*]
small pox, viruela [*vee-roo-eh'-lah*]
smart [alert], listo [*lees'-toh*]
smash *v.*, aplastar [*ah-plahs-tahr'*]
smell *n.*, olor (m) [*oh-lohr'*]
smell *v.*, oler (irreg) [*oh-lehr'*]
smile *n.*, sonrisa [*sohn-ree'-sah*]
smile *v.*, sonreir (irreg) [*sohn-reh-eer'*]
smoke *n.*, humo [*oo'-moh*]
smoke *v.*, fumar [*foo-mahr'*]
smooth, terso [*tehr'-soh*]
snail, caracol (m) [*kah-rah-kohl'*]
snake, culebra [*koo-leh'-brah*]
sneeze *v.*, estornudar [*ehs-tohr-noo-dahr'*]
snore *v.*, roncar [*rohn-kahr'*]

snow *n.*, nieve (f) [*nee-eh'-veh*]
snow *v.*, nevar (irreg) [*neh-vahr'*]
snowflake, copo de nieve [*koh'-poh deh nee-eh'-veh*]
so, así, tan, muy [*ah-see', tahn, moo-ee'*]
  so far, hasta ahora [*ahs'-tah ah-oh'-rah*]
  so forth, así sucesivamente [*ah-see' soo-theh-see-vah-mehn'-teh*]
  so much, tanto [*tahn'-toh*]
  so so, así así [*ah-see' ah-see'*]
  so that, de modo que [*deh moh'-doh keh*]
  I think so, Creo que sí [*kreh'-oh keh see*]
soap, jabón [*hah-bohn'*]
sober, sobrio [*soh'-bree-oh*]
social, social [*soh-thee-ahl'*]
socialist, socialista (m, f) [*soh-thee-ah-lees'-tah*]
society, sociedad (f) [*soh-thee-eh-dahd'*]
sock [apparel], calcetín (m) [*kahl-theh-teen'*]
soda, gaseosa [*gah-seh-oh'-sah*]
sofa, sofá (m) [*soh-fah'*]
soft, suave, blando [*soo-ah'-veh, blahn'-doh*]
softness, suavidad (f) [*soo-ah-vee-dahd'*]
soldier, soldado [*sohl-dah'-doh*]
sole [of shoe] *n.*, suela [*soo-eh'-lah*]
sole [fish] *n.*, lenguado [*lehn-goo-ah'-doh*]
sole *adj.*, único [*oo'-nee-koh*]
solid, sólido [*soh'-lee-doh*]
solution, solución (f) [*soh-loo-thee-ohn'*]
solve *v.*, resolver (irreg) [*reh-sohl-vehr'*]
some, algún, alguna, algo [*ahl-goon', ahl-goo'-nah, ahl'-goh*]
someone, alguno, alguien [*ahl-goo'-noh, ahl'-ghee-ehn*]
something, algo [*ahl'-goh*]
sometime, alguna vez [*ahl-goo'-nah vehth*]
sometimes, algunas veces (m) [*ahl-goo'-nahs veh'-thehs*]
somewhat, un tanto [*oon tahn'-toh*]
somewhere, en alguna parte [*ehn ahl-goo'-nah pahr'-teh*]
somewhere else, en alguna otra parte [*ehn ahl-goo'-nah oh'-trah pahr'-teh*]
son, hijo [*ee'-hoh*]

son-in-law, yerno [*yehr'-noh*]

song, canción (f) [*kahn-thee-ohn'*]

soon, pronto [*prohn'-toh*]

  as soon as, tan pronto como [*tahn prohn'-toh koh'-moh*]

  sooner or later, tarde o temprano [*tahr'-deh oh tehm-prah'-noh*]

sore *adj.,* dolorido [*doh-loh-rée-doh*]

sore throat, dolor (m) de garganta [*doh-lohr' deh gahr-gahn'-tah*]

sorrow, pena [*peh'-nah*]

sorrowful, triste [*trees'-teh*]

sorry, arrepentido [*ah-rreh-pehn-tee'-doh*]

  be sorry, sentir (irreg) [*sehn-teer'*]

sort *n.,* clase (f) [*klah'-seh*]

soul, (el) alma (f) [*ahl'-mah*]

sound *n.,* sonido [*soh-nee'-doh*]

sound *adj.,* cuerdo [*koo-ehr'-doh*]

sound *v.,* sonar (irreg) [*soh-nahr'*]

soup, sopa [*soh'-pah*]

sour, agrio [*ah'-gree-oh*]

south, sur (m) [*soor*]

South America, América del Sur [*ah-meh'-ree-kah dehl soor*]

South American, suramericano [*soo-rah-meh-ree-kah'-noh*]

souvenir, recuerdo [*reh-koo-ehr'-doh*]

space, espacio [*ehs-pah'-thee-oh*]

spacious, espacioso [*ehs-pah-thee-oh'-soh*]

Spain, España [*ehs-pah'-nyah*]

Spaniard, Spanish, español [*ehs-pah-nyohl'*]

spare [extra], de sobra [*deh soh'-brah*]

spare parts, piezas de repuesto [*pee-eh'-thahs deh reh-poo-ehs'-toh*]

spare tire, neumático de repuesto [*neh-oo-mah'-tee-koh deh reh-poo-ehs'-toh*]

sparkle *n.,* chispa [*chees'-pah*]

spark plug, bujía [*boo-hee'-ah*]

speak, *v.,* hablar [*ah-blahr'*]

Do you speak English? ¿Habla usted inglés? [*ah'blah oos-tehd' een-glehs'*]

special, especial [*ehs-peh-thee-ahl'*]

specialist, especialista (m, f) *ehs-peh-thee-ah-lees'-tah*]

specialty, especialidad (f) [*ehs-peh-thee-ah-lee-dahd'*]

spectacle, espectáculo [*ehs-pehk-tah'-koo-loh*]

spectator, espectador (m) [*ehs-pehk-tah-dohr'*]

speech [address] *n.,* discurso [*dees-koor'-soh*]

speed *n.,* velocidad (f) [*veh-loh-thee-dahd'*]

full speed ahead, a toda velocidad [*ah toh'-dah veh-loh-thee-dahd'*]

speed *v.,* acelerar [*ah-theh-leh-rahr'*]

speed limit, límite (m) de velocidad [*lee'-mee-teh deh veh-loh-thee-dahd'*]

speedy, veloz [*veh-lohth'*]

spell *v.,* deletrear [*deh-leh-treh-ahr'*]

spelling, deletreo [*deh-leh-treh'-oh*]

spend [consume] *v.,* gastar [*gahs-tahr'*]

spend [time] *v.,* pasar [*pah-sahr'*]

spice, especia [*ehs-peh'-thee-ah*]

spider, araña [*ah-rah'-nyah*]

spin *v.,* girar [*hee-rahr'*]

spinach, espinaca [*ehs-pee-nah'-kah*]

spine, columna bertebral [*koh-loom'-nah behr-teh-brahl'*]

spirit, espíritu (m) [*ehs-pee'-ree-too*]

spiritual, espiritual [*ehs-pee-ree-too-ahl'*]

spite: in spite of, a pesar de [*ah peh-sahr' deh*]

splendid, espléndido [*ehs-plehn'-dee-doh*]

split *v.,* rajar, dividir [*rah-hahr', dee-vee-deer'*]

spoil *v.,* estropear [*ehs-troh-peh-ahr'*]

sponge, esponja [*ehs-pohn'-hah*]

spontaneous, espontáneo [*ehs-pohn-tah'-neh-oh*]

spoon, cuchara [*koo-chah'-rah*]

teaspoon, cucharilla [*koo-chah-ree'-yah*]

spoonful, cucharada [*koo-chah-rah'-dah*]

sport, deporte (m) [*deh-pohr'-teh*]

spot [place], lugar (m) [*loo-gahr'*]

spot [stain], mancha [*mahn'-chah*]

spouse, esposo [*ehs-poh'-soh*]
sprain *n.*, torcedura [*tohr-theh-doo'-rah*]
sprain *v.*, torcer (irreg) [*tohr-thehr'*]
spray *v.*, rociar [*roh-thee-ahr'*]
spread *v.*, extender (irreg) [*ehks-tehn-dehr'*]
spring [season] *n.*, primavera [*pree-mah-veh'-rah*]
spring [coil] *n.*, muelle (m) [*moo-eh'-yeh*]
spring *v.*, saltar, brincar [*sahl-tahr', breen-kahr'*]
spy *n.*, espía (m, f) [*ehs-pee'-ah*]
spy *v.*, espiar [*ehs-pee-ahr'*]
square [public], plaza [*plah'-thah*]
square [plane figure], cuadrado [*koo-ah-drah'-doh*]
squeak *v.*, chirriar [*chee-rree-ahr'*]
squeeze *v.*, exprimir [*ehks-pree-meer'*]
stab *v.*, apuñalar [*ah-poo-nyah-lahr'*]
stable *n.*, establo [*ehs-tah'-bloh*]
stable *adj.*, estable [*ehs-tah'-bleh*]
stadium, estadio [*ehs-tah'-dee-oh*]
stage, escenario [*ehs-theh-nah'-ree-oh*]
stain *n.*, mancha [*mahn'-chah*]
stairs, escalera [*ehs-kah-leh'-rah*]
stall [auto] *v.*, atascar [*ah-tahs-kahr'*]
stamp *n.*, sello [*seh'-yoh*]
stand *n.*, puesto [*poo-ehs'-toh*]
stand *v.*, estar de pie [*ehs-tahr' deh pee-eh'*]
    stand up, levantarse [*leh-vahn-tahr'-seh*]
standard *adj.*, corriente [*koh-rree-ehn'-teh*]
standing, de pie [*deh pee-eh'*]
standpoint, punto de vista [*poon'-toh deh vees'-tah*]
star, estrella [*ehs-treh'-yah*]
starch, almidón (m) [*ahl-mee-dohn'*]
start *n.*, principio [*preen-thee'-pee-oh*]
start *v.*, empezar (irreg) [*ehm-peh-thahr'*]
starter [auto], botón (m) de arranque [*boh-tohn' deh ah-rrahn'-keh*]
starve *v.*, morir de hambre [*moh-reer' deh ahm'-breh*]
state *n.*, estado [*ehs-tah'-doh*]
state *v.*, exponer (irreg) [*ehks-poh-nehr'*]

statement, declaración (f) [*deh-klah-rah-thee-ohn'*]
stateroom, camarote (m) [*kah-mah-roh'-teh*]
statesman, estadista (m) [*ehs-tah-dees'-tah*]
station, estación (f) [*ehs-tah-thee-ohn'*]
   railway station, estación de ferrocarril [*ehs-tah-thee-ohn' deh feh-rroh-kah-rreel'*]
stationery, papelería [*pah-peh-leh-ree'-ah*]
statue, estatua [*ehs-tah'-too-ah*]
stay *v.,* quedar(se) [*keh-dahr'-seh*]
steady, invariable [*een-vah-ree-ah'-bleh*]
steak, biftec (m) [*beef-tehk'*]
steal *v.,* robar [*roh-bahr'*]
steam, vapor (m) [*vah-pohr'*]
steel, acero [*ah-theh'-roh*]
steering wheel, volante (m) [*voh-lahn'-teh*]
stenographer, taquígrafo [*tah-kee'-grah-foh*]
step *n.,* paso [*pah'-soh*]
step *v.,* dar un paso [*dahr oon pah'-soh*]
   step on *v.,* pisar [*pee-sahr'*]
stepfather, padrastro [*pah-drahs'-troh*]
stepmother, madrastra [*mah-drahs'-trah*]
sterilized, esterilizado [*ehs-teh-ree-lee-thah'-doh*]
stern [of boat] *n.,* popa [*poh'-pah*]
stern *adj.,* austero [*ah-oos-teh'-roh*]
steward, camarero, mesero [*kah-mah-reh'-roh, meh-seh'-roh*]
stewardess, camarera, azafata [*kah-mah-reh'-rah, ah-thah-fah'-tah*]
stick *n.,* palo [*pah'-loh*]
stick [adhere] *v.,* pegar [*peh-gahr'*]
stick [prick] *v.,* picar, aguzar [*pee-kahr', ah-goo-thahr'*]
stiff, tieso [*tee-eh'-soh*]
still [yet], todavía [*toh-dah-vee'-ah*]
stimulant, estimulante (m) [*ehs-tee-moo-lahn'-teh*]
sting *n.,* picadura [*pee-kah-doo'-rah*]
sting *v.,* picar [*pee-kahr'*]
stir *v.,* revolver (irreg) [*reh-vohl-vehr'*]
stock, existencias (pl) [*ehk-sees-tehn'-thee-ahs*]

stockbroker, corredor (m) de bolsa [*koh-rreh-dohr′ deh bohl′-sah*]

stock exchange, bolsa [*bohl′-sah*]

stocking, media [*meh′-dee-ah*]

stolen, robado [*roh-bah′-doh*]

stomach, estómago [*ehs-toh′-mah-goh*]

stomach ache, dolor (m) de estómago [*doh-lohr′ deh ehs-toh′-mah-goh*]

stone, piedra [*pee-eh′-drah*]

stop v., parar [*pah-rahr′*]

  Stop here, Pare aquí [*pah′-reh ah-kee′*]

storage, almacenaje (m) [*ahl-mah-theh-nah′-heh*]

store n., tienda, almacenes (m, pl) [*tee-ehn′-dah, ahl-mah-theh′-nehs*]

store v., almacenar [*ahl-mah-theh-nahr′*]

storm, tormenta [*tohr-mehn′-tah*]

story [tale], cuento [*koo-ehn′-toh*]

story [floor], piso [*pee′-soh*]

stove, estufa, cocina [*ehs-too′-fah, koh-thee′-nah*]

straight, recto [*rehk′-toh*]

  straight ahead, derecho [*deh-reh′-choh*]

strain, tírantez (f), tension (f) [*tee-rahn-teth′, tehn-see-ohn′*]

strange, extraño [*ehks-trah′-nyoh*]

stranger, extranjero [*ehks-trahn-heh′-roh*]

strap, correa [*koh-rreh′-ah*]

straw, paja [*pah′-hah*]

strawberry, fresa [*freh′-sah*]

stream, arroyo [*ah-rroh′-yoh*]

street, calle (f) [*kah′-yeh*]

  one-way street, calle de una sola dirección [*kah′-yeh deh oo′-nah soh′-lah dee-rehk-thee-ohn′*]

streetcar, tranvía (m) [*trahn-vee′-ah*]

strength, fuerza [*foo-ehr′-thah*]

strengthen v., fortalecer (irreg) [*fohr-tah-leh-thehr′*]

stress, acento [*ah-thehn′-toh*]

stretch v., estirar [*ehs-tee-rahr′*]

strict, estricto [*ehs-treek′-toh*]

strictly, estrictamente [*ehs-treek-tah-mehn′-teh*]

strike *n.*, huelga [*oo-ehl'-gah*]
strike [hit] *v.*, pegar [*peh-ghahr'*]
string, cordel (m) [*kohr-dehl'*]
stripe, raya [*rah'-yah*]
strong, fuerte [*foo-ehr'-teh*]
structure, estructura [*ehs-trook-too'-rah*]
struggle *n.*, lucha [*loo'-chah*]
struggle *v.*, luchar [*loo-chahr'*]
stubborn, terco [*tehr'-koh*]
student, estudiante (m, f) [*ehs-too-dee-ahn'-teh*]
study *n.*, estudio [*ehs-too'-dee-oh*]
study *v.*, estudiar [*ehs-too-dee-ahr'*]
stuff, cosas (pl) [*koh'-sahs*]
stumble *v.*, tropezar (irreg) [*troh-peh-thahr'*]
stupid, estúpido [*ehs-too'-pee-doh*]
style, estilo [*ehs-tee'-loh*]
subject, materia [*mah-teh'-ree-ah*]
submarine, submarino [*soob-mah-ree'-noh*]
submit *v.*, someter [*soh-meh-tehr'*]
substantial, substancial [*soobs-tahn-thee-ahl'*]
substitute *v.*, substituir (irreg) [*soobs-tee-too-eer'*]
substitution, substitución (f) [*soobs-tee-too-thee-ohn'*]
subtraction, sustracción (f) [*soos-trahk-thee-ohn'*]
suburbs, afueras [*ah-foo-eh'-rahs*]
subway, metro [*meh'-troh*]
succeed *v.*, tener (irreg) éxito [*teh-nehr' ehks'-ee-toh*]
success, éxito [*ehks'-ee-toh*]
successive, sucesivo [*soo-theh-see'-voh*]
such, tal [*tahl*]
sudden, repentino [*reh-pehn-tee'-noh*]
suddenly, de repente [*deh reh-pehn'-teh*]
suffer *v.*, sufrir [*soo-freer'*]
sufficient, suficiente [*soo-fee-thee-ehn'-teh*]
sugar, azúcar (m) [*ah-thoo'-kahr*]
sugar bowl, azucarero [*ah-thoo-kah-reh'-roh*]
suggest *v.*, sugerir (irreg) [*soo-heh-reer'*]
suggestion, sugerencia [*soo-heh-rehn'-thee-ah*]

suicide, suicidio [*soo-ee-thee'-dee-oh*]
suit [of clothes] *n.*, traje (m) [*trah'-heh*]
suit *v.*, convenir (irreg) [*kohn-veh-neer'*]
suitable, conveniente [*kohn-veh-nee-ehn'-teh*]
suitcase, maleta [*mah-leh'-tah*]
sum *n.*, suma [*soo'-mah*]
summary, sumario [*soo-mah'-ree-oh*]
summer, verano [*veh-rah'-noh*]
summit, cima [*thee'-mah*]
summons, citación (f) [*thee-tah-thee-ohn'*]
sun, sol (m) [*sohl*]
sunburn, quemadura de sol [*keh-mah-doo'-rah deh sohl*]
sunburned, tostado [*tohs-tah'-doh*]
Sunday, domingo [*doh-meen'-goh*]
sunglasses, gafas de sol [*gah'-fahs deh sohl*]
sunrise, salida del sol [*sah-lee'-dah dehl sohl*]
sunset, puesta del sol [*poo-ehs'-tah dehl sohl*]
sunshine, luz (f) del sol [*looth dehl sohl*]
suntanned, bronceado [*brohn-theh-ah'-doh*]
superb, soberbio [*soh-behr'-bee-oh*]
superficial, superficial [*soo-pehr-fee-thee-ahl'*]
superior *adj. & n.*, superior (m) [*soo-peh-ree-ohr'*]
superstitious, supersticioso [*soo-pehrs-tee-thee-oh'-soh*]
supper, cena [*theh'-nah*]
  have supper, cenar [*theh-nahr'*]
supply *n.*, provisión (f) [*proh-vee-see-ohn'*]
supply *v.*, suministrar [*soo-mee-nees-trahr'*]
support *v.*, sostener (irreg), apoyar [*sohs-teh-nehr', ah-poh-yahr'*]
suppose *v.*, suponer (irreg) [*soo-poh-nehr'*]
supreme, supremo [*soo-preh'-moh*]
sure, seguro [*seh-goo'-roh*]
surely, seguramente [*seh-goo-rah-mehn'-teh*]
surf, oleaje (m) [*oh-leh-ah'-heh*]
surface *n.*, superficie (f) [*soo-pehr-fee'-thee-eh*]
surgeon, cirujano [*thee-roo-hah'-noh*]
surgery, operación (f) [*oh-peh-rah-thee-ohn'*]

surprise *n.*, sorpersa [*sohr-preh'-sah*]
surprise *v.*, sorprender [*sohr-prehn-dehr'*]
surprising, sorprendente [*sohr-prehn-dehn'-teh*]
surrender *v.*, rendir(se) (irreg) [*rehn-deer'(-seh)*]
surround *v.*, rodear [*roh-deh-ahr'*]
surroundings, alrededores (m) [*ahl-reh-deh-doh'-rehs*]
survive *v.*, sobrevivir [*soh-breh-vee-veer'*]
survivor, superviviente (m, f) [*soo-pehr-vee-vee-ehn'-teh*]
suspect *v.*, sospechar [*sohs-peh-chahr'*]
suspicion, sospecha [*sohs-peh'-chah*]
suspicious, sospechoso [*sohs-peh-choh'-soh*]
swallow *v.*, tragar [*trah-gahr'*]
swan, cisne (m) [*thees'-neh*]
swear *v.*, jurar [*hoo-rahr'*]
sweater, sueter (m) [*soo-eh'-tehr*]
Sweden, Suecia [*soo-eh'-thee-ah*]
Swedish, sueco [*soo-eh'-koh*]
sweep *v.*, barrer [*bah-rrehr'*]
sweet *n. & adj.*, dulce (m) [*dool'-theh*]
sweetheart, querido [*keh-ree'-doh*]
sweet potato, batata [*bah-tah'-tah*]
swell *v.*, hinchar [*een-chahr'*]
swim *v.*, nadar [*nah-dahr'*]
swimmer, nadador (m) [*nah-dah-dohr'*]
swimming pool, piscina [*pees-thee'-nah*]
swimming suit, bañador (m) [*bah-nyah-dohr'*]
Swiss, suizo [*soo-ee'-thoh*]
switch *n.*, llave (f) eléctrica [*yah'-veh eh-lehk'-tree-kah*]
Switzerland, Suiza [*soo-ee'-thah*]
swollen, hinchado [*een-chah'-doh*]
sword, espada [*ehs-pah'-dah*]
sympathy, condolencia [*kohn-doh-lehn'-thee-ah*]
symphony, sinfonía [*seen-foh-nee'-ah*]
symptom, síntoma [*seen'-toh-mah*]
synthetic, sintético [*seen-teh'-tee-koh*]
system, sistema (m) [*sees-teh'-mah*]
systematic, sistemático [*sees-teh-mah'-tee-koh*]

T

table, mesa [*meh'-sah*]
  set the table, poner la mesa [*poh-nehr' lah meh'-sah*]
tablecloth, mantel (m) [*mahn-tehl'*]
tablespoon, cuchera grande [*koo-chah'-rah grahn'-deh*]
tablet, tableta [*tah-bleh'-tah*]
tack *n.,* tachuela [*tah-choo-eh'-lah*]
tact, tacto [*tahk'-toh*]
tail, cola [*koh'-lah*]
tailor, sastre (m) [*sahs'-treh*]
tailor shop, sastrería [*sahs-treh-ree'-ah*]
take *v.,* tomar [*toh-mahr'*]
  Take it, Tómelo [*toh'-meh-loh*]
  take advantage of, aprovecharse de [*ah-proh-veh-chahr'-seh deh*]
  take a walk, dar un paseo [*dahr oon pah-seh'-oh*]
  take away, quitar [*kee-tahr'*]
  take care of, cuidar de [*koo-ee-dahr' deh*]
  take leave, despedirse (irreg [*dehs-peh-deer'-seh*]
  take notice, notar [*noh-tahr'*]
  take off, despegar [*dehs-peh-gahr'*]
  take out, sacar [*sah-kahr'*]
  take place, tener lugar [*teh-nehr' loo-ghahr'*]
  take the opportunity, aprovechar la oportunidad [*ah-proh-veh-chahr' lah oh-pohr-too-nee-dahd'*]
take [carry] *v.,* llevar [*yeh-vahr'*]
talent, talento [*tah-lehn'-toh*]
talk *n.,* conversación (f) [*kohn-vehr-sah-thee-ohn'*]
talk *v.,* conversar, hablar [*kohn-vehr-sahr', ah-blahr'*]
tall, alto [*ahl'-toh*]
tame, manso [*mahn'-soh*]
tan, bronceado [*brohn-theh-ah'-doh*]
tape, cinta [*theen'-tah*]

139

tapestry, tapiz (m) [*tah-peeth'*]

tariff, tarifa [*tah-ree'-fah*]

taste *n.*, gusto [*goos'-toh*]

taste *v.*, gustar [*goos-tahr'*]

  This tastes good, Esto sabe bien [*ehs'-toh sah'-beh bee-ehn'*]

tasty, sabroso [*sah-broh'-soh*]

tax, impuesto [*eem-poo-ehs'-toh*]

tax-free, libre de impuesto [*lee'-breh deh eem-poo-ehs'-toh*]

taxi, taxi (m) [*tahk'-see*]

tea, té (m) [*teh*]

  iced tea, té con hielo [*teh kohn ee-eh'-loh*]

teach *v.*, enseñar [*ehn-seh-nyahr'*]

teacher, maestro [*mah-ehs'-troh*]

teaching, enseñanza [*ehn-seh-nyahn'-thah*]

teacup, taza paraté [*tah'-thah pah-rah-teh'*]

team, equipo [*eh-kee'-poh*]

teapot, tetera [*teh-teh'-rah*]

tear *v.*, rasgar [*rahs-gahr'*]

teardrop, lágrima [*lah'-gree-mah*]

teaspoon, cucharilla [*koo-chah-ree'-yah*]

technical, técnico [*tehk'-nee-koh*]

telegram, telegrama (m) [*teh-leh-grah'-mah*]

telephone *n.*, teléfono [*teh-leh'-foh-noh*]

telephone *v.*, telefonear [*teh-leh-foh-neh-ahr'*]

telephone book, guía telefónica [*ghee'-ah teh-leh-foh'-nee-kah*]

telephone booth, cabina telefónica [*kah-bee'-nah teh-leh-foh'-nee-kah*]

telephone call, llamada telefónica [*yah-mah'-dah teh-leh-foh'-nee-kah*]

telephone number, número de teléfono [*noo'-meh-roh deh teh-leh'-foh-noh*]

telephone operator, telefonista [*teh-leh-foh-nees'-tah*]

television, televisión (f) [*teh-leh-vee-see-ohn'*]

television set, televisor (m) [*teh-leh-vee-sohr'*]

tell *v.*, decir (irreg) [*deh-theer'*]

  Tell me, Dígame [*dee'-ghah-meh*]

temperature, temperatura [*tehm-peh-rah-too'-rah*]

temple [church], templo [*tehm'-ploh*]
temporary, temporal [*tehm-poh-rahl'*]
temptation, tentación (f) [*tehn-tah-thee-ohn'*]
ten, diez [*dee-ehth'*]
tenant, inquilino [*een-kee-lee'-noh*]
tendency, tendencia [*tehn-dehn'-thee-ah*]
tender, tierno [*tee-ehr'-noh*]
tennis, tenis (m) [*teh'-nees*]
tenth, décimo [*deh'-thee-moh*]
term [name], termino [*tehr-mee'-noh*]
term [time], plazo [*plah'-thoh*]
terminal, terminal (f) [*tehr-mee-nahl'*]
terrace, terraza [*teh-rrah'-thah*]
terrible, terrible [*teh-rree'-bleh*]
terribly, terriblemente [*teh-rree-bleh-mehn'-teh*]
terrify *v.*, aterrorizar [*ah-teh-rroh-ree-thahr'*]
territory, territorio [*teh-rree-toh'-ree-oh*]
terror, terror (m) [*teh-rrohr'*]
test *n.*, prueba [*proo-eh'-bah*]
test *v.*, probar (irreg) [*proh-bahr'*]
testify *v.*, atestiguar [*ah-tehs-tee-goo-ahr'*]
text, texto [*tehks'-toh*]
textile, tejido [*teh-hee'-doh*]
than, que [*keh*]
thank *v.*, agradecer (irreg) [*ah-grah-deh-thehr'*]
   Thank you, Gracias [*grah'-thee-ahs*]
thankful, agradecido [*ah-grah-deh-thee'-doh*]
that *adj.*, ese, aquel [*eh'-seh, ah-kehl'*]
that *dem. & rel. pron.*, ése, aquél [*eh'-seh, ah-kehl'*]
that *conj.*, que [*keh*]
   that which, lo que [*loh keh*]
the, el, la (sing); los, las (pl) [*ehl, lah, lohs, lahs*]
theater, teatro [*teh-ah'-troh*]
theft, robo [*roh'-boh*]
their, su, sus [*soo, soos*]
theirs, suyo, suya, de ellos, de ellas [*soo'-yoh, soo'-yah, deh
   eh'-yohs, deh eh'-yahs*]
them, los, las, les [*lohs, lahs, lehs*]

themselves, ellos mismos, ellas mismas [*eh'-yohs mees'-mohs, eh'-yahs mees'-mahs*]

then, entonces [*ehn-tohn'-thehs*]
  now and then, de vez en cuando [*deh vehth ehn koo-ahn'-doh*]

theory, teoría [*teh-oh-ree'-ah*]

there, ahí, allí, allá [*ah-ee', ah-yee', ah-yah'*]
  there is, there are, hay [*ah'-ee*]

therefore, por lo tanto [*pohr loh tahn'-toh*]

thermometer, termómetro [*tehr-moh'-meh-troh*]

these, estos, estas [*ehs'-tohs, ehs'-tahs*]

they, ellos, ellas [*eh'-yohs, eh'-yahs*]

thick, espeso, grueso [*ehs-peh'-soh, groo-eh'-soh*]

thief, ladrón (m) [*lah-drohn'*]

thin, delgado [*dehl-gah'-doh*]

thing, cosa [*koh'-sah*]

think *v.*, pensar (irreg) [*pehn-sahr'*]

third, tercero [*tehr-theh'-roh*]

thirsty, sediento [*seh-dee-ehn'-toh*]
  be thirsty, tener sed [*teh-nehr' sehd*]

thirteen, trece [*treh'-theh*]

thirty, treinta [*treh'-een-tah*]

this *adj.*, este, esta, esto [*ehs'-teh, ehs'-tah, ehs'-toh*]

this *pron.*, éste, esta, esto [*ehs'-teh, ehs'-tah, ehs'-toh*]

thorn, espina [*ehs-pee'-nah*]

thoroughly, completamente [*kohm-pleh-tah-mehn'-teh*]

those, esos, aquellos [*eh'-sohs, ah-keh'-yohs*]

though, aunque [*ah-oon'-keh*]

thought, pensamiento [*pehn-sah-mee-ehn'-toh*]

thoughtful, atento [*ah-tehn'-toh*]

thoughtless, desconsiderado [*dehs-kohn-see-deh-rah'-doh*]

thousand, mil [*meel*]

thread, hilo [*ee'-loh*]

threat, amenaza [*ah-meh-nah'-thah*]

threaten *v.*, amenazar [*ah-meh-nah-thahr'*]

three, tres [*trehs*]

thrifty, ahorrativo [*ah-oh-rrah-tee'-voh*]

thrilled, estremecido [*ehs-treh-meh-thee'-doh*]

throat, garganta [*gahr-gahn'-tah*]

throb *v.*, latir [*lah-teer'*]

throne, trono [*troh'-noh*]

through *prep.*, a través de [*ah trah-vehs' deh*]

through [finished], terminado [*tehr-mee-nah'-doh*]

throughout, por todo [*pohr toh'-doh*]

throw *v.*, tirar [*tee-rahr'*]

thumb, pulgar (m) [*pool-gahr'*]

thunder, trueno [*troo-eh'-noh*]

thunderstorm, tormenta [*tohr-mehn'-tah*]

Thursday, jueves (m) [*hoo-eh'-vehs*]

thus, así [*ah-see'*]

ticket, billete (m), entrada, boleto [*bee-yeh'-teh, ehn-trah'-dah, boh-leh'-toh*]

  one-way ticket, billete de ida [*bee-yeh'-teh deh ee'-dah*]

  round trip ticket, billete de ida y vuelta [*bee-yeh'-teh deh ee'-dah ee voo-ehl'-tah*]

ticket window, taquilla [*tah-kee'-yah*]

tide, marea [*mah-reh'-ah*]

tie [apparel] *n.*, corbata [*kohr-bah'-tah*]

tie *v.*, atar [*ah-tahr'*]

tight, apretado [*ah-preh-tah'-doh*]

tighten *v.*, apretar (irreg) [*ah-preh-tahr'*]

tile, teja [*teh'-hah*]

till [until], hasta [*ahs'-tah*]

time [instance], vez (f) [*vehth*]

  at times, a veces [*ah veh'-thehs*]

time [duration], tiempo [*tee-ehm'-poh*]

  at the same time, al mismo tiempo [*ahl mees'-moh tee-ehm'-poh*]

  Have a good time! ¡Diviértase! [*dee-vee-ehr'-tah-seh*]

  on time, a tiempo [*ah tee-ehm'-poh*]

  What time is it? ¿Qué hora es? [*keh oh'-rah ehs*]

timetable, itinerario [*ee-tee-neh-rah'-ree-oh*]

timid, tímido [*tee'-mee-doh*]

tin, estaño [*ehs-tah'-nyoh*]

tiny, diminuto [*dee-mee-noo'-toh*]

tip [gratuity], propina [*proh-pee'-nah*]

tip [point], punta [*poon'-tah*]

tire [automobile] *n.*, neumático [*neh-oo-mah'-tee-koh*]

  flat tire, rueda pinchada [*roo-eh'-dah peen-chah'-dah*]

tired, cansado [*kahn-sah'-doh*]

tiresome, aburrido [*ah-boo-rree'-doh*]

tissue paper, papel (m) de seda [*pah-pehl' deh seh'-dah*]

title, título [*tee'-too-loh*]

to, a [*ah*]

  to and fro, de acá para allá [*deh ah-kah' pah'-rah ah-yah'*]

toast [bread] *n.*, tostada [*tohs-tah'-dah*]

toast [compliment] *n.*, brindis (m) [*breen'-dees*]

toaster, tostador (m) [*tohs-tah-dohr'*]

tobacco, tabaco [*tah-bah'-koh*]

tobacco store, tabaqueria, estanco [*tah-bah-keh-ree'-ah,*
  ehs-tahn'-koh]

today, hoy [*oh'-ee*]

toe, dedo del pie [*deh'-doh dehl pee-eh'*]

together, juntos [*hoon'-tohs*]

toilet, excusado [*ehks-koo-sah'-doh*]

tolerate *v.*, tolerar [*toh-leh-rahr'*]

toll [fee], peaje (m) [*peh-ah'-heh*]

tomato, tomate (m) [*toh-mah'-teh*]

tomato juice, jugo de tomate [*hoo'-goh deh toh-mah'-teh*]

tomb, tumba [*toom'-bah*]

tomorrow, mañana [*mah-nyah'-nah*]

tomorrow evening, mañana por la tarde [*mah-nyah'-nah*
  pohr lah tahr''deh]

  tomorrow morning, mañana por la mañana [*mah-nyah'-*
  nah pohr lah mah-nyah'-nah]

ton, tonelada [*toh-neh-lah'-dah*]

tone, tono [*toh'-noh*]

tongue, lengua [*lehn'-goo-ah*]

tonight, esta noche (f) [*ehs'-tah noh'-cheh*]

tonsils, amígdalas [*ah-meeg'-dah-lahs*]

too, también [*tahm-bee-ehn'*]

too much, demasiado [*deh-mah-see-ah'-doh*]

tool, herramienta [*eh-rrah-mee-ehn'-tah*]

tooth, diente (m), muela [*dee-ehn'-teh, moo-eh'-lah*]

toothache, dolor (m) de muelas [*doh-lohr' deh moo-eh'-lahs*]
toothbrush, cepillo de dientes [*theh-pee'-yoh deh dee-ehn'-tehs*]
toothpaste, pasta de dientes [*pahs'-tah deh dee-ehn'-tehs*]
toothpick, palillo de dientes [*pah-lee'-yoh deh dee-ehn'-tehs*]
top [highest point] *n.*, cima, pico [*thee'-mah, pee'-koh*]
  on top of, encima de [*ehn-thee'-mah deh*]
top [cover, lid] *n.*, tapa [*tah'-pah*]
topic, tópico, tema (m) [*toh'-pee-koh, teh'-mah*]
toreador, torero [*toh-reh'-roh*]
torn, roto [*roh'-toh*]
tornado, tornado [*tohr-nah'-doh*]
torture *n.*, tortura [*tohr-too'-rah*]
toss *v.*, tirar [*tee-rahr'*]
total *n.*, total (m) [*toh-tahl'*]
touch *n.*, toque (m) [*tóh-keh*]
touch *v.*, tocar [*toh-kahr'*]
touching, conmovedor [*kohn-moh-veh-dohr'*]
touchy, susceptible [*soos-thehp-tee'-bleh*]
tough, duro [*doo'-roh*]
tour *n.*, jira [*hee'-rah*]
tourist, turista (m, f) [*too-rees'-tah*]
tourist office, oficina de turismo [*oh-fee-thee'-nah deh too-rees'-moh*]
tow *v.*, remolcar [*reh-mohl-kahr'*]
tow truck, remolcador (m) [*reh-mohl-kah-dohr'*]
toward, hacia [*ah'-thee-ah*]
towel, toalla [*toh-ah'-yah*]
tower, torre (f) [*toh'-rreh*]
town, pueblo, ciudad (f) [*poo-eh'-bloh, thee-oo-dahd'*]
town hall, ayuntamiento [*ah-yoon-tah-mee-ehn'-toh*]
toy, juguete (m) [*hoo-gheh'-teh*]
trace *n.*, rastro [*rahs'-troh*]
track *n.*, vía [*vee'-ah*]
trade *n.*, comercio [*koh-mehr'-thee-oh*]
trade *v.*, comerciar [*koh-mehr-thee-ahr'*]
trademark, marca de fábrica [*mahr'-kah deh fah'-bree-kah*]
tradition, tradición (f) [*trah-dee-thee-ohn'*]

traditional, tradicional [*trah-dee-thee-oh-nahl'*]
traffic, tráfico [*trah'-fee-koh*]
tragedy, tragedia [*trah-heh'-dee-ah*]
tragic, trágico [*trah'-hee-koh*]
trail, sendero [*sehn-deh'-roh*]
train *n.,* tren (m) [*trehn*]
train *v.,* adiestrar [*ah-dee-ehs-trahr'*]
training, adiestramiento [*ah-dee-ehs-trah-mee-ehn'-toh*]
trait, rasgo [*rahs'-goh*]
traitor, traidor (m) [*trah-ee-dohr'*]
tranquil, tranquilo [*trahn-kee'-loh*]
transfer [move] *v.,* trasladar [*trahs-lah-dahr'*]
transfer [change] *v.,* transbordar [*trahns-bohr-dahr'*]
transform *v.,* transformar [*trahns-fohr-mahr'*]
transient, transeúnte [*trahn-seh-oon'-teh*]
translate *v.,* traducir (irreg) [*trah-doo-theer'*]
translation, traducción (f) [*trah-dook-thee-ohn'*]
translator, traductor (m) [*trah-dook-tohr'*]
transmission, transmisión (f) [*trahns-mee-see-ohn'*]
transmit *v.,* transmitir [*trahns-mee-teer'*]
transportation, transporte (m) [*trahns-pohr'-teh*]
trap *n.,* trampa [*trahm'-pah*]
trap *v.,* atrapar [*ah-trah-pahr'*]
travel *n.,* viaje (m) [*vee-ah'-heh*]
travel *v.,* viajar [*vee-ah-hahr'*]
travel agency, agencia de viajes [*ah-hehn'-thee-ah deh vee-ah'-hehs*]
traveler, viajero [*vee-ah-heh'-roh*]
traveler's check, cheque (m) de viaje [*cheh'-keh deh vee-ah'-heh*]
tray, bandeja [*bahn-deh'-hah*]
treasure *n.,* tesoro [*teh-soh'-roh*]
treasurer, tesorero [*teh-soh-reh'-roh*]
treasury, tesorería [*teh-soh-reh-ree'-ah*]
treat *v.,* tratar [*trah-tahr'*]
treatment, tratamiento [*trah-tah-mee-ehn'-toh*]
treaty, tratado [*trah-tah'-doh*]
tree, árbol (m) [*ahr'-bohl*]

tremble *v.*, temblar (irreg) [*tehm-blahr'*]
tremendous, tremendo [*treh-mehn'-doh*]
trespass [on property] *v.*, violar [*vee-oh-lahr'*]
trial, juicio, prueba [*hoo-ee'-thee-oh, proo-eh'-bah*]
triangle, triángulo [*tree-ahn'-goo-loh*]
tribe, tribu (f) [*tree'-boo*]
trick *n.*, treta [*treh'-tah*]
trim *v.*, recortar [*reh-kohr-tahr'*]
trip [journey], viaje (m) [*vee-ah'-heh*]
triumphant, triunfante [*tree-oon-fahn'-teh*]
trivial, trivial [*tree-vee-ahl'*]
troop, tropa [*troh'-pah*]
tropical, tropical [*troh-pee-kahl'*]
trouble *n.*, dificultad (f) [*dee-fee-kool-tahd'*]
trouble *v.*, molestar [*moh-lehs-tahr'*]
trousers, pantalones (m, pl) [*pahn-tah-loh'-nehs*]
trout, trucha [*troo'-chah*]
truck, camión (m) [*kah-mee-ohn'*]
true, verdadero [*vehr-dah-deh'-roh*]
trunk [container], baúl (m) [*bah-ool'*]
trust [in] *n.*, confiar (en) [*kohn-fee-ahr' (ehn)*]
truth, verdad (f) [*vehr-dahd'*]
try *v.*, tratar [*trah-tahr'*]
  try on, probarse (irreg) [*proh-bahr'-seh*]
tub, bañera [*bah-nyeh'-rah*]
tube, tubo [*too'-boh*]
tuberculosis, tuberculosis (f) [*too-behr-koo-loh'-sees*]
Tuesday, martes (m) [*mahr'-tehs*]
tugboat, remolcador (m) [*reh-mohl-kah-dohr'*]
tune [melody], tonada [*toh-nah'-dah*]
tunnel, túnel (m) [*too'-nehl*]
turkey, pavo [*pah'-voh*]
Turkey, Turquía [*toor-kee'-ah*]
Turkish, turco [*toor'-koh*]
turn *n.*, turno, viraje (m) [*toor'-noh, vee-rah'-heh*]
turn *v.*, virar [*vee-rahr'*]
  turn around, dar la vuelta [*dahr lah voo-ehl'-tah*]

turn away, apartar, despedir (irreg) [*ah-pahr-tahr'*, *dehs-peh-deer'*]
turn back, retroceder [*reh-troh-theh-dehr'*]
turn off [light], apagar [*ah-pah-gahr'*]
turn on [light], encender (irreg) [*ehn-thehn-dehr'*]
turn over, volcar(se) (irreg) [*vohl-kahr'-seh*]
turnip, nabo [*nah'-boh*]
twelfth, doceavo [*doh-theh-ah'-voh*]
twelve, doce [*doh'-theh*]
twenty, veinte [*veh'-een-teh*]
twice, dos veces [*dohs veh'-thehs*]
twilight, crepúsculo [*kreh-poos'-koo-loh*]
twin *n. & adj.*, gemelo [*heh-meh'-loh*]
twine, cuerda [*koo-ehr'-dah*]
twist *v.*, torcer (irreg) [*tohr-thehr'*]
two, dos [*dohs*]
type *n.*, tipo [*tee'-poh*]
typewriter, máquina de escribir [*mah'-kee-nah deh ehs-kree-beer'*]
typical, típico [*tee'-pee-koh*]
typist, mecanógrafo [*meh-kah-noh'-grah-foh*]
tyranny, tiranía [*tee-rah-nee'-ah*]
tyrant, tirano [*tee-rah'-noh*]

U

ugly, feo [*feh'-oh*]
ultimate, último [*ool'-tee-moh*]
umbrella, paraguas (m) [*pah-rah'-goo-ahs*]
unable, incapaz [*een-kah-pahth'*]
unanimous, unánime [*oo-nah'-nee-meh*]
unbearable, insoportable [*een-soh-pohr-tah'-bleh*]
uncertain, incierto [*een-thee-ehr'-toh*]
uncle, tío [*tee'-oh*]
uncomfortable, incómodo [*een-koh'-moh-doh*]

unconscious, inconsciente [*een-kohns-thee-ehn'-teh*]
uncover *v.,* descubrir [*dehs-koo-breer'*]
undecided, indeciso [*een-deh-thee'-soh*]
under, debajo [*deh-bah'-hoh*]
underground, subterráneo [*soob-teh-rrah'-neh-oh*]
underwear, ropa interior [*roh'-pah een-teh-ree-ohr'*]
understand *v.,* comprender [*kohm-prehn-dehr'*]
  Do you understand? ¿Comprende usted? [*kohm-prehn'-deh oos-tehd'*]
undertake *v.,* emprender [*ehm-prehn-dehr'*]
undertaking, empresa [*ehm-preh'-sah*]
underwear, ropa interior [*roh'-pah een-teh-ree-ohr'*]
undo *v.,* deshacer (irreg) [*dehs-ah-thehr'*]
undress *v.,* desnudar(se) [*dehs-noo-dahr'-seh*]
uneasy, inquieto [*een-kee-eh'-toh*]
unemployed, desempleado [*deh-sehm-pleh-ah'-doh*]
unequal, desigual [*deh-see-goo-ahl'*]
unexpected, inesperado [*ee-nehs-peh-rah'-doh*]
unfair, injusto [*een-hoos'-toh*]
unfaithful, infiel (m, f) [*een-fee-ehl'*]
unfavorable, desfavorable [*dehs-fah-voh-rah'-bleh*]
unfit, inepto [*ee-nehp'-toh*]
unforeseen, imprevisto [*eem-preh-vees'-toh*]
unforgettable, inolvidable [*ee-nohl-vee-dah'-bleh*]
unfortunate, desgraciado [*dehs-grah-thee-ah'-doh*]
unfortunately, desgraciadamente [*dehs-grah-thee-ah-dah-mehn'-teh*]
ungrateful, desagradecido [*deh-sah-grah-deh-thee'-doh*]
unhappy, infeliz [*een-feh-leeth'*]
unharmed, ileso [*ee-leh'-soh*]
unhealthy, enfermizo [*ehn-fehr-mee'-thoh*]
uniform, uniforme (m) [*oo-nee-fohr'-meh*]
unimportant, sin importancia [*seen eem-pohr-tahn'-thee-ah*]
union, unión (f) [*oo-nee-ohn'*]
unit, unidad (f) [*oo-nee-dahd'*]
unite *v.,* unir [*oo-neer'*]
United States, Estados Unidos [*ehs-tah'-dohs oo-nee'-dohs*]
universal, universal [*oo-nee-vehr-sahl'*]

universe, universo [*oo-nee-vehr'-soh*]

university, universidad (f) [*oo-nee-vehr-see-dahd'*]

unjust, injusto [*een-hoos'-toh*]

unkind, descortés [*dehs-kohr-tehs'*]

unknown, desconocido [*dehs-koh-noh-thee'-doh*]

unlawful, ilegal [*ee-leh-gahl'*]

unless, a menos que [*ah meh'-nohs keh*]

unload *v.,* descargar [*dehs-kahr-gahr'*]

unlock, abrir [*ah-breer'*]

unlucky, desafortunado [*deh-sah-fohr-too-nah'-doh*]

unoccupied, desocupado [*deh-soh-koo-pah'-doh*]

unpack *v.,* desempaquetar [*deh-sehm-pah-keh-tahr'*]

unpleasant, desagradable [*deh-sah-grah-dah'-bleh*]

unsafe, inseguro [*een-seh-goo'-roh*]

unselfish, desinteresado [*deh-seen-teh-reh-sah'-doh*]

until, hasta [*ahs'-tah*]

untrue, falso [*fahl'-soh*]

unusual, raro [*rah'-roh*]

unwilling, reacio [*reh-ah'-thee-oh*]

up, arriba [*ah-rree'-bah*]

   go up, subir [*soo-beer'*]

uphill, cuesta arriba [*koo-ehs'-tah ah-rree'-bah*]

upon, sobre [*soh'-breh*]

upper, superior [*soo-peh-ree-ohr'*]

upper floor, piso de arriba [*pee'-soh deh ah-rree'-bah*]

upset *v.,* trastornar [*trahs-tohr-nahr'*]

upside down, al revés [*ahl reh-vehs'*]

upstairs, arriba [*ah-rree'-bah*]

up to now, hasta ahora [*ahs'-tah ah-oh'-rah*]

upward, hacia arriba [*ah'-thee-ah ah-rree'-bah*]

up-to-date, moderno [*moh-dehr'-noh*]

urgent, urgente [*oor-hehn'-teh*]

Uruguay, Uruguay [*oo-roo-goo-ah'-ee*]

Uruguayan, uruguayo [*oo-roo-goo-ah'-yoh*]

us, nos [*nohs*]

   for us, para nosotros [*pah'-rah noh-soh'-trohs*]

use *n.,* uso [*oo'-soh*]

use *v.,* usar [*oo-sahr'*]

be used to, estar acostumbrado a [*ehs-tahr' ah-kohs-toom-brah'-doh ah*]
used, usado [*oo-sah'-doh*]
useful, útil [*oo'-teel*]
useless, inútil [*ee-noo'-teel*]
usher, acomodador (m) [*ah-koh-moh-dah-dohr'*]
usual, corriente [*koh-rree-ehn'-teh*]
usually, generalmente [*heh-neh-rahl-mehn'-teh*]
utility, utilidad (f) [*oo-tee-lee-dahd'*]

V

vacancy, vacante (f) [*vah-kahn'-teh*]
  no vacancy, completo [*kohm-pleh'-toh*]
vacant, libre [*lee'-breh*]
vacation, vacaciones (f, pl) [*vah-kah-thee-oh'-nehs*]
vaccination, vacuna [*vah-koo'-nah*]
vacuum cleaner, aspiradora [*ahs-pee-rah-doh'-rah*]
vagabond, vagabundo [*vah-gah-boon'-doh*]
vague, vago [*vah'-goh*]
vain, vanidoso [*vah-nee-doh'-soh*]
  in vain, en vano [*ehn vah'-noh*]
valid, válido [*vah'-lee-doh*]
valley, valle (m) [*vah'-yeh*]
valuable, valioso [*vah-lee-oh'-soh*]
value *n.,* valor (m) [*vah-lohr'*]
value *v.,* valorar [*vah-loh-rahr'*]
valve, válvula [*vahl'-voo-lah*]
vanilla, vainilla [*vah-ee-nee'-yah*]
vanish *v.,* desvanecerse (irreg) [*dehs-vah-neh-thehr'-seh*]
vanity, vanidad (f) [*vah-nee-dahd'*]
variety, variedad (f) [*vah-ree-eh-dahd'*]
various, varios [*vah'-ree-ohs*]
vary *v.,* variar [*vah-ree-ahr'*]
vast, vasto [*vahs'-toh*]

Vatican, Vaticano [*vah-tee-kah'-noh*]
vault, bóveda [*boh'-veh-dah*]
veal, ternera [*tehr-neh'-rah*]
vegetables, verduras [*vehr-doo'-rahs*]
vehicle, vehículo [*veh-ee'-koo-loh*]
veil, velo [*veh'-loh*]
vein, vena [*veh'-nah*]
velvet, terciopelo [*tehr-thee-oh-peh'-loh*]
Venezuela, Venezuela [*veh-neh-thoo-eh'-lah*]
Venezuelan, venezolano [*veh-neh-thoh-lah'-noh*]
ventilator, ventilador (m) [*vehn-tee-lah-dohr'*]
verb, verbo [*vehr'-boh*]
verify *v.*, verificar [*veh-ree-fee-kahr'*]
verse, verso [*vehr'-soh*]
vertical, vertical [*vehr-tee-kahl'*]
very, muy [*moo-ee'*]
   very much, mucho [*moo'-choh*]
   very well, muy bien [*moo-ee' bee-ehn'*]
vest, chaleco [*chah-leh'-koh*]
veterinarian, veterinario [*veh-teh-ree-nah'-ree-oh*]
vibrate *v.*, vibrar [*vee-brahr'*]
vice, vicio [*vee'-thee-oh*]
vicinity, vecindad (f) [*veh-theen-dahd'*]
vicious, vicioso [*vee-thee-oh'-soh*]
victim, víctima [*veek'-tee-mah*]
victory, victoria [*veek-toh'-ree-ah*]
view *n.*, vista [*vees'-tah*]
viewpoint, punto de vista [*poon'-toh deh vees'-tah*]
vigorous, vigoroso [*vee-goh-roh'-soh*]
village, aldea, pueblecito [*ahl-deh'-ah, poo-eh-bleh-thee'-toh*]
vine, vid (f) [*veed*]
vinegar, vinagre (m) [*vee-nah'-greh*]
vineyard, viña [*vee'-nyah*]
violate *v.*, violar [*vee-oh-lahr'*]
violence, violencia [*vee-oh-lehn'-thee-ah*]
violet, violeta [*vee-oh-leh'-teh*]
violin, violín (m) [*vee-oh-leen'*]
virgin, virgen (f) [*veer'-hehn*]

virtue, virtud (f) [*veer-tood'*]
virtuous, virtuoso [*veer-too-oh'-soh*]
visa, visado [*vee-sah'-doh*]
visible, visible [*vee-see'-bleh*]
visit *n.,* visita [*vee-see'-tah*]
visit *v.,* visitar [*vee-see-tahr'*]
visitor, visitante (m, f) [*vee-see-tahn'-teh*]
vitamin, vitamina [*vee-tah-mee'-nah*]
vocabulary, vocabulario [*voh-kah-boo-lah'-ree-oh*]
vocalist, vocalista (m, f) [*voh-kah-lees'-tah*]
vocation, vocación (f) [*voh-kah-thee-ohn'*]
voice, voz (f) [*vohth*]
volcano, volcán (m) [*vohl-kahn'*]
volume, volumen (m) [*voh-loo'-mehn*]
voluntary, voluntario [*voh-loon-tah'-ree-oh*]
vomit *v.,* vomitar [*voh-mee-tahr'*]
vote *n.,* voto [*voh'-toh*]
vote *v.,* votar [*voh-tahr'*]
vowel, vocal (f) [*voh-kahl'*]
voyage *n.,* viaje (m) [*vee-ah'-heh*]
vulgar, vulgar [*vool-gahr'*]
vulture, buitre (m) [*boo-ee'-treh*]

W

wages, sueldo [*soo-ehl'-doh*]
wagon, carreta [*kah-rreh'-tah*]
waist, cintura [*theen-too'-rah*]
wait *n.,* espera [*ehs-peh'-rah*]
wait *v.,* esperar [*ehs-peh-rahr'*]
   Wait a moment, Espere un momento [*ehs-peh'-reh oon moh-mehn'-toh*]
   Wait for me, Espéreme [*ehs-peh'-reh-meh*]
waiter, camarero, mesero [*kah-mah-reh'-roh, meh-seh'-roh*]
waiting room, sala de espera [*sah'-lah deh ehs-peh'-rah*]

waitress, camarera [*kah-mah-reh'-rah*]

wake [up] *v.*, despertar(se) (irreg) [*dehs-pehr-tahr'-seh*]

walk *n.*, paseo [*pah-seh'-oh*]

  take a walk, dar un paseo [*dahr oon pah-seh'-oh*]

walk *v.*, caminar, pasear [*kah-mee-nahr', pah-seh-ahr'*]

wall, pared (f) [*pah-rehd'*]

wallet, cartera [*kahr-teh'-rah*]

walnut, nogal (m) [*noh-gahl'*]

wander *v.*, vagar [*vah-gahr'*]

want *v.*, querer (irreg) [*keh-rehr'*]

war, guerra [*gheh'-rrah*]

wardrobe, guardarropa (m) [*goo-ahr-dah-rroh'-pah*]

warehouse, almacén (m) [*ahl-mah-thehn'*]

warm, templado, cordial [*tehm-plah'-doh, kohr-dee-ahl'*]

warm [up] *v.*, calentar (irreg) [*kah-lehn-tahr'*]

warn *v.*, advertir (irreg) [*ahd-vehr-teer'*]

warning, aviso [*ah-vee'-soh*]

warship, barco de guerra [*bahr'-koh deh gheh'-rrah*]

wash *v.*, lavar [*lah-vahr'*]

washbasin, lavabo [*lah-vah'-boh*]

washing machine, máquina de lavar [*mah'-kee-nah deh lah-vahr'*]

wasp, avispa [*ah-vees'-pah*]

waste *v.*, mal gastar [*mahl gahs-tahr'*]

wastebasket, papelera [*pah-peh-leh'-rah*]

watch *n.*, reloj (m) [*reh-lohh'*]

  wristwatch, reloj de pulsera [*reh-lohh' deh pool-seh'-rah*]

watch *v.*, observar [*ohb-sehr-vahr'*]

  Watch out, ¡Cuidado! [*koo-ee-dah'-doh*]

watchmaker, relojero [*reh-loh-heh'-roh*]

watchman, vigilante (m) [*vee-hee-lahn'-teh*]

water, agua [*ah'-goo-ah*]

  fresh water, agua dulce [*ah'-goo-ah dool'-theh*]

  mineral water, agua mineral [*ah'-goo-ah mee-neh-rahl'*]

  running water, agua corriente [*ah'-goo-ah koh-rree-ehn'-teh*]

waterfall, cascada [*kahs-káh-dah*]

watermelon, sandía [*sahn-dee'-ah*]

waterproof, impermeable [*eem-pehr-meh-ah'-bleh*]
wave *n.*, onda, ola [*ohn'-dah, oh'-lah*]
wave [undulate] *v.*, ondear [*ohn-deh-ahr'*]
wave [signal] *v.*, hacer señas [*ah-thehr' seh'-nyahs*]
wax, cera [*theh'-rah*]
way [route], vía [*vee'-ah*]
  one-way street, dirección única [*dee-rehk-thee-ohn' oo'-nee-kah*]
way [manner], modo, manera [*moh'-doh, mah-neh'-rah*]
  by the way, a propósito [*ah proh-poh'-see-toh*]
  in no way, de ninguna manera [*deh neen-goo'-nah mah-neh'-rah*]
  in this way, de esta manera [*deh ehs'-tah mah-neh'-rah*]
we, nosotros [*noh-soh'-trohs*]
weak, débil [*deh'-beel*]
weakness, debilidad (f) [*deh-bee-lee-dahd'*]
wealth, riqueza [*ree-keh'-thah*]
wealthy, rico [*ree'-koh*]
weapon, arma [*ahr'-mah*]
wear *v.*, llevar, usar [*yeh-vahr', oo-sahr'*]
wear out, *v.*, gastar (se) [*gahs-tahr'*-seh]
weather, tiempo [*tee-ehm'-poh*]
web, telaraña [*teh-lah-rah'-nyah*]
wedding, boda [*boh'-dah*]
Wednesday, miércoles (m) [*mee-ehr'-koh-lehs*]
week, semana [*seh-mah'-nah*]
weekend, fin (m) de semana [*feen deh seh-mah'-nah*]
weekly, semanal [*seh-mah-nahl'*]
weep *v.*, llorar [*yoh-rahr'*]
weigh *v.*, pesar [*peh-sahr'*]
weight, peso [*peh'-soh*]
welcome *n.*, bienvenido [*bee-ehn-veh-nee'-doh*]
well [for water] *n.*, pozo [*poh'-thoh*]
well *adv.*, bien [*bee-ehn'*]
  Very well, ¡Está bien! [*ehs-tah' bee-ehn'*]
well-bred, bien educado [*bee-ehn' eh-doo-kah'-doh*]
well-known, muy conocido [*moo-ee' koh-noh-thee'-doh*]
well-off, acomodado [*ah-koh-moh-dah'-doh*]

west, oeste (m) [*oh-ehs'-teh*]
western, occidental [*ohk-thee-dehn-tahl'*]
West Indies, las Antillas [*lahs ahn-tee'-yahs*]
wet, mojado [*moh-hah'-doh*]
whale, ballena [*bah-yeh'-nah*]
wharf, embarcadero [*ehm-bahr-kah-deh'-roh*]
what, que [*keh*]
   what else? ¿qué más? [*keh mahs*]
   what for? ¿para qué? [*pah'-rah keh*]
   What is the matter? ¿Qué pasa? [*keh pah'-sah*]
whatever, cualquiera [*koo-ahl-kee-eh'-rah*]
wheat, trigo [*tree'-goh*]
wheel, rueda [*roo-eh'-dah*]
   steering wheel, volante (m) [*voh-lahn'-teh*]
when, cuando [*koo-ahn'-doh*]
   since when, desde cuando [*dehs'-deh koo-ahn'-doh*]
where, donde [*dohn'-deh*]
wherever, dondequiera [*dohn-deh-kee-eh'-rah*]
whether, si [*see*]
which *rel. pron.*, que, (el/la) cual, (los/las) cuales [*keh, ehl/lah koo-ahl', lohs/lahs koo-ah-lehs*]
which? ¿cual? ¿cuales? ¿que? [*koo-ahl', koo-ah'-lehs, keh*]
while, mientras [*mee-ehn'-trahs*]
whipped cream, crema batida [*kreh'-mah bah-tee'-dah*]
whisper *v.*, susurrar [*soo-soo-rrahr'*]
whistle *n.*, silbido, silbato [*seel-bee'-doh, seel-bah'-toh*]
white, blanco [*blahn'-koh*]
who *rel. pron.*, que, quien, quienes [*keh, kee-ehn', kee-eh'-nehs*]
who? ¿quien? ¿quienes? [*kee-ehn', kee-eh'-nehs*]
whoever, quienquiera [*kee-ehn-kee-eh'-rah*]
whole, entero [*ehn-teh'-roh*]
wholesale, al por mayor [*ahl pohr mah-yohr'*]
whom, a quien, a quienes [*ah kee-ehn', ah kee-eh'-nehs*]
whose *rel. pron.*, de quien, de quienes, cujo [*deh kee-ehn', de kee-eh'-nehs, koo'-yoh*]
whose? ¿de quién? ¿de quienes? [*deh kee-ehn', deh kee-eh'-nehs*]

why? ¿por qué? [*pohr keh'*]
  why not? ¿por qué no? [*pohr keh noh*]
wide, ancho [*ahn'-choh*]
widow, viuda [*vee-oo'-dah*]
widower, viudo [*vee-oo'-doh*]
width, anchura [*ahn-choo'-rah*]
wife, esposa [*ehs-poh'-sah*]
wig, peluca [*peh-loo'-kah*]
wild, salvaje [*sahl-vah'-heh*]
will [volition] *n.*, voluntad (f) [*voh-loon-tahd'*]
will [testament] *n.*, testamento [*tehs-tah-mehn'-toh*]
willing, deseoso [*deh-seh-oh'-soh*]
willingly, de buena gana [*deh boo-eh'-nah gah'-nah*]
win *v.*, ganar [*gah-nahr'*]
wind, viento [*vee-ehn'-toh*]
  be windy, hacer viento [*ah-thehr' vee-ehn'-toh*]
windmill, molino de viento [*moh-lee'-noh deh vee-ehn'-toh*]
windshield, parabrisas (m) [*pah-rah-bree'-sahs*]
window, ventana [*vehn-tah'-nah*]
wine, vino [*vee'-noh*]
  red wine, vino tinto [*vee'-noh teen'-toh*]
  white wine, vino blanco [*vee'-noh blahn'-koh*]
wing, ala [*ah'-lah*]
winner, vencedor (m) [*vehn-theh-dohr'*]
winter, invierno [*een-vee-ehr'-noh*]
wipe *v.*, secar [*seh-kahr'*]
wire [filament] *n.*, alambre (m) [*ah-lahm'-breh*]
wire *v.*, telegrafiar [*teh-leh-grah-fee-ahr'*]
wisdom, sabiduría [*sah-bee-doo-ree'-ah*]
wise, sabio [*sah'-bee-oh*]
wish *n.*, deseo [*deh-seh'-oh*]
wish *v.*, desear [*deh-seh-ahr'*]
wit, ingenio [*een-heh'-nee-oh*]
witch, bruja [*broo'-hah*]
with, con [*kohn*]
withdraw *v.*, retirar [*reh-tee-rahr'*]
withhold *v.*, retener (irreg) [*reh-teh-nehr'*]
within, dentro de [*dehn'-troh deh*]

without, sin [*seen*]
witness *n.,* testigo [*tehs-tee'-goh*]
witness *v.,* presenciar [*preh-sehn-thee-ahr'*]
witty, gracioso [*grah-thee-oh'-soh*]
wolf, lobo [*loh'-boh*]
woman, mujer (f) [*moo-hehr'*]
wonder *v.,* preguntarse [*preh-goon-tahr'-seh*]
wonderful, maravilloso [*mah-rah-vee-yoh'-soh*]
wood, madera [*mah-deh'-rah*]
wooden, de madera [*deh mah-deh'-rah*]
woods, bosque (m) [*bohs'-keh*]
wool, lana [*lah'-nah*]
woolen, de lana [*deh lah'-nah*]
word, palabra [*pah-lah'-brah*]
work *n.,* trabajo [*trah-bah'-hoh*]
work *v.,* trabajar [*trah-bah-hahr'*]
worker, obrero [*oh-breh'-roh*]
world, mundo [*moon'-doh*]
world war, guerra mundial [*gheh'-rrah moon-dee-ahl'*]
worm, gusano [*goo-sah'-noh*]
worn out, gastado, agotado [*gahs-tah'-doh, ah-goh-tah'-doh*]
worried, preocupado [*preh-oh-koo-pah'-doh*]
worry *n.,* preocupación (f) [*preh-oh-koo-pah-thee-ohn'*]
worry *v.,* preocuparse [*preh-oh-koo-pahr'-seh*]
worse, peor [*peh-ohr'*]
  worse than, peor que [*peh-ohr' keh*]
worst, el peor [*ehl peh-ohr'*]
worth, valor (m) [*vah-lohr'*]
worthy, valioso [*vah-lee-oh'-soh*]
wound [injury], herida [*ee-ree'-dah*]
wounded, herido [*eh-ree'-doh*]
wrap [up] *v.,* envolver (irreg) [*ehn-vohl-vehr'*]
wrench [tool], llave (f) inglesa [*yah'-veh een-gleh'-sah*]
wrestling, lucha libre [*loo'-chah lee'-breh*]
wrinkle *n.,* arruga [*ah-rroo'-gah*]
wrinkle *v.,* arrugar(se) [*ah-rroo-gahr'(-seh)*]
wrist, muñeca [*moo-nyeh'-kah*]

wristwatch, reloj (m) de pulsera [*reh-lokh' deh pool-seh'-rah*]
write *v.*, escribir [*ehs-kree-beer'*]
writer, escritor (m) [*ehs-kree-tohr'*]
writing, escritura [*ehs-kree-too'-rah*]
writing paper, papel (m) de escribir [*pah-pehl' deh ehs-kree-beer'*]
wrong *adj.*, equivocado [*eh-kee-voh-kah'-doh*]
wrong, equivocado [*eh-kee-voh-kah'-doh*]
  be wrong, estar equivocado [*ehs-tahr' eh-kee-voh-kah'-doh*]

X

x ray, rayos (m, pl) equis [*rah'-yohs eh'-kees*]

Y

yacht, yate (m) [*yah'-teh*]
yard [court], patio [*pah'-tee-oh*]
yard [measure], yarda, cercado [*yahr'-dah, thehr-kah'-doh*]
yawn *v.*, bostezar [*bohs-teh-thahr'*]
year, año [*ah'-nyoh*]
  last year, el año pasado [*ehl ah'-nyoh pah-sah'-doh*]
  next year, el año que viene [*ehl ah'-nyoh keh vee-eh'-neh*]
yearly, anualmente [*ah-noo-ahl-mehn'-teh*]
yell *v.*, gritar [*gree-tahr'*]
yellow, amarillo [*ah-mah-ree'-yoh*]
yes, sí [*see*]
  Yes indeed! ¡Ya lo creo! [*yah loh kreh'-oh*]
yesterday, ayer [*ah-yehr'*]
  the day before yesterday, anteayer [*ahn-teh-ah-yehr'*]

yet [still], todavía [*toh-dah-vee'-ah*]
yet [however], sin embargo [*seen ehm-bahr'-goh*]
yield *v.*, ceder [*theh-dehr'*]
you, tú (fam), usted, ustedes (formal) [*too, oos-tehd', oos-tehd'-ehs*]
young, joven [*hoh'-vehn*]
  young person, joven (m, f) [*hoh'-vehn*]
your, su, sus, tu, tus [*soo, soos, too, toos*]
yours, tuyo, suyo [*too'-yoh, soo'-yoh*]
yourself, tú mismo, usted mismo [*too mees'-moh, oos-tehd' mees'-moh*]
yourselves, vosotros mismos, ustedes mismos [*voh-soh'-trohs mees'-mohs, oos-teh'-dehs mees'-mohs*]
youth, juventud (f) [*hoo-vehn-tood'*]
youthful, juvenil [*hoo-veh-neel'*]

Z

zebra, cebra [*theh'-brah*]
zero, cero [*theh'-roh*]
zipper, cremallera [*kreh-mah-yeh'-rah*]
zone, zona [*thoh'-nah*]
zoo, jardín (m) zoológico [*hahr-deen' thoh-oh-loh'-hee-koh*]

Spanish/English

A

a [*ah*] to, at
  a bordo [*ah bohr'-doh*] aboard
  a la mano [*ah lah mah'-noh*] at hand
  a las dos [*ah lahs dohs*] at two o'clock
  a menos que [*ah meh'-nohs keh*] unless
  a menudo [*ah meh-noo'-doh*] often
  a pesar de [*ah peh-sahr' deh*] in spite of
  a pie [*ah pee-eh'*] on foot
  a toda velocidad [*ah toh'-dah veh-loh-thee-dahd'*]
    full speed ahead
  a través de [*ah trah-vehs' deh*] across, through
  a veces [*ah veh'-thehs*] at times
abajo [*ah-bah'-hoh*] down, downstairs, below
  ¡Abajo con . . . ! [*ah-bah'-hoh kohn*] Down with . . . !
abandonado [*ah-bahn-doh-nah'-doh*] abandoned
abandonar *v.* [*ah-bahn-doh-nahr'*] abandon
abanico [*ah-bah-nee'-koh*] fan [manual]
abarcar *v.* [*ah-bahr-kahr'*] encompass
abastecer *v. irreg.* [*ah-bahs-teh-thehr'*] supply
abastecimiento [*ah-bahs-teh-thee-mee-ehn'-toh*] supply,
    provision
abatido [*ah-bah-tee'-doh*] gloomy
abeja [*ah-beh'-hah*] bee
abierto [*ah-bee-ehr'-toh*] open
ablandar *v.* [*ah-blahn-dahr'*] soften
abochornado [*ah-boh-chohr-nah'-doh*] embarrassed
abogado [*ah-boh-gah'-doh*] lawyer, attorney
abogar *v.* [*ah-boh-gahr'*] plead
abolengo [*ah-boh-lehn'-goh*] lineage, ancestry
abolir *v.* [*ah-boh-leer'*] abolish
abolladura [*ah-boh-yah-doo'-rah*] bump
abonado [*ah-boh-nah'-doh*] subscriber

abonar *v.* [*ah-boh-nahr'*] make a payment

abotonar *v.* [*ah-boh-toh-nahr'*] button up

abrazar *v.* [*ah-brah-thahr'*] embrace

abrazo [*ah-brah'-thoh*] embrace, hug

abrelatas *m. sing.* [*ah-breh-lah'-tahs*] can opener

abreviatura [*ah-breh-vee-ah-too'-rah*] abbreviation

abrigo [*ah-bree'-goh*] coat

   abrigo de pieles [*ah-bree'-goh deh pee-eh'-lehs*] fur coat

abril *m.* [*ah-breel'*] April

abrir *v.* [*ah-breer'*] open

abrochar *v.* [*ah-broh-chahr'*] fasten, button

absolutamente [*ahb-soh-loo-tah-mehn'-teh*] absolutely

absoluto [*ahb-soh-loo'-toh*] absolute

absolver *v. irreg.* [*ahb-sohl-vehr'*] acquit, absolve

absorber *v.* [*ahb-sohr-behr'*] absorb

absorto [*ahb-sohr'-toh*] absorbed

abstenerse *v. irreg.* [*ahbs-teh-nehr'-seh*] refrain, restrain

abstracción *f.* [*ahbs-trahk-thee-ohn'*] abstraction

abstracto [*ahbs-trahk'-toh*] abstract

absurdo [*ahb-soor -doh*] absurd

abuela [*ah-boo-eh'-lah*] grandmother

abuelo [*ah-boo-eh'-loh*] grandfather

abultado [*ah-bool-tah'-doh*] bulky

abundancia [*ah-boon-dahn'-thee-ah*] abundance

abundante [*ah-boon-dahn'-teh*] abundant

abundar *v.* [*ah-boon-dahr'*] abound

aburrido [*ah-boo-rree'doh*] tiresome, boring

aburrir *v.* [*ah-boo-rreer'*] bore

aburrirse *v.* [*ah-boo-rreer'-seh*] become bored

abusar *v.* [*ah-boo-sahr'*] abuse

abuso *n.* [*ah-boo'-soh*] abuse

acá [*ah-kah'*] here, over here

acabado [*ah-kah-bah'-doh*] over, finished

acabar *v.* [*ah-kah-bahr'*] end, finish

   acabar de [*ah-kah-bahr' deh*] to have just

academia [*ah-kah-deh'-mee-ah*] academy

acalorado [*ah-kah-loh-rah'-doh*] excited

acampar *v.* [*ah-kahm-pahr'*] camp

acariciar *v.* [*ah-kah-ree-thee-ahr'*] caress
acatarrarse *v.* [*ah-kah-tah-rrahr'-seh*] catch cold
accesible [*ahk-theh-see'-bleh*] accessible
acceso [*ahk-theh'-soh*] access, entrance
accidental [*ahk-thee-dehn-tahl'*] accidental
accidente *m.* [*ahk-thee-dehn'-teh*] accident
acción *f.* [*ahk-thee-ohn'*] action
aceite *m.* [*ah-theh'-ee-teh*] oil
   aceite de oliva [*ah-theh'-ee-teh deh oh-lee'-vah*] olive oil
aceituna [*ah-theh-ee-too'-nah*] olive
acelerador *m.* [*ah-theh-leh-rah-dohr'*] accelerator
acelerar *v.* [*ah-theh-leh-rahr'*] accelerate, speed
acento [*ah-thehn'-toh*] accent
acentuar *v.* [*ah-thehn-too-ahr'*] accent, stress
aceptable [*ah-thehp-tah'-bleh*] acceptable
aceptación *f.* [*ah-thehp-tah-thee-ohn'*] acceptance
aceptar *v.* [*ah-thehp-tahr'*] accept
acera [*ah-theh'-rah*] sidewalk
acerca de *prep.* [*ah-thehr'-kah deh*] about
acercamiento [*ah-thehr-kah-mee-ehn'-toh*] approach
acercar *v.* [*ah-thehr-kahr'*] approach
acero [*ah-theh'-roh*] steel
acertar *v.* [*ah-thehr-tahr'*] hit upon, find by chance
ácido *n. & adj.* [*ah'-thee-doh*] acid
aclarar *v.* [*ah-klah-rahr'*] clear, explain, rinse
aclimatar *v.* [*ah-klee-mah-tahr'*] acclimatize
acomodación *f.* [*ah-koh-moh-dah-thee-ohn'*]
   accommodation
acomodado [*ah-koh-moh-dah'-doh*] well off
acomodador *m.* [*ah-koh-moh-dah-dohr'*] usher
acomodar *v.* [*ah-koh-moh-dahr'*] accommodate, lodge
acompañante *m.,f.* [*ah-kohm-pah-nyahn'-teh*] companion
acompañar *v.* [*ah-kohm-pah-nyahr'*] accompany
aconsejar *v.* [*ah-kohn-seh-hahr'*] advise
acontecimiento [*ah-kohn-teh-thee-mee-ehn'-toh*] event,
   happening
acortar *v.* [*ah-kohr-tahr'*] shorten
acostado [*ah-kohs-tah'-doh*] in bed, lying down

acostarse *v.* [*ah-kohs-tahr'-seh*] go to bed
acostumbrar *v.* [*ah-kohs-toom-brahr'*] accustom
acostumbrarse *v.* [*ah-kohs-toom-brahr'-seh*] get used to
acreedor *m.* [*ah-kreh-eh-dohr'*] creditor
actitud *f.* [*ahk-tee-tood'*] attitude
actividad *f.* [*ahk-tee-vee-dahd'*] activity
activo [*ahk-tee'-voh*] active
acto [*ahk'-toh*] act, action, deed
  en el acto [*ehn ehl ahk'-toh*] immediately
actor *m.* [*ahk-tohr'*] actor
actriz *f.* [*ahk-treeth'*] actress
actual [*ahk-too-ahl'*] actual, present
actualmente [*ahk-too-ahl-mehn'-teh*] at present, nowadays
actuar *v.* [*ahk-too-ahr'*] act
acudir *v.* [*ah-koo-deer'*] go, come, be present
acuerdo [*ah-koo-ehr'-doh*] agreement
acusación *f.* [*ah-koo-sah-thee-ohn'*] accusation
acusado [*ah-koo-sah'-doh*] accused
acusar *v.* [*ah-koo-sahr'*] accuse
acuse (de recibo) *m.* [*ah-koo'-seh (deh reh-thee'-boh)*]
   acknowledgment (of receipt)
adaptar *v.* [*ah-dahp-tahr'*] adapt
adecuado [*ah-deh-koo-ah'-doh*] adequate
adelantado [*ah-deh-lahn-tah'-doh*] ahead, advanced
adelantar *v.* [*ah-deh-lahn-tahr'*] move forward, advance
adelante [*ah-deh-lahn'-teh*] forward
adelgazar *v.* [*ah-dehl-gah-thahr'*] get thin
además [*ah-deh-mahs'*] moreover, besides
adentro [*ah-dehn'-troh*] inside, indoors
adepto [*ah-dehp'-toh*] adept
adherir *v. irreg.* [*ahd-eh-reer'*] adhere, stick
adición *f.* [*ah-dee-thee-ohn'*] addition
adicional [*ah-dee-thee-oh-nahl'*] additional
adiestramiento [*ah-dee-ehs-trah-mee-ehn'-toh*] training
adiestrar *v.* [*ah-dee-ehs-trahr'*] train
adinerado [*ah-dee-neh-rah'-doh*] wealthy
adiós [*ah-dee-ohs'*] good-bye
adivinar *v.* [*ah-dee-vee-nahr'*] guess

adjetivo [*ahd-heh-tee'-voh*] adjective
adjudicar *v.* [*ahd-hoo-dee-kahr'*] award
administración *f.* [*ahd-mee-nees-trah-thee-ohn'*]
    administration
administrador *m.* [*ahd-mee-nees-trah-dohr'*] manager
administrar *v.* [*ahd-mee-nees-trahr'*] administer, manage
admirable [*ahd-mee-rah'-bleh*] admirable
admiración *f.* [*ahd-mee-rah-thee-ohn'*] admiration
admirador *m.* [*ahd-mee-rah-dohr'*] admirer
admirar *v.* [*ahd-mee-rahr'*] admire
admisión *f.* [*ahd-mee-see-ohn'*] admission, admittance
admitir *v.* [*ahd-mee-teer'*] admit, let in
¿Adónde? [*ah-dohn'-deh*] Where to?
adopción *f.* [*ah-dohp-thee-ohn'*] adoption
adoptar *v.* [*ah-dohp-tahr'*] adopt
adorar *v.* [*ah-doh-rahr'*] adore
adornar *v.* [*ah-dohr-nahr'*] adorn
adorno [*ah-dohr'-noh*] ornament
adquirir *v. irreg.* [*ahd-kee-reer'*] acquire
adquisición *f.* [*ahd-kee-see-thee-ohn'*] acquisition
adrede [*ah-dreh'-deh*] on purpose
aduana [*ah-doo-ah'-nah*] customs
aduanero [*ah-doo-ah-neh'-roh*] customs officer
adulto *n. & adj.* [*ah-dool'-toh*] adult
adverbio [*ahd-vehr'-bee-oh*] adverb
adversario [*ahd-vehr-sah'-ree-oh*] adversary
adversidad *f.* [*ahd-vehr-see-dahd'*] adversity
adverso [*ahd-vehr'-soh*] adverse
advertencia [*ahd-vehr-tehn'-thee-ah*] warning, notice
advertir *v. irreg.* [*ahd-vehr-teer'*] warn, notice
adyacente [*ahd-yah-thehn'-teh*] adjacent
aéreo [*ah-eh'-reh-oh*] aerial, airborne
    correo aéreo [*koh-rreh'-oh ah-eh'-reh-oh*] air mail
aeropuerto [*ah-eh-roh-poo-ehr'-toh*] airport
afán *m.* [*ah-fahn'*] eagerness
afectado [*ah-fehk-tah'-doh*] affected
afectar *v.* [*ah-fehk-tahr'*] affect
afecto [*ah-fehk'-toh*] affection

afectuoso [*ah-fehk-too-oh'-soh*] affectionate
afeitar *v.* [*ah-feh-ee-tahr'*] shave
  máquina de afeitar [*mah'-kee-nah deh ah-feh-ee-tahr'*]
    electric razor
  navaja de afeitar [*nah-vah'-hah deh ah-feh-ee-tahr'*] razor
afición *f.* [*ah-fee-thee-ohn'*] fondness, inclination
afilar *v.* [*ah-fee-lahr'*] sharpen
afirmar *v.* [*ah-feer-mahr'*] affirm
afirmativo [*ah-feer-mah-tee'-voh*] affirmative
aflicción *f.* [*ah-fleek-thee-ohn'*] grief
afligir *v.* [*ah-flee-heer'*] afflict, distress
aflojar *v.* [*ah-floh-hahr'*] loosen
aflojamiento [*ah-floh-hah-mee-ehn'-toh*] relaxation
afortunadamente [*ah-fohr-too-nah-dah-mehn'-teh*] fortunately
afortunado [*ah-fohr-too-nah'-doh*] lucky, fortunate
afrentoso [*ah-frehn-toh'-soh*] outrageous
Africa [*ah'-free-kah*] Africa
afrontar *v.* [*ah-frohn-tahr'*] face
afuera *adv.* [*ah-foo-eh'-rah*] outside
afueras *f. pl.* [*ah-foo-eh'-rahs*] outskirts
agacharse *v.* [*ah-gah-chahr'-seh*] bend down
agarradero [*ah-gah-rrah-deh'-roh*] grip, handle
agarrar *v.* [*ah-gah-rrahr'*] seize, grab
agencia [*ah-hehn'-thee-ah*] agency
  agencia de viajes [*ah hehn'-thee-ah deh vee-ah'-hehs*]
    travel agency
agente *m.* [*ah-hehn'-teh*] agent
ágil [*ah'-heel*] agile
agitar *v.* [*ah-hee-tahr'*] fidget
aglomeración *f.* [*ah-gloh-meh-rah-thee-ohn'*] conglomeration
agonía [*ah-goh-nee'-ah*] agony
agosto [*ah-gohs'-toh*] August
agotado [*ah-goh-tah'-doh*] worn out, exhausted
agraciado *adj.* [*ah-grah-thee-ah'-doh*] graceful
agraciado *n.* [*ah-grah-thee-ah'-doh*] winner
agradable [*ah-grah-dah'-bleh*] pleasant
agradar *v.* [*ah-grah-dahr'*] please
agradecer *v. irreg.* [*ah-grah-deh-thehr'*] thank, be grateful

agradecido [*ah-grah-deh-thee'-doh*] thankful, grateful
agradecimiento [*ah-grah-deh-thee-mee-ehn'-toh*] gratitude
agravar *v.* [*ah-grah-vahr'*] aggravate
agresión *f.* [*ah-greh-see-ohn'*] aggression
agresivo [*ah-greh-see'-voh*] aggressive
agricultura [*ah-gree-kool-too'-rah*] agriculture
agrio [*ah'-gree-oh*] sour
(el) agua *f.* [*ah'-goo-ah*] water
  agua corriente [*ah'-goo-ah koh-rree-ehn'-teh*] running water
  agua dulce [*ah'-goo-ah dool'- theh*] fresh water
  agua mineral [*ah'-goo-ah mee-neh-rahl'*] mineral water
aguantar *v.* [*ah-goo-ahn-tahr'*] endure, bear
aguardar *v.* [*ah-goo-ahr-dahr'*] wait
agudo [*ah-goo'-doh*] sharp, acute
aguja [*ah-goo'-hah*] needle
agujerear *v.* [*ah-goo-heh-reh-ahr'*] perforate
agujero [*ah-goo-heh'-roh*] hole
ahí [*ah-ee'*] there
ahogar *v.* [*ah-oh-gahr'*] drown
ahora [*ah-oh'-rah*] now
  ahora mismo [*ah-oh'-rah mees'-moh*] right now, right away
ahorrar *v.* [*ah-oh-rrahr'*] save
ahorrativo [*ah-oh-rrah-tee'-voh*] thrifty
ahorros *m. pl.* [*ah-oh'-rrohs*] savings
aire *m.* [*ah'-ee-reh*] air
  aire acondicionado [*ah'-ee-reh ah-kohn-dee-thee-oh-nah'-doh*] air-conditioned
ajedrez *m.* [*ah-heh-drehth'*] chess
ajeno [*ah-heh'-noh*] another's; foreign, alien
ají *m.* [*ah-hee'*] chili pepper
ajo [*ah'-hoh*] garlic
ajustar *v.* [*ah-hoos-tahr'*] adjust, tighten
ajuste *m.* [*ah-hoos'-teh*] adjustment, fit
al (a el) [*ahl*] to the
  al agua [*ahl ah'-goo-ah*] overboard
  al aire libre [*ahl ah'-ee-reh lee'-breh*] outdoors
  al fin [*ahl feen*] at last
  al fin y al cabo [*ahl feen ee ahl kah'-boh*] after all

al menos [*ahl meh'-nohs*] at least
al mismo tiempo [*ahl mees'-moh tee-ehm'-poh*] at the same time
al por mayor [*ahl pohr mah-yohr'*] wholesale
al por menor [*ahl pohr meh-nohr'*] retail
al principio [*ahl preen-thee'-pee-oh*] at first
al revés [*ahl reh-vehs'*] inside out, upside down
ala [*ah'-lah*] wing
alabar *v.* [*ah-lah-bahr'*] praise
alambre *m.* [*ah-lahm'-breh*] wire
alargar *v.* [*ah-lahr-gahr'*] lengthen, prolong
alarma [*ah-lahr'-mah*] alarm
alarmar *v.* [*ah-lahr-mahr'*] alarm
albaricoque *m.* [*ahl-bah-ree-koh'-keh*] apricot
albóndiga [*ahl-bohn'-dee-gah*] meat ball
alcalde *m.* [*ahl-kahl'-deh*] mayor
alcance *m.* [*ahl-kahn'-theh*] range, scope, reach
alcanzar *v.* [*ahl-kahn-thahr'*] reach, achieve
alcoba [*ahl-koh'-bah*] bedroom
alcohol *m.* [*ahl-koh'-ohl*] alcohol
aldea [*ahl-deh'-ah*] village
alegrar *v.* [*ah-leh-grahr'*] cheer up
alegrarse *v.* [*ah-leh-grahr'-seh*] be glad
alegre [*ah-leh'-greh*] happy, cheerful, merry
alegría [*ah-leh-gree'-ah*] happiness, cheer
alejarse *v.* [*ah-leh-hahr'-seh*] move away
alemán *m.* [*ah-leh-mahn'*] German
Alemania [*ah-leh-mah'-nee-ah*] Germany
alerta *n.* [*ah-lehr'-tah*] alert
alertar *v.* [*ah-lehr-tahr'*] alert
alfabeto [*ahl-fah-beh'-toh*] alphabet
alfiler *m.* [*ahl-fee-lehr'*] pin
alfombra [*ahl-fohm'-brah*] carpet, rug
algo [*ahl'-goh*] something, anything
algodón *m.* [*ahl-goh-dohn'*] cotton
alguien [*ahl'-ghee-ehn*] someone, somebody
algún *m.* [*ahl-goon'*] some, someone
   alguna vez [*ahl-goo'-nah vehth*] sometime, ever

aliado [*ah-lee-ah'-doh*] allied
aliento [*ah-lee-ehn'-toh*] breath
alimentar *v.* [*ah-lee-mehn-tahr'*] feed
alimento [*ah-lee-mehn'-toh*] food, nourishment
alistar *v.* [*ah-lees-tahr'*] enroll
alivio [*ah-lee'-vee-oh*] relief
(el) alma *f.* [*ahl'-mah*] soul
almacén *m.* [*ahl-mah-thehn'*] warehouse
almacenaje *m.* [*ahl-mah-theh-nah'-heh*] storage
almacenes *m. pl.* [*ahl-mah-theh'-nehs*] department store
almeja [*ahl-meh'-hah*] clam
almendra [*ahl-mehn'-drah*] almond
almidón *m.* [*ahl-mee-dohn'*] starch
almirante *m.* [*ahl-mee-rahn'-teh*] admiral
almohada [*ahl-moh-ah'-dah*] pillow
almohadón *m.* [*ahl-moh-ah-dohn'*] cushion
almuerzo [*ahl-moo-ehr'-thoh*] lunch
alojamiento [*ah-loh-hah-mee-ehn'-toh*] lodging
alquilar *v.* [*ahl-kee-lahr'*] rent
  se alquila una habitación [*seh ahl-kee'-lah oo'-nah
    ah-bee-tah-thee-ohn'*] room for rent
alquiler *m.* [*ahl-kee-lehr'*] rent
alrededor *adv.* [*ahl-reh-deh-dohr'*] around
alrededores *m. pl.* [*ahl-reh-deh-doh'-rehs*] surroundings
altar *m.* [*ahl-tahr'*] altar
altavoz *m.* [*ahl-tah-vohth'*] loudspeaker
alterar *v.* [*ahl-teh-rahr'*] alter
altitud *f.* [*ahl-tee-tood'*] altitude
alto [*ahl'-toh*] high, tall, loud
!Alto! [*ahl'-toh*] Halt!
altura [*ahl-too'-rah*] height, altitude
alubias *f. pl.* [*ah-loo'-bee-ahs*] beans
alumno [*ah-loom'-noh*] pupil, student
alza *m.* [*ahl'-thah*] rise
allá, allí [*ah-yah', ah-yee'*] there, over there
  más allá [*mahs ah-yah'*] farther
amabilidad *f.* [*ah-mah-bee-lee-dahd'*] kindness
amable [*ah-mah'-bleh*] kind

amanecer *m.* [*ah-mah-neh-thehr'*] dawn
amante *m.,f.* [*ah-mahn'-teh*] lover
amar *v.* [*ah-mahr'*] love
amargo [*ah-mahr'-goh*] bitter
amarillo [*ah-mah-ree'-yoh*] yellow
ámbar *m.* [*ahm'-bahr*] amber
ambición *f.* [*ahm-bee-thee-ohn'*] ambition
ambicioso [*ahm-bee-thee-oh'-soh*] ambitious
ambiente *m.* [*ahm-bee-ehn'-teh*] environment
   medio ambiente [*meh'-dee-oh ahm-bee-ehn'-teh*]
   environment
ambos [*ahm'-bohs*] both
ambulancia [*ahm-boo-lahn'-thee-ah*] ambulance
amenaza [*ah-meh-nah'-thah*] threat
amenazar *v.* [*ah-meh-nah-thahr'*] threaten
América [*ah-meh'-ree-kah*] America
   Norte América [*nohr'-teh ah-meh'-ree-kah*] North America
   Sudamérica [*sood-ah-meh'-ree-kah*] South America
americano [*ah-meh-ree-kah'-noh*] American
amígdalas *f. pl.* [*ah-meeg'-dah-lahs*] tonsils
amigo [*ah-mee'-goh*] friend
amistad *f.* [*ah-mees-tahd'*] friendship
amo [*ah'-moh*] owner, boss
amonestar *v.* [*ah-moh-nehs-tahr'*] admonish
amontonar *v.* [*ah-mohn-toh-nahr'*] pile up
amor *m.* [*ah-mohr'*] love
amplio [*ahm'-plee-oh*] broad
ampolla [*ahm-poh'-yah*] blister
amueblar *v.* [*ah-moo-eh-blahr'*] furnish
analfabeto [*ah-nahl-fah-beh'-toh*] illiterate
análisis *m.* [*ah-nah'-lee-sees*] analysis
anarquía [*ah-nahr-kee'-ah*] anarchy
anciano [*ahn-thee-ah'-noh*] old man
ancla [*ahn'-klah*] anchor
ancho [*ahn'-choh*] wide, broad
anchura [*ahn-choo'-rah*] width
andar *v.* [*ahn-dahr'*] walk
anécdota [*ah-nehk'-doh-tah*] anecdote

anfitrión *m.* [*ahn-fee-tree-ohn'*] host
ángel *m.* [*ahn'-hehl*] angel
ángulo [*ahn'-goo-loh*] angle
angustia [*ahn-goos'-tee-ah*] anguish
anhelo [*ahn-eh'-loh*] longing
anillo [*ah-nee'-yoh*] ring [circular band]
animado [*ah-nee-mah'-doh*] animated, brisk
animal *m.* [*ah-nee-mahl'*] animal
animar *v.* [*ah-nee-mahr'*] cheer, encourage
ánimo [*ah'-nee-moh*] courage
aniversario [*an-nee-vehr-sah'-ree-oh*] anniversary
anoche [*ah-noh'-cheh*] last night
anochecer *m.* [*ah-noh-cheh-thehr'*] nightfall
anónimo [*ah-noh'-nee-moh*] anonymous
anormal [*ah-nohr-mahl'*] abnormal
ansioso [*ahn-see-oh'-soh*] anxious, eager
ante [*ahn'-teh*] before
   ante todo [*ahn'-teh toh'-doh*] above all
   de antemano [*deh ahn-teh-mah'-noh*] beforehand
antena [*ahn-teh'-nah*] antenna
anteojos *m. pl.* [*ahn-teh-oh'-hohs*] eyeglasses
antepasado [*ahn-teh-pah-sah'-doh*] ancestor
anterior [*ahn-teh-ree-ohr'*] prior, former
antes [*ahn'-tehs*] before
anticipar *v.* [*ahn-tee-thee-pahr'*] anticipate
   por anticipado [*pohr ahn-tee-thee-pah'-doh*] in advance
antídoto [*ahn-tee'-doh-toh*] antidote
antigüedad *f.* [*ahn-tee-goo-eh-dahd'*] antiquity
antiguo [*ahn-tee'-goo-oh*] ancient, old
anual [*ah-noo-ahl'*] annual
anualmente [*ah-noo-ahl-mehn'-teh*] yearly
anulado [*ah-noo-lah'-doh*] void
anunciar *v.* [*ah-noon-thee-ahr'*] advertise, announce
anuncio [*ah-noon'-thee-oh*] announcement, advertisement
añadir *v.* [*ah-nyah-deer'*] add
año [*ah'-nyoh*] year
   el año pasado [*ehl ah'-nyoh pah-sah'-doh*] last year
   el año que viene [*ehl ah'-nyoh keh vee-eh'-neh*] next year

¿Cuántos años tiene usted? [*koo-ahn'-tohs ah'-nyohs tee-eh'-neh oos-tehd'*] How old are you?

apagar *v.* [*ah-pah-gahr'*] turn off (light)

aparador *m.* [*ah-pah-rah-dohr'*] cupboard

aparato [*ah-pah-rah'-toh*] apparatus

aparecer *v. irreg.* [*ah-pah-reh-thehr'*] appear

aparente [*ah-pah-rehn'-teh*] apparent

aparentemente [*ah-pah-rehn-teh-mehn'-teh*] apparently

apariencia [*ah-pah-ree-ehn'-thee-ah*] look, appearance

apartamento [*ah-pahr-tah-mehn'-toh*] apartment

apartar *v.* [*ah-pahr-tahr'*] remove, set apart

aparte [*ah-pahr'-teh*] apart

apasionado [*ah-pah-see-oh-nah'-doh*] passionate

apellido [*ah-peh-yee'-doh*] last name

apenas [*ah-peh'-nahs*] hardly

apendicitis *m.* [*ah-pehn-dee-thee'-tees*] appendicitis

aperitivo [*ah-peh-ree-tee'-voh*] appetizer

apertura [*ah-pehr-too'-rah*] opening

apetito [*ah-peh-tee'-toh*] appetite

aplastar *v.* [*ah-plahs-tahr'*] crush, smash

aplaudir *v.* [*ah-plah-oo-deer'*] applaud

aplauso [*ah-plah'-oo-soh*] applause

aplazar *v.* [*ah-plah-thahr'*] postpone

aplicar *v.* [*ah-plee-kahr'*] apply

apoderarse *v.* [*ah-poh-deh-rahr'-seh*] seize

apodo [*ah-poh'-doh*] nickname

apostar *v. irreg.* [*ah-pohs-tahr'*] bet

apoyarse *v.* [*ah-poh-yahr'-seh*] lean

apreciar *v.* [*ah-preh-thee-ahr'*] appreciate

aprender *v.* [*ah-prehn-dehr'*] learn

aprendiz *m.* [*ah-prehn-deeth'*] apprentice

aprendizaje *m.* [*ah-prehn-dee-thah'-heh*] learning

apresurarse *v.* [*ah-preh-soo-rahr'-seh*] rush, hurry

apretado [*ah-preh-tah'-doh*] tight

apretar *v. irreg.* [*ah-preh-tahr'*] tighten, press

aprisa [*ah-pree'-sah*] fast, swiftly

aprobación *f.* [*ah-proh-bah-thee-ohn'*] approval

aprobar *v. irreg.* [*ah-proh-bahr'*] approve

apropiado [*ah-proh-pee-ah'-doh*] appropriate

  apropiado para [*ah-proh-pee-ah'-doh pah'-rah*] fit for

apropiarse *v.* [*ah-proh-pee-ahr'-seh*] take possession of

aprovechar *v.* [*ah-proh-veh-chahr'*] profit

  approvechar la oportunidad [*ah-proh-veh-chahr' lah oh-pohr-too-nee-dahd'*] take the opportunity

  approvecharse de [*ah-proh-veh-chahr'-seh deh*] take advantage of

aproximadamente [*ah-prohk-see-mah-dah-mehn'-teh*] approximately

apuesta [*ah-poo-ehs'-tah*] bet

apuntar *v.* [*ah-poon-tahr'*] aim, point at, sketch

apuñalar *v.* [*ah-poo-nyah-lahr'*] stab

aquel *m.*, **aquella** *f.* [*ah-kehl', ah-keh'-yah*] that

aquellos *m.*, **aquellas** *f.* [*ah-keh'-yohs, ah-keh'-yahs*] those

aquí [*ah-kee'*] here

  Aquí está [*ah-kee' ehs-tah'*] Here it is

árabe [*ah'-rah-beh*] Arab

araña [*ah-rah'-nyah*] spider

arar *v.* [*uh-rahr'*] plow

arbitrario [*ahr-bee-trah'-ree-oh*] arbitrary

árbitro [*ahr'- bee-troh*] referee

árbol *m.* [*ahr'-bohl*] tree

arbusto [*ahr-boos'-toh*] bush

arco [*ahr'-koh*] bow, arc

arco iris [*ahr'-koh ee'-rees*] rainbow

archivo [*ahr-chee'-voh*] file

arder *v.* [*ahr-dehr'*] burn

ardid *m.* [*ahr-deed'*] device, trick

área [*ah'-reh-ah*] area

arena [*ah-reh'-nah*] sand

Argentina [*ahr-hehn-tee'-nah*] Argentina

argentino [*ahr-hehn-tee'-noh*] Argentine, Argentinian

argüir *v. irreg.* [*ahr-goo-eer'*] argue

árido [*ah'-ree-doh*] arid

aristócrata *m., f.* [*ah-rees-toh'-krah-tah*] aristocrat

aristocrático [*ah-rees-toh-krah'-tee-koh*] aristocratic

arma [*ahr'-mah*] weapon, arm

armar *v.* [*ahr-mahr'*] arm

armario [*ahr-mah'-ree-oh*] wardrobe

armazón *m.* [*ahr-mah-thohn'*] frame

arpa [*ahr'-pah*] harp

arquitecto [*ahr-kee-tehk'-toh*] architect

arquitectura [*ahr-kee-tehk-too'-rah*] architecture

arrancar *v.* [*ah-rrahn-kahr'*] pull out, start

   mecanismo de arranque [*meh-kah-nees'-moh deh ah-rrahn'-keh*] starter

arrastrar *v.* [*ah-rrahs-trahr'*] drag

arreglar *v.* [*ah-rreh-glahr'*] fix, settle

arrendar *v. irreg.* [*ah-rrehn-dahr'*] rent

arrepentido [*ah-rreh-pehn-tee'-doh*] sorry

arrestar *v.* [*ah-rrehs-tahr'*] arrest

arresto [*ah-rrehs'-toh*] arrest

arriba [*ah-rree'-bah*] above, upstairs

   de arriba abajo [*deh ah-rree'-bah ah-bah'-hoh*] from top to bottom

arriendo, arrendamiento [*ah-rree-ehn'-doh, ah-rrehn-dah-mee-ehn'-toh*] rent, lease

arriesgar *v.* [*ah-rree-ehs-gahr'*] risk

arrodillarse *v.* [*ah-rroh-dee-yahr'-seh*] kneel

arrogancia [*ah-rroh-gahn'-thee-ah*] arrogance

arrojar *v.* [*ah-rroh-hahr'*] throw

arroyo [*ah-rroh'-yoh*] stream

arroz *m.* [*ah-rrohth'*] rice

arruga [*ah-rroo'-gah*] wrinkle

arrugar *v.* [*ah-rroo-gahr'*] wrinkle

arte *m., f.* [*ahr'-teh*] art

arteria [*ahr-teh'-ree-ah*] artery

artesano [*ahr-teh-sah'-noh*] craftsman

artículo [*ahr-tee'-koo-loh*] article, item

artificial [*ahr-tee-fee-thee-ahl'*] artificial

artista *m, f.* [*ahr-tees'-tah*] artist

artístico [*ahr-tees'-tee-koh*] artistic

asado [*ah-sah'-doh*] roasted

   poco asado [*poh'-koh ah-sah'doh*] rare

asaltar *v.* [*ah-sahl-tahr'*] assault

asamblea [*ah-sahm-bleh'-ah*] assembly
asar *v.* [*ah-sahr'*] roast
  asar a la parrilla [*ah-sahr' ah lah pah-rree'-yah*] broil
ascender *v. irreg.* [*ahs-thehn-dehr'*] rise
  ascender a [*ahs-thehn-dehr' ah*] amount to
ascenso [*ahs-thehn'-soh*] promotion, ascent
ascensor *m.* [*ahs-thehn-sohr'*] elevator
asegurar *v.* [*ah-seh-goo-rahr'*] make sure, assure, insure
aseo [*ah-seh'-oh*] cleaning
asesinar *v.* [*ah-seh-see-nahr'*] murder
asesino [*ah-seh-see'-noh*] murderer
así [*ah-see'*] thus, like this
  así así [*ah-see' ah-see'*] so-so
  así sucesivamente [*ah-see' soo-theh-see-vah-mehn'-teh*] so forth
Asia [*ah'-see-ah*] Asia
asiento [*ah-see-ehn'-toh*] seat
  Tome asiento [*toh'-meh ah-see-ehn'-toh*] Have a seat
asignación *f.* [*ah-seeg-nah-thee-ohn'*] assignment, salary
asignar *v.* [*ah-seeg-nahr'*] assign
asistencia [*ah-sees-tehn'-thee-ah*] assistance, attendance
asistente *m.,f.* [*ah-sees-tehn'-teh*] attendant, assistant
asistir *v.* [*ah-sees-teer'*] assist, attend
asociado [*ah-soh-thee-ah'-doh*] associate
asociar *v.* [*ah-soh-thee-ahr'*] associate
asomarse *v.* [*ah-soh-mahr'-seh*] look out
asombrar *v.* [*ah-sohm-brahr'*] astonish
asombroso [*ah-sohm-broh'-soh*] astonishing
áspero [*ahs'-peh-roh*] rough, harsh
aspiración *f.* [*ahs-pee-rah-thee-ohn'*] aspiration
aspiradora [*ahs-pee-rah-doh'-rah*] vacuum cleaner
aspirar *v.* [*ahs-pee-rahr'*] aspire
aspirina [*ahs-pee-ree'-nah*] aspirin
astronomía [*ahs-troh-noh-mee'-ah*] astronomy
astuto [*ahs-too'-toh*] cunning
asumir *v.* [*ah-soo-meer'*] assume
asunto [*ah-soon'-toh*] subject matter, topic
asustado [*ah-soos-tah'-doh*] afraid

asustar *v.* [*ah-soos-tahr'*] frighten, scare
atacar *v.* [*ah-tah-kahr'*] attack
ataque *m.* [*ah-tah'-keh*] attack
atar *v.* [*ah-tahr'*] tie, bind, fasten
atavío [*ah-tah-vee'-oh*] attire
atención *f.* [*ah-tehn-thee-ohn'*] attention
atender *v. irreg.* [*ah-tehn-dehr'*] pay attention, attend to
atento [*ah-tehn'-toh*] thoughtful
aterrizaje *m.* [*ah-teh-rree-thah'-heh*] landing
aterrizar *v.* [*ah-teh-rree-thahr'*] land
aterrorizar *v.* [*ah-teh-rroh-ree-thahr'*] terrify
atestado [*ah-tehs-tah'-doh*] crowded
atestiguar *v.* [*ah-tehs-tee-goo-ahr'*] testify
ático [*ah'-tee-koh*] attic
Atlántico [*aht-lahn'-tee-koh*] Atlantic
atletismo [*aht-leh-tees'-moh*] athletics
atmósfera [*aht-mohs'-feh-rah*] atmosphere
atracar *v.* [*ah-trah-kahr'*] dock, land, assault
atracción *f.* [*ah-trahk-thee-ohn'*] attraction
atractivo [*ah-trahk-tee'-voh*] attractive
atraer *v. irreg.* [*ah-trah-ehr'*] attract, appeal
atrapar *v.* [*ah-trah-pahr'*] trap
atrás *adv.* [*ah-trahs'*] back
atrasado [*ah-trah-sah'-doh*] late, backward, behind
atravesar *v. irreg.* [*ah-trah-veh-sahr'*] cross
atrever *v.* [*ah-treh-vehr'*] dare, risk
atrevido [*ah-treh-vee'-doh*] daring
atropellar *v.* [*ah-troh-peh-yahr'*] run over
audaz [*ah-oo-dahth'*] bold
audiencia [*ah-oo-dee-ehn'-thee-ah*] audience
aula [*ah'-oo-lah*] classroom
aumentar *v.* [*ah-oo-mehn-tahr'*] increase
aumento [*ah-oo-mehn'-toh*] increase
aun [*ah-oon'*] even, still, yet
  aun así [*ah-oon' ah-see'*] even so
  aun cuando [*ah-oon' koo-ahn'-doh*] even though
  aun si [*ah-oon' see*] even if
aunque [*ah-oon'-keh*] although

ausencia [*ah-oo-sehn'-thee-ah*] absence
ausente [*ah-oo-sehn'-teh*] absent, missing
austero [*ah-oos-teh'-roh*] stern, austere
Australia [*ah-oos-trah'-lee-ah*] Australia
australiano [*ah-oos-trah-lee-ah'-noh*] Australian
Austria [*ah-oos'-tree-ah*] Austria
austríaco [*ah-oos-tree'-ah-koh*] Austrian
auténtico [*ah-oo-tehn'-tee-koh*] authentic
autobús *m.* [*ah-oo-toh-boos'*] bus
automático [*ah-oo-toh-mah'-tee-koh*] automatic
automóvil *m.* [*ah-oo-toh-moh'-veel*] automobile
autor [*ah-oo-tohr'*] author
autoridad *f.* [*ah-oo-toh-ree-dahd'*] authority
autorización *f.* [*ah-oo-toh-ree-thah-thee-ohn'*] permit
autorizar *v.* [*ah-oo-toh-ree-thahr'*] authorize
auxiliar *v.* [*ah-ook-see-lee-ahr'*] aid, help
auxilio [*ah-ook-see'-lee-oh*] help, aid
  primeros auxilios [*pree-meh'-rohs ah-ook-see'-lee-ohs*]
    first aid
avalancha [*ah-vah-lahn'-chah*] avalanche
avance *m.* [*ah-vahn'-theh*] advance
avanzar *v.* [*ah-vahn-thahr'*] advance, come forward
avenida [*ah-veh-nee'-dah*] avenue
aventura [*ah-vehn-too'-rah*] adventure
avergonzado [*ah-vehr-gohn-thah'-doh*] ashamed
avión *m.* [*ah-vee-ohn'*] airplane
  por avión [*pohr ah-vee-ohn'*] air mail, by plane
aviso [*ah-vee'-soh*] notice, warning
avispa [*ah-vees'-pah*] wasp
ayer [*ah-yehr'*] yesterday
  anteayer [*ahn-teh-ah-yehr'*] the day before yesterday
ayuda [*ah-yoo'-dah*] aid, help
ayudante *m., f.* [*ah-yoo-dahn'-teh*] assistant
ayudar *v.* [*ah-yoo-dahr'*] help
ayunar *v.* [*ah-yoo-nahr'*] fast
ayuntamiento [*ah-yoon-tah-mee-ehn'-toh*] city hall
azafata [*ah-thah-fah'-tah*] stewardess
azar *m.* [*ah-thahr'*] chance, random

azteca *m., f.* [*ahth-teh'-kah*] Aztec
azúcar *m.* [*ah-thoo'-kahr*] sugar
azucarero [*ah-thoo-kah-reh'-roh*] sugarbowl
azul [*ah-thool'*] blue

B

bachiller *m., f.* [*bah-chee-yehr'*] bachelor
bahía [*bah-ee'-ah*] bay
bailar *v.* [*bah-ee-lahr'*] dance
bailarín *m.* [*bah-ee-lah-reen'*] dancer
baile *m.* [*bah'-ee-leh*] dance
bajada [*bah-hah'-dah*] descent, slope
bajar *v.* [*bah-hahr'*] come down, go down
bajarse *v.* [*bah-hahr'-seh*] get off
bajo [*bah'-hoh*] short, low
balance *m.* [*bah-lahn'-theh*] balance
balcón *m.* [*bahl-kohn'*] balcony
baldosa [*bahl-doh'-sah*] floor tile
ballena [*bah-yeh'-nah*] whale
ballet *m.* [*bah-leht'*] ballet
banco [*bahn'-koh*] bank, bench
banda [*bahn'-dah*] band, ribbon
bandeja [*bahn-deh'-hah*] tray
bandera [*bahn-deh'-rah*] flag
banquete *m.* [*bahn-keh'-teh*] banquet
bañador *m.* [*bah-nyah-dohr'*] swimming suit
bañar *v.* [*bah-nyahr'*] bathe
bañarse *v.* [*bah-nyahr'-seh*] take a bath
bañera [*bah-nyeh'-rah*] bathtub
baño [*bah'-nyoh*] bath
bar *m.* [*bahr*] bar, taproom
barato [*bah-rah'-toh*] cheap, inexpensive
barba [*bahr'-bah*] beard
barbero [*bahr-beh'-roh*] barber

barca [*bahr'-kah*] boat, launch
  barca de pasaje [*bahr'-kah deh pah-sah'-heh*] ferryboat
barco [*bahr'-koh*] ship, boat
  barco de guerra [*bahr'-koh deh gheh'-rrah*] warship
  barco de vela [*bahr'koh deh veh'-lah*] sailboat
barra [*bah'-rrah*] bar, rod
barrer *v.* [*bah-rrehr'*] sweep
barricada [*bah-rree-kah'-dah*] barricade
barril *m.* [*bah-rreel'*] barrel
barro [*bah'-rroh*] mud
base *f.* [*bah'-seh*] base, basis
básico [*bah'-see-koh*] basic
bastante [*bahs-tahn'-teh*] enough
bastar *v.* [*bahs-tahr'*] be enough
  ¡Basta! [*bahs'-tah*] That's enough!
bastón *m.* [*bahs-tohn'*] cane
basura [*bah-soo'-rah*] garbage
bata [*bah'-tah*] housecoat
batalla [*bah-tah'-yah*] battle
batería [*bah-teh-ree'-ah*] battery
batir *v.* [*bah-teer'*] beat
baúl *m.* [*bah-ool'*] trunk [container]
bautismo [*bah-oo-tees'-moh*] baptism
bayeta [*bah-yeh'-tah*] flannel
beber *v.* [*beh-behr'*] drink
bebida [*beh-bee'-dah*] drink
beca [*beh'-kah*] scholarship
belga *m., f.* [*behl'-gah*] Belgian
Bélgica [*behl'-hee-kah*] Belgium
belleza [*beh-yeh'-thah*] beauty
bello [*beh'-yoh*] beautiful
bendecir *v. irreg.* [*behn-deh-theer'*] bless
bendición *f.* [*behn-dee-thee-ohn'*] blessing
beneficio [*beh-neh-fee'-thee-oh*] profit
besar *v.* [*beh-sahr'*] kiss
beso [*beh'-soh*] kiss
bestia [*behs'-tee-ah*] beast
Biblia [*bee'-blee-ah*] Bible

biblioteca [*bee-blee-oh-teh'-kah*] library
bicho [*bee'-choh*] bug
bicicleta [*bee-thee-kleh'-tah*] bicycle
bien [*bee-ehn'*] well
  más bien [*mahs bee-ehn'*] rather
bienes *m. pl.* [*bee-eh'-nehs*] estate
  bienes inmuebles [*bee-eh'-nehs een-moo-eh'-blehs*] real estate
bienvenido [*bee-ehn-veh-nee'-doh*] welcome
bigote *m.* [*bee-goh'-teh*] mustache
billete *m.* [*bee-yeh'-teh*] ticket, bill
  billete de ida y vuelta [*bee-yeh'-teh deh ee'-dah ee voo-ehl'-tah*] round trip ticket
bizcocho [*beeth-koh'-choh*] biscuit
blanco [*blahn'-koh*] white
blando [*blahn'-doh*] smooth, soft
blanquear *v.* [*blahn-keh-ahr'*] bleach
blusa [*bloo'-sah*] blouse
boca [*boh'-kah*] mouth
bocadillo [*boh-kah-dee'-yoh*] sandwich
boceto [*boh-theh'-toh*] sketch
bocina [*boh-thee'-nah*] horn [sounding device]
boda [*boh'-dah*] wedding
bodega [*boh-deh'-gah*] cellar
bofetada [*boh-feh-tah'-dah*] slap
bola [*boh'-lah*] ball
boletín *m.* [*boh-leh-teen'*] bulletin
boleto [*boh-leh'-toh*] ticket
Bolivia [*boh-lee'-vee-ah*] Bolivia
boliviano [*boh-lee-vee-ah'-noh*] Bolivian
bolsa [*bohl'-sah*] bag
  bolsa de mano [*bohl'-sah deh mah'-noh*] handbag
bolsillo [*bohl-see'-yoh*] pocket
bolso [*bohl'-soh*] purse
bomba [*bohm'-bah*] bomb, pump
bombero [*bohm-beh'-roh*] fireman
bombilla [*bohm-bee'-yah*] bulb
bondad *f.* [*bohn-dahd'*] kindness, goodness
bonito [*boh-nee'-toh*] pretty

bono [*boh'-noh*] bond
bordado [*bohr-dah'-doh*] embroidery
borde *m.* [*bohr'-deh*] border
borracho [*boh-rrah'-choh*] drunk
borrador *m.* [*boh-rrah-dohr'*] eraser
borrar *v.* [*boh-rrahr'*] erase
bosque *m.* [*bohs'-keh*] woods
bostezar *v.* [*bohs-teh-thahr'*] yawn
bota [*boh'-tah*] boot
botella [*boh-teh'-yah*] bottle
botón *m.* [*boh-tohn'*] button
botones *m. sing.* [*boh-toh'-nehs*] bellboy
bóveda [*boh'-veh-dah*] vault [arched roof]
boxeo [*bohk-seh'-oh*] boxing
Brasil *m.* [*brah-seel'*] Brazil
brasileño [*brah-see-leh'-nyoh*] Brazilian
bravo [*brah'-voh*] brave
brazalete *m.* [*brah-thah-leh'-teh*] bracelet
brazo [*brah'-thoh*] arm
breve [*breh'-veh*] brief, short
brillante [*bree-yahn'-teh*] bright, brilliant
brillar *v.* [*bree-yahr'*] shine
brindar *v.* [*breen-dahr'*] toast [compliment]
brisa [*bree'-sah*] breeze
británico [*bree-tah'-nee-koh*] British
broche *m.* [*broh'-cheh*] brooch
broma [*broh'-mah*] jest, joke
bromear *v.* [*broh-meh-ahr'*] joke, kid
bronce *m.* [*brohn'-theh*] bronze
bronceado [*brohn-theh-ah'-doh*] tan
brote *m.* [*broh'-teh*] blossom
bruja [*broo'-hah*] witch
brújula [*broo'-hoo-lah*] compass [instrument]
bruma [*broo'-mah*] fog
brumoso [*broo-moh'-soh*] foggy
brusco [*broos'-koh*] rough
brutalidad *f.* [*broo-tah-lee-dahd'*] brutality
bueno [*boo-eh'-noh*] good

buenos días [*boo-eh'-nohs dee'-ahs*] good morning
buenas noches [*boo-eh'-nahs noh'-chehs*] good evening, good night
buena suerte [*boo-eh'-nah soo-ehr'-teh*] good luck
buenas tardes [*boo-eh'-nahs tahr'-dehs*] good afternoon, good evening
de buen parecer [*deh boo-ehn' pah-reh-thehr'*] clean-cut
bufanda [*boo-fahn'-dah*] scarf
bulto [*bool'-toh*] bulk, lump
burlarse *v.* [*boor-lahr'-seh*] make fun, ridicule
burro [*boo'-rroh*] donkey
buscar *v.* [*boos-kahr'*] look for, search
buscar a tientas [*boos-kahr' ah tee-ehn'-tahs*] fumble
búsqueda [*boos'-keh-dah*] search
buzón *m.* [*boo-thohn'*] letter box, mailbox

C

caballero [*kah-bah-yeh'-roh*] gentleman
caballero andante [*kah-bah-yeh'-roh ahn-dahn'-teh*] knight
caballo [*kah-bah'-yoh*] horse
cabaret *m.* [*kah-bah-reht'*] nightclub
cabello [*kah-beh'-yoh*] hair
tónico para el cabello [*toh'-nee-koh pah'-rah ehl kah-beh'-yoh*] hair tonic
caber *v. irreg.* [*kah-behr'*] fit into, have room
cabeza [*kah-beh'-thah*] head
dolor *m.* **de cabeza** [*doh-lohr' deh kah-beh'-thah*] headache
cabida [*kah-bee'-dah*] room, space
cabina [*kah-bee'-nah*] cabin
cable *m.* [*kah'-bleh*] cable [wire]
cabo [*kah'-boh*] cape
cacahuete *m.* [*kah-kah-oo-eh'-teh*] peanut
cacao [*kah-kah'-oh*] cocoa
cada [*kah'-dah*] each, every

cada uno [*kah'-dah oo'-noh*] each one
cadena [*kah-deh'-nah*] chain
cadera [*kah-deh'-rah*] hip
caer *v. irreg.* [*kah-ehr'*] fall (down)
café *m.* [*kah-feh'*] coffee, café
  granizada de café [*grah-nee-thah'-dah deh kah-feh'*]
    iced coffee
caída [*kah-ee'-dah*] fall
  caída de la tarde [*kah-ee'-dah deh lah tahr'-deh*] dusk
caja [*kah'-hah*] box, case
cajero [*kah-heh'-roh*] cashier
cajón *m.* [*kah-hohn'*] drawer
calabaza [*kah-lah-bah'-thah*] pumpkin
calabozo [*kah-lah-boh'-thoh*] dungeon
calavera [*kah-lah-veh'-rah*] skull
calcetín *m.* [*kahl-theh-teen'*] sock
cálculo [*kahl'-koo-loh*] calculus, calculation
caldo [*kahl'-doh*] broth
calefacción *f.* [*kah-leh-fahk-thee-ohn'*] heating
calendario [*kah-lehn-dah'-ree-oh*] calendar
calentar *v. irreg.* [*kah-lehn-tahr'*] warm (up), heat
calidad *f.* [*kah-lee-dahd'*] quality
caliente [*kah-lee-ehn'-teh*] hot
calificación *f.* [*kah-lee-fee-kah-thee-ohn'*] qualification, grade
calma [*kahl'-mah*] calm
calor *m.* [*kah-lohr'*] heat
calumnia [*kah-loom'-nee-ah*] slander
calvo [*kahl'-voh*] bald
calzarse *v. irreg.* [*kahl-thahr'-seh*] put on shoes
callado [*kah-yah'-doh*] quiet
callar *v.* [*kah-yahr'*] be silent, keep silent
  ¡Cállese! [*kah'yeh-seh*] Keep quiet!
calle *f.* [*kah'-yeh*] street
  calle de una sola dirección [*kah'-yeh deh oo'-nah soh'-la*
    dee-rehk-thee-ohn'] one-way street
callejón *m.* [*kah-yeh-hohn'*] alley
cama [*kah'-mah*] bed
  camita de niño [*kah-mee'-tah deh nee'-nyoh*] crib

cámara [*kah'-mah-rah*] camera, chamber
camarera [*kah-mah-reh'-rah*] waitress
camarero [*kah-mah-reh'-roh*] waiter
camarón *m.* [*kah-mah-rohn'*] shrimp
camarote *m.* [*kah-mah-roh'-teh*] stateroom
cambiar *v.* [*kahm-bee-ahr'*] change, exchange, shift
cambio [*kahm'-bee-oh*] change, exchange
  a cambio de [*ah kahm'-bee-oh deh*] in exchange for
caminar *v.* [*kah-mee-nahr'*] walk
camino [*kah-mee'-noh*] way, road
camión *m.* [*kah-mee-ohn'*] truck, lorry
camisa [*kah-mee'-sah*] shirt
camisón *m.* [*kah-mee-sohn'*] nightgown
campamento [*kahm-pah-mehn'-toh*] camp
campana [*kahm-pah'-nah*] bell
campeón *m.* [*kahm-peh-ohn'*] champion
campesino [*kahm-peh-see'-noh*] country man, peasant
campo [*kahm'-poh*] field, country
Canadá *m.* [*kah-nah-dah'*] Canada
canadiense [*kah-nah-dee-ehn'-seh*] Canadian
canal *m.* [*kah-nahl'*] canal, channel
canasta [*kah-nahs'-tah*] basket
cancelar *v.* [*kahn-theh-lahr'*] cancel
cancha [*kahn'-chah*] court [sports area]
canción *f.* [*kahn-thee-ohn'*] song
candidato [*kahn-dee-dah'-toh*] candidate
cangrejo [*kahn-greh'-hoh*] crab
cansado [*kahn-sah'-doh*] tired
cantante *m., f.* [*kahn-tahn'-teh*] singer
cantar *v.* [*kahn-tahr'*] sing
cantidad *f.* [*kahn-tee-dahd'*] quantity, amount
caña [*kah'-nyah*] cane
caoba [*kah-oh'-bah*] mahogany
capa [*kah'-pah*] cape
capacidad *f.* [*kah-pah-thee-dahd'*] ability, capacity
capaz [*kah-pahth'*] able, capable
capital *m.* [*kah-pee-tahl'*] capital [money]
capital *f.* [*kah-pee-tahl'*] capital [city]

capitán *m.* [*kah-pee-tahn'*] captain
capítulo [*kah-pee'-too-loh*] chapter
capricho [*kah-pree'-choh*] caprice
cara [*kah'-rah*] face
caracol *m.* [*kah-rah-kohl'*] snail
carácter *m.* [*kah-rahk'-tehr*] character
característico [*kah-rahk-teh-rees'-tee-koh*] characteristic
carbón *m.* [*kahr-bohn'*] coal
cárcel *f.* [*kahr'-thehl*] jail
carecer *v. irreg.* [*kah-reh-thehr'*] lack
carente [*kah-rehn'-teh*] lacking
carga [*kahr'-gah*] cargo, burden, load
cargar *v.* [*kahr-gahr'*] load
cargo [*kahr'-goh*] position
caricia [*kah-ree'-thee-ah*] caress
cariñosamente [*kah-ree-nyoh-sah-mehn'-teh*] dearly
carnaval *m.* [*kahr-nah-vahl'*] carnival
carne *f.* [*kahr'-neh*] meat, flesh
   carne de vaca [*kahr'-neh deh vah'-kah*] beef
carnicero [*kahr-nee-theh'-roh*] butcher
caro [*kah'-roh*] expensive
carpintero [*kahr-peen-teh'-roh*] carpenter
carrera [*kah-rreh'-rah*] career, race
   carrera de caballos [*kah-rreh'-rah deh kah-bah'-yohs*]
     horse race
carreta [*kah-rreh'-tah*] wagon
carrete *m.* [*kah-rreh'-teh*] reel
carretera [*kah-rreh-teh'-rah*] highway, road
carruaje *m.* [*kah-rroo-ah'-heh*] carriage
carta [*kahr'-tah*] letter [missive]
   carta certificada [*kahr'-tah thehr-tee-fee-kah'-dah*]
     registered letter
   carta de presentación [*kahr'-tah deh preh-sehn-tah-thee-ohn'*] letter of introduction
cartel *m.* [*kahr-tehl'*] poster
cartera [*kahr-teh'-rah*] pocketbook, portfolio
carterista *m., f.* [*kahr-teh-rees'-tah*] pickpocket
cartero [*kahr-teh'-roh*] mailman

cartón *m.* [*kahr-tohn'*] carton
casa [*kah'-sah*] house, home
  casa de campo [*kah'-sah deh kahm'-poh*] cottage
  casa de empeños [*kah'-sah deh ehm-peh'-nyohs*] pawnshop
  en casa [*ehn kah'-sah*] at home
  Está en su casa [*ehs-tah' ehn soo kah'-sah*] Make
    yourself at home
  estar *v.* **en casa** [*ehs-tahr' ehn kah'-sah*] be at home, be in
casarse *v.* [*kah-sahr'-seh*] get married
cascada [*kahs-kah'-dah*] waterfall
cáscara [*kahs'-kah-rah*] shell
casera [*kah-seh'-rah*] housekeeper
casi [*kah'-see*] almost
caso [*kah'-soh*] case, matter
  en caso de urgencia (emergencia) [*ehn kah'-soh deh
    oor-hehn'-thee-ah (eh-mehr-hehn'-thee-ah)*] in case of
    emergency
  en ese caso [*ehn eh'-seh kah'-soh*] in that case
  en todo caso [*ehn toh'-doh kah'-soh*] in any case
caspa [*kahs'-pah*] dandruff
castaño [*kahs-tah'-nyoh*] brown
castigar *v.* [*kahs-tee-gahr'*] punish
castigo [*kahs-tee'-goh*] punishment
castillo [*kahs-tee'-yoh*] castle
casualidad *f.* [*kah-soo-ah-lee-dahd'*] chance
  por casualidad [*pohr kah-soo-ah-lee-dahd'*] by chance
catálogo [*kah-tah'-loh-goh*] catalog
catarro [*kah-tah'-rroh*] cold
catedral *f.* [*kah-teh-drahl'*] cathedral
categoria [*kah-teh-goh-ree'-ah*] category
católico *n. & adj.* [*kah-toh'-lee-koh*] Catholic
catorce [*kah-tohr'-theh*] fourteen
catre *m.* [*kah'-treh*] cot
causa [*kah'-oo-sah*] cause
  a causa de [*ah kah'-oo-sah deh*] because of
causar *v.* [*kah-oo-sahr'*] cause
cavar *v.* [*kah-vahr'*] dig
cavidad *f.* [*kah-vee-dahd'*] cavity

cazador *m*. [*kah-thah-dohr'*] hunter
cazar *v*. [*kah-thahr'*] hunt, chase
cazuela [*kah-thoo-eh'-lah*] pan
cebo [*theh'-boh*] bait, lure
cebolla [*theh-boh'-yah*] onion
ceder *v*. [*theh-dehr'*] yield, give in
ceguera [*theh-gheh'-rah*] blindness
ceja [*theh'-hah*] eyebrow
celda [*thehl'-dah*] cell [prison, small room]
celebración *f*. [*theh-leh-brah-thee-ohn'*] celebration
celebrar *v*. [*theh-leh-brahr'*] celebrate
célebre [*theh'-leh-breh*] famous
celoso [*theh-loh'-soh*] jealous
cementerio [*theh-mehn-teh'-ree-oh*] cemetery
cemento [*theh-mehn'-toh*] cement, concrete
cena [*theh'-nah*] supper
cenicero [*theh-nee-theh'-roh*] ashtray
ceniza [*theh-nee'-thah*] ash
censura [*thehn-soo'-rah*] censorship
centavo [*thehn-tah'-voh*] cent
centenario [*thehn-teh-nah'-ree-oh*] centennial
centro [*thehn'-troh*] center
ceñir *v. irre*g. [*theh-nyeer'*] girdle, tighten
cepillar *v*. [*theh-pee-yahr'*] brush
cepillo [*theh-pee'-yoh*] brush
cera [*theh'-rah*] wax
cerámica [*theh-rah'-mee-kah*] pottery
cerca *n*. [*thehr'-kah*] fence, enclosure
cerca *adv*. [*thehr'-kah*] near, close
cercado [*thehr-kah'-doh*] yard, enclosure
cercano [*thehr-kah'-noh*] nearby
cercar *v*. [*thehr-kahr'*] circle
cerdo [*thehr'-doh*] pig, pork
cerebro [*theh-reh'-broh*] brain
ceremonia [*theh-reh-moh'-nee-ah*] ceremony
cereza [*theh-reh'-thah*] cherry
cerilla [*theh-ree'-yah*] match
cero [*theh'-roh*] zero

cerrado [*theh-rrah'-doh*] closed, locked, shut
cerradura [*theh-rrah-doo'-rah*] lock
cerrar *v. irreg.* [*theh-rrahr'*] close
cerrojo [*theh-rroh'-hoh*] bolt
certificado [*thehr-tee-fee-kah'-doh*] certificate
cerveza [*thehr-veh'-thah*] beer
cesar *v.* [*theh-sahr'*] cease
césped *m.* [*thehs'-pehd*] lawn
cesta [*thehs'-tah*] basket
cicatriz *f.* [*thee-kah-treeth'*] scar
ciego [*thee-eh'-goh*] blind
cielo [*thee-eh'-loh*] heaven, sky
cien, ciento [*thee-ehn', thee-ehn'-toh*] one hundred
  por ciento [*pohr thee-ehn'-toh*] per cent
ciencia [*thee-ehn'-thee-ah*] science
científico [*thee-ehn-tee'-fee-koh*] scientist
ciertamente [*thee-ehr-tah-mehn'-teh*] certainly
cierto [*thee-ehr'-toh*] certain
  hasta cierto punto [*ahs'-tah thee-ehr'-toh poon'-toh*]
    to a certain extent
cifra [*thee'-frah*] cipher, numeral
cigarrillo [*thee-gah-rree'-yoh*] cigarette
cigarro [*thee-gah'-rroh*] cigar
cigüeña [*thee-goo-eh'-nyah*] stork
cilindro [*thee-leen'-droh*] cylinder
cima [*thee'-mah*] summit, peak
cinco [*theen'-koh*] five
cincuenta [*theen-koo-ehn'-tah*] fifty
cine *m.* [*thee'-neh*] movies
cinta [*theen'-tah*] ribbon, tape
cintura [*theen-too'-rah*] waist
cinturón *m.* [*theen-too-rohn'*] belt
circo [*theer'-koh*] circus
circulación *f.* [*theer-koo-lah-thee-ohn'*] circulation
círculo [*theer'-koo-loh*] circle
circunstancia [*theer-koons-tahn'-thee-ah*] circumstance
ciruela [*thee-roo-eh'-lah*] prune, plum
cirujano [*thee-roo-hah'-noh*] surgeon

cita [*thee'-tah*] appointment, date

citación *f.* [*thee-tah-thee-ohn'*] summons

citar *v.* [*thee-tahr'*] make a date/appointment, quote

ciudad *f.* [*thee-oo-dahd'*] city, town

ciudadanía [*thee-oo-dah-dah-nee'-ah*] citizenship

ciudadano [*thee-oo-dah-dah'-noh*] citizen

cívico [*thee'-vee-koh*] civic

civilización *f.* [*thee-vee-lee-thah-thee-ohn'*] civilization

claro [*klah'-roh*] clear, light

   ¡Claro que sí! [*klah'-roh keh see'*] Yes indeed!

clase *f.* [*klah'-seh*] class, classroom, kind

clásico [*klah'-see-koh*] classic

clasificar *v.* [*klah-see-fee-kahr'*] classify

clavar *v.* [*klah-vahr'*] nail

clave *f.* [*klah'-veh*] key

clavo [*klah'-voh*] nail [carpenter's]

clero [*kleh'-roh*] clergy

cliente *m.* [*klee-ehn'-teh*] customer, client

clima *m.* [*klee'-mah*] climate

clínica [*klee'-nee-kah*] clinic

cobarde *m., f.* [*koh-bahr'-deh*] coward

cobrar *v.* [*koh-brahr'*] cash, collect

cobre *m.* [*koh'-breh*] copper

cocer *v. irreg.* [*koh-thehr'*] cook, boil

cocina [*koh-thee'-nah*] kitchen

cocinar *v.* [*koh-thee-nahr'*] cook

   cocinar al horno [*koh-thee-nahr' ahl ohr'-noh*] bake

cocinero [*koh-thee-neh'-roh*] cook

coco [*koh'-koh*] coconut

coche *m.* [*koh'-cheh*] car, coach

   coche dormitorio [*koh'-cheh dohr-mee-toh'-ree-oh*]
      sleeping car

   coche restaurante [*koh'-cheh rehs-tah-oo-rahn'-teh*]
      dining car

codicioso [*koh-dee-thee-oh'-soh*] greedy

codo [*koh'-doh*] elbow

coger *v.* [*koh-hehr'*] catch

coincidencia [*koh-een-thee-dehn'-thee-ah*] coincidence

cojín *m.* [*koh-heen'*] cushion, pad
cojo [*koh'-hoh*] lame, one-legged
col *f.* [*kohl*] cabbage
cola [*koh'-lah*] tail, line, glue
colcha [*kohl'-chah*] bedspread
colchón *m.* [*kohl-chohn'*] mattress
colección *f.* [*koh-lehk-thee-ohn'*] collection
coleccionar *v.* [*koh-lehk-thee-oh-nahr'*] collect
colega *m.*, *f.* [*koh-leh'-gah*] colleague
cólera [*koh'-leh-rah*] anger
colgar *v. irreg.* [*kohl-gahr'*] hang
colina [*koh-lee'-nah*] hill
colindante [*koh-leen-dahn'-teh*] adjoining
colisión *f.* [*koh-lee-see-ohn'*] collision, clash
colocar *v.* [*koh-loh-kahr'*] set, put, place
Colombia [*koh-lohm'-bee-ah*] Colombia
colombiano [*koh-lohm-bee-ah'-noh*] Colombian
colonia [*koh-loh'-nee-ah*] colony
color *m.* [*koh-lohr'*] color
colorado [*koh-loh-rah'-doh*] red
colorete *m.* [*koh-loh-reh'-teh*] rouge
columna [*koh-loom'-nah*] column
　　columna vertebral [*koh-loom'-nah vehr-teh-brahl'*] spine
collar *m.* [*koh-yahr'*] necklace
　　collar de perlas [*koh-yahr' deh pehr'-lahs*] pearl necklace
combinación *f.* [*kohm-bee-nah-thee-ohn'*] combination
combustible *m.* [*kohm-boos-tee'-bleh*] fuel
combustible *adj.* [*kohm-boos-tee'-bleh*] combustible
comedia [*koh-meh'-dee-ah*] comedy
comediante *m.*, *f.* [*koh-meh-dee-ahn'-teh*] comedian
comedor *m.* [*koh-meh-dohr'*] dining room
comentar *v.* [*koh-mehn-tahr'*] comment
comentario [*koh-mehn-tah'-ree-oh*] commentary, comment
comenzar *v. irreg.* [*koh-mehn-thahr'*] begin
comer *v.* [*koh-mehr'*] eat, dine
comercial [*koh-mehr-thee-ahl'*] commercial
comerciante *m.*, *f.* [*koh-mehr-thee-ahn'-teh*] merchant
comerciar *v.* [*koh-mehr-thee-ahr'*] trade

comercio [*koh-mehr'-thee-oh*] trade
comestible [*koh-mehs-tee'-bleh*] edible
cometa *m.* [*koh-meh'-tah*] comet
cometa *f.* [*koh-meh'-tah*] kite
cómico [*koh'-mee-koh*] funny
comida [*koh-mee'-dah*] food, meal
comienzo [*koh-mee-ehn'-thoh*] beginning
comillas *f. pl.* [*koh-mee'-yahs*] quotation marks
comisión *f.* [*koh-mee-see-ohn'*] commission
comité *m.* [*koh-mee-teh'*] committee
como [*koh'-moh*] as, like, such as
¿Cómo? [*koh'-moh*] How?
   ¿Cómo está Usted? [*koh'-moh ehs-tah' oos-tehd'*]
    How do you do?
   ¿Cómo se llama? [*koh'-moh seh yah'-mah*] What is your
    name?
cómoda [*koh'-moh-dah*] chest of drawers
comodidad *f.* [*koh-moh-dee-dahd'*] comfort
cómodo [*koh'-moh-doh*] comfortable
compañero [*kohm-pah-nyeh'-roh*] mate, fellow
   compañero de clase [*kohm-pah-nyeh'-roh deh klah'-seh*]
    classmate
   compañero de juego [*kohm-pah-nyeh'-roh deh hoo-eh'-goh*]
    playmate
compañía [*kohm-pah-nyee'-ah*] company
comparación *f.* [*kohm-pah-rah-thee-ohn'*] comparison
comparar *v.* [*kohm-pah-rahr'*] compare
compartimiento [*kohm-pahr-tee-mee-ehn'-toh*] compartment
compartir *v.* [*kohm-pahr-teer'*] share
compasión *f.* [*kohm-pah-see-ohn'*] compassion, pity
compatriota *m., f.* [*kohm-pah-tree-oh'-tah*] countryman
compensación *f.* [*kohm-pehn-sah-thee-ohn'*] compensation
competente [*kohm-peh-tehn'-teh*] competent
competición *f.* [*kohm-peh-tee-thee-ohn'*] competition
complejo [*kohm-pleh'-hoh*] complex
completamente [*kohm-pleh-tah-mehn'-teh*] completely,
   thoroughly
completar *v.* [*kohm-pleh-tahr'*] complete

completo [*kohm-pleh'-toh*] complete
complicado [*kohm-plee-kah'-doh*] complicated
complicar v. [*kohm-plee-kahr'*] complicate
complot m. [*kohm-ploht'*] plot, scheme
componer v. irreg. [*kohm-poh-nehr'*] compose
comportarse v. [*kohm-pohr-tahr'-seh*] behave
compositor m. [*kohm-poh-see-tohr'*] composer
compostura [*kohm-pohs-too'-rah*] composure
compra [*kohm'-prah*] purchase
  ir v. irreg. **de compras** [*eer deh kohm'-prahs*] go shopping
comprar v. [*kohm-prahr'*] buy, purchase
comprender v. [*kohm-prehn-dehr'*] understand
comprobante m. [*kohm-proh-bahn'-teh*] voucher
comprobar v. irreg. [*kohm-proh-bahr'*] check, test
comprometerse v. [*kohm-proh-meh-tehr'-seh*] commit
  oneself, become engaged
compromiso [*kohm-proh-mee'-soh*] engagement
compuesto n. [*kohm-poo-ehs'-toh*] compound
compuesto adj. [*kohm-poo-ehs'-toh*] composed, fixed, calm
común [*koh-moon'*] common
comunicación f. [*koh-moo-nee-kah-thee-ohn'*] communication
comunicar v. [*koh-moo-nee-kahr'*] communicate
comunidad f. [*koh-moo-nee-dahd'*] community
comunista m., f. [*koh-moo-nees'-tah*] communist
con [*kohn*] with
  con respecto a [*kohn rehs-pehk'-toh ah*] in respect to
  con tal que [*kohn tahl keh*] provided that
concebir v. irreg. [*kohn-theh-beer'*] conceive
conceder v. [*kohn-theh-dehr'*] concede, grant
concentrar v. [*kohn-thehn-trahr'*] concentrate
conciencia [*kohn-thee-ehn'-thee-ah*] conscience
concienzudo [*kohn-thee-ehn-thoo'-doh*] conscientious
concierto [*kohn-thee-ehr'-toh*] concert
conciso [*kohn-thee'-soh*] concise
conclusión f. [*kohn-kloo-see-ohn'*] conclusion
concurso [*kohn-koor'-soh*] contest
concha [*kohn'-chah*] shell
conde m. [*kohn'-deh*] count [title]

condenar v. [*kohn-deh-nahr'*] condemn
condensar v. [*kohn-dehn-sahr'*] condense
condición f. [*kohn-dee-thee-ohn'*] condition
condicional [*kohn-dee-thee-oh-nahl'*] conditional
condimentar v. [*kohn-dee-mehn-tahr'*] season
condolencia [*kohn-doh-lehn'-thee-ah*] sympathy
conducir v. irreg. [*kohn-doo-theer'*] conduct, drive
conducta [*kohn-dook'-tah*] behavior
conductor m. [*kohn-dook-tohr'*] driver
conejo [*koh-neh'-hoh*] rabbit
conexión f. [*koh-nek-see-ohn'*] connection
conferencia [*kohn-feh-rehn'-thee-ah*] lecture, long-distance call
  dar v. **una conferencia** [*dahr oo'-nah kohn-feh-rehn'-thee-ah*] lecture
conferir v. irreg. [*kohn-feh-reer'*] confer
confesar v. irreg. [*kohn-feh-sahr'*] confess
confesión f. [*kohn-feh-see-ohn'*] confession
confiado [*kohn-fee-ah'-doh*] confident
confiar v. [*kohn-fee-ahr'*] trust
  confiar en [*kohn-fee-ahr' ehn*] count on
confidencial [*kohn-fee-dehn-thee-ahl'*] confidential
confirmar v. [*kohn-feer-mahr'*] confirm
conflicto [*kohn-fleek'-toh*] conflict
conforme [*kohn-fohr'-meh*] in agreement
confusión f. [*kohn-foo-see-ohn'*] confusicn
congelado [*kohn-heh-lah'-doh*] frozen
congelar v. [*kohn-heh-lahr'*] freeze
congreso [*kohn-greh'-soh*] congress
conjunto [*kohn-hoon'-toh*] set, group
conmigo [*kohn-mee'-goh*] with me
conmovedor adj. [*kohn-moh-veh-dohr'*] touching
conmoción f. [*kohn-moh-thee-ohn'*] commotion
conmover v. irreg. [*kohn-moh-vehr'*] move [affect emotionally]
conocer v. irreg. [*koh-noh-thehr'*] know [someone]
  ¡Encantado de conocerle! [*ehn-kahn-tah'-doh deh koh-noh-thehr'-leh*] Glad to meet you!
conocido [*koh-noh-thee'-doh*] known

muy conocido [*moo'-ee koh-noh-thee'-doh*] well known

conocimiento [*koh-noh-thee-mee-ehn'-toh*] acquaintance, knowledge

conquistar *v.* [*kohn-kees-tahr'*] conquer

consciente [*kohns-thee-ehn'-teh*] conscious

consecuencia [*kohn-seh-koo-ehn'-thee-ah*] consequence

consecuente [*kohn-seh-koo-ehn'-teh*] consequent

consejo [*kohn-seh'-hoh*] advice, council

consentimiento [*kohn-sehn-tee-mee-ehn'-toh*] consent

consentir *v. irreg.* [*kohn-sehn-teer'*] consent

conseguir *v. irreg.* [*kohn-seh-gheer'*] get

conserje *m.* [*kohn-sehr'-heh*] janitor

conservador [*kohn-sehr-vah-dohr'*] conservative

conservas *f. pl.* [*kohn-sehr'-vahs*] preserves

considerable [*kohn-see-deh-rah'-bleh*] considerable

considerar *v.* [*kohn-see-deh-rahr'*] consider

consistente [*kohn-sees-tehn'-teh*] consistent

consistir *v.* [*kohn-sees-teer'*] consist

consolar *v. irreg.* [*kohn-soh-lahr'*] console

constante [*kohns-tahn'-teh*] constant

constituir *v. irreg.* [*kohns-tee-too-eer'*] constitute

construcción *f.* [*kohns-trook-thee-ohn'*] construction

construir *v. irreg.* [*kohns-troo-eer'*] construct, build

cónsul *m.* [*kohn'-sool*] consul

consulado [*kohn-soo-lah'-doh*] consulate

consultar *v.* [*kohn-sool-tahr'*] consult

consumir *v.* [*kohn-soo-meer'*] consume

contacto [*kohn-tahk'-toh*] contact

contagioso [*kohn-tah-hee-oh'-soh*] contagious

contar *v. irreg.* [*kohn-tahr'*] count, tell

    contar con [*kohn-tahr' kohn*] rely on

contemporáneo [*kohn-tehm-poh-rah'-neh-oh*] contemporary

contener *v. irreg.* [*kohn-teh-nehr'*] contain

contenido [*kohn-teh-nee'-doh*] contents

contestar *v.* [*kohn-tehs-tahr'*] reply, answer

continente *m.* [*kohn-tee-nehn'-teh*] continent

continuación *f.* [*kohn-tee-noo-ah-thee-ohn'*] continuation

continuar *v.* [*kohn-tee-noo-ahr'*] continue

contra [*kohn'-trah*] against

  pros y contras [*prohs ee kohn'-trahs*] pros and cons

contradicción *f.* [*kohn-trah-deek-thee-ohn'*] contradiction

contrario [*kohn-trah'-ree-oh*] contrary

contraste *m.* [*kohn-trahs'-teh*] contrast

contratar *v.* [*kohn-trah-tahr'*] hire

contrato [*kohn-trah'-toh*] contract

contribuir *v. irreg.* [*kohn-tree-boo-eer'*] contribute

control *m.* [*kohn-trohl'*] control

controlar *v.* [*kohn-troh-lahr'*] control

controversia [*kohn-troh-vehr'-see-ah*] controversy

contusión *f.* [*kohn-too-see-ohn'*] bruise

convencer *v.* [*kohn-vehn-thehr'*] convince

conveniente [*kohn-veh-nee-ehn'-teh*] convenient

convenio [*kohn-veh'-nee-oh*] pact, agreement

convento [*kohn-vehn'-toh*] convent

conversación *f.* [*kohn-vehr-sah-thee-ohn'*] conversation

conversar *v.* [*kohn-vehr-sahr'*] talk, converse

convertir *v. irreg.* [*kohn-vehr-teer'*] convert

convidar *v.* [*kohn-vee-dahr'*] invite

coñac *m.* [*koh-nyahk'*] brandy

cooperación *f.* [*koh-oh-peh-rah-thee-ohn'*] cooperation

copa [*koh'-pah*] goblet

copia [*koh'-pee-ah*] copy

copiar *v.* [*koh-pee-ahr'*] copy

coquetear *v.* [*koh-keh-teh-ahr'*] flirt

corazón *m.* [*koh-rah-thohn'*] heart

  enfermedad *f.* **de corazón** [*ehn-fehr-meh-dahd' deh koh-rah-thohn'*] heart disease

corbata [*kohr-bah'-tah*] necktie

corcho [*kohr'-choh*] cork

cordel *m.* [*kohr-dehl'*] string

cordero [*kohr-deh'-roh*] lamb

cordial [*kohr-dee-ahl'*] warm, cordial

cordillera [*kohr-dee-yeh'-rah*] mountain range

corona [*koh-roh'-nah*] crown

corporación *f.* [*kohr-poh-rah-thee-ohn'*] corporation

corral *m.* [*koh-rrahl'*] farmyard
correa [*koh-rreh'-ah*] strap, belt
correción *f.* [*koh-rrehk-thee-ohn'*] correction
correcto [*koh-rrehk'-toh*] correct, proper
corredor *m.* [*koh-rreh-dohr'*] corridor
corregir *v. irreg.* [*koh-rreh-heer'*] correct
correo [*koh-rreh'-oh*] mail
  correo aéreo [*koh-rreh'-oh ah-eh'-reh-oh*] air mail
correos [*koh-rreh'-ohs*] post office
  apartado de correos [*ah-pahr-tah'-doh deh koh-rreh'-ohs*
    post office box
correr *v.* [*koh-rrehr'*] run
  correr un albur [*koh-rrehr' oon ahl-boor'*] take a chance
correspondencia [*koh-rrehs-pohn-dehn'-thee-ah*]
  correspondence
corresponder *v.* [*koh-rrehs-pohn-dehr'*] correspond,
  reciprocate
corriente *f.* [*koh-rree-ehn'-teh*] current
corriente *adj.* [*koh-rree-ehn'-teh*] current, usual
corrientemente [*koh-rree-ehn-teh-mehn'-teh*] fluently
corrompido [*koh-rrohm-pee'-doh*] corrupt
corrupción *f.* [*koh-rroop-thee-ohn'*] corruption
cortar *v.* [*kohr-tahr'*] cut
corte *m.* [*kohr'-teh*] cut
cortejar *v.* [*kohr-teh-hahr'*] court
cortés [*kohr-tehs'*] polite
cortina [*kohr-tee'-nah*] curtain
corto [*kohr'-toh*] short
  corto de vista [*kohr'-toh deh vees'-tah*] shortsighted
cosa [*koh'-sah*] thing, matter
cosecha [*koh-seh'-chah*] harvest
coser *v.* [*koh-sehr'*] sew
  máquina de coser [*mah'-kee-nah deh koh-sehr'*] sewing
    machine
cosmético [*kohs-meh'-tee-koh*] cosmetic
costa [*kohs'-tah*] coast
costar *v. irreg.* [*kohs-tahr'*] cost

coste *m.* **de vida** [*kohs'-teh deh vee'-dah*] cost of living

¿Cuánto cuesta esto? [*koo-ahn'-toh koo-ehs'-tah ehs'-toh*] How much does this cost?

Costa Rica [*kohs'-tah ree'-kah*] Costa Rica

costarricense [*kohs-tah-rree-thehn'-seh*] Costa Rican

costilla [*kohs-tee'-yah*] rib

costo [*kohs'-toh*] cost

costoso [*kohs-toh'-soh*] costly

costumbre *f.* [*kohs-toom'-breh*] custom, habit

costura [*kohs-too'-rah*] seam, sewing

cotidiano [*koh-tee-dee-ah'-noh*] daily

creación *f.* [*kreh-ah-thee-ohn'*] creation

crear *v.* [*kreh-ahr'*] create

crecer *v. irreg.* [*kreh-thehr'*] grow

crédito [*kreh'-dee-toh*] credit

creencia [*kreh-ehn'-thee-ah*] belief

creer *v.* [*kreh-ehr'*] believe

crema [*kreh'-mah*] cream

crema batida [*kreh'-mah bah-tee'-dah*] whipped cream

cremallera [*kreh-mah-yeh'-rah*] zipper

crepúsculo [*kreh-poos'-koo-loh*] twilight

criada [*kree-ah'-dah*] maid

criar *v.* [*kree-ahr'*] raise, nurse, breed

criatura [*kree-ah-too'-rah*] creature, child

crimen *m.* [*kree'-mehn*] crime

criminal *n. f. & adj.* [*kree-mee-nahl'*] criminal

criollo [*kree-oh'-yoh*] Creole

crisis *f.* [*kree'-sees*] crisis

cristal *m.* [*krees-tahl'*] crystal

cristiano *n. & adj.* [*krees-tee-ah'-noh*] Christian

criticar *v.* [*kree-tee-kahr'*] criticize, gossip

crítico [*kree'-tee-koh*] critical

cruce *m.* [*kroo'-theh*] cross, crossing

crudo [*kroo'-doh*] raw, uncooked

cruel [*kroo-ehl'*] cruel

crueldad *f.* [*kroo-ehl-dahd'*] cruelty

crujido [*kroo-hee'-doh*] crack

cruz *f.* [*krooth*] cross
  Cruz Roja [*krooth roh'-hah*] Red Cross
cruzar *v.* [*kroo-thahr'*] cross
cuaderno [*koo-ah-dehr'-noh*] notebook
cuadrado [*koo-ah-drah'-doh*] square
cuadro [*koo-ah'-droh*] picture
cual [*koo-ahl'*] which
cualidad [*koo-ah-lee-dahd'*] quality
cualquiera [*koo-ahl-kee-eh'-rah*] either (one), anyone
  en cualquier parte [*ehn koo-ahl-kee-ehr' pahr'-teh*]
    anywhere
  de cualquier modo [*deh koo-ahl-kee-ehr' moh'-doh*]
    anyway
cuando [*koo-ahn'-doh*] when
cuanto [*koo-ahn'-toh*] as much as
  cuanto antes [*koo-ahn'-toh ahn'-tehs*] as soon as possible
¿Cuánto . . . ? [*koo-ahn'-toh*] How much . . . ?
  ¿Cuántos? [*koo-ahn'-tohs*] How many?
  ¿Cuánto tiempo? [*koo-ahn'-toh tee-ehm'-poh*] How long?
cuarenta [*koo-ah-rehn'-tah*] forty
cuarto [*koo-ahr'-toh*] fourth
  cuarto de hora [*koo-ahr'-toh deh oh'-rah*] quarter hour
cuarto [*koo-ahr'-toh*] room, quart
  cuarto de baño [*koo-ahr'-toh deh bah'-nyoh*] bathroom
cuatro [*koo-ah'-troh*] four
Cuba [*koo'-bah*] Cuba
cubano [*koo-bah'-noh*] Cuban
cubierta [*koo-bee-ehr'-tah*] cover, deck
cubo [*koo'-boh*] cube, bucket
cubrir *v.* [*koo-breer'*] cover
cuchara [*koo-chah'-rah*] spoon
cucharada [*koo-chah-rah'-dah*] spoonful
cucharilla [*koo-chah-ree'-yah*] teaspoon
cuchillo [*koo-chee'-yoh*] knife
cuello [*koo-eh'-yoh*] neck, collar
cuenta [*koo-ehn'-tah*] account, bill
  cuenta corriente [*koo-ehn'-tah koh-rree-ehn'-teh*] bank
    account

cuento [*koo-ehn'-toh*] tale
cuerda [*koo-ehr'-dah*] cord, rope
cuerdo [*koo-ehr'-doh*] sane
cuerno [*koo-ehr'-noh*] horn [made of or shaped like horn]
cuero [*koo-eh'-roh*] leather
cuerpo [*koo-ehr'-poh*] body
cuesta [*koo-ehs'-tah*] hill, slope
  cuesta abajo [*koo-ehs'-tah ah-bah'-hoh*] downhill
  cuesta arriba [*koo-ehs'-tah ah-rree'-bah*] uphill
cuestionario [*koo-ehs-tee-oh-nah'-ree-oh*] questionnaire
cueva [*koo-eh'-vah*] cave
cuidado [*koo-ee-dah'-doh*] care
  ¡Cuidado! [*koo-ee-dah'-doh*] Watch out!, Look out!
cuidadosamente [*koo-ee-dah-doh-sah-mehn'-teh*] carefully
cuidadoso [*koo-ee-dah-doh'-soh*] careful
cuidar v. [*koo-ee-dahr'*] care
  cuidar de [*koo-ee-dahr' deh*] take care of
culebra [*koo-leh'-brah*] snake
culpa [*kool'-pah*] blame
culpable [*kool-pah'-bleh*] guilty
culpar v. [*kool-pahr'*] blame
cultivar v. [*kool-tee-vahr'*] grow crops
culto [*kool'-toh*] cult, worship
cultura [*kool-too'-rah*] culture
cumpleaños [*koom-pleh-ah'-nyohs*] birthday
  Feliz cumpleaños [*feh-leeth' koom-pleh-ah'-nyohs*]
    Happy birthday
cumplido [*koom-plee'-doh*] compliment
cumplir v. [*koom-pleer'*] fulfill
cuna [*koo'-nah*] cradle
cuneta [*koo-neh'-tah*] gutter
cuñada [*koo-nyah'-dah*] sister-in-law
cuñado [*koo-nyah'-doh*] brother-in-law
cúpula [*koo'-poo-lah*] dome
cura [*koo'-rah*] cure
curar v. [*koo-rahr'*] cure
curiosidad f. [*koo-ree-oh-see-dahd'*] curiosity

curso [*koor'-soh*] course
curva [*koor'-vah*] curve
   curva peligrosa [*koor'-vah peh-lee-groh'-sah*] dangerous
     curve
cutis *m.* [*koo'-tees*] complexion
cuyo [*koo'-yoh*] whose

CH

chaleco [*chah-leh'-koh*] vest
champú *m.* [*chahm-poo'*] shampoo
chaqueta [*chah-keh'-tah*] jacket
charco [*chahr'-koh*] puddle
charlar *v.* [*chahr-lahr'*] chat
chato [*chah'-toh*] flat-nosed
cheque *m.* [*cheh'-keh*] check
chicle *m.* [*chee'-kleh*] chewing gum
chico [*chee'-koh*] boy, small
Chile [*chee'-leh*] Chile
chileno [*chee-leh'-noh*] Chilean
chillar *v.* [*chee-yahr'*] shriek, scream
chimenea [*chee-meh-neh'-ah*] fireplace, chimney
China [*chee'-nah*] China
chino [*chee'-noh*] Chinese
chirriar *v.* [*chee-rree-ahr'*] squeak
chisme *m.* [*chees'-meh*] gossip, gadget
chismorrear *v.* [*chees-moh-rreh-ahr'*] gossip
chispa [*chees'-pah*] spark
chiste *m.* [*chees'-teh*] joke
chocar *v.* [*choh-kahr'*] collide, crash
chocolate *m.* [*choh-koh-lah'-teh*] chocolate
chófer *m.* [*choh'-fehr*] driver, chauffeur
choque *m.* [*choh'-keh*] shock, collision
chorro [*choh'-rroh*] jet
chupar *v.* [*choo-pahr'*] suck

D

dados *m. pl.* [*dah'-dohs*] dice
dama [*dah'-mah*] lady
  dama de honor [*dah'-mah deh oh-nɔhr'*] bridesmaid
dañar *v.* [*dah-nyahr'*] harm, hurt
danés [*dah-nehs'*] Danish
danza [*dahn'-thah*] dance
dañado [*dah-nyah'-doh*] damaged
dañino [*dah-nyee'-noh*] harmful
daño [*dah'-nyoh*] damage
dar *v. irreg.* [*dahr*] give
  dar a luz [*dahr ah looth*] give birth, bear
  dar la mano [*dahr lah mah'-noh*] shake hands
  dar un paseo [*dahr oon pah-seh'-oh*] take a walk
  darse cuenta [*dahr'-seh koo-ehn'-tah*] realize
de [*deh*] of, by
  de confianza [*deh kohn-fee-ahn'-thah*] reliable
  de modo que [*deh moh'-doh keh*] so that
  de vez en cuando [*deh vehth ehn koo-ahn'-doh*] now and
    then, from time to time
debajo [*deh-bah'-hoh*] underneath, below
  debajo de [*deh-bah'-hoh deh*] under
deber *m.* [*deh-behr'*] duty
deber *v.* [*deh-behr'*] owe
  deber de [*deh-behr' deh*] ought to
  ¿Cuánto le debo? [*koo-ahn'-toh leh deh'-boh*] How much
    do I owe you?
debido [*deh-bee'-doh*] due
  debido a [*deh-bee'-doh ah*] owing to
débil [*deh'-beel*] weak
debilidad *f.* [*deh-bee-lee-dahd'*] weakness
década [*deh'-kah-dah*] decade
decaer *v. irreg.* [*deh-kah-ehr'*] decay

decaimiento [*deh-kah-ee-mee-ehn'-toh*] decay

decencia [*deh-thehn'-thee-ah*] decency

decente [*deh-thehn'-teh*] decent

decepcionado [*deh-thehp-thee-oh-nah'-doh*] disappointed

decepcionar v. [*deh-thehp-thee-oh-nahr'*] disappoint

decidir v. [*deh-thee-deer'*] decide

   decidirse [*deh-thee-deer'-seh*] make up one's mind

décimo [*deh'-thee-moh*] tenth

decir v. irreg. [*deh-theer'*] say, tell

decisión f. [*deh-thee-see-ohn'*] decision

declaración f. [*deh-klah-rah-thee-ohn'*] declaration, statement

declarar v. [*deh-klah-rahr'*] declare

   declarar culpable [*deh-klah-rahr' kool-pah'-bleh*]
      convict

declinar v. [*deh-klee-nahr'*] decline

decoración f. [*deh-koh-rah-thee-ohn'*] decoration

decorar v. [*deh-koh-rahr'*] decorate

dedicado [*deh-dee-kah'-doh*] dedicated

dedicar v. [*deh-dee-kahr'*] dedicate

dedo [*deh'-doh*] finger

   dedo del pie [*deh'-doh dehl pee-eh'*] toe

deducir v. irreg. [*deh-doo-theer'*] deduce

defecto [*deh-fehk'-toh*] defect

defectuoso [*deh-fehk-too-oh'-soh*] defective

defender v. irreg. [*deh-fehn-dehr'*] defend

deficiente [*deh-fee-thee-ehn'-teh*] deficient

definición f. [*deh-fee-nee-thee-ohn'*] definition

definido [*deh-fee-nee'-doh*] definite

definir v. [*deh-fee-neer'*] define

definitivo [*deh-fee-nee-tee'-voh*] definitive

dejar v. [*deh-hahr'*] leave

del (de el) [*dehl*] of the

delantal m. [*deh-lahn-tahl'*] apron

delante [*deh-lahn'-teh*] ahead

delantero [*deh-lahn-teh'-roh*] leading

deleitar v. [*deh-leh-ee-tahr'*] delight

deleite m. [*deh-leh'-ee-teh*] delight

deletrear v. [*deh-leh-treh-ahr'*] spell

delgado [*dehl-gah'-doh*] thin
deliberado [*deh-lee-beh-rah'-doh*] deliberate
delicado [*deh-lee-kah'-doh*] delicate
delicioso [*deh-lee-thee-oh'-soh*] delicious
demasiado [*deh-mah-see-ah'-doh*] too much
democracia [*deh-moh-krah'-thee-ah*] democracy
demorar *v.* [*deh-moh-rahr'*] delay
demostración *f.* [*deh-mohs-trah-thee-ohn'*] demonstration, proof
demostrar *v. irreg.* [*deh-mohs-trahr'*] demonstrate
densidad *f.* [*dehn-see-dahd'*] density
denso [*dehn'-soh*] dense, thick
dentista *m., f.* [*dehn-tees'-tah*] dentist
dentro [*dehn'-troh*] inside, into
  dentro de [*dehn'-troh deh*] within
  dentro de poco (tiempo) [*dehn'-troh deh poh'-koh (tee-ehm'-poh)*] presently
departamento [*deh-pahr-tah-mehn'-toh*] department
depender *v.* [*deh-pehn-dehr'*] depend
  depender de [*deh-pehn-dehr' deh*] depend on
  eso depende [*eh'-soh deh-pehn'-deh*] that depends
dependiente *m., f.* [*deh-pehn-dee-ehn'-teh*] clerk
deporte *m.* [*deh-pohr'-teh*] sport
depositar *v.* [*deh-poh-see-tahr'*] deposit
depósito [*deh-poh'-see-toh*] deposit, depot
depreciar *v.* [*deh-preh-thee-ahr'*] depreciate
derecha [*deh-reh'-chah*] right [direction]
  a la dercha [*ah lah deh-reh'-chah*] to the right
derecho *n. & adj.* [*deh-reh'-choh*] straight, right, law
  derechos de aduana [*deh-reh'-chohs deh ah-doo-ah'-nah*] customs duty
derretir *v. irreg.* [*deh-rreh-teer'*] melt
derrota [*deh-rroh'-tah*] defeat
derrotar *v.* [*deh-rroh-tahr'*] defeat
desacreditar *v.* [*deh-sah-kreh-dee-tahr'*] disgrace
desacuerdo [*deh-sah-koo-ehr'-doh*] disagreement
desafiar *v.* [*deh-sah-fee-ahr'*] challenge
desafío [*deh-sah-fee'-oh*] challenge

desafortunado [*deh-sah-fohr-too-nah'-doh*] unlucky
desagradable [*deh-sah-grah-dah'-bleh*] unpleasant
desagradecido [*deh-sah-grah-deh-thee'-doh*] ungrateful
desagüe *m.* [*deh-sah'-goo-eh*] drain
desalentado [*deh-sah-lehn-tah'-doh*] discouraged
desalentar *v. irreg.* [*deh-sah-lehn-tahr'*] discourage
desalentarse *v. irreg.* [*deh-sah-lehn-tahr'-seh*] get
    discouraged
desaparecer *v. irreg.* [*deh-sah-pah-reh-thehr'*] disappear
desaprovar *v. irreg.* [*deh-sah-proh-vahr'*] disapprove
desarrollar *v.* [*deh-sah-rroh-yahr'*] develop
desarrollo [*deh-sah-rroh'-yoh*] development
desastre *m.* [*deh-sahs'-treh*] disaster
desatar *v.* [*deh-sah-tahr'*] untie
desayuno [*deh-sah-yoo'-noh*] breakfast
descalzo [*dehs-kahl'-thoh*] barefoot
descansar *v.* [*dehs-kahn-sahr'*] rest
descanso [*dehs-kahn'-soh*] rest
descarado [*dehs-kah-rah'-doh*] bold, shameless
descargar *v.* [*dehs-kahr-gahr'*] unload
descargo [*dehs-kahr'-goh*] discharge
descarriar *v.* [*dehs-kah-rree-ahr'*] mislead
descender *v. irreg.* [*dehs-thehn-dehr'*] descend
descolorar *v.* [*dehs-koh-loh-rahr'*] fade
desconcertar *v. irreg.* [*dehs-kohn-thehr-tahr'*] embarrass
desconfianza [*dehs-kohn-fee-ahn'-thah*] distrust
desconfiar *v.* [*dehs-kohn-fee-ahr'*] distrust
desconocido [*dehs-koh-noh-thee'-doh*] unknown
desconsiderado [*dehs-kohn-see-deh-rah'-doh*] thoughtless
descortés [*dehs-kohr-tehs'*] impolite, unkind
describir *v.* [*dehs-kree-beer'*] describe
descripción *f.* [*dehs-kreep-thee-ohn'*] description
descubrimiento [*dehs-koo-bree-mee-ehn'-toh*] discovery
descubrir *v.* [*dehs-koo-breer'*] discover, uncover
descuidado [*dehs-koo-ee-dah'-doh*] careless
descuidar *v.* [*dehs-koo-ee-dahr'*] neglect
descuido [*dehs-koo-ee'-doh*] oversight
desde [*dehs'-deh*] since, from

desde ahora en adelante [*dehs'-deh ah-oh'-rah ehn ah-deh-lahn'-teh*] from now on

desde lejos [*dehs'-deh leh'-hohs*] from afar

deseable [*deh-seh-ah'-bleh*] desirable

desear *v.* [*deh-seh-ahr'*] desire, wish

desempaquetar *v.* [*deh-sehm-pah-keh-tahr'*] unpack

desempleado [*deh-sehm-pleh-ah'-doh*] unemployed

deseo [*deh-seh'-oh*] desire, wish

deseoso [*deh-seh-oh'-soh*] willing

desertar *v.* [*deh-sehr-tahr'*] desert

desesperación *f.* [*deh-sehs-peh-rah-thee-ohn'*] despair

desesperado [*deh-sehs-peh-rah'-doh*] desperate

desesperar *v.* [*deh-sehs-peh-rahr'*] despair

desfavorable [*dehs-fah-voh-rah'-bleh*] unfavorable

desfile *m.* [*dehs-fee'-leh*] parade

desgracia [*dehs-grah'-thee-ah*] disgrace

desgraciadamente [*dehs-grah-thee-ah-dah-mehn'-teh*] unfortunately

desgraciado [*dehs-grah-thee-ah'-doh*] unfortunate

deshacer *v. irreg.* [*dehs-ah-thehr'*] undo

deshacerse de [*dehs-ah-thehr'-seh deh*] get rid of

deshonesto [*dehs-oh-nehs'-toh*] dishonest

desierto [*deh-see-ehr'-toh*] desert

designar *v.* [*deh-seeg-nahr'*] appoint

desigual [*deh-see-goo-ahl'*] unequal

desilusión *f.* [*deh-see-loo-see-ohn'*] disillusion, disappointment

desinteresado [*deh-seen-teh-reh-sah'-doh*] unselfish

deslizar *v.* [*dehs-lee-thahr'*] slide

desmayar *v.* [*dehs-mah-yahr'*] faint

desmayo [*dehs-mah'-yoh*] dismay

desnudarse *v.* [*dehs-noo-dahr'-seh*] undress

desnudo [*dehs-noo'-doh*] naked

desobedecer *v. irreg.* [*deh-soh-beh-deh-thehr'*] disobey

desorden *m.* [*deh-sohr'-dehn*] disorder

desorden público [*deh-sohr'-dehn poo'-blee-koh*] riot

despacio [*dehs-pah'-thee-oh*] slowly

desparramar *v.* [*dehs-pah-rrah-mahr'*] scatter, spread

despedida [*dehs-peh-dee'-dah*] farewell

despedir v. irreg. [dehs-peh-deer'] say good-bye, fire, dismiss
despedirse v. irreg. [dehs-peh-deer'-seh] say good-bye
despegar v. [dehs-peh-gahr'] take off, detach
despertador m. [dehs-pehr-tah-dohr'] alarm clock
despertarse v. irreg. [dehs-pehr-tahr'-seh] wake up
desplomarse v. [dehs-ploh-mahr'-seh] collapse
despreciar v. [dehs-preh-thee-ahr'] scorn
desprecio [dehs-preh'-thee-oh] contempt, scorn
después [dehs-poo-ehs'] afterwards, after
destapar v. [dehs-tah-pahr'] uncover
destello [dehs-teh'-yoh] flare
destinar v. [dehs-tee-nahr'] destine
destino [dehs-tee'-noh] destiny, destination, fate
destituido [dehs-tee-too-ee'-doh] destitute
destornillador m. [dehs-tohr-nee-yah-dohr'] screwdriver
destreza [dehs-treh'-thah] skill
destrucción f. [dehs-trook-thee-ohn'] destruction
destruir v. irreg. [dehs-troo-eer'] destroy
desván m. [dehs-vahn'] garret
desvanecerse v. irreg. [dehs-vah-neh-thehr'-seh] faint
desventaja [dehs-vehn-tah'-hah] disadvantage, handicap
desviación f. [dehs-vee-ah-thee-ohn'] detour
detalle m. [deh-tah'-yeh] detail
detener v. irreg. [deh-teh-nehr'] arrest, stop
detenerse v. [deh-teh-nehr'-seh] stop
detenido [deh-teh-nee'-doh] detained
determinar v. [deh-tehr-mee-nahr'] determine
detrás [deh-trahs'] behind
deuda [deh'-oo-dah] debt
devoción f. [deh-voh-thee-ohn'] devotion
devolver v. irreg. [deh-vohl-vehr'] give back
día m. [dee'-ah] day
  Buenos días [boo-eh'-nohs dee'-ahs] Good morning
  día de fiesta [dee'-ah deh fee-ehs'-tah] holiday
diablo [dee-ah'-bloh] devil
diagrama m. [dee-ah-grah'-mah] diagram
dialecto [dee-ah-lehk'-toh] dialect
diálogo [dee-ah'-loh-goh] dialogue

diamante *m.* [*dee-ah-mahn'-teh*] diamond
diario [*dee-ah'-ree-oh*] diary, journal
dibujar *v.* [*dee-boo-hahr'*] draw, sketch
diccionario [*deek-thee-oh-nah'-ree-oh*] dictionary
diciembre *m.* [*dee-thee-ehm'-breh*] December
dicho [*dee'-choh*] said
dictado [*deek-tah'-doh*] dictation
dictar *v.* [*deek-tahr'*] dictate
diecinueve [*dee-eh-thee-noo-eh'-veh*] nineteen
dieciocho [*dee-eh-thee-oh'-choh*] eighteen
dieciséis [*dee-eh-thee-seh'-ees*] sixteen
diecisiete [*dee-eh-thee-see-eh'-teh*] seventeen
diente *m.* [*dee-ehn'-teh*] tooth
  cepillo de dientes [*theh-pee'-yoh deh dee-ehn'-tehs*]
    toothbrush
  palillo de dientes [*pah-lee'-yoh deh dee-ehn'-tehs*]
    toothpick
diestro [*dee-ehs'-troh*] skillful
dieta [*dee-eh'-tah*] diet
diez [*dee-ehth'*] ten
diferencia [*dee-feh-rehn'-thee-ah*] difference
diferente [*dee-feh-rehn'-teh*] different
difícil [*dee-fee'-theel*] difficult
dificultad *f.* [*dee-fee-kool-tahd'*] difficulty
difunto [*dee-foon'-toh*] deceased
digestión *f.* [*dee-hehs-tee-ohn'*] digestion
dignidad *f.* [*deeg-nee-dahd'*] dignity
dimensión *f.* [*dee-mehn-see-ohn'*] dimension
diminuto [*dee-mee-noo'-toh*] tiny
dimisión *f.* [*dee-mee-see-ohn'*] resignation
dinero [*dee-neh'-roh*] money
  dinero effectivo [*dee-neh'-roh eh-fehk-tee'-voh*] cash
  dinero suelto [*dee-neh'-roh soo-ehl'-toh*] small change
Dios [*dee-ohs'*] God
diploma *m.* [*dee-ploh'-mah*] diploma
diplomático *n.* [*dee-ploh-mah'-tee-koh*] diplomat
diplomático *adj.* [*dee-ploh-mah'-tee-koh*] diplomatic
diputado [*dee-poo-tah'-doh*] deputy

dirección *f.* [*dee-rehk-thee-ohn'*] direction, address
directamente [*dee-rehk-tah-mehn'-teh*] directly
directo [*dee-rehk'-toh*] direct
director *m.* [*dee-rehk-tohr'*] director
dirigir *v.* [*dee-ree-heer'*] direct
discernimiento [*dees-thehr-nee-mee-ehn'-toh*] insight
disciplina [*dees-thee-plee'-nah*] discipline
discípulo [*dees-thee'-poo-loh*] pupil
disco [*dees'-koh*] record
discontinuar *v.* [*dees-kohn-tee-noo-ahr'*] discontinue
disculpa [*dees-kool'-pah*] apology
discurso [*dees-koor'-soh*] speech
discusión *f.* [*dees-koo-see-ohn'*] discussion, argument
discutir *v.* [*dees-koo-teer'*] discuss
disentería [*dee-sehn-teh-ree'-ah*] dysentery
disfraz *m.* [*dees-frahth'*] disguise
disgustado [*dees-goos-tah'-doh*] disgusted
disimular *v.* [*dee-see-moo-lahr'*] feign
disminuir *v. irreg.* [*dees-mee-noo-eer'*] decrease, diminish
disparar *v.* [*dees-pah-rahr'*] shoot
disparate *m.* [*dees-pah-rah'-teh*] nonsense
disparo [*dees-pah'-roh*] shot
dispensar *v.* [*dees-pehn-sahr'*] excuse
   Dispénseme [*dees-pehn'-seh-meh*] Excuse me
disponer *v. irreg.* [*dees-poh-nehr'*] arrange
disponible [*dees-poh-nee'-bleh*] available
disposición *f.* [*dees-poh-see-thee-ohn'*] arrangement
disputa [*dees-poo'-tah*] dispute
distancia [*dees-tahn'-thee-ah*] distance
   ¿A qué distancia? [*ah keh dees-tahn'-thee-ah*] How far?
distante [*dees-tahn'-teh*] distant
distinguido [*dees-teen-ghee'-doh*] distinguished
distinguir *v.* [*dees-teen-gheer'*] distinguish
distinto [*dees-teen'-toh*] distinct, different
distraído [*dees-trah-ee'-doh*] absent-minded
distribución *f.* [*dees-tree-boo-thee-ohn'*] distribution
distribuir *v. irreg.* [*dees-tree-boo-eer'*] distribute
distrito [*dees-tree'-toh*] district

disturbio [*dees-toor'-bee-oh*] riot, disturbance
diversión *f.* [*dee-vehr-see-ohn'*] amusement, fun
divertir *v. irreg.* [*dee-vehr-teer'*] amuse
   Diviértase [*dee-vee-ehr'-tah-seh*] Have a good time
dividir *v.* [*dee-vee-deer'*] divide, split
divino [*dee-vee'-noh*] divine
división *f.* [*dee-vee-see-ohn'*] division
divorciarse *v.* [*dee-vohr-thee-ahr'-seh*] divorce
divorcio [*dee-vohr'-thee-oh*] divorce
doblar *v.* [*doh-blahr'*] fold, bend
doble [*doh'-bleh*] double
doce [*doh'-theh*] twelve
doceavo [*doh-theh-ah'-voh*] twelfth
docena [*doh-theh'-nah*] dozen
doctor *m.* [*dohk-tohr'*] doctor
documento [*doh-koo-mehn'-toh*] document
dólar *m.* [*doh'-lahr*] dollar
doler *v. irreg.* [*doh-lehr'*] hurt, ache, feel pain
dolor *m.* [*doh-lohr'*] ache, pain
   dolor de cabeza [*doh-lohr' deh kah-beh'-thah*] headache
   dolor de garganta [*doh-lohr' deh gahr-gahn'-tah*] sore
    throat
dolorido [*doh-loh-ree'-doh*] sore
doloroso [*doh-loh-roh'-soh*] painful
doméstico *n. & adj.* [*doh-mehs'-tee-koh*] domestic
dominar *v.* [*doh-mee-nahr'*] dominate
domingo [*doh-meen'-goh*] Sunday
dominicano [*doh-mee-nee-kah'-noh*] Dominican
donde [*dohn'-deh*] where
dondequiera [*dohn-deh-kee-eh'-rah*] wherever
dorado [*doh-rah'-doh*] golden
dormido [*dohr-mee'-doh*] asleep
dormir *v. irreg.* [*dohr-meer'*] sleep
dormirse *v. irreg.* [*dohr-meer'-seh*] fall asleep
dormitar *v.* [*dohr-mee-tahr'*] doze
dormitorio [*dohr-mee-toh'-ree-oh*] dormitory
dos [*dohs*] two
dosis *f.* [*doh'-sees*] dose

drama *m.* [*drah'-mah*] drama
dramático [*drah-mah'-tee-koh*] dramatic
droga [*droh'-gah*] drug
ducha [*doo'-chah*] shower
duda [*doo'-dah*] doubt
  sin duda [*seen doo'-dah*] doubtless
dudar *v.* [*doo-dahr'*] doubt
dudoso [*doo-doh'-soh*] doubtful
duende *m.* [*doo-ehn'-deh*] ghost
dueña [*doo-eh'-nyah*] landlady
dueño [*doo-eh'-nyoh*] owner, landlord
dulce *n. m. & adj.* [*dool'-theh*] sweet, candy
duque *m.* [*doo'-keh*] duke
duquesa [*doo-keh'-sah*] duchess
duradero [*doo-rah-deh'-roh*] durable
durante [*doo-rahn'-teh*] during
durar *v.* [*doo-rahr'*] last, endure
duro [*doo'-roh*] hard, tough

E

eco [*eh'-koh*] echo
economía [*eh-koh-noh-mee'-ah*] economy
económico [*eh-koh-noh'-mee-koh*] economical, inexpensive
Ecuador *m.* [*eh-koo-ah-dohr'*] Ecuador
ecuatoriano [*eh-koo-ah-toh-ree-ah'-noh*] Ecuadorian
echar *v.* [*eh-chahr'*] throw
  echar de menos [*eh-chahr' deh meh'-nohs*] miss
echarse *v.* [*eh-chahr'-seh*] lie down
  echarse atrás [*eh-chahr'-seh ah-trahs'*] lie back
edad *f.* [*eh-dahd'*] age
edición *f.* [*eh-dee-thee-ohn'*] edition
edificio [*eh-dee-fee'-thee-oh*] building
editor *m.* [*eh-dee-tohr'*] editor
educación *f.* [*eh-doo-kah-thee-ohn'*] education

educar *v.* [*eh-doo-kahr'*] educate, bring up
  bien educado [*bee-ehn' eh-doo-kah'-doh*] well-bred
efecto [*eh-fehk'-toh*] effect
eficaz [*eh-fee-kahth'*] effective
eficiente [*eh-fee-thee-ehn'-teh*] efficient
egipcio [*eh-heep'-thee-oh*] Egyptian
Egipto [*eh-heep'-toh*] Egypt
egoísta *m., f.* [*eh-goh-ees'-tah*] selfish
eje *m.* [*eh'-heh*] axis, axle
ejecutar *v.* [*eh-heh-koo-tahr'*] execute, perform
ejemplo [*eh-hehm'-ploh*] example
  por ejemplo [*pohr eh-hehm'-ploh*] for example
ejercer *v.* [*eh-hehr-thehr'*] exert
ejercicio [*eh-hehr-thee'-thee-oh*] exercise
ejército [*eh-hehr'-thee-toh*] army
el *m. sing.* [*ehl*] the
  el uno al otro [*ehl oo'-noh ahl oh'-troh*] each other
él [*ehl'*] he
  él mismo [*ehl mees'-moh*] himself
El Salvador [*ehl sahl-vah-dohr'*] Salvador
elaborado [*eh-lah-boh-rah'-doh*] elaborate
elástico *n. & adj.* [*eh-lahs'-tee-koh*] elastic
elección *f.* [*eh-lehk-thee-ohn'*] election, choice
electricidad *f.* [*eh-lehk-tree-thee-dahd'*] electricity
eléctrico [*eh-lehk'-tree-koh*] electric
elefante *m.* [*eh-leh-fahn'-teh*] elephant
elegante [*eh-leh-gahn'-teh*] elegant
elegir *v. irreg.* [*eh-leh-heer'*] elect
elemental [*eh-leh-mehn-tahl'*] elementary
elemento [*eh-leh-mehn'-toh*] element
elevar *v.* [*eh-leh-vahr'*] lift
eliminar *v.* [*eh-lee-mee-nahr'*] eliminate
elogiar *v.* [*eh-loh-hee-ahr'*] praise
elogio [*eh-loh'-hee-oh*] praise
ella [*eh'-yah*] she
  ella misma [*eh'-yah mees'-mah*] herself
ello [*eh'-yoh*] it
embajada [*ehm-bah-hah'-dah*] embassy

embajador *m.* [*ehm-bah-hah-dohr'*] ambassador
embalaje *m.* [*ehm-bah-lah'-heh*] packing
embarazada [*ehm-bah-rah-thah'-dah*] pregnant
embarcadero [*ehm-bahr-kah-deh'-roh*] wharf, pier
embarcar *v.* [*ehm-bahr-kahr'*] embark, ship
embargo [*ehm-bahr'-goh*] embargo
emborracharse *v.* [*ehm-boh-rrah-chahr'-seh*] become drunk
embustero [*ehm-boos-teh'-roh*] liar
emergencia [*eh-mehr-hehn'-thee-ah*] emergency
emigración *f.* [*eh-mee-grah-thee-ohn'*] emigration
emigrante *m., f.* [*eh-mee-grahn'-teh*] emigrant
emoción *f.* [*eh-moh-thee-ohn'*] emotion
empacar *v.* [*ehm-pah-kahr'*] pack
empalme *m.* [*ehm-pahl'-meh*] connection, junction
empaquetar *v.* [*ehm-pah-keh-tahr'*] pack
emparedado [*ehm-pah-reh-dah'-doh*] sandwich
empatar *v.* [*ehm-pah-tahr'*] equal
empeñar *v.* [*ehm-peh-nyahr'*] pawn
empeñarse *v.* [*ehm-peh-nyahr'-seh*] persist
empeorar *v.* [*ehm-peh-oh-rahr'*] grow worse
emperador *m.* [*ehm-peh-rah-dohr'*] emperor
empezar *v.* [*ehm-peh-thahr'*] begin
empleo [*ehm-pleh'-oh*] employment
  agencia de empleos [*ah-hehn'-thee-ah deh ehm-pleh'-ohs*]
    employment agency
emprender *v.* [*ehm-prehn-dehr'*] undertake
empresa [*ehm-preh'-sah*] enterprise
empujar *v.* [*ehm-poo-hahr'*] push
en [*ehn*] in, on, at, into
  en alguna parte [*ehn ahl-goo'-nah pahr'-teh*] somewhere
  en alguna otra parte [*ehn ahl-goo'-nah oh'-trah pahr'-teh*]
    somewhere else
  en blanco [*ehn blahn'-koh*] blank
  en caso de [*ehn kah'-soh deh*] in the event of
  en conformidad [*ehn kohn-fohr-mee-dahd'*] accordingly
  en lugar de [*ehn loo-gahr' deh*] instead of
  en parte [*ehn pahr'-teh*] partly
  en poco tiempo [*ehn poh'-koh tee-ehm'-poh*] in a short

    time

en vano [*ehn vah'-noh*] in vain

enamorarse *v.* [*eh-nah-moh-rahr'-seh*] fall in love

encaje *m.* [*ehn-kah'-heh*] lace

encantador [*ehn-kahn-tah-dohr'*] charming, lovely

encanto [*ehn-kahn'-toh*] charm

encargar *v.* [*ehn-kahr-gahr'*] charge, commission

encargo [*ehn-kahr'-goh*] charge, request, message

encendedor *m.* [*ehn-thehn-deh-dohr'*] lighter

encender *v. irreg.* [*ehn-thehn-dehr'*] light, put on

encerrar *v. irreg.* [*ehn-theh-rrahr'*] lock up

encía [*ehn-thee'-ah*] gum [anat.]

encima [*ehn-thee'-mah*] above, over, on

  encima de [*ehn-thee'-mah deh*] on top of

encinta [*ehn-theen'-tah*] pregnant

encoger *v.* [*ehn-koh-hehr'*] shrink

encontrar *v. irreg.* [*ehn-kohn-trahr'*] find

encontrarse *v.* [*ehn-kohn-trahr'-seh*] meet

  encontrarse con [*ehn-kohn-trahr'-seh kohn*] encounter

encrucijada [*ehn-kroo-thee-hah'-dah*] crossroads

encuentro [*ehn-koo-ehn'-troh*] encounter

enchufe *m.* [*ehn-choo'-feh*] plug

endurecer *v. irreg.* [*ehn-doo-reh-thehr'*] harden

enemigo [*eh-neh-mee'-goh*] enemy

energía [*eh-nehr-hee'-ah*] energy

enero [*eh-neh'-roh*] January

enfadarse *v.* [*ehn-fah-dahr'-seh*] become angry

énfasis *m.* [*ehn'-fah-sees*] emphasis

  dar *v.* **énfasis** [*dahr ehn'-fah-sees*] emphasize

enfermedad *f.* [*ehn-fehr-meh-dahd'*] illness, sickness, disease

enfermera [*ehn-fehr-meh'-rah*] nurse

enfermizo [*ehn-fehr-mee'-thoh*] unhealthy

enfermo [*ehn-fehr'-moh*] ill, sick

enfrente [*ehn-frehn'-teh*] in front, facing

enfriar *v.* [*ehn-free-ahr'*] cool

engañar *v.* [*ehn-gah-nyahr'*] deceive

engaño [*ehn-gah'-nyoh*] deceit

engordar *v.* [*ehn-gohr-dahr'*] fatten

engranaje *m.* [*ehn-grah-nah'-heh*] gear
engrasar *v.* [*ehn-grah-sahr'*] oil
enjuagar *v.* [*ehn-hoo-ah-gahr'*] rinse
enmienda [*ehn-mee-ehn'-dah*] amends
enojado [*eh-noh-hah'-doh*] angry
enorme [*eh-nohr'-meh*] enormous, huge
ensalada [*ehn-sah-lah'-dah*] salad
ensayo [*ehn-sah'-yoh*] rehearsal, essay
enseguida [*ehn-seh-ghee'-dah*] at once
enseñanza [*ehn-seh-nyahn'-thah*] teaching
  segunda enseñanza [*seh-goon'-dah ehn-seh-nyahn'-thah*]
    secondary education
enseñar *v.* [*ehn-seh-nyahr'*] teach
entender *v. irreg.* [*ehn-tehn-dehr'*] understand
  ¿Entiende usted? [*ehn-tee-ehn'-deh oos-tehd'*] Do you
    understand?
enterado [*ehn-teh-rah'-doh*] aware, acquainted
enteramente [*ehn-teh-rah-mehn'-teh*] entirely
entero [*ehn-teh'-roh*] entire, whole
enterrar *v. irreg.* [*ehn-teh-rrahr'*] bury
entidad *f.* [*ehn-tee-dahd'*] entity
entierro [*ehn-tee-eh'-rroh*] burial
entonces [*ehn-tohn'-thehs*] then
  para entonces [*pah'-rah ehn-tohn'-thehs*] by then
entrada [*ehn-trah'-dah*] entrance, entrance ticket
entrar *v.* [*ehn-trahr'*] enter, go in
  no entre [*noh ehn'-treh*] keep out
entre [*ehn'-treh*] between, among
entreabierto [*ehn-treh-ah-bee-ehr'-toh*] half open
entreacto [*ehn-treh-ahk'-toh*] intermission
entrecejo [*ehn-treh-theh'-hoh*] frown
entrega [*ehn-treh'-gah*] delivery
entregar *v.* [*ehn-treh-gahr'*] deliver
entremés *m.* [*ehn-treh-mehs'*] side dish
entrenador *m.* [*ehn-treh-nah-dohr'*] coach, trainer
entretener *v. irreg.* [*ehn-treh-teh-nehr'*] entertain
entretenido [*ehn-treh-teh-nee'-doh*] entertaining
entretenimiento [*ehn-treh-teh-nee-mee-ehn'-toh*] entertainment,

    amusement

entrevista [*ehn-treh-vees'-tah*] interview

entristecerse *v. irreg.* [*ehn-trees-teh-thehr'-seh*] sadden

entrometerse *v.* [*ehn-troh-meh-tehr'-seh*] intrude

entusiasmo [*ehn-too-see-ahs'-moh*] enthusiasm

envase *m.* [*ehn-vah'-seh*] can, container

envejecer *v. irreg.* [*ehn-veh-heh-thehr'*] grow old

enviar *v.* [*ehn-vee-ahr'*] send

   enviar por correo [*ehn-vee-ahr' pohr koh-rreh'-oh*]
    mail

envidia [*ehn-vee'-dee-ah*] envy

envío [*ehn-vee'-oh*] remittance

envolver *v. irreg.* [*ehn-vohl-vehr'*] wrap up

equilibrar *v.* [*eh-kee-lee-brahr'*] balance

equipaje *m.* [*eh-kee-pah'-heh*] luggage

equipo [*eh-kee'-poh*] equipment, team

equivalente [*eh-kee-vah-lehn'-teh*] equivalent

equivocación *f.* [*eh-kee-voh-kah-thee-ohn'*] mistake

equivocado [*eh-kee-voh-kah'-doh*] wrong

equivocar *v.* [*eh-kee-voh-kahr'*] mistake

equivocarse *v.* [*eh-kee-voh-kahr'-seh*] make a mistake

   estar *v.* **equivocado** [*ehs-tahr' eh-kee-voh-kah'-doh*] be
    wrong

errar *v. irreg.* [*eh-rrahr'*] err

error *m.* [*eh-rrohr'*] error

erudición *f.* [*eh-roo-dee-thee-ohn'*] learning

erudito [*eh-roo-dee'-toh*] learned

esbelto [*ehs-behl'-toh*] slender

escala [*ehs-kah'-lah*] scale

escalar *v.* [*ehs-kah-lahr'*] climb

escalera [*ehs-kah-leh'-rah*] stairs, ladder

escándalo [*ehs-kahn'-dah-loh*] scandal

escapar *v.* [*ehs-kah-pahr'*] escape

escaparate *m.* [*ehs-kah-pah-rah'-teh*] shop window

escarcha [*ehs-kahr'-chah*] frost

escarmentar *v. irreg.* [*ehs-kahr-mehn-tahr'*] take warning

escaso [*ehs-kah'-soh*] scarce

escena [*ehs-theh'-nah*] scene

escenario [*ehs-theh-nah'-ree-oh*] stage
esclavitud *f.* [*ehs-klah-vee-tood'*] slavery
esclavo [*ehs-klah'-voh*] slave
escoba [*ehs-koh'-bah*] broom
escocés *m.* [*ehs-koh-thehs'*] Scot, Scotsman
Escocia [*ehs-koh'-thee-ah*] Scotland
escoger *v.* [*ehs-koh-hehr'*] pick, choose
escogido [*ehs-koh-hee'-doh*] chosen
esconder *v.* [*ehs-kohn-dehr'*] hide
escribir *v.* [*ehs-kree-beer'*] write
escritor *m.* [*ehs-kree-tohr'*] writer
escritorio [*ehs-kree-toh'-ree-oh*] desk
escritura [*ehs-kree-too'-rah*] writing
escuchar *v.* [*ehs-koo-chahr'*] listen
escudo [*ehs-koo'-doh*] shield
escuela [*ehs-koo-eh'-lah*] school
  escuela secundaria [*ehs-koo-eh'-lah seh-koon-dah'-ree-ah*]
    high school
  maestro de escuela [*mah-ehs'-troh deh ehs-koo-eh'-lah*]
    schoolteacher
escultura [*ehs-kool-too'-rah*] sculpture
escupir *v.* [*ehs-koo-peer'*] spit
ese [*eh'-seh*] that
esencial [*eh-sehn-thee-ahl'*] essential
esfera [*ehs-feh'-rah*] sphere, dial
esfuerzo [*ehs-foo-ehr'-thoh*] effort
esgrima [*ehs-gree'-mah*] fencing
esmeralda [*ehs-meh-rahl'-dah*] emerald
esos *m.*, **esas** *f.* [*eh'-sohs, eh'-sahs*] those
espacio [*ehs-pah'-thee-oh*] space
espacioso [*ehs-pah-thee-oh'-soh*] spacious, roomy
espada [*ehs-pah'-dah*] sword
espalda [*ehs-pahl'-dah*] back, shoulders
espantoso [*ehs-pahn-toh'-soh*] dreadful
España [*ehs-pah'-nyah*] Spain
español [*ehs-pah-nyohl'*] Spanish, Spaniard
especia [*ehs-peh'-thee-ah*] spice
especial [*ehs-peh-thee-ahl'*] special

especialidad *f.* [*ehs-peh-thee-ah-lee-dahd'*] specialty

especialista *m., f.* [*ehs-peh-thee-ah-lees'-tah*] specialist

especialmente [*ehs-peh-thee-ahl-mehn'-teh*] especially

espectáculo [*ehs-pehk-tah'-koo-loh*] spectacle

espectador *m.* [*ehs-pehk-tah-dohr'*] onlooker, spectator

espejo [*ehs-peh'-hoh*] mirror

esperanza [*ehs-peh-rahn'-thah*] hope

  sin esperanza [*seen ehs-peh-rahn'-thah*] hopeless

esperanzado [*ehs-peh-rahn-thah'-doh*] hopeful

esperar *v.* [*ehs-peh-rahr'*] wait, hope, expect

  Espéreme [*ehs-peh'-reh-meh*] Wait for me

  Espere un momento [*ehs-peh'-reh oon moh-mehn'-toh*]
    Wait a moment

  sala de espera [*sah'-lah deh ehs-peh'-rah*] waiting room

espeso [*ehs-peh'-soh*] thick

espía *m., f.* [*ehs-pee'-ah*] spy

espiar *v.* [*ehs-pee-ahr'*] spy

espina [*ehs-pee'-nah*] thorn

espinaca [*ehs-pee-nah'-kah*] spinach

espíritu *m.* [*ehs-pee'-ree-too*] spirit, ghost

espiritual [*ehs-pee-ree-too-ahl'*] spiritual

espléndido [*ehs-plehn'-dee-doh*] splendid

esponja [*ehs-pohn'-hah*] sponge

espontáneo [*ehs-pohn-tah'-neh-oh*] spontaneous

esposa [*ehs-poh'-sah*] wife

esposo [*ehs-poh'-soh*] husband

espuma [*ehs-poo'-mah*] foam

esqueleto [*ehs-keh-leh'-toh*] skeleton

esquema *m.* [*ehs-keh'-mah*] scheme

esquiar *v.* [*ehs-kee-ahr'*] ski

esquina [*ehs-kee'-nah*] corner

estable [*ehs-tah'-bleh*] stable

establecer *v. irreg.* [*ehs-tah-bleh-thehr'*] establish

establecerse *v.* [*ehs-tah-bleh-thehr'-seh*] settle

establecimiento [*ehs-tah-bleh-thee-mee-ehn'-toh*]
    establishment, store

establo [*ehs-tah'-bloh*] stable

estación *f.* [*ehs-tah-thee-ohn'*] station, season

estación de ferrocarril [*ehs-tah-thee-ohn' deh feh-rroh-kah-rreel'*] railway station

estacionar *v.* [*ehs-tah-thee-oh-nahr'*] park

estadio [*ehs-tah'-dee-oh*] stadium

estadista *m.* [*ehs-tah-dees'-tah*] statesman

estado [*ehs-tah'-doh*] state, condition

  en buen estado [*ehn boo-ehn' ehs-tah'-doh*] in good condition

  estado mayor [*ehs-tah'-doh mah-yohr'*] headquarters

Estados Unidos [*ehs-tah'-dohs oo-nee'-dohs*] United States

estafador *m.* [*ehs-tah-fah-dohr'*] crook

estante *m.* [*ehs-tahn'-teh*] shelf, bookcase

estaño [*ehs-tah'-nyoh*] tin

estar *v. irreg.* [*ehs-tahr'*] be

  Está bien [*ehs-tah' bee-ehn'*] All right

  estar acostumbrado a [*ehs-tahr' ah-kohs-toom-brah'-doh ah*] be used to

  estar de acuerdo [*ehs-tahr' deh ah-koo-ehr'-doh*] agree

  no estar de acuerdo [*noh ehs-tahr' deh ah-koo-ehr'-doh*] disagree

  estar de parto [*ehs-tahr' deh pahr'-toh*] be in labor

  estar de pie [*ehs-tahr' deh pee-eh'*] stand

  estar de servicio [*ehs-tahr' deh sehr-vee'-thee-oh*] be on duty

  estar equivocado [*ehs-tahr' eh-kee-voh-kah'-doh*] be mistaken

  ¿Como está usted? [*koh'-moh ehs-tah' oos-tehd'*] How do you do?

estatua [*ehs-tah'-too-ah*] statue

estatura [*ehs-tah-too'-rah*] height

este *m.* [*ehs'-teh*] east

este *m.*, **esta** *f.* [*ehs'-teh, ehs'-tah*] this

esterilizado [*ehs-teh-ree-lee-thah'-doh*] sterilized

estilo [*ehs-tee'-loh*] style

estimar *v.* [*ehs-tee-mahr'*] esteem, estimate

estimulante *m.* [*ehs-tee-moo-lahn'-teh*] stimulant

estímulo [*ehs-tee'-moo-loh*] encouragement

estipular *v.* [*ehs-tee-poo-lahr'*] stipulate

estirar *v.* [*ehs-tee-rahr'*] stretch
esto [*ehs'-toh*] this
estofado [*ehs-toh-fah'-doh*] stew
estómago [*ehs-toh'-mah-goh*] stomach
   dolor *m.* **de estómago** [*doh-lohr' deh ehs-toh'-mah-goh*]
    stomachache
estorbar *v.* [*ehs-tohr-bahr'*] obstruct, hinder
estornudar *v.* [*ehs-tohr-noo-dahr'*] sneeze
estos [*ehs'-tohs*] these
estrecho [*ehs-treh'-choh*] narrow
estrella [*ehs-treh'-yah*] star
estrellarse *v.* [*ehs-treh-yahr'-seh*] crash
estremecido [*ehs-treh-meh-thee'-doh*] thrilled
estrictamente [*ehs-treek-tah-mehn'-teh*] strictly
estricto [*ehs-treek'-toh*] strict
estropeado [*ehs-troh-peh-ah'-doh*] disabled, lame
estropear *v.* [*ehs-troh-peh-ahr'*] spoil
estructura [*ehs-trook-too'-rah*] structure
estrujar *v.* [*ehs-troo-hahr'*] squeeze
estudiante *m., f.* [*ehs-too-dee-ahn'-teh*] student
estudiar *v.* [*ehs-too-dee-ahr'*] study
estudio [*ehs-too'-dee-oh*] study
estufa [*ehs-too'-fah*] stove
estupendo [*ehs-too-pehn'-doh*] fine
estúpido [*ehs-too'-pee-doh*] stupid
etapa [*eh-tah'-pah*] stage, stop
eterno [*eh-tehr'-noh*] eternal
ética [*eh'-tee-kah*] ethics
etiqueta [*eh-tee-keh'-tah*] label
Europa [*eh-oo-roh'-pah*] Europe
europeo [*eh-oo-roh-peh'-oh*] European
evacuar *v.* [*eh-vah-koo-ahr'*] evacuate
evadir *v.* [*eh-vah-deer'*] evade
eventualmente [*eh-vehn-too-ahl-mehn'-teh*] eventually
evidencia [*eh-vee-dehn'-thee-ah*] evidence
evidente [*eh-vee-dehn'-teh*] evident
evidentemente [*eh-vee-dehn-teh-mehn'-teh*] evidently
evitar *v.* [*eh-vee-tahr'*] avoid

exactamente [*ehk-sahk-tah-mehn'-teh*] exactly
exacto [*ehk-sahk'-toh*] exact
exageración *f.* [*ehk-sah-heh-rah-thee-ohn'*] exaggeration
exagerar *v.* [*ehk-sah-heh-rahr'*] exaggerate
examen *m.* [*ehk-sah'-mehn*] examination
examinar *v.* [*ehk-sah-mee-nahr'*] examine
exceder *v.* [*ehks-theh-dehr'*] exceed
excederse *v.* [*ehks-theh-dehr'-seh*] overdo
excelente [*ehks-theh-lehn'-teh*] excellent
excepción *f.* [*ehks-thehp-thee-ohn'*] exception
excepto [*ehks-thehp'-toh*] except
exceso [*ehks-theh'-soh*] excess
excitado [*ehks-thee-tah'-doh*] excited
excitar *v.* [*ehks-thee-tahr'*] excite
 ¡No se excite! [*noh seh ehks-thee'-teh*] Don't get excited!
excluir *v. irreg.* [*ehks-kloo-eer'*] exclude
exclusivo [*ehks-kloo-see'-voh*] exclusive
excursión *f.* [*ehks-koor-see-ohn'*] excursion
excusa [*ehks-koo'-sah*] excuse
excusado [*ehks-koo-sah'-doh*] toilet
excusar *v.* [*ehks-koo-sahr'*] excuse
excusarse *v.* [*ehks-koo-sahr'-seh*] apologize
exento [*ehk-sehn'-toh*] exempt, free
exhibición *f.* [*ehk-see-bee-thee-ohn'*] exhibition
exhibir *v.* [*ehk-see-beer'*] exhibit, display
exigencia [*ehk-see-hehn'-thee-ah*] demand
existencia [*ehk-sees-tehn'-thee-ah*] existence
existir *v.* [*ehk-sees-teer'*] exist
éxito [*ehk'-see-toh*] success
 tener *v. irreg.* **éxito** [*teh-nehr' ehk'-see-toh*] succeed
expedición *f.* [*ehks-peh-dee-thee-ohn'*] expedition
experiencia [*ehks-peh-ree-ehn'-thee-ah*] experience
experimento [*ehks-peh-ree-mehn'-toh*] experiment
experto *n. & adj.* [*ehks-pehr'-toh*] expert
explicación *f.* [*ehks-plee-kah-thee-ohn'*] explanation
explicar *v.* [*ehks-plee-kahr'*] explain
explorar *v.* [*ehks-ploh-rahr'*] explore
explosión *f.* [*ehks-ploh-see-ohn'*] explosion

exponer *v. irreg.* [*ehks-poh-nehr'*] state, show
exportar *v.* [*ehks-pohr-tahr'*] export
exposición *f.* [*ehks-poh-see-thee-ohn'*] exposition, show
expresar *v.* [*ehks-preh-sahr'*] express
expresivo [*ehks-preh-see'-voh*] expressive
expreso [*ehks-preh'-soh*] express
exprimir *v.* [*ehks-pree-meer'*] squeeze
expulsar *v.* [*ehks-pool-sahr'*] expel
exquisito [*ehks-kee-see'-toh*] dainty
extender *v. irreg.* [*ehks-tehn-dehr'*] spread
extenderse *v.* [*ehks-tehn-dehr'-seh*] extend
extensión *f.* [*ehks-tehn-see-ohn'*] extent, extension
exterior *m.* [*ehks-teh-ree-ohr'*] exterior
externo [*ehks-tehr'-noh*] external
extinguir *v.* [*ehks-teen-gheer'*] extinguish
extra [*ehks' trah*] extra
extraer *v. irreg.* [*ehks-trah-ehr'*] extract
extranjero [*ehks-trahn-heh'-roh*] foreign
　en el extranjero [*ehn ehl ehks-trahn-heh'-roh*] abroad
extrañarse *v.* [*ehks-trah-nyahr'-seh*] wonder at
extraño [*ehks-trah'-nyoh*] strange
extraordinario [*ehks-trah-ohr-dee-nah'-ree-oh*]
　　extraordinary
extravagante [*ehks-trah-vah-gahn'-teh*] extravagant
extraviar *v.* [*ehks-trah-vee-ahr'*] misplace, misguide
extremadamente [*ehks-treh-mah-dah-mehn'-teh*] extremely
extremo [*ehks-treh'-moh*] extreme

F

fábrica [*fah'-bree-kah*] factory
fabricante *m.* [*fah-bree-kahn'-teh*] manufacturer
fabricar *v.* [*fah-bree-kahr'*] manufacture
fácil [*fah'-theel*] easy
facilidad *f.* [*fah-thee-lee-dahd'*] ease

fácilmente [*fah'-theel-mehn-teh*] easily
factible [*fahk-tee'-bleh*] feasible
factor *m.* [*fahk-tohr'*] factor
factura [*fahk-too'-rah*] invoice, bill
   factura de equipaje [*fahk-too'-rah deh eh-kee-pah'-heh*]
     baggage check
facultad *f.* [*fah-kool-tahd'*] faculty, ability
fachada [*fah-chah'-dah*] façade
faena [*fah-eh'-nah*] task
faja [*fah'-hah*] girdle
fajo [*fah'-hoh*] bundle
falda [*fahl'-dah*] skirt
falsedad *f.* [*fahl-seh-dahd'*] falsehood
falso [*fahl'-soh*] false, untrue
falta [*fahl'-tah*] fault
faltar *v.* [*fahl-tahr'*] be missing
fallar *v.* [*fah-yahr'*] fail
fama [*fah'-mah*] fame
familia [*fah-mee'-lee-ah*] family
familiar [*fah-mee-lee-ahr'*] familiar
familiarizar *v.* [*fah-mee-lee-ah-ree-thahr'*] acquaint
famoso [*fah-moh'-soh*] famous
fanático *n. & adj.* [*fah-nah'-tee-koh*] fanatic
fanfarrón *m.* [*fahn-fah-rrohn'*] braggart
fango [*fahn'-goh*] mud
fangoso [*fahn-goh'-soh*] muddy
fantasía [*fahn-tah-see'-ah*] fancy
fantasma [*fahn-tahs'-mah*] ghost
fantástico [*fahn-tahs'-tee-koh*] fantastic
fardo [*fahr'-doh*] bundle
farmacéutico [*fahr-mah-theh'-oo-tee-koh*] pharmacist
farmacia [*fahr-mah'-thee-ah*] drugstore, pharmacy
faro [*fah'-roh*] lighthouse
fascinante [*fahs-thee-nahn'-teh*] fascinating
fascinar *v.* [*fahs-thee-nahr'*] fascinate
fase *f.* [*fah'-seh*] phase
fatiga [*fah-tee'-gah*] fatigue
favor *m.* [*fah-vohr'*] favor

por favor [*pohr fah-vohr'*] please
favorecer *v. irreg.* [*fah-voh-reh-thehr'*] favor
favorito [*fah-voh-ree'-toh*] favorite
fe *f.* [*feh*] faith
febrero [*feh-breh'-roh*] February
febril [*feh-breel'*] feverish
fecha [*feh'-chah*] date
federal [*feh-deh-rahl'*] federal
felicidad *f.* [*feh-lee-thee-dahd'*] happiness
felicitaciones *f.* [*feh-lee-thee-tah-thee-oh'-nehs*]
    congratulations
felicitar *v.* [*feh-lee-thee-tahr'*] congratulate
feliz [*feh-leeth'*] happy
  Felices Pascuas [*feh-lee'-thehs pahs'-koo-ahs*] Merry
    Christmas
  Feliz Año Nuevo [*feh-leeth' ah'-nyoh noo-eh'-voh*]
    Happy New Year
  Feliz Cumpleaños [*feh-leeth' koom-pleh-ah'-nyohs*]
    Happy Birthday
femenino [*feh-meh-nee'-noh*] feminine
feo [*feh'-oh*] ugly
ferretería [*feh-rreh-teh-ree'-ah*] hardware store
ferrocarril *m.* [*feh-rroh-kah-rreel'*] railroad
festín *m.* [*fehs-teen'*] feast
festival *m.* [*fehs-tee-vahl'*] festival
fiarse *v.* [*fee-ahr'-seh*] rely on
fibra [*fee'-brah*] fiber
ficción *f.* [*feek-thee-ohn'*] fiction
fiebre *f.* [*fee-eh'-breh*] fever
fiel [*fee-ehl'*] faithful
fiero [*fee-eh'-roh*] fierce
fiesta [*fee-ehs'-tah*] party
figura [*fee-goo'-rah*] figure, shape
fijar *v.* [*fee-hahr'*] fasten, set up
fila [*fee'-lah*] row
filete *m.* [*fee-leh'-teh*] steak
filosofía [*fee-loh-soh-fee'-ah*] philosophy
filósofo [*fee-loh'-soh-foh*] philosopher

filtro [*feel'-troh*] filter
fin *m.* [*feen*] end, purpose
final [*fee-nahl'*] final
finalmente [*fee-nahl-mehn'-teh*] finally
financiero [*fee-nahn-thee-eh'-roh*] financial
finca [*feen'-kah*] real estate, ranch
fingir *v.* [*feen-heer'*] pretend
fino [*fee'-noh*] fine, delicate
firma [*feer'-mah*] signature, firm, company
firmar *v.* [*feer-mahr'*] sign
firme *adj.* [*feer'-meh*] firm
físico [*fee'-see-koh*] physical
flaco [*flah'-koh*] skinny
flamante [*flah-mahn'-teh*] brand-new
flan *m.* [*flahn*] custard
flauta [*flah'-oo-tah*] flute
flecha [*fleh'-chah*] arrow
flete *m.* [*fleh'-teh*] freight
flexible [*flehk-see'-bleh*] flexible
flojo [*floh'-hoh*] loose
flor *f.* [*flohr*] flower
florecer *v. irreg.* [*floh-reh-thehr'*] blossom, flourish
florería [*floh-reh-ree'-ah*] flowershop
flota [*floh'-tah*] fleet
flotar *v.* [*floh-tahr'*] float
fluente [*floo-ehn'-teh*] fluent
flúido [*floo'-ee-doh*] fluid
fluir *v. irreg.* [*floo-eer'*] flow
foca [*foh'-kah*] seal [animal]
foco [*foh'-koh*] focus
folleto [*foh-yeh'-toh*] pamphlet
fondo [*fohn'-doh*] bottom
fondos *m. pl.* [*fohn'-dohs*] funds
fontanero [*fohn-tah-neh'-roh*] plumber
forastero [*foh-rahs-teh'-roh*] outsider
forma [*fohr'-mah*] shape, form
   dar *v.* **forma** [*dahr fohr'-mah*] shape
formal [*fohr-mahl'*] formal

formalidad *f.* [*fohr-mah-lee-dahd'*] formality
formar *v.* [*fohr-mahr'*] form
fórmula [*fohr'-moo-lah*] formula
forro [*foh'-rroh*] lining
fortalecer *v. irreg.* [*fohr-tah-leh-thehr'*] strengthen
fortaleza [*fohr-tah-leh'-thah*] fortress, vigor
fortuna [*fohr-too'-nah*] fortune
forzar *v. irreg.* [*fohr-thahr'*] force
fósforo [*fohs'-foh-roh*] match [for cigarette]
fotografía [*foh-toh-grah-fee'-ah*] photograph
fotografiar *v.* [*foh-toh-grah-fee-ahr'*] photograph, take a
     picture
fotógrafo [*foh-toh'-grah-foh*] photographer
fracasar *v.* [*frah-kah-sahr'*] fail
fracaso [*frah-kah'-soh*] failure
fractura [*frahk-too'-rah*] fracture
fragancia [*frah-gahn'-thee-ah*] fragrance
frágil [*frah'-heel*] fragile
fraile *m.* [*frah'-ee-leh*] friar
Francia [*frahn'-thee-ah*] France
francés [*frahn-thehs'*] French
franco [*frahn'-koh*] frank
franela [*frah-neh'-lah*] flannel
franqueo [*frahn-keh'-oh*] postage
frasco [*frahs'-koh*] flask
frase *f.* [*frah'-seh*] sentence
fraude *m.* [*frah'-oo-deh*] fraud
frazada [*frah-thah'-dah*] blanket
frecuente [*freh-koo-ehn'-teh*] frequent
frecuentemente [*freh-koo-ehn-teh-mehn'-teh*] frequently
freír *v. irreg.* [*freh-eer'*] fry
frenar *v.* [*freh-nahr'*] brake
frenético [*freh-neh'-tee-koh*] frantic
freno [*freh'-noh*] brake
frente *m.* [*frehn'-teh*] front
frente *f.* [*frehn'-teh*] forehead
fresa [*freh'-sah*] strawberry

fresco [*frehs'-koh*] fresh, cool
frialdad *f.* [*free-ahl-dahd'*] coldness
frigorífico [*free-goh-ree'-fee-koh*] refrigerator
frijol *m.* [*free-hohl'*] bean
frío [*free'-oh*] cold, chilly
   tener *v. irreg.* **frío** [*teh-nehr' free'-oh*] be cold
frito [*free'-toh*] fried
frontera [*frohn-teh'-rah*] frontier, border
frotar *v.* [*froh-tahr'*] rub
fruncir *v.* [*froon-theer'*] frown
frustración *f.* [*froos-trah-thee-ohn'*] frustration
fruta [*froo'-tah*] fruit
   ensalada de frutas [*ehn-sah-lah'-dah deh froo'-tahs*]
    fruit salad
frutería [*froo-teh-ree'-ah*] fruit store
fuego [*foo-eh'-goh*] fire
fuente *f.* [*foo-ehn'-teh*] fountain
fuera [*foo-eh'-rah*] outside, out, off
   fuera de servicio [*foo-eh'-rah deh sehr-vee'-thee-oh*]
    out of order
   hacia fuera [*ah'-thee-ah foo-eh'-rah*] outward
fuerte [*foo-ehr'-teh*] strong
fuerza [*foo-ehr'-thah*] strength, force
fuga [*foo'-gah*] escape
fugarse *v.* [*foo-gahr'-seh*] run away
fugitivo *n. & adj.* [*foo-hee-tee'-voh*] runaway
fumar *v.* [*foo-mahr'*] smoke
función *f.* [*foon-thee-ohn'*] function, show
funcionar *v.* [*foon-thee-oh-nahr'*] work, run
funda [*foon'-dah*] cover
fundación *f.* [*foon-dah-thee-ohn'*] foundation
funeral *m.* [*foo-neh-rahl'*] funeral
furioso [*foo-ree-oh'-soh*] furious
fusil *m.* [*foo-seel'*] gun
fútbol *m.* [*foot'-bohl*] football
futuro *n. & adj.* [*foo-too'-roh*] future
   en el futuro [*ehn ehl foo-too'-roh*] in the future

G

gafas *f. pl.* [*gah'-fahs*] eyeglasses
  gafas de sol [*gah'-fahs deh sohl*] sunglasses
galón *m.* [*gah-lohn'*] gallon
galleta [*gah-yeh'-tah*] cracker, cookie
gallina [*gah-yee'-nah*] hen
gana [*gah'-nah*] desire, appetite
  de buena gana [*deh boo-eh'-nah gah'-nah*] willingly
ganado [*gah-nah'-doh*] cattle
ganancia [*gah-nahn'-thee-ah*] gain
ganar *v.* [*gah-nuhr'*] gain, earn, win
gancho [*gahn'-choh*] hook
ganga [*gahn'-gah*] bargain
garage *m.* [*gah-rah'-heh*] garage
garantía [*gah-rahn-tee'-ah*] guarantee, warranty
garantizar *v.* [*gah-rahn-tee-thahr'*] guarantee
garganta [*gahr-gahn'-tah*] throat
gas *m.* [*gahs*] gas
gaseosa [*gah-seh-oh'-sah*] soda
gasolina [*gah-soh-lee'-nah*] gasoline
gasolinera [*gah-soh-lee-neh'-rah*] gasoline station
gastado [*gahs-tah'-doh*] worn out
gastar *v.* [*gahs-tahr'*] spend
  malgastar *v.* [*mahl-gahs-tahr'*] waste
gasto [*gahs'-toh*] expense
gato [*gah'-toh*] cat
gaveta [*gah-veh'-tah*] drawer
gelatina [*heh-lah-tee'-nah*] jelly
gema [*heh'-mah*] gem
gemelo [*heh-meh'-loh*] twin
gemido [*heh-mee'-doh*] groan
gemir *v. irreg.* [*heh-meer'*] groan
generación *f.* [*heh-neh-rah-thee-ohn'*] generation

general *m.* [*heh-neh-rahl'*] general
general *adj.* [*heh-neh-rahl'*] general
generalmente [*heh-neh-rahl-mehn'-teh*] generally, usually
género [*heh'-neh-roh*] gender
generoso [*heh-neh-roh'-soh*] generous
genio [*heh'-nee-oh*] genius, temper
  de mal genio [*deh mahl heh'-nee-oh*] bad-tempered
gente *f.* [*hehn'-teh*] people
gentío [*hehn-tee'-oh*] crowd
genuino [*heh-noo-ee'-noh*] genuine
geografía [*heh-oh-grah-fee'-ah*] geography
gerente *m.* [*heh-rehn'-teh*] manager
germen *m.* [*hehr'-mehn*] germ
gestionar *v.* [*hehs-tee-oh-nahr'*] take steps
gesto [*hehs'-toh*] grimace, gesture
gimnasio [*heem-nah'-see-oh*] gymnasium
ginebra [*hee-neh'-brah*] gin
girar *v.* [*hee-rahr'*] revolve, spin
giro [*hee'-roh*] draft, money order
gitano [*hee-tah'-noh*] gypsy
glándula [*glahn'-doo-lah*] gland
globo [*gloh'-boh*] balloon, globe
  globo del ojo [*gloh'-boh dehl oh'-hoh*] eyeball
gloria [*gloh'-ree-ah*] glory
gobernador *m.* [*goh-behr-nah-dohr'*] governor
gobernante *m., f.* [*goh-behr-nahn'-teh*] ruler
gobernar *v. irreg.* [*goh-behr-nahr'*] rule
gobierno [*goh-bee-ehr'-noh*] government
golfo [*gohl'-foh*] gulf
golpe *m.* [*gohl'-peh*] blow, bruise, attack, knock
  golpe de vista [*gohl'-peh deh vees'-tah*] glance
golpear *v.* [*gohl-peh-ahr'*] hit, knock
goma [*goh'-mah*] rubber
gordo [*gohr'-doh*] fat
gorra [*gohr'-rrah*] cap
gota [*goh'-tah*] drop
gotear *v.* [*goh-teh-ahr'*] drip
gotera [*goh-teh'-rah*] leak

gozar *v.* [*goh-thahr'*] enjoy
gozo [*goh'-thoh*] enjoyment
gozoso [*goh-thoh'-soh*] elated
grabado [*grah-bah'-doh*] engraving
gracia [*grah'-thee-ah*] grace
gracias [*grah'-thee-ahs*] thank you
gracioso [*grah-thee-oh'-soh*] graceful, funny
grado [*grah'-doh*] grade, degree
graduación *f.* [*grah-doo-ah-thee-ohn'*] graduation, military
    rank
graduado [*grah-doo-ah'-doh*] graduate
gradualmente [*grah-doo-ahl-mehn'-teh*] gradually
graduarse *v.* [*grah-doo-ahr'-seh*] graduate
gramática [*grah-mah'-tee-kah*] grammar
gramo [*grah'-moh*] gram
gran, grande [*grahn, grahn'-deh*] great, large, big
    una gran cantidad [*oo'-nah grahn kahn-tee-dahd'*] a lot of
    de gran valor [*deh grahn vah-lohr'*] invaluable
Gran Bretaña [*grahn breh-tah'-nyah*] Great Britain
grandeza [*grahn-deh'-thah*] greatness
granero [*grah-neh'-roh*] barn
granja [*grahn'-hah*] farm
granjero [*grahn-heh'-roh*] farmer
grano [*grah'-noh*] grain
grasa [*grah'-sah*] grease
gratis [*grah'-tees*] free
gratitud *f.* [*grah-tee-tood'*] gratitude
gravedad *f.* [*grah-veh-dahd'*] gravity
Grecia [*greh'-thee-ah*] Greece
griego [*gree-eh'-goh*] Greek
grifo [*gree'-foh*] faucet
gris *m., f.* [*grees*] gray
gritar *v.* [*gree-tahr'*] scream, yell, shout
grito [*gree'-toh*] shout, cry
grosero [*groh-seh'-roh*] rude, gross
grueso [*groo-eh'-soh*] thick, fat
grupo [*groo'-poh*] group
guante *m.* [*goo-ahn'-teh*] glove

guapa [*goo-ah'-pah*] pretty, good-looking
guarda *m.* [*goo-ahr'-dah*] guard, keeper
  guardabarros *m.* [*goo-ahr-dah-bah'-rrohs*] fender
  guardarropa *m.* [*goo-ahr-dah-rroh'-pah*] closet, wardrobe
guardar *v.* [*goo-ahr-dahr'*] keep, guard
guardia *m.* [*goo-ahr'-dee-ah*] guard
Guatemala [*goo-ah-teh-mah'-lah*] Guatemala
guatemalteco [*goo-ah-teh-mahl-teh'-koh*] Guatemalan
guerra [*gheh'-rrah*] war
  guerra mundial [*gheh'-rrah moon-dee-ahl'*] world war
guía *m., f.* [*ghee'-ah*] guide
guía telefónica *f.* [*ghee'-ah teh-leh-foh'-nee-kah*] telephone
  book
guiñar *v.* [*ghee-nyahr'*] wink
guisante *m.* [*ghee-sahn'-teh*] pea
guitarra [*ghee-tah'-rrah*] guitar
gusano [*goo-sah'-noh*] worm
gustar *v.* [*goos-tahr'*] like, care for, enjoy
  no gustar [*noh goos-tahr'*] dislike
gusto [*goos'-toh*] taste
  mucho gusto [*moo'-choh goos'-toh*] glad to meet you

H

haber *v. irreg.* [*ah-behr'*] have
hábil [*ah'-beel*] able, skillful
habitación *f.* [*ah-bee-tah-thee-ohn'*] room, lodging
  habitación amueblada [*ah-bee-tah-thee-ohn' ah-moo-eh-
  blah'-dah*] furnished room
habitante *m.* [*ah-bee-tahn'-teh*] inhabitant
habitar *v.* [*ah-bee-tahr'*] inhabit
hábito [*ah'-bee-toh*] habit
habitual [*ah-bee-too-ahl'*] customary
hablar *v.* [*ah-blahr'*] speak, talk
hacer *v. irreg.* [*ah-thehr'*] make, do

hacer auto-stop [*ah-thehr' ah-oo'-toh-stohp*] hitchhike

hace dos semanas [*ah'-theh dohs seh-mah'-nahs*] two weeks ago

hacer un cumplido [*ah-thehr' oon koom-plee'-doh*] pay a compliment

hacer viento [*ah-thehr' vee-ehn'-toh*] be windy

Hágame el favor de . . . [*ah'-gah-meh ehl fah-vohr' deh . . .* Do me the favor of . . .

hacerse *v. irreg.* [*ah-thehr'-seh*] become

hacia [*ah'-thee-ah*] toward

hacia adelante [*ah'-thee-ah ah-deh-lahn'-teh*] forward

hacia arriba [*ah'-thee-ah ah-rree'-bah*] upward

hacia atrás [*ah'-thee-ah ah-trahs'*] backward

hacia atrás y hacia adelante [*ah'-thee-ah ah-trahs' ee ah'-thee-ah ah-deh-lahn'-teh*] back and forth

hacha [*ah'-chah*] ax

hallar *v.* [*ah-yahr'*] find

hambre *m.* [*ahm'-breh*] hunger

tener *v. irreg.* **hambre** [*teh-nehr' ahm'-breh*] be hungry

hambriento [*ahm-bree-ehn'-toh*] hungry

harina [*ah-ree'-nah*] flour

harto [*ahr'-toh*] full, fed up

hasta [*ahs'-tah*] till, until

hasta ahora [*ahs'-tah ah-oh'-rah*] so far, up to now

hay [*ah'-ee*] there is, there are

Hay sitio . . . [*ah'-ee see'-tee-oh*] There is room . . .

hebilla [*eh-bee'-yah*] buckle

hebreo [*eh-breh'-oh*] Hebrew

hecho *n.* [*eh'-choh*] fact, event

hecho *adj.* [*eh'-choh*] done, made

hecho a mano [*eh'-choh ah mah'-noh*] handmade

helado [*eh-lah'-doh*] ice cream

hélice *f.* [*eh'-lee-theh*] propeller

hembra [*ehm'-brah*] female

heredar *v.* [*eh-reh-dahr'*] inherit

heredera [*eh-reh-deh'-rah*] heiress

heredero [*eh-reh-deh'-roh*] heir

herencia [*eh-rehn'-thee-ah*] inheritance

herida [*eh-ree'-dah*] wound
herido [*eh-ree'-doh*] wounded
hermana [*ehr-mah'-nah*] sister
hermano [*ehr-mah'-noh*] brother
hermoso [*ehr-moh'-soh*] beautiful
héroe [*eh'-roh-eh*] hero
heroína [*eh-roh-ee'-nah*] heroine
herramienta [*eh-rrah-mee-ehn'-tah*] tool
herrumbre *f.* [*eh-rroom'-breh*] rust
hervir *v. irreg.* [*ehr-veer'*] boil
hielo [*ee-eh'-loh*] ice
hierba [*ee-ehr'-bah*] grass
hierro [*ee-eh'-rroh*] iron [metal]
hígado [*ee'-gah-doh*] liver
higiene *f.* [*ee-hee-eh'-neh*] hygiene
higo [*ee'-goh*] fig
hija [*ee'-hah*] daughter
hijo [*ee'-hoh*] son
hilo [*ee'-loh*] thread
himno [*eem'-noh*] hymn
hinchar *v.* [*een-chahr'*] swell
hipócrita *m., f.* [*ee-poh'-kree-tah*] hypocrite
hipoteca [*ee-poh-teh'-kah*] mortgage
hispano [*ees-pah'-noh*] Hispanic
historia [*ees-toh'-ree-ah*] history
hogar *m.* [*oh-gahr'*] home, fireplace
hoguera [*oh-gheh'-rah*] bonfire
hoja [*oh'-hah*] leaf, blade, sheet
hola [*oh'-lah*] hello
Holanda [*oh-lahn'-dah*] Holland
holandés [*oh-lahn-dehs'*] Dutch
holgazán [*ohl-gah-thahn'*] lazy
hombre *m.* [*ohm'-breh*] man
hombro [*ohm'-broh*] shoulder
hondo [*ohn'-doh*] deep
Honduras [*ohn-doo'-rahs*] Honduras
hondureño [*ohn-doo-reh'-nyoh*] Honduran
honesto [*oh-nehs'-toh*] honest

honor *m.* [*oh-nohr'*] honor
honorarios *m.pl.* [*oh-noh-rah'-ree-ohs*] fee
honrado [*ohn-rah'-doh*] honest
honrar *v.* [*ohn-rahr'*] honor
hora [*oh'-rah*] hour, time
  horas extra [*oh'-rahs ehks'-trah*] overtime
  por hora [*pohr oh'-rah*] hourly
  Es hora de . . . [*ehs oh'-rah deh . . .*] It is time to . . .
  ¿Qué hora es? [*keh' oh'-rah ehs*] What time is it?
horario [*oh-rah'-ree-oh*] schedule
horizontal [*oh-ree-thohn-tahl'*] horizontal
hormiga [*ohr-mee'-gah*] ant
horno [*ohr'-noh*] oven
horquilla [*ohr-kee'-yah*] hairpin
horrible [*oh-rree'-bleh*] awful, horrible
horripilante [*oh-rree-pee-lahn'-teh*] hideous
hortalizas *f. pl.* [*ohr-tah-lee'-thahs*] vegetables
hospedar *v.* [*ohs-peh-dahr'*] lodge
hospital *m.* [*ohs-pee-tahl'*] hospital
hospitalidad *f.* [*ohs-pee-tah-lee-dahd'*] hospitality
hostil [*ohs-teel'*] hostile
hotel *m.* [*oh-tehl'*] hotel
  habitación de hotel [*ah-bee-tah-thee-ohn' deh oh-tehl'*]
    hotel room
hoy [*oh'-ee*] today
  hoy día [*oh'-ee dee'-ah*] nowadays
huelga [*oo-ehl'-gah*] strike [work stoppage]
huella [*oo-eh'-yah*] trace, footprint
  huella digital [*oo-eh'-yah dee-hee-tahl'*] fingerprint
huérfano [*oo-ehr'-fah-noh*] orphan
huerto [*oo-ehr'-toh*] orchard, garden
hueso [*oo-eh'-soh*] bone
huésped *m.* [*oo-ehs'-pehd*] guest
huevo [*oo-eh'-voh*] egg
  huevos duros [*oo-eh'-vohs doo'-rohs*] hard-boiled eggs
  huevos fritos [*oo-eh'-vohs free'-tohs*] fried eggs
  huevos pasados por agua [*oo-eh'-vohs pah-sah'-dohs
    pohr ah'-goo-ah*] soft-boiled eggs

huevos revueltos [*oo-eh'-vohs reh-voo-ehl'-tohs*] scrambled eggs
huir *v. irreg.* [*oo-eer'*] flee
humanidad *f.* [*oo-mah-nee-dahd'*] humanity
humano [*oo-mah'-noh*] human
humedad *f.* [*oo-meh-dahd'*] moisture, humidity
húmedo [*oo'-meh-doh*] humid, wet, damp
humilde [*oo-meel'-deh*] humble
humo [*oo'-moh*] smoke
humor *m.* [*oo-mohr'*] mood
   de mal humor [*deh mahl oo-mohr'*] in a bad mood
humorístico [*oo-moh-rees'-tee-koh*] humorous
hundir *v.* [*oon-deer'*] sink
Hungría [*oon-gree'-ah*] Hungary

I

ida [*ee'-dah*] departure
   billete *m.* **de ida y vuelta** [*bee-yeh'-teh deh ee'-dah ee voo-ehl'-tah*] round-trip ticket
idea [*ee-deh'-ah*] idea, concept
ideal *m.* [*ee-deh-ahl'*] ideal
idéntico [*ee-dehn'-tee-koh*] identical
identidad *f.* [*ee-dehn-tee-dahd'*] identity
   tarjeta de identidad [*tahr-heh'-tah deh ee-dehn-tee-dahd'*] identification card
identificar *v.* [*ee-dehn-tee-fee-kahr'*] identify
idioma *m.* [*ee-dee-oh'-mah*] language
iglesia [*ee-gleh'-see-ah*] church
ignorante [*eeg-noh-rahn'-teh*] ignorant
igual [*ee-goo-ahl'*] equal
igualdad *f.* [*ee-goo-ahl-dahd'*] equality
ilegal [*ee-leh-gahl'*] illegal, unlawful
ileso [*ee-leh'-soh*] unharmed
ilícito [*ee-lee'-thee-toh*] illicit

iluminar *v.* [*ee-loo-mee-nahr'*] light, illuminate
ilustración *f.* [*ee-loos-trah-thee-ohn'*] illustration
imagen *f.* [*ee-mah'-hehn*] image
imaginación *f.* [*ee-mah-hee-nah-thee-ohn'*] imagination
imaginar *v.* [*ee-mah-hee-nahr'*] imagine
imitación *f.* [*ee-mee-tah-thee-ohn'*] imitation
imitar *v.* [*ee-mee-tahr'*] imitate
impaciente [*eem-pah-thee-ehn'-teh*] impatient
impar [*eem-pahr'*] odd [not even]
imparcial [*eem-pahr-thee-ahl'*] impartial
impedir *v. irreg.* [*eem-peh-deer'*] impede, prevent
imperfecto [*eem-pehr-fehk'-toh*] imperfect
impermeable *m.* [*eem-pehr-meh-ah'-bleh*] raincoat
impermeable *adj.* [*eem-pehr-meh-ah'-bleh*] waterproof
imponente [*eem-poh-nehn'-teh*] impressive
importado [*eem-pohr-tah'-doh*] imported
importancia [*eem-pohr-tahn'-thee-ah*] importance
importante [*eem-pohr-tahn'-teh*] important
importar *v.* [*eem-pohr-tahr'*] import, concern, matter
　No importa [*noh eem-pohr'-tah*] It doesn't matter
importe *m.* [*eem-pohr'-teh*] amount
imposible [*eem-poh-see'-bleh*] impossible
impresión *f.* [*eem-preh-see-ohn'*] impression
impresionante [*eem-preh-see-oh-nahn'-teh*] impressive
impresor *m.* [*eem-preh-sohr'*] printer
imprevisto [*eem-preh-vees'-toh*] unforeseen
imprimir *v.* [*eem-pree-meer'*] print
improbable [*eem-proh-bah'-bleh*] unlikely
impuesto [*eem-poo-ehs'-toh*] tax
　impuesto sobre ingresos [*eem-poo-ehs'-toh soh'-breh een-greh'-sohs*] income tax
impulso [*eem-pool'-soh*] impulse
incapacidad *f.* [*een-kah-pah-thee-dahd'*] disability
incapacitado [*een-kah-pah-thee-tah'-doh*] disabled
incapaz [*een-kah-pahth'*] unable
incendio [*een-thehn'-dee-oh*] fire
incidentalmente [*een-thee-dehn-tahl-mehn'-teh*] incidentally
incidente *m.* [*een-thee-dehn'-teh*] incident

incierto [*een-thee-ehr'-toh*] uncertain
inclinación *f.* [*een-klee-nah-thee-ohn'*] inclination, tendency
inclinar *v.* [*een-klee-nahr'*] lean
incluído [*een-kloo-ee'-doh*] included, enclosed
incluir *v. irreg.* [*een-kloo-eer'*] include
incombustible [*een-kohm-boos-tee'-bleh*] fireproof
incomodidad *f.* [*een-koh-moh-dee-dahd'*] discomfort
incómodo [*een-koh'-moh-doh*] uncomfortable
incompleto [*een-kohm-pleh'-toh*] incomplete
inconfundible [*een-kohn-foon-dee'-bleh*] unmistakable
inconsciente [*een-kohns-thee-ehn'-teh*] unconscicus
incorrecto [*een-koh-rrehk'-toh*] incorrect
increíble [*een-kreh-ee'-bleh*] incredible
incursión *f.* [*een-koor-see-ohn'*] raid
indagar *v.* [*een-dah-gahr'*] find out
indecente [*een-deh-thehn'-teh*] indecent
indeciso [*een-deh-thee'-soh*] undecided
indefinido [*een-deh-fee-nee'-doh*] indefinite
indemnización *f.* [*een-dehm-nee-thah-thee-ohn'*] compensation
independencia [*een-deh-pehn-dehn'-thee-ah*] independence
independiente [*een-deh-pehn-dee-ehn'-teh*] independent
India [*een'-dee-ah*] India
indicador *m.* [*een-dee-kah-dohr'*] gauge
indicar *v.* [*een-dee-kahr'*] point out, indicate
índice *m.* [*een'-dee-theh*] index
indiferente [*een-dee-feh-rehn'-teh*] indifferent
indigestión *f.* [*een-dee-hehs-tee-ohn'*] indigestion
indignado [*een-deeg-nah'-doh*] indignant
indio [*een'-dee-oh*] Indian
indirecto [*een-dee-rehk'-toh*] indirect
indiscreto [*een-dees-kreh'-toh*] indiscreet
indiscutible [*een-dees-koo-tee'-bleh*] unquestionable
individuo *n. & adj.* [*een-dee-vee'-doo-oh*] individual
industria [*een-doos'-tree-ah*] industry
industrial [*een-doos-tree-ahl'*] industrial
ineficaz [*ee-neh-fee-kahth'*] inefficient
inepto [*ee-nehp'-toh*] unfit
inesperado [*ee-nehs-peh-rah'-doh*] unexpected

inevitable [*ee-neh-vee-tah′-bleh*] unavoidable

inexacto [*ee-nehk-sahk′-toh*] inaccurate

infantil [*een-fahn-teel′*] childish

infección *f.* [*een-fehk-thee-ohn′*] infection

infeliz [*een-feh-leeth′*] unhappy

inferior *m., f.* [*een-feh-ree-ohr′*] inferior

infiel [*een-fee-ehl′*] unfaithful

infierno [*een-fee-ehr′-noh*] hell

infinitivo [*een-fee-nee-tee′-voh*] infinitive

infinito [*een-fee-nee′-toh*] infinite

influencia [*een-floo-ehn′-thee-ah*] influence

influir *v. irreg.* [*een-floo-eer′*] influence

información *f.* [*een-fohr-mah-thee-ohn′*] information

informar *v.* [*een-fohr-mahr′*] inform

informe *m.* [*een-fohr′-meh*] report, account

infortunio [*een-fohr-too′-nee-oh*] misfortune

infundado [*een-foon-dah′-doh*] groundless

ingeniero [*een-heh-nee-eh′-roh*] engineer

ingenio [*een-heh′-nee-oh*] wit

ingenuo [*een-heh′-noo-oh*] naïve

Inglaterra [*een-glah-teh′-rrah*] England

inglés [*een-glehs′*] English

ingratitud *f.* [*een-grah-tee-tood′*] ingratitude

ingrediente *m.* [*een-greh-dee-ehn′-teh*] ingredient

ingresos *m. pl.* [*een-greh′-sohs*] income

inicial [*een-nee-thee-ahl′*] initial

injusticia [*een-hoos-tee′-thee-ah*] injustice

injusto [*een-hoos′-toh*] unfair, unjust

inmaduro [*een-mah-doo′-roh*] immature

inmediatamente [*een-meh-dee-ah-tah-mehn′-teh*] immediately

inmediato [*een-meh-dee-ah′-toh*] immediate

inmenso [*een-mehn′-soh*] immense

inmigración *f.* [*een-mee-grah-thee-ohn′*] immigration

inmigrante *m., f.* [*een-mee-grahn′-teh*] immigrant

inminente [*een-mee-nehn′-teh*] impending

inmoral [*een-moh-rahl′*] immoral

inmortal [*een-mohr-tahl′*] immortal

inmóvil [*een-moh'-veel*] motionless
inmunidad *f.* [*een-moo-nee-dahd'*] immunity
innumerable [*een-noo-meh-rah'-bleh*] innumerable
inocente [*ee-noh-thehn'-teh*] innocent
inolvidable [*ee-nohl-vee-dah'-bleh*] unforgettable
inquieto [*een-kee-eh'-toh*] restless, uneasy
inquilino [*een-kee-lee'-noh*] tenant
inscribir *v.* [*eens-kree-beer'*] register
insecto [*een-sehk'-toh*] insect
inseguro [*een-seh-goo'-roh*] unsafe
inservible [*een-sehr-vee'-bleh*] useless
insignia [*een-seeg'-nee-ah*] badge
insinuar *v.* [*een-see-noo-ahr'*] hint
insistir *v.* [*een-sees-teer'*] insist
insólito [*een-soh'-lee-toh*] unusual
inspección *f.* [*eens-pehk-thee-ohn'*] inspection
inspeccionar *v.* [*eens-pehk-thee-oh-nahr'*] inspect
inspector *m.* [*eens-pehk-tohr'*] inspector
inspiración *f.* [*eens-pee-rah-thee-ohn'*] inspiration
instalar *v.* [*eens-tah-lahr'*] install
instantáneo [*eens-tahn-tah'-neh-oh*] instant, instantaneous
instante *m.* [*eens-tahn'-teh*] jiffy
instinto [*eens-teen'-toh*] instinct
institución *f.* [*eens-tee-too-thee-ohn'*] institution
instituto [*eens-tee-too'-toh*] high school
instrucción *f.* [*eens-trook-thee-ohn'*] instruction
instructor *m.* [*eens-trook-tohr'*] instructor
instruir *v. irreg.* [*eens-troo-eer'*] instruct
instrumento [*eens-troo-mehn'-toh*] tool, instrument
insuficiente [*een-soo-fee-thee-ehn'-teh*] insufficient
insulso [*een-sool'-soh*] dull
insultar *v.* [*een-sool-tahr'*] insult
insulto [*een-sool'-toh*] insult
intelectual [*een-teh-lehk-too-ahl'*] intellectual
inteligente [*een-teh-lee-hehn'-teh*] intelligent, clever
intención *f.* [*een-tehn-thee-ohn'*] intention
intenso [*een-tehn'-soh*] intense

intentar *v.* [*een-tehn-tahr'*] intend, try
intento [*een-tehn'-toh*] aim, intent
interés *m.* [*een-teh-rehs'*] interest
interesante [*een-teh-reh-sahn'-teh*] interesting
interesar *v.* [*een-teh-reh-sahr'*] interest
interesarse *v.* [*een-teh-reh-sahr'-seh*] be interested in
interferir *v. irreg.* [*een-tehr-feh-reer'*] interfere
interior *m.* [*een-teh-ree-ohr'*] interior
interior *adj.* [*een-teh-ree-ohr'*] inner
internacional [*een-tehr-nah-thee-oh-nahl'*] international
interno [*een-tehr'-noh*] internal
intérprete *m., f.* [*een-tehr'-preh-teh*] interpreter
interrogar *v.* [*een-teh-rroh-gahr'*] interrogate
interruptor *m.* [*een-teh-rroop-tohr'*] switch
intersección *f.* [*een-tehr-sehk-thee-ohn'*] intersection
intervalo [*een-tehr-vah'-loh*] interval
íntimo [*een'-tee-moh*] intimate
introducción *f.* [*een-troh-dook-thee-ohn'*] introduction
intuición *f.* [*een-too-ee-thee-ohn'*] intuition
inundación *f.* [*ee-noon-dah-thee-ohn'*] flood
inútil [*ee-noo'-teel*] useless
invadir *v.* [*een-vah-deer'*] invade
inválido [*een-vah'-lee-doh*] invalid
invariable [*een-vah-ree-ah'-bleh*] steady
invasión *f.* [*een-vah-see-ohn'*] invasion
invención *f.* [*een-vehn-thee-ohn'*] invention
inventor *m.* [*een-vehn-tohr'*] inventor
invertir *v. irreg.* [*een-vehr-teer'*] invest
investigación *f.* [*een-vehs-tee-gah-thee-ohn'*] research
investigar *v.* [*een-vehs-tee-gahr'*] investigate
invierno [*een-vee-ehr'-noh*] winter
invisible [*een-vee-see'-bleh*] invisible
invitación *f.* [*een-vee-tah-thee-ohn'*] invitation
invitar *v.* [*een-vee-tahr'*] invite
involuntario [*een-voh-loon-tah'-ree-oh*] involuntary
inyección *f.* [*een-yehk-thee-ohn'*] injection
ir *v. irreg.* [*eer*] go

Irlanda [*eer-lahn'-dah*] Ireland
irlandés [*eer-lahn-dehs'*] Irish
irregular [*ee-rreh-goo-lahr'*] irregular
irresistible [*ee-rreh-sees-tee'-bleh*] irresistible
irritar *v.* [*ee-rree-tahr'*] irritate
irse *v.* [*eer'-seh*] go, quit
　¡**Váyase!** [*vah'-yah-seh*] Go away!
isla [*ees'-lah*] island
Italia [*ee-tah'-lee-ah*] Italy
italiano [*ee-tah-lee-ah'-noh*] Italian
itinerario [*ee-tee-neh-rah'-ree-oh*] itinerary, schedule
izquierda [*eeth-kee-ehr'-dah*] left [direction]

J

jabón *m.* [*hah-bohn'*] soap
jactarse *v.* [*hahk-tahr'-seh*] brag
jadear *v.* [*hah-deh-ahr'*] pant
jamás [*hah-mahs'*] never
jamón *m.* [*hah-mohn'*] ham
Japón [*hah-pohn'*] Japan
japonés [*hah-poh-nehs'*] Japanese
jardín *m.* [*hahr-deen'*] garden
　jardín zoológico [*har-deen' thoh-oh-loh'-hee-koh*] zoo
jardinero [*hahr-dee-neh'-roh*] gardener
jarra [*hah'-rrah*] pitcher, jar
jaula [*hah'-oo-lah*] cage
jefe *m.* [*heh'-feh*] chief, leader, boss
jerez *m.* [*heh-rehth'*] sherry wine
jerga [*hehr'-gah*] slang
jira [*hee'-rah*] tour
jornada [*hohr-nah'-dah*] journey
joven *n. m., f.* [*hoh'-vehn*] young man, young woman
joven *adj.* [*hoh'-vehn*] young

más joven [*mahs hoh'-vehn*] junior
joya [*hoh'-yah*] jewel
joyería [*hoh-yeh-ree'-ah*] jewelry store
jubilarse *v.* [*hoo-bee-lahr'-seh*] retire
judía [*hoo-dee'-ah*] bean
judío *n. & adj.* [*hoo-dee'-oh*] Jew, Jewish
juego [*hoo-eh'-goh*] play, game, set
    juego de naipes [*hoo-eh'-goh deh nah'-ee-pehs*] pack of
      cards
jueves *m.* [*hoo-eh'-vehs*] Thursday
juez *m.* [*hoo-ehth'*] judge
jugar *v. irreg.* [*hoo-gahr'*] play, gamble
jugo [*hoo'-goh*] juice
juguete *m.* [*hoo-gheh'-teh*] toy
juicio [*hoo-ee'-thee-oh*] trial, judgment
julio [*hoo'-lee-oh*] July
junio [*hoo'-nee-oh*] June
junta [*hoon'-tah*] board, council, meeting
juntarse *v.* [*hoon-tahr'-seh*] join
junto a [*hoon'-toh ah*] beside, near to
juntos [*hoon'-tohs*] together
jurado [*hoo-rah'-doh*] jury
juramento [*hoo-rah-mehn'-toh*] oath
jurar *v.* [*hoo-rahr'*] swear
justicia [*hoos-tee'-thee-ah*] fairness, justice
justificar *v.* [*hoos-tee-fee-kahr'*] justify
justo [*hoos'-toh*] fair, just
juvenil [*hoo-veh-neel'*] youthful, juvenile
juventud *f.* [*hoo-vehn-tood'*] youth
juzgar *v.* [*hooth-gahr'*] judge

K

kilogramo [*kee-loh-grah'-moh*] kilogram
kilómetro [*kee-loh'-meh-troh*] kilometer

L

la *f. sing.* [*lah*] the
labio [*lah'-bee-oh*] lip
laboratorio [*lah-boh-rah-toh'-ree-oh*] laboratory
lácteo [*lahk'-teh-oh*] milky
lado [*lah'-doh*] side
  a un lado [*ah oon lah'-doh*] aside
  al lado de [*ahl lah'-doh deh*] next to
ladrar *v.* [*lah-drahr'*] bark
ladrillo [*lah-dree'-yoh*] brick
ladrón *m.* [*lah-drohn'*] thief, burglar, robber
lago [*lah'-goh*] lake
lágrima [*lah'-gree-mah*] tear
lamentar *v.* [*lah-mehn-tahr'*] regret
lamentarse *v.* [*lah-mehn-tahr'-seh*] grieve
lámpara [*lahm'-pah-rah*] lamp
lana [*lah'-nah*] wool
  de lana [*deh lah'-nah*] woolen
lancha [*lahn'-chah*] launch
langosta [*lahn-gohs'-tah*] lobster
lápiz *m.* [*lah'-peeth*] pencil
  lápiz de labios [*lah'-peeth deh lah'-bee-ohs*] lipstick
largo [*lahr'-goh*] long
  a lo largo de [*ah loh lahr'-goh deh*] along
las *f. pl.* [*lahs*] the, them
lástima [*lahs'-tee-mah*] pity
  ¡Qué lástima! [*keh lahs'-tee-mah*] What a pity!
lata [*lah'-tah*] can
lateral [*lah-teh-rahl'*] lateral, side
latido [*lah-tee'-doh*] beat, throb
latín [*lah-teen'*] Latin
latir *v.* [*lah-teer'*] beat, throb
latón *m.* [*lah-tohn'*] brass

244

lavable [*lah-vah'-bleh*] washable
lavabo [*lah-vah'-boh*] washbasin
lavandería [*lah-vahn-deh-ree'-ah*] laundry
lavar v. [*lah-vahr'*] wash
le [*leh*] him, to him
leal [*leh-ahl'*] loyal
lección f. [*lehk-thee-ohn'*] lesson, assignment
lectura [*lehk-too'-rah*] reading
leche f. [*leh'-cheh*] milk
lechería [*leh-cheh-ree'-ah*] dairy
lechuga [*leh-choo'-gah*] lettuce
leer v. [*leh-ehr'*] read
legal [*leh-gahl'*] lawful, legal
legislación f. [*leh-hees-lah-thee-ohn'*] legislation
legítimo [*leh-hee'-tee-moh*] legitimate
legumbre f. [*leh-goom'-breh*] vegetable
lejos [*leh'-hohs*] away, far
   más lejos [*mahs leh'-hohs*] further
   muy lejos [*moo-ee' leh'-hohs*] far away
lengua [*lehn'-goo-ah*] tongue
lenguado [*lehn-goo-ah'-doh*] sole
lenguaje m. [*lehn-goo-ah'-heh*] language
lente f. [*lehn'-teh*] lens
lento [*lehn'-toh*] slow
león m. [*leh-ohn'*] lion
les [*lehs*] to them, to you
lesión f. [*leh-see-ohn'*] injury
lesionar v. [*leh-see-oh-nahr'*] injure
letra [*leh'-trah*] letter [written character]
letrero [*leh-treh'-roh*] sign
levantar v. [*leh-vahn-tahr'*] lift, raise
levantarse [*leh-vahn-tahr'-seh*] get up, stand up
ley f. [*leh'-ee*] law
leyenda [*leh-yehn'-dah*] legend
liberal n. & adj. [*lee-beh-rahl'*] liberal
libertad f. [*lee-behr-tahd'*] liberty, freedom
libertar v. [*lee-behr-tahr'*] free, set free
libra [*lee'-brah*] pound [weight]

librar *v.* [*lee-brahr'*] relieve
libre [*lee'-breh*] free, vacant
   libre de impuestos [*lee'-breh deh eem-poo-ehs'-tohs*
     tax free
librería [*lee-breh-ree'-ah*] bookstore
libro [*lee'-broh*] book
licencia [*lee-thehn'-thee-ah*] license
   licencia para conducir [*lee-thehn'-thee-ah pah'-rah kohn-*
    doo-theer'] driving license
licor *m.* [*lee-kohr'*] liquor
liga [*lee'-gah*] league
ligero [*lee-heh'-roh*] light [weight]
límite *m.* [*lee'-mee-teh*] limit, boundary
   límite de velocidad [*lee'-mee-teh deh veh-loh-thee-dahd'*]
    speed limit
limón *m.* [*lee-mohn'*] lemon
limonada [*lee-moh-nah'-dah*] lemonade
limpiabotas *m. sing.* [*leem-pee-ah-boh'-tahs*] shoeshine boy
limpiar *v.* [*leem-pee-ahr'*] clean
limpieza [*leem-pee-eh'-thah*] cleaning
limpio [*leem'-pee-oh*] clean
lindo [*leen'-doh*] pretty
línea [*lee'-neh-ah*] line
   línea aérea [*lee'-neh-ah ah-eh'-reh-ah*] airline
linterna [*leen-tehr'-nah*] lantern
lío [*lee'-oh*] mess
líquido [*lee'-kee-doh*] liquid
liso [*lee'-soh*] flat
lisonja [*lee-sohn'-hah*] flattery
lisonjero [*lee-sohn-heh'-roh*] flatterer
lista [*lees'-tah*] list
   lista de precios [*lees'-tah deh preh'-thee-ohs*] price list
listo [*lees'-toh*] ready, smart, clever
litera [*lee-teh'-rah*] litter, berth
literalmente [*lee-teh-rahl-mehn'-teh*] literally
literatura [*lee-teh-rah-too'-rah*] literature
litro [*lee'-troh*] liter
lo [*loh*] him, you, it

lo que [*loh keh*] that which
lobo [*loh'-boh*] wolf
local *m.* [*loh-kahl'*] premises
local *adj.* [*loh-kahl'*] local
localidad *f.* [*loh-kah-lee-dahd'*] locality, location; seat
loco [*loh'-koh*] crazy, insane, mad
locomotora [*loh-koh-moh-toh'-rah*] locomotive
lodo [*loh'-doh*] mud
lógico [*loh'-hee-koh*] logical
lograr *v.* [*loh-grahr'*] attain
longitud *f.* [*lohn-hee-tood'*] length
los *m. pl.* [*lohs*] the, them
lubricar *v.* [*loo-bree-kahr'*] lubricate
lucha [*loo'-chah*] struggle, fight
   lucha libre [*loo'-chah lee'-breh*] wrestling
luchar *v.* [*loo-chahr'*] struggle, fight
luego [*loo-eh'-goh*] afterwards, soon, then
lugar *m.* [*loo-gahr'*] place. location
   en lugar de [*ehn loo-gahr' deh*] in place of
   tener *v. irreg.* **lugar** [*teh-nehr' loo-gahr'*] take place
lúgubre [*loo'-goo-breh*] dismal
lujo [*loo'-hoh*] luxury
lujoso [*loo-hoh'-soh*] luxurious
luna [*loo'-nah*] moon
lunes *m.* [*loo'-nehs*] Monday
lustrar *v.* [*loos-trahr'*] polish
luto [*loo'-toh*] mourning
luz *f.* [*looth*] light
   luz de la luna [*looth deh lah loo'-nah*] moonlight

LL

llama [*yah'-mah*] flame
llamada [*yah-mah'-dah*] call
   llamada telefónica [*yah-mah'-dah teh-leh-foh'-nee-kah*]

telephone call
llamar *v.* [*yah-mahr'*] call
  llamar a la puerta [*yah-mahr' ah lah poo-ehr'-tah*] knock
llamativo [*yah-mah-tee'-voh*] showy
llano *adj.* [*yah'-noh*] flat, plain
llanta [*yahn'-tah*] tire
llave *f.* [*yah'-veh*] key
  llave eléctrica [*yah'-veh eh-lehk'-tree-kah*] switch
  llave inglesa [*yah'-veh een-gleh'-sah*] wrench
llavero [*yah-veh'-roh*] key ring
llegada [*yeh-gah'-dah*] arrival
llegar *v.* [*yeh-gahr'*] arrive
  llegar a [*yèh-gahr' ah*] get to
  llegar a ser [*yeh-gahr' ah sehr*] become, get
llenar *v.* [*yeh-nahr'*] fill
lleno [*yeh'-noh*] full
llevar *v.* [*yeh-vahr'*] carry, bear, wear
  llevar a cabo [*yeh-vahr' ah kah'-boh*] achieve
llorar *v.* [*yoh-rahr'*] cry, weep
llover *v. irreg.* [*yoh-vehr'*] rain
lluvia [*yoo'-vee-ah*] rain

M

macarrones *m. pl.* [*mah-kah-rroh'-nehs*] macaroni
macho [*mah'-choh*] male
madera [*mah-deh'-rah*] wood
  de madera [*deh mah-deh'-rah*] wooden
madrastra [*mah-drahs'-trah*] stepmother
madre *f.* [*mah'-dreh*] mother
madrugar *v.* [*mah-droo-gahr'*] rise early
maduro [*mah-doo'-roh*] mature, ripe
maestro [*mah-ehs'-troh*] teacher
mágico *adj.* [*mah'-hee-koh*] magic
magnífico [*mahg-nee'-fee-koh*] magnificent

maíz *m.* [*mah-eeth'*] corn
mal *m.* [*mahl*] evil
mal *adv.* [*mahl*] badly
  mal hecho [*mahl eh'-choh*] sloppy
malamente [*mah-lah-mehn'-teh*] badly
maldecir *v. irreg.* [*mahl-deh-theer'*] curse
maleficio [*mah-leh-fee'-thee-oh*] curse
malentendido [*mah-lehn-tehn-dee'-doh*] misunderstanding
maleta [*mah-leh'-tah*] suitcase
maletero [*mah-leh-teh'-roh*] porter
malgastar *v.* [*mahl-gahs-tahr'*] waste
malo [*mah'-loh*] bad
mancha [*mahn'-chah*] stain, spot
mandar *v.* [*mahn-dahr'*] command, send, order
  mandar a buscar [*mahn-dahr' ah boos-kahr'*] send for
mandíbula [*mahn-dee'-boo-lah*] jaw
manejar *v.* [*mah-neh-hahr'*] handle, drive
manera [*mah-neh'-rah*] manner, way
  de esta manera [*deh ehs'-tah mah-neh'-rah*] in this way
  de ninguna manera [*deh neen-goo'-nah mah-neh'-rah*]
   in no way
manga [*mahn'-gah*] sleeve
manguera [*mahn-gheh'-rah*] hose
manía [*mah-nee'-ah*] fad
manicura [*mah-nee-koo'-rah*] manicure
manifestación *f.* [*mah-nee-fehs-tah-thee-ohn'*] demonstration
mano *f.* [*mah'-noh*] hand
manso [*mahn'-soh*] meek, tame
manta [*mahn'-tah*] blanket
mantel *m.* [*mahn-tehl'*] tablecloth
mantener *v. irreg.* [*mahn-teh-nehr'*] maintain
mantequilla [*mahn-teh-kee'-yah*] butter
mantón *m.* [*mahn-tohn'*] shawl
manual *m.* [*mah-noo-ahl'*] manual
manual *adj.* [*mah-noo-ahl'*] manual
manuscrito [*mah-noos-kree'-toh*] manuscript
manzana [*mahn-thah'-nah*] apple
  pastel *m.* **de manzana** [*pahs-tehl' deh mahn-thah'-nah*] apple

pie
mañana [*mah-nyah'-nah*] tomorrow, morning
  pasado mañana [*pah-sah'-doh mah-nyah'-nah*] day after tomorrow
  por la mañana [*pohr lah mah-nyah'-nah*] in the morning
  mañana por la mañana [*mah-nyah'-nah pohr lah mah-nyah'-nah*] tomorrow morning
mapa *m.* [*mah'-pah*] map, chart
máquina [*mah'-kee-nah*] machine
  máquina de escribir [*mah'-kee-nah deh ehs-kree-beer'*] typewriter
maquinaria [*mah-kee-nah'-ree-ah*] machinery
mar *m., f.* [*mahr*] sea
maravilloso [*mah-rah-vee-yoh'-soh*] marvelous, wonderful
marca [*mahr'-kah*] brand, mark
  marca de fábrica [*mahr'-kah deh fah'-bree-kah*] trademark
marcar *v.* [*mahr-kahr'*] mark
marco [*mahr'-koh*] frame
marchar *v.* [*mahr-chahr'*] march
  poner *v. irreg.* **en marcha** [*poh-nehr' ehn mahr'-chah*] start
  marcha atrás [*mahr'-chah ah-trahs'*] reverse
marcharse *v.* [*mahr-chahr'-seh*] leave
marea [*mah-reh'-ah*] tide
mareado [*mah-reh-ah'-doh*] dizzy, seasick
marfil *m.* [*mahr-feel'*] ivory
marido [*mah-ree'-doh*] husband
marina [*mah-ree'-nah*] navy
marinero [*mah-ree-neh'-roh*] sailor
mariposa [*mah-ree-poh'-sah*] butterfly
mármol *m.* [*mahr'-mohl*] marble
martes *m.* [*mahr'-tehs*] Tuesday
martillo [*mahr-tee'-yoh*] hammer
marzo [*mahr'-thoh*] March
más [*mahs*] more, plus, else
  alguien más [*ahl'-ghee-ehn mahs*] someone else
  el más . . . [*ehl mahs*] the most . . .
  más allá [*mahs ah-yah'*] beyond
  más bien [*mahs bee-ehn'*] rather

más o menos [*mahs oh meh'-nohs*] more or less
una vez más [*oo'-nah vehth mahs*] once more
masa [*mah'-sah*] mass [quantity]
masage *m.* [*mah-sah'-heh*] massage
máscara [*mahs'-kah-rah*] mask
masticar *v.* [*mahs-tee-kahr'*] chew
matar *v.* [*mah-tahr'*] kill
matemáticas *f. pl.* [*mah-teh-mah'-tee-kahs*] mathematics
materia [*mah-teh'-ree-ah*] matter, subject
materia prima [*mah-teh'-ree-ah pree'-mah*] raw material
material *m.* [*mah-teh-ree-ahl'*] material
maternal [*mah-tehr-nahl'*] maternal
maternidad *f.* [*mah-tehr-nee-dahd'*] maternity, motherhood
matrimonio [*mah-tree-moh'-nee-oh*] marriage
mayo [*mah'-yoh*] May
mayor [*mah-yohr'*] bigger, older, elder
la mayor parte de [*lah mah-yohr' pahr'-teh deh*] most of
mayoría [*mah-yoh-ree'-ah*] majority
me [*meh*] me
mecánico *n.* [*meh-kah'-nee-koh*] mechanic
mecánico *adj.* [*meh-kah'-nee-koh*] mechanical
mecanógrafo [*meh-kah-noh'-grah-fo*] typist
mecedora [*meh-theh-doh'-rah*] rocking chair
medalla [*meh-dah'-yah*] medal
media [*meh'-dee-ah*] average
medianoche *f.* [*meh-dee-ah-noh'-cheh*] midnight
medias [*meh'-dee-ahs*] stockings
medicina [*meh-dee-thee'-nah*] medicine, drug
médico *n.* [*meh'-dee-koh*] doctor, physician
médico *adj.* [*meh'-dee-koh*] medical
medida [*meh-dee'-dah*] measure
medio [*meh'-dee-oh*] middle, medium
medio camino [*meh'-dee-oh kah-mee'-noh*] halfway
las dos y media [*lahs dohs ee meh'-dee-ah*] half past two
mediodía *m.* [*meh-dee-oh-dee'-ah*] noon
medir *v. irreg.* [*meh-deer'*] measure
mediterráneo [*meh-dee-teh-rrah'-neh-oh*] Mediterranean
mejicano [*meh-hee-kah'-noh*] Mexican

Méjico, México [*meh'-hee-koh*] Mexico
mejilla [*meh-hee'-yah*] cheek
mejor [*meh-hohr'*] better
mejora [*meh-hoh'-rah*] improvement
mejorar *v.* [*meh-hoh-rahr'*] improve
melocotón *m.* [*meh-loh-koh-tohn'*] peach
melodía [*meh-loh-dee'-ah*] melody
melón *m.* [*meh-lohn'*] melon
memoria [*meh-moh'-ree-ah*] memory
  de memoria [*deh meh-moh'-ree-ah*] by heart
mencionar *v.* [*mehn-thee-oh-nahr'*] mention
menor [*meh-nohr'*] smaller, younger
  menor de edad [*meh-nohr' deh eh-dahd'*] minor
menos [*meh'-nohs*] less, fewer, minus
mensaje *m.* [*mehn-sah'-heh*] message
mensajero [*mehn-sah-heh'-roh*] messenger
mensual [*mehn-soo-ahl'*] monthly
mental [*mehn-tahl'*] mental
mente *f.* [*mehn'-teh*] mind
mentir *v. irreg.* [*mehn-teer'*] lie
mentira [*mehn-tee'-rah*] lie
mentiroso [*mehn-tee-roh'-soh*] liar
mentón *m.* [*mehn-tohn'*] chin
menú *m.* [*meh-noo'*] menu
meramente [*meh-rah-mehn'-teh*] merely
mercado [*mehr-kah'-doh*] market
mercancía [*mehr-kahn-thee'-ah*] merchandise, goods
mercería [*mehr-theh-ree'-ah*] notions, dry goods
merecer *v. irreg.* [*meh-reh-thehr'*] deserve, merit
merendar *v. irreg.* [*meh-rehn-dahr'*] have an afternoon snack
mérito [*meh'-ree-toh*] merit
mes *m.* [*mehs*] month
mesa [*meh'-sah*] table
mesero [*meh-seh'-roh*] waiter
mesonero [*meh-soh-neh'-roh*] innkeeper
meta [*meh'-tah*] goal
metal *m.* [*meh-tahl'*] metal
meter *v.* [*meh-tehr'*] put in

meterse *v.* [*meh-tehr'-seh*] get in
método [*meh'-toh-doh*] method
metro [*meh'-troh*] meter [measure]
metro [*meh'-troh*] subway, underground
mezcla [*mehth'-klah*] mixture
mezclar *v.* [*mehth-klahr'*] mix
mi *sing.*, **mis** *pl.* [*mee, mees*] my
micrófono [*mee-kroh'-foh-noh*] microphone
miedo [*mee-eh'-doh*] fear
  sin miedo [*seen mee-eh'-doh*] fearless
  tener *v. irreg.* **miedo** [*teh-nehr' mee-eh'-doh*] fear
miel *f.* [*mee-ehl'*] honey
  luna de miel [*loo'-nah deh mee-ehl'*] honeymoon
miembro [*mee-ehm'-broh*] member, limb
mientras [*mee-ehn'-trahs*] while
  mientras tanto [*mee-ehn'-trahs tahn'-toh*] meantime,
    meanwhile
miércoles *m.* [*mee-ehr'-koh-lehs*] Wednesday
miga [*mee'-gah*] crumb
mil [*meel*] thousand
militar [*mee-lee-tahr'*] military
  servicio militar [*sehr-vee'-thee-oh mee-lee-tahr'*] military
    service
milla [*mee'-yah*] mile
millón *m.* [*mee-yohn'*] million
millonario [*mee-yoh-nah'-ree-oh*] millionaire
mina *n.* [*mee'-nah*] mine
  mina de carbón [*mee'-nah deh kahr-bohn'*] coalmine
mineral *m.* [*mee-neh-rahl'*] mineral
minero [*mee-neh'-roh*] miner
mínimo [*mee'-nee-moh*] least, minimum
ministerio [*mee-nees-teh'-ree-oh*] ministry, office
  ministerio de negocios extranjeros [*mee-nees-teh'-ree-oh
    deh neh-goh'-thee-ohs ehks-trahn-heh'-rohs*] foreign
    office
ministro [*mee-nees'-troh*] minister
  ministro de relaciones exteriores [*mee-nees'-troh deh
    reh-lah-thee-oh'-nehs ehks-teh-ree-oh'-rehs*] foreign

minister

minoría [*mee-noh-ree'-ah*] minority

minuto [*mee-noo'-toh*] minute

mío [*mee'-oh*] mine

  ¿Cuál es mío? [*koo-ahl' ehs mee'-oh*] Which is mine?

mirar *v.* [*mee-rahr'*] look

  ¡Mire! [*mee'-reh*] Look!

mirón *m.* [*mee-rohn'*] onlooker

misa [*mee'-sah*] mass [eccles.]

miserable [*mee-seh-rah'-bleh*] miserable

miseria [*mee-seh'-ree-ah*] misery

misericordia [*mee-seh-ree-kohr'-dee-ah*] mercy, pity

misión *f.* [*mee-see-ohn'*] mission

misionero [*mee-see-oh-neh'-roh*] missionary

mismo [*mees'-moh*] same, self

  Lo mismo me da [*loh mees'-moh meh dah*] It's all the same to me

misterio [*mees-teh'-ree-oh*] mystery

misterioso [*mees-teh-ree-oh'-soh*] mysterious

místico [*mees'-tee-koh*] mystic

mitad *f.* [*mee-tahd'*] middle, half

  mitad de camino [*mee-tahd' deh kah-mee'-noh*] midway

mobiliario [*moh-bee-lee-ah'-ree-oh*] furniture

moción *f.* [*moh-thee-ohn'*] motion

moda [*moh'-dah*] fashion

  de moda [*deh moh'-dah*] fashionable

modales *m. pl.* [*moh-dah'-lehs*] manners

modelo *m., f.* [*moh-deh'-loh*] model

moderno [*moh-dehr'-noh*] modern

modestia [*moh-dehs'-tee-ah*] modesty

modesto [*moh-dehs'-toh*] modest

modista [*moh-dees'-tah*] dressmaker

modo [*moh'-doh*] way

  de ningún modo [*deh neen-goon' moh'-doh*] by no means

  de todos modos [*deh toh'-dohs moh'-dohs*] by all means, anyhow

mofar *v.* [*moh-fahr'*] jeer

mojado [*moh-hah'-doh*] wet

mojón *m.* [*moh-hohn'*] landmark
molde *m.* [*mohl'-deh*] mold, cast, model
moler *v. irreg.* [*moh-lehr'*] grind
molestar *v.* [*moh-lehs-tahr'*] disturb, bother, annoy
molestia [*moh-lehs'-tee-ah*] bother, inconvenience
molesto [*moh-lehs'-toh*] bothering, annoying
molino [*moh-lee'-noh*] mill
   molino de viento [*moh-lee'-noh deh vee-ehn'-toh*] windmill
momento [*moh-mehn'-toh*] moment
monarquía [*moh-nahr-kee'-ah*] monarchy
monasterio [*moh-nahs-teh'-ree-oh*] monastery
mondadientes *m.* [*mohn-dah-dee-ehn'-tehs*] toothpick
moneda [*moh-neh'-dah*] coin
   moneda corriente [*moh-neh'-dah koh-rree-ehn'-teh*]
   currency
monja [*mohn'-hah*] nun
monje *m.* [*mohn'-heh*] monk
mono [*moh'-noh*] monkey
monótono [*moh-noh'-toh-noh*] monotonous
monstruoso [*mohns-troo-oh'-soh*] monstrous
montaña [*mohn-tah'-nyah*] mountain
montar *v.* [*mohn-tahr'*] ride, assemble, mount
montón *m.* [*mohn-tohn'*] pile, heap
monumento [*moh-noo-mehn'-toh*] monument
morado [*moh-rah'-doh*] purple, violet
moral *m. f. & adj.* [*moh-rahl'*] moral, ethics
moralidad *f.* [*moh-rah-lee-dahd'*] morality
morboso [*mohr-boh'-soh*] morbid
mordaza [*mohr-dah'-thah*] gag, muzzle
morder *v. irreg.* [*mohr-dehr'*] bite
moreno [*moh-reh'-noh*] brown, brunette; dark
morir *v. irreg.* [*moh-reer'*] die
   morir de hambre [*moh-reer' deh ahm'-breh*] starve
mortal [*mohr-tahl'*] deadly
mortalidad *f.* [*mohr-tah-lee-dahd'*] mortality
mosaico [*moh-sah'-ee-koh*] mosaic
mosca [*mohs'-kah*] fly
mosquito [*mohs-kee'-toh*] mosquito

mostaza [*mohs-tah'-thah*] mustard
mostrador *m.* [*mohs-trah-dohr'*] counter
mostrar *v. irreg.* [*mohs-trahr'*] show
  ¡**Muéstreme!** [*moo-ehs'-treh-meh*] Show me!
motivo [*moh-tee'-voh*] motive
motocicleta [*moh-toh-thee-kleh'-tah*] motorcycle
motor *m.* [*moh-tohr'*] engine, motor
mover *v. irreg.* [*moh-vehr'*] move
mozo *adj.* [*moh'-thoh*] young, youthful
  buen mozo [*boo-ehn' moh'-thoh*] handsome
mozo *n.* [*moh'-thoh*] porter
muchacha [*moo-chah'-chah*] girl
muchacho [*moo-chah'-choh*] boy
mucho [*moo'-choh*] much, very much, a lot
muchos [*moo'-chohs*] many
mudarse *v.* [*moo-dahr'-seh*] move
mudo [*moo'-doh*] dumb, mute, silent
muebles *m. pl.* [*moo-eh'-blehs*] furniture
muela [*moo-eh'-lah*] molar
  dolor *m.* **de muelas** [*doh-lohr' deh moo-eh'-lahs*] toothache
muelle *m.* [*moo-eh'-yeh*] spring [mech.], wharf, dock
muerte *f.* [*moo-ehr'-teh*] death
muerto [*moo-ehr'-toh*] dead
muestra [*moo-ehs'-trah*] sample
mujer *f.* [*moo-hehr'*] woman
  mujer de su casa [*moo-hehr' deh soo kah'-sah*] housewife
multa [*mool'-tah*] fine
multitud *f.* [*mool-tee-tood'*] crowd
mundo [*moon'-doh*] world
munición *f.* [*moo-nee-thee-ohn'*] ammunition
muñeca [*moo-nyeh'-kah*] wrist, doll
muñeco [*moo-nyeh'-koh*] puppet
muralla [*moo-rah'-yah*] wall
murmullo [*moor-moo'-yoh*] murmur
músculo [*moos'-koo-loh*] muscle
museo [*moo-seh'-oh*] museum
música [*moo'-see-kah*] music
musical [*moo-see-kahl'*] musical

músico [*moo'-see-koh*] musician
mutuo [*moo'-too-oh*] mutual
muy [*moo-ee'*] very, so
  muy bien [*moo-ee' bee-ehn'*] very well

N

nabo [*nah'-boh*] turnip
nacer *v. irreg.* [*nah-thehr'*] be born
nacimiento [*nah-thee-mee-ehn'-toh*] birth
nación *f.* [*nah-thee-ohn'*] nation
nacional [*nah-thee-oh-nahl'*] national
nacionalidad *f.* [*nah-thee-oh-nah-lee-dahd'*] nationality
nada [*nah'-dah*] nothing
  nada más [*nah'-dah mahs*] nothing else
nadar *v.* [*nah-dahr'*] swim
nadie [*nah'-dee-eh*] nobody, no one
naipes *m. pl.* [*nah'-ee-pehs*] playing cards
naranja [*nah-rahn'-hah*] orange [fruit]
  jugo de naranja [*hoo'-goh deh nah-rahn'-hah*] orange juice
nariz *f.* [*nah-reeth'*] nose
narrar *v.* [*nah-rrahr'*] narrate
natilla [*nah-tee'-yah*] custard
nativo *adj.* [*nah-tee'-voh*] native
natural [*nah-too-rahl'*] native, natural
naturaleza [*nah-too-rah-leh'-thah*] nature
naturalmente [*nah-too-rahl-mehn'-teh*] naturally
naufragio [*nah-oo-frah'-hee-oh*] shipwreck
náusea [*nah'-oo-seh-ah*] nausea
naval [*nah-vahl'*] naval
navegar *v.* [*nah-veh-gahr'*] sail
Navidad [*nah-vee-dahd'*] Christmas
neblina [*neh-blee'-nah*] fog
necesario [*neh-theh-sah'-ree-oh*] necessary
necesitar *v.* [*neh-theh-see-tahr'*] need

necio [*neh'-thee-oh*] foolish
negar *v. irreg.* [*neh-gahr'*] deny, refuse
negativa [*neh-gah-tee'-vah*] refusal, denial
negativo [*neh-gah-tee'-voh*] negative
negociante *m., f.* [*neh-goh-thee-ahn'-teh*] dealer
negocio [*neh-goh'-thee-oh*] business
  hombre *m.* **de negocios** [*ohm'-breh deh neh-goh'-thee-ohs*]
    businessman
negro [*neh'-groh*] black, Negro
nene *m.* [*neh'-neh*] baby
nervioso [*nehr-vee-oh'-soh*] nervous
neumático [*neh-oo-mah'-tee-koh*] tire
  neumático de repuesto [*neh-oo-mah'-tee-koh deh reh-poo-*
    ehs'-toh] spare tire
neutral [*neh-oo-trahl'*] neutral
nevada [*neh-vah'-dah*] snowfall
nevar *v. irreg.* [*neh-vahr'*] snow
nevera [*neh-veh'-rah*] refrigerator
ni [*nee*] nor
  ni . . . ni [*nee nee*] neither . . . nor
  ni siquiera [*nee see-kee-eh'-rah*] not even
  ni uno [*nee oo'-noh*] not one
Nicaragua [*nee-kah-rah'-goo-ah*] Nicaragua
nicaragüense [*nee-kah-rah-goo-ehn'-seh*] Nicaraguan
niebla [*nee-eh'-blah*] fog, mist
nieto [*nee-eh'-toh*] grandchild
nieve *f.* [*nee-eh'-veh*] snow
  copo de nieve [*koh'-poh deh nee-eh'-veh*] snowflake
ninguno [*neen-goo'-noh*] nobody, none
  de ningún modo [*deh neen-goon' moh'-doh*] not at all
  ninguno de los dos [*neen-goo'-noh deh lohs dohs*] neither
    one
niña [*nee'-nyah*] girl
niñez *f.* [*nee-nyehth'*] childhood
niño [*nee'-nyoh*] child
nivel *m.* [*nee-vehl'*] level
no [*noh*] no, not
  ¡No importa! [*noh eem-pohr'-tah*] Never mind!

no menos [*noh meh'-nohs*] nonetheless

noble *adj.* [*noh'-bleh*] noble

noción *f.* [*noh-thee-ohn'*] notion

noche *f.* [*noh'-cheh*] night

   buenas noches [*boo-eh'-nahs noh'-chehs*] good night, good evening

   esta noche [*ehs'-tah noh'-cheh*] tonight

   Nochebuena [*noh-cheh-boo-eh'-nah*] Christmas Eve

nogal *m.* [*noh-gahl'*] walnut

nombrar *v.* [*nohm-brahr'*] nominate, name

nombre *m.* [*nohm'-breh*] name

   nombre de pila [*nohm'-breh deh pee'-lah*] first name

nordeste *m.* [*nohr-dehs'-teh*] northeast

normal [*nohr-mahl'*] normal

noroeste *m.* [*noh-roh-ehs'-teh*] northwest

norte *m.* [*nohr'-teh*] north

Noruega [*noh-roo-eh'-gah*] Norway

norteamericano [*nohr-tch-ah-meh-ree-kah'-noh*] North American

nos [*nohs*] us

nosotros [*noh-soh'-trohs*] we, us

   para nosotros [*pah'-rah noh-soh'-trohs*] for us

nota [*noh'-tah*] note, remark; grade

notable [*noh-tah'-bleh*] remarkable

notar *v.* [*noh-tahr'*] note, notice

noticias *f. pl.* [*noh-tee'-thee-ahs*] news

notificar *v.* [*noh-tee-fee-kahr'*] notify

novedad *f.* [*noh-veh-dahd'*] novelty

novela [*noh-veh'-lah*] novel

noveno [*noh-veh'-noh*] ninth

noventa [*noh-vehn'-tah*] ninety

novia [*noh'-vee-ah*] bride, fiancée

noviembre *m.* [*noh-vee-ehm'-breh*] November

novio [*noh'-vee-oh*] bridegroom, fiancé

nube *f.* [*noo'-beh*] cloud

nublado [*noo-blah'-doh*] cloudy

nudo [*noo'-doh*] knot

nuera [*noo-eh'-rah*] daughter-in-law

nuestro [*noo-ehs'-troh*] our
  el nuestro, los nuestros [*ehl noo-ehs'-troh, lohs noo-ehs'-trohs*] ours
nueve [*noo-eh'-veh*] nine
nuevo [*noo-eh'-voh*] new
nuez *f.* [*noo-ehth'*] nut
número [*noo'-meh-roh*] number
  número par [*noo'-meh-roh pahr*] even number
  calificación numérica [*kah-lee-fee-kah-thee-ohn' noo-meh'-ree-kah*] score
numeroso [*noo-meh-roh'-soh*] numerous
nunca [*noon'-kah*] never
  nunca más [*noon'-kah mahs*] nevermore, never again
nutritivo [*noo-tree-tee'-voh*] nourishing

O

o [*oh*] or
obedecer *v. irreg.* [*oh-beh-deh-thehr'*] obey
obediente [*oh-beh-dee-ehn'-teh*] obedient
obispo [*oh-bees'-poh*] bishop
objeción *f.* [*ohb-heh-thee-ohn'*] objection
objetar *v.* [*ohb-heh-tahr'*] object
objeto [*ohb-heh'-toh*] object
obligación *f.* [*oh-blee-gah-thee-ohn'*] obligation
obligar *v.* [*oh-blee-gahr'*] compel, obligate
obra [*oh'-brah*] work
  obra de arte [*oh'-brah deh ahr'-teh*] work of art
  obra maestra [*oh'-brah mah-ehs'-trah*] masterpiece
  obra de teatro [*oh'-brah deh teh-ah'-troh*] play
obrero [*oh-breh'-roh*] worker
obsceno [*ohbs-theh'-noh*] obscene
obscuridad *f.* [*ohbs-koo-ree-dahd*] darkness
obscuro [*ohbs-koo'-roh*] dim
observación *f.* [*ohb-sehr-vah-thee-ohn'*] remark

observar v. [ohb-sehr-vahr'] observe, watch
obstáculo [ohbs-tah'-koo-loh] obstacle
obtener v. irreg. [ohb-teh-nehr'] obtain
obvio [ohb'-vee-oh] obvious
ocasión f. [oh-kah-see-ohn'] occasion
ocasionalmente [oh-kah-see-oh-nahl-mehn'-teh] occasionally
occidental [ohk-thee-dehn-tahl'] occidental, western
océano [oh-theh'-ah-noh] ocean
ocio [oh'-thee-oh] leisure
octavo [ohk-tah'-voh] eighth
octubre m. [ohk-too'-breh] October
oculista m., f. [oh-koo-lees'-tah] eye doctor, oculist
ocultar v. [oh-kool-tahr'] conceal
ocupado [oh-koo-pah'-doh] busy, occupied
ocupar v. [oh-koo-pahr'] occupy
ocurrir v. [oh-koo-rreer'] happen
ochenta [oh-chehn'-tah] eighty
ocho [oh'-choh] eight
odiar v. [oh-dee-ahr'] hate
odio [oh'-dee-oh] hatred
oeste m. [oh-ehs'-teh] west
ofender v. [oh-fehn-dehr'] offend
ofensivo [oh-fehn-see'-voh] offensive
oferta [oh-fehr'-tah] bid, offer
oficial m. [oh-fee-thee-ahl'] officer
oficial [oh-fee-thee-ahl'] official
oficina [oh-fee-thee'-nah] office, bureau
oficio [oh-fee'-thee-oh] position, function
ofrecer v. irreg. [oh-freh-thehr'] offer, bid
oír v. irreg. [oh-eer'] hear
ojo [oh'-hoh] eye
ola [oh'-lah] wave
oleaje m. [oh-leh-ah'-heh] surf
óleo [oh'-leh-oh] oil painting
oler v. irreg. [oh-lehr'] smell
oliva [oh-lee'-vah] olive
olor m. [oh-lohr'] smell
olvidar v. [ohl-vee-dahr'] forget

no me olvides [*noh meh ohl-vee'-dehs*] forget-me-not
olla [*oh'-yah*] pot
omisión *f.* [*oh-mee-see-ohn'*] omission
omitir *v.* [*oh-mee-teer'*] omit
ómnibus *m.* [*ohm'-nee-boos*] bus
once [*ohn'-theh*] eleven
onda [*ohn'-dah*] wave
   onda corta [*ohn'-dah kohr'-tah*] short wave
ondear *v.* [*ohn-deh-ahr'*] wave
onza [*ohn'-thah*] ounce
ópera [*oh'-peh-rah*] opera
operación *f.* [*oh-peh-rah-thee-ohn'*] operation, surgery
operar *v.* [*oh-peh-rahr'*] operate
opinión *f.* [*oh-pee-nee-ohn'*] opinion
oponer *v. irreg.* [*oh-poh-nehr'*] oppose
oportunidad *f.* [*oh-pohr-too-nee-dahd'*] chance, opportunity
optimista *m., f.* [*ohp-tee-mees'-tah*] optimist
óptimo [*ohp'-tee-moh*] best
opuesto [*oh-poo-ehs'-toh*] opposite
oración *f.* [*oh-rah-thee-ohn'*] prayer; sentence [grammar]
oral [*oh-rahl'*] oral
orden *f.* [*ohr'-dehn*] order, command
orden *m.* [*ohr'-dehn*] order, arrangement
ordenado [*ohr-deh-nah'-doh*] orderly, ordered
ordenar *v.* [*ohr-deh-nahr'*] order
ordinariamente [*ohr-dee-nah-ree-ah-mehn'-teh*] ordinarily
ordinario [*ohr-dee-nah'-ree-oh*] ordinary
oreja [*oh-reh'-hah*] ear
orgánico [*ohr-gah'-nee-koh*] organic
organización *f.* [*ohr-gah-nee-thah-thee-ohn'*] organization
organizar *v.* [*ohr-gah-nee-thahr'*] organize, arrange
órgano [*ohr'-gah-noh*] organ
orgullo [*ohr-goo'-yoh*] pride
orgulloso [*ohr-goo-yoh'-soh*] proud
oriental [*oh-ree-ehn-tahl'*] oriental
origen *m.* [*oh-ree'-hehn*] origin
original [*oh-ree-hee-nahl'*] original
originalmente [*oh-ree-hee-nahl-mehn'-teh*] originally

orilla [*oh-ree'-yah*] shore, edge
ornamento [*ohr-nah-mehn'-toh*] ornament
oro [*oh'-roh*] gold
orquesta [*ohr-kehs'-tah*] orchestra
oscuridad *f.* [*ohs-koo-ree-dahd'*] darkness
oscuro [*ohs-koo'-roh*] dark
ostra [*ohs'-trah*] oyster
otoño [*oh-toh'-nyoh*] autumn, fall
otorgar *v.* [*oh-tohr-gahr'*] grant
otro [*oh'-troh*] other, another
  de otro modo [*deh oh'-troh moh'-doh*] otherwise
  otra vez [*oh'-trah vehth*] again
ovalado [*oh-vah-lah'-doh*] oval
oxidado [*ohk-see-dah'-doh*] rusty
oxígeno [*ohk-see'-heh-noh*] oxygen

P

paciencia [*pah-thee-ehn'-thee-ah*] patience
paciente [*pah-thee-ehn'-teh*] patient
pacífico [*pah-thee'-fee-koh*] peaceful
padrastro [*pah-drahs'-troh*] stepfather
padre *m.* [*pah'-dreh*] father
padres *m. pl.* [*pah'-drehs*] parents
pagado [*pah-gah'-doh*] paid
pagar *v.* [*pah-gahr'*] pay
  pagar al contado [*pah-gahr' ahl kohn-tah'-doh*] pay cash
  pagar a plazos [*pah-gahr' ah plah'-thohs*] pay by
    installments
  pagar una multa [*pah-gahr' oo'-nah mool'-tah*] pay a fine
página [*pah'-hee-nah*] page
pago [*pah'-goh*] payment
país *m.* [*pah-ees'*] country
paisaje *m.* [*pah-ee-sah'-heh*] landscape, scenery
paja [*pah'-hah*] straw

pájaro [*pah'-hah-roh*] bird
pala [*pah'-lah*] shovel
palabra [*pah-lah'-brah*] word
palacio [*pah-lah'-thee-oh*] palace
palangana [*pah-lahn-gah'-nah*] basin
pálido [*pah'-lee-doh*] pale
palma [*pahl'-mah*] palm
palmatoria [*pahl-mah-toh'-ree-ah*] candlestick
palmera [*pahl-meh'-rah*] palm tree
palo [*pah'-loh*] stick
paloma [*pah-loh'-mah*] dove
pan *m.* [*pahn*] bread, loaf
panadería [*pah-nah-deh-ree'-ah*] bakery
Panamá [*pah-nah-mah'*] Panama
panameño [*pah-nah-meh'-nyoh*] Panamanian
pánico [*pah'-nee-koh*] panic
pantalla [*pahn-tah'-yah*] screen
pantalones *m. pl.* [*pahn-tah-loh'-nehs*] trousers, slacks, pants
paño [*pah'-nyoh*] cloth
pañuelo [*pah-nyoo-eh'-loh*] handkerchief
papel *m.* [*pah-pehl'*] paper
  papel de escribir [*pah-pehl' deh ehs-kree-beer'*] writing
    paper
  papel de seda [*pah-pehl' deh seh'-dah*] tissue paper
  papeles de archivo [*pah-peh'-lehs deh ahr-chee'-voh*]
    records
  papel higiénico [*pah-pehl' ee-hee-eh'-nee-koh*] toilet paper
papelera [*pah-peh-leh'-rah*] waste basket
papelería [*pah-peh-leh-ree'-ah*] stationery
paquete *m.* [*pah-keh'-teh*] package, parcel
par *m.* [*pahr*] pair
para [*pah'-rah*] for, in order to
  para que [*pah'-rah keh*] in order to
  para siempre [*pah'-rah see-ehm'-preh*] forever
paracaídas *m. sing. & pl.* [*pah-rah-kah-ee'-dahs*] parachute
parachoques *m. sing. & pl.* [*pah-rah-choh'-kehs*] bumper
parada [*pah-rah'-dah*] stop
paraguas *m. sing. & pl.* [*pah-rah'goo-ahs*] umbrella

Paraguay [*pah-rah-goo-ah'-ee*] Paraguay
paraguayo [*pah-rah-goo-ah'-yoh*] Paraguayan
paraíso [*pah-rah-ee'-soh*] paradise
paralelo [*pah-rah-leh'-loh*] parallel
paralizar *v.* [*pah-rah-lee-thahr'*] paralyze
parar *v.* [*pah-rahr'*] stop
  ¡Pare aquí! [*pah'-reh ah-kee'*] Stop here!
parcialmente [*pahr-thee-ahl-mehn'-teh*] partially
parecer *v. irreg.* [*pah-reh-thehr'*] seem
  me parece [*meh pah-reh'-theh*] it seems to me
parecerse *v. irreg.* [*pah-reh-thehr'-seh*] look like
parecido *n.* [*pah-reh-thee'-doh*] resemblance
parecido *adj.* [*pah-reh-thee'-doh*] alike
pared *f.* [*pah-rehd'*] wall
pareja [*pah-reh'-hah*] couple
parejo [*pah-reh'-hoh*] even
parentesco [*pah-rehn-tehs'-koh*] relationship
parientes *m. pl.* [*pah-ree-ehn'-tehs*] relatives
parlamento [*pahr-lah-mehn'-toh*] parliament
párpado [*pahr'-pah-doh*] eyelid
parque *m.* [*pahr'-keh*] park
párrafo [*pah'-rrah-foh*] paragraph
parrilla [*pah-rree'-yah*] grill, broiler
  a la parrilla [*ah lah pah-rree'-yah*] broiled, grilled
parroquia [*pah-rroh'-kee-ah*] parish
parte *f.* [*pahr'-teh*] part, share
  parte superior [*pahr'-teh soo-peh-ree-ohr'*] top
participar *v.* [*pahr-tee-thee-pahr'*] participate
particular [*pahr-tee-koo-lahr'*] particular
particularmente [*pahr-tee-koo-lahr-mehn'-teh*] particularly
partida [*pahr-tee'-dah*] departure
partido [*pahr-tee'-doh*] match, game; faction
partir *v.* [*pahr-teer'*] part, depart
parto [*pahr'-toh*] childbirth
pasado [*pah-sah'-doh*] past
pasaje *m.* [*pah-sah'-heh*] passage
pasajero [*pah-sah-heh'-roh*] passenger
pasaporte *m.* [*pah-sah-pohr'-teh*] passport

pasar *v.* [*pah-sahr'*] pass, occur, happen
  pasar por encima de [*pah-sahr' pohr ehn-thee'-mah deh*]
    go over
Pascua [*pahs'-koo-ah*] Easter
pase *m.* [*pah'-seh*] permit
pasear *v.* [*pah-seh-ahr'*] walk
paseo [*pah-seh'-oh*] walk
  dar *v.* **un paseo** [*dahr oon pah-seh'-oh*] take a walk
pasillo [*pah-see'-yoh*] corridor, aisle
pasión *f.* [*pah-see-ohn'*] passion
pasivo [*pah-see'voh*] passive
paso [*pah'-soh*] pass, step, passing
  paso de peatones [*pah'-soh deh peh-ah-toh'-nehs*]
    crosswalk
  dar *v.* **un paso** [*dahr oon pah'-soh*] step
  paso a nivel [*pah'-soh ah nee-vehl'*] railroad crossing
pasta [*pahs'-tah*] paste, noodles
pastel *m.* [*pahs-tehl'*] cake, pie
pastelería [*pahs-teh-leh-ree'-ah*] pastry
pastilla [*pahs-tee'-yah*] tablet
pata [*pah'-tah*] leg
patata [*pah-tah'-tah*] potato
patear *v.* [*pah-teh-ahr'*] kick
patinar *v.* [*pah-tee-nahr'*] skate
patio [*pah'-tee-oh*] patio, courtyard
pato [*pah'-toh*] duck
patriótico [*pah-tree-oh'-tee-koh*] patriotic
patrón *m.* [*pah-trohn'*] employer, pattern
patrulla [*pah-troo'-yah*] patrol
pausa [*pah'-oo-sah*] pause
pavimento [*pah-vee-mehn'-toh*] pavement
pavo [*pah'-voh*] turkey
paz *f.* [*pahth*] peace
peaje *m.* [*peh-ah'-heh*] toll
peatón *m.* [*peh-ah-tohn'*] pedestrian
pecado [*peh-kah'-doh*] sin
peculiar [*peh-koo-lee-ahr'*] peculiar
pecho [*peh'-choh*] breast, chest

pedacito [*peh-dah-thee'-toh*] bit
pedazo [*peh-dah'-thoh*] piece
pedir *v. irreg.* [*peh-deer'*] ask for
pegar *v.* [*peh-gahr'*] hit, beat
peinar *v.* [*peh-ee-nahr'*] comb
peine *m.* [*peh'-ee-neh*] comb
pelea [*peh-leh'-ah*] fight
pelear *v.* [*peh-leh-ahr'*] fight
peletería [*peh-leh-teh-ree'-ah*] fur store
película [*peh-lee'-koo-lah*] film
peligro [*peh-lee'-groh*] danger
peligroso [*peh-lee-groh'-soh*] dangerous
pelo [*peh'-loh*] hair
  corte *m.* **de pelo** [*kohr'-teh deh peh'-loh*] haircut
pelota [*peh-loh'-tah*] ball
peluca [*peh-loo'-kah*] wig
peluquería [*peh-loo-keh-ree'-ah*] barbershop, hairdresser's
    shop
peluquero [*peh-loo-keh'-roh*] barber, hairdresser
pellizcar *v.* [*peh-yeeth-kahr'*] pinch
pena [*peh'-nah*] sorrow
pendiente *m.* [*pehn-dee-ehn'-teh*] earring
península [*peh-neen'-soo-lah*] peninsula
pensamiento [*pehn-sah-mee-ehn'-toh*] thought
pensar *v. irreg.* [*pehn-sahr'*] think
pensión *f.* [*pehn-see-ohn'*] boarding house
  pensión completa [*pehn-see-ohn' kohm-pleh'-tah*]
    room and board
penúltimo [*peh-nool'-tee-moh*] next to the last
peor [*peh-ohr'*] worse
  peor que [*peh-ohr' keh*] worse than
  el peor [*ehl peh-ohr'*] the worst
pepino [*peh-pee'-noh*] cucumber
pequeño [*peh-keh'-nyoh*] little, small
pera [*peh'-rah*] pear
percibir *v.* [*pehr-thee-beer'*] perceive
percha [*pehr'-chah*] hanger
perder *v. irreg.* [*pehr-dehr'*] lose

pérdida [*pehr'-dee-dah*] loss
perdido [*pehr-dee'-doh*] lost
perdón *m.* [*pehr-dohn'*] pardon
perdonar *v.* [*pehr-doh-nahr'*] forgive
   Perdóneme [*pehr-doh'-neh-meh*] Pardon me
perejil [*peu-reh-heel'*] parsley
perezoso [*peh-reh-thoh'-soh*] lazy
perfección *f.* [*pehr-fehk-thee-ohn'*] perfection
perfecto [*pehr-fehk'-toh*] perfect
perfil *m.* [*pehr-feel'*] profile
perfume *m.* [*pehr-foo'-meh*] perfume
periódico [*peh-ree-oh'-dee-koh*] newspaper
periodista *m.,f.* [*peh-ree-oh-dees'-tah*] journalist
período [*peh-ree'-oh-doh*] period
perla [*pehr'-lah*] pearl
permanecer *v. irreg.* [*pehr-mah-neh-thehr'*] remain, stay
permanente [*pehr-mah-nehn'-teh*] permanent wave
permanentemente [*pehr-mah-nehn-teh-mehn'-teh*]
    permanently
permiso [*pehr-mee'-soh*] permission, permit
permitir *v.* [*pehr-mee-teer'*] let, allow, permit
pero [*peh'-roh*] but
perpendicular [*pehr-pehn-dee-koo-lahr'*] perpendicular
perplejo [*pehr-pleh'-hoh*] puzzled
perro [*peh'-rroh*] dog
persa *m., f.* [*pehr'-sah*] Persian
perseguir *v., irreg.* [*pehr-seh-gheer'*] pursue
persiana [*pehr-see-ah'-nah*] shutter
persistir *v.* [*pehr-sees-teer'*] persist
persona [*pehr-soh'-nah*] person
personal *m.* [*pehr-soh-nahl'*] personnel
personal *adj.* [*pehr-soh-nahl'*] personal
personalidad *f.* [*pehr-soh-nah-lee-dahd'*] personality
personalmente [*pehr-soh-nahl-mehn'-teh*] personally
persuasivo [*pehr-soo-ah-see'-voh*] persuasive
persuadir *v.* [*pehr-soo-ah-deer'*] persuade
pertenecer *v. irreg.* [*pehr-teh-neh-thehr'*] belong
pertenencias [*pehr-teh-nehn'-thee-ahs*] belongings

Perú [*peh-roo'*] Peru
peruano [*peh-roo-ah'-noh*] Peruvian
pesadilla [*peh-sah-dee'-yah*] nightmare
pesado [*peh-sah'-doh*] heavy
pesar *v.* [*peh-sahr'*] weigh
pesca [*pehs'-kah*] fishing
   barco de pesca [*bahr'-koh deh pehs'-kah*] fishing boat
pescado [*pehs-kah'-doh*] fish
pescador *m.* [*pehs-kah-dohr'*] fisherman
pescar *v.* [*pehs-kahr'*] fish
pesimista *m., f.* [*peh-see-mees'-tah*] pessimistic
peso [*peh'-soh*] weight
pestañas *f. pl.* [*pehs-tah'-nyahs*] eyelashes
petición *f.* [*peh-tee-thee-ohn'*] request
pez *m.* [*pehth*] fish
pezón *m.* [*peh-thohn'*] nipple
piano [*pee-ah'-noh*] piano
pianista *m., f.* [*pee-ah-nees'-tah*] pianist
picante [*pee-kahn'-teh*] spicy, hot
picar *v.* [*pee-kahr'*] itch, bite
pie *m.* [*pee-eh'*] foot
   de pie [*deh pee-eh'*] standing
piedad *f.* [*pee-eh-dahd'*] pity
piedra [*pee-eh'-drah*] stone
piel *f.* [*pee-ehl'*] skin, fur
pierna [*pee-ehr'-nah*] leg
pieza [*pee-eh'-thah*] part, piece
   piezas de repuesto [*pee-eh'-thahs deh reh-poo-ehs'-toh*]
     spare parts
pijama *m.* [*pee-hah'-mah*] pajamas
pila [*pee'-lah*] pile
píldora [*peel'-doh-rah*] pill
piloto [*pee-loh'-toh*] pilot
pimienta [*pee-mee-ehn'-tah*] pepper
pimiento [*pee-mee-ehn'-toh*] green pepper
pintar *v.* [*peen-tahr'*] paint
pintor *m.* [*peen-tohr'*] painter
pintoresco [*peen-toh-rehs'-koh*] picturesque

pintura [*peen-too'-rah*] painting, paint
piña [*pee'-nyah*] pineapple
pipa [*pee'-pah*] pipe
pirámide *f.* [*pee-rah'-mee-deh*] pyramid
pisar *v.* [*pee-sahr'*] step on
piscina [*pees-thee'-nah*] swimming pool
piso [*pee'-soh*] floor, story
  piso de arriba [*pee'-soh deh ah-rree'-bah*] upper floor
  piso bajo [*pee'-soh bah'-hoh*] ground floor
pista [*pees'-tah*] track
pistola [*pees-toh'-lah*] pistol
placer *m.* [*plah-thehr'*] pleasure
plan *m.* [*plahn*] plan
planchar *v.* [*plahn-chahr'*] iron
planear *v.* [*plah-neh-ahr'*] plan
planeta *m.* [*plah-neh'-tah*] planet
plano [*plah'-noh*] plan
planta [*plahn'-tah*] plant
plantar *v.* [*plahn-tahr'*] plant
plástico *n. & adj.* [*plahs'-tee-koh*] plastic
plata [*plah'-tah*] silver
plataforma [*plah-tah-fohr'-mah*] platform
plátano [*plah'-tah-noh*] banana
platillo [*plah-tee'-yoh*] saucer
plato [*plah'-toh*] plate, dish
playa [*plah'-yah*] beach
plaza [*plah'-thah*] square, plaza
pleito [*pleh'-ee-toh*] litigation
plomo [*ploh'-moh*] lead [metal]
pluma [*ploo'-mah*] feather, pen
  pluma estilográfica [*ploo'-mah ehs-tee-loh-grah'-fee-kah*]
    fountain pen
plural *m.* [*ploo-rahl'*] plural
población *f.* [*poh-blah-thee-ohn'*] population
pobre [*poh'-breh*] poor
pobreza [*poh-breh'-thah*] poverty
poco [*poh'-koh*] little
  muy poco [*moo-ee' poh'-koh*] very little

poco a poco [*poh'-koh ah poh'-koh*] little by little
  un poquito [*oon poh-kee'-toh*] a little bit
pocos [*poh'-kohs*] few
poder *m.* [*poh-dehr'*] power
poder *v. irreg.* [*poh-dehr'*] can, may
  Puede ser [*poo-eh'-deh sehr*] It may be
  Puedo correr [*poo-eh'-doh koh-rrehr'*] I can run
  No puedo correr [*noh poo-eh'-doh koh-rrehr'*] I can't run
  podría [*poh-dree'-ah*] might, could
  ¿Puedo...? [*poo-eh'-doh*] May I...?
poderoso [*poh-deh-roh'-soh*] powerful
poema *m.* [*poh-eh'-mah*] poem
poesía [*poh-eh-see'-ah*] poetry
poeta *m., f.* [*poh-heh'-tah*] poet
policía *m., f.* [*poh-lee-thee'-ah*] police
  comisaría de policía [*koh-mee-sah-ree'-ah deh poh-lee-thee'-ah*] police station
política [*poh-lee'-tee-kah*] politics, policy
  política exterior [*poh-lee'-tee-kah ehks-teh-ree-ohr'*] foreign policy
político *m.* [*poh-lee'-tee-koh*] politician
político *adj.* [*poh-lee'-tee-koh*] political
polo [*poh'-loh*] pole
Polonia [*poh-loh'-nee-ah*] Poland
polvo [*pohl'-voh*] powder, dust
pollo [*poh'-yoh*] chicken
poner *v. irreg.* [*poh-nehr'*] put, place
  poner la mesa [*poh-nehr' lah meh'-sah*] set the table
ponerse *v. irreg.* [*poh-nehr'-seh*] put on
  ponerse en contacto [*poh-nehr'-seh ehn kohn-tahk'-toh*] contact
popa [*poh'-pah*] stern [of boat]
popular [*poh-poo-lahr'*] popular
popularidad *f.* [*poh-poo-lah-ree-dahd'*] popularity
por [*pohr*] by, for
  por consiguiente [*pohr kohn-see-ghee-ehn'-teh*] consequently
  por el momento [*pohr ehl moh-mehn'-toh*] for the moment

por lo tanto [*pohr loh tahn'-toh*] therefore
por otra parte [*pohr oh'-trah pahr'-teh*] on the other hand
por persona [*pohr pehr-soh'-nah*] apiece, per person
por supuesto [*pohr soo-poo-ehs'-toh*] of course
por todo [*pohr toh'-doh*] throughout, all over
porcentaje *m.* [*pohr-thehn-tah'-heh*] percentage
porche *m.* [*pohr'-cheh*] porch
porque [*pohr'-keh*] because
¿por qué? [*pohr keh'*] why?
  ¿por qué no? [*pohr keh' noh*] why not?
portátil [*pohr-tah'-teel*] portable
portorriqueño [*pohr-toh-rree-keh'-nyoh*] Puerto Rican
Portugal *m.* [*pohr-too-gahl'*] Portugal
portugués *m.* [*pohr-too-ghehs'*] Portuguese
posada [*poh-sah'-dah*] inn
poseer *v.* [*poh-seh-ehr'*] possess, own
posesión *f.* [*poh-seh-see-ohn'*] possession
posibilidad *f.* [*poh-see-bee-lee-dahd'*] possibility
posible [*poh-see'-bleh*] possible
posiblemente [*poh-see-bleh-mehn'-teh*] possibly
posición *f.* [*poh-see-thee-ohn'*] position
positivo [*poh-see-tee'-voh*] positive
postal *f.* [*pohs-tahl'*] postcard
poste *m.* [*pohs'-teh*] pole, post
posterior [*pohs-teh-ree-ohr'*] rear
postre *m.* [*pohs'-treh*] dessert
postura [*pohs-too'-rah*] posture, position
potencia [*poh-tehn'-thee-ah*] power
pozo *n.* [*poh'-thoh*] well
práctica [*prahk'-tee-kah*] practice
practicar *v.* [*prahk-tee-kahr'*] practice
prado [*prah'-doh*] meadow
precaución *f.* [*preh-kah-oo-thee-ohn'*] precaution
preceder *v.* [*preh-theh-dehr'*] precede
precio [*preh'-thee-oh*] price
  precio fijo [*preh'-thee-oh fee'-hoh*] fixed price
precioso [*preh-thee-oh'-soh*] precious
precisamente [*preh-thee-sah-mehn'-teh*] precisely

precisión *f.* [*preh-thee-see-ohn'*] accuracy
preciso [*preh-thee'-soh*] precise, accurate
predicar *v.* [*preh-dee-kahr'*] preach
preferencia [*preh-feh-rehn'-thee-ah*] preference, liking
preferible [*pre-feh-ree'-bleh*] preferable
preferir *v. irreg.* [*preh-feh-reer'*] prefer
pregunta [*preh-goon'-tah*] question
preguntar *v.* [*preh-goon-tahr'*] ask
preguntarse *v.* [*preh-goon-tahr'-seh*] wonder
prejuicio [*preh-hoo-ee'-thee-oh*] prejudice
prematuro [*preh-mah-too'-roh*] premature
premio [*preh'-mee-oh*] prize, award
prenda [*prehn'-dah*] garment
prender *v.* [*prehn-dehr'*] apprehend
prensa [*prehn'-sah*] press
preocupación *f.* [*preh-oh-koo-pah-thee-ohn'*] worry
preocupado [*preh-oh-koo-pah'-doh*] worried
preocupar *v.* [*preh-oh-koo-pahr'*] worry
preparación *f.* [*preh-pah-rah-thee-ohn'*] preparation
preparar *v.* [*preh-pah-rahr'*] prepare
presa [*preh'-sah*] dam
presencia [*preh'-sehn'-thee-ah*] presence
presenciar *v.* [*preh-sehn-thee-ahr'*] witness
presentar *v.* [*preh-sehn-tahr'*] present, introduce
presente [*preh-sehn'-teh*] present
presentimiento [*preh-sehn-tee-mee-ehn'-toh*] premonition
preservar *v.* [*preh-sehr-vahr'*] preserve
presidente *m.* [*preh-see-dehn'-teh*] president
presidiario [*preh-see-dee-ah'-ree-oh*] inmate
presión *f.* [*preh-see-ohn'*] pressure
presionar *v.* [*preh-see-oh-nahr'*] press
préstamo [*prehs'-tah-moh*] loan
prestar *v.* [*prehs-tahr'*] lend
 pedir *v. irreg.* **prestado** [*peh-deer' prehs-tah'-doh*] borrow
prestigio [*prehs-tee'-hee-oh*] prestige
presunción *f.* [*preh-soon-thee-ohn'*] conceit
presupuesto [*preh-soo-poo-ehs'-toh*] budget
pretender *v.* [*preh-tehn-dehr'*] pretend

pretexto [*preh-tehks'-toh*] pretext
prevención *f.* [*preh-vehn-thee-ohn'*] prevention
prevenir *v. irreg.* [*preh-veh-neer'*] prevent
prever *v. irreg.* [*preh-vehr'*] anticipate
previo [*preh'-vee-oh*] previous
primavera [*pree-mah-veh'-rah*] spring [season]
primero [*pree-meh'-roh*] first
  primeros auxilios [*pree-meh'-rohs ah-ook-see'-lee-ohs*]
    first aid
primo [*pree'-moh*] cousin
princesa [*preen-theh'-sah*] princess
principal [*preen-thee-pahl'*] principal, main
  calle *f.* **principal** [*kah'-yeh preen-thee-pahl'*] main street
  oficina principal [*oh-fee-thee'-nah preen-thee-pahl'*]
    main office
principalmente [*preen-thee-pahl-mehn'-teh*] mainly
príncipe *m.* [*preen'-thee-peh*] prince
principio [*preen-thee'-pee-oh*] beginning, start, principle
  al principio [*ahl preen-thee'-pee-oh*] at first
prisa [*pree'-sah*] hurry, haste
  ¡Dese prisa! [*deh'-seh pree'-sah*] Hurry up!
  tener *v. irreg.* **prisa** [*teh-nehr' pree'-sah*] be in a hurry
prisión *f.* [*pree-see-ohn'*] prison
prisionero [*pree-see-oh-neh'-roh*] prisoner
privacidad *f.* [*pree-vah-thee-dahd'*] privacy
privado [*pree-vah'-doh*] private; unconscious
privar *v.* [*pree-vahr'*] deprive
privilegio [*pree-vee-leh'-hee-oh*] privilege
proa [*proh'-ah*] prow
probablemente [*proh-bah-bleh-mehn'-teh*] probably
problema *m.* [*proh-bleh'-mah*] problem
probar *v. irreg.* [*proh-bahr'*] prove
probarse *v. irreg.* [*proh-bahr'-seh*] try on
proceder *v.* [*proh-theh-dehr'*] proceed, come from
procedimiento [*proh-theh-dee-mee-ehn'-toh*] procedure
proceso [*proh-theh'-soh*] process
producción *f.* [*proh-dook-thee-ohn'*] production
  producción en masa [*proh-dook-thee-ohn' ehn mah'-sah*]

mass production
producir v. irreg. [*proh-doo-theer'*] produce
producto [*proh-dook'-toh*] product
profesión f. [*proh-feh-see-ohn'*] profession
profesor m. [*proh-feh-sohr'*] professor
profundidad f. [*proh-foon-dee-dahd'*] depth
profundo [*proh-foon'-doh*] deep
programa m. [*proh-grah'-mah*] program
progresar v. [*proh-greh-sahr'*] progress
progresista m., f. [*proh-greh-sees'-tah*] progressive
progreso [*proh-greh'-soh*] progress
prohibido [*proh-ee-bee'-doh*] forbidden, prohibited
  ¡Prohibido el paso! [*proh-ee-bee'-doh ehl pah'-soh*] Do not
    enter!
prohibir v. [*proh-ee-beer'*] forbid, prohibit
  se prohibe entrar [*seh proh-ee'-beh ehn-trahr'*] no
    admittance
  se prohibe estacionar [*seh proh-ee'-beh ehs-tah-thee-oh-
    nahr'*] no parking
promedio [*proh-meh'-dee-oh*] average
promesa [*proh-meh'-sah*] promise
prometer v. [*proh-meh-tehr'*] promise
prominente [*proh-mee-nehn'-teh*] prominent
promoción f. [*proh-moh-thee-ohn'*] promotion
pronombre m. [*proh-nohm'-breh*] pronoun
pronóstico [*proh-nohs'-tee-koh*] forecast, prediction
pronto [*prohn'-toh*] soon
  tan pronto como sea posible [*tahn prohn'-toh koh'-moh
    seh'-ah poh-see'-bleh*] as soon as possible
pronunciación f. [*proh-noon-thee-ah-thee-ohn'*]
    pronunciation
pronunciar v. [*proh-noon-thee-ahr'*] pronounce
  ¿Cómo se pronuncia . . . ? [*koh-'moh seh proh-noon'-
    thee-ah*] How do you pronounce . . . ?
propaganda [*proh-pah-gahn'-dah*] propaganda
propiedad f. [*proh-pee-eh-dahd'*] property
propina [*proh-pee'-nah*] tip
propio [*proh'-pee-oh*] proper, own

proponer *v. irreg.* [*proh-poh-nehr'*] propose
proporción *f.* [*proh-pohr-thee-ohn'*] proportion
proporcionar *v.* [*proh-pohr-thee-oh-nahr'*] supply
proposición *f.* [*proh-poh-see-thee-ohn'*] proposition
propósito [*proh-poh'-see-toh*] purpose
  a propósito [*ah proh-poh'-see-toh*] by the way
propuesta [*proh-poo-ehs'-tah*] proposal
prosperidad *f.* [*prohs-peh-ree-dahd'*] prosperity
próspero [*prohs'-peh-roh*] prosperous
protección *f.* [*proh-tehk-thee-ohn'*] protection
proteger *v.* [*proh-teh-hehr'*] protect
protesta [*proh-tehs'-tah*] protest
protestante [*proh-tehs-tahn'-teh*] Protestant
protestar *v.* [*proh-tehs-tahr'*] protest
provecho [*proh-veh'-choh*] profit
proveer *v. irreg.* [*proh-veh-ehr'*] provide, supply
provenir *v. irreg.* [*proh-veh-neer'*] come from
proverbio [*proh-vehr'-bee-oh*] proverb
provincia [*proh-veen'-thee-ah*] province
provisiones *f. pl.* [*proh-vee-see-oh'-nehs*] provisions, supplies
próximo [*prohk'-see-moh*] next
  el mes próximo [*ehl mehs prohk'-see-moh*] next month
proyecto [*proh-yehk'-toh*] project
prueba [*proo-eh'-bah*] test, proof
psicoanálisis *m.* [*psee-koh-ah-nah'-lee-sees*] psychoanalysis
psicológico [*psee-koh-loh'-hee-koh*] psychological
psiquiatra *m., f.* [*psee-kee-ah'-trah*] psychiatrist
publicación *f.* [*poo-blee-kah-thee-ohn'*] publication
publicar *v.* [*poo-blee-kahr'*] publish
publicidad *f.* [*poo-blee-thee-dahd'*] publicity
público *n. & adj.* [*poo'-blee-koh*] public
pueblo [*poo-eh'-bloh*] village, people
puente *m.* [*poo-ehn'-teh*] bridge
puerta [*poo-ehr'-tah*] door, gate
puerto [*poo-ehr'-toh*] port, harbor
  puerto de mar [*poo-ehr'-toh deh mahr*] seaport
Puerto Rico [*poo-ehr'-toh ree'-koh*] Puerto Rico
puesto [*poo-ehs'-toh*] place, position, booth

pulcro [*pool'-kroh*] neat
pulga [*pool'-gah*] flea
pulgada [*pool-gah'-dah*] inch
pulgar *m.* [*pool-gahr'*] thumb
pulmón *m.* [*pool-mohn'*] lung
pulso [*pool'-soh*] pulse
punta [*poon'-tah*] point [sharp end]
punto [*poon'-toh*] point
  punto de vista [*poon'-toh deh vees'-tah*] point of view,
    viewpoint
puntual [*poon-too-ahl'*] punctual, exact
puñal *m.* [*poo-nyahl'*] dagger
puñetazo [*poo-nyeh-tah'-thoh*] punch
puño [*poo'-nyoh*] fist
puro [*poo'-roh*] pure

Q

que [*keh*] what, that, which, than
  ¿Qué hora es? [*keh oh'-rah ehs*] What time is it?
  ¿Qué más? [*keh mahs*] What else?
  ¿Qué pasa? [*keh pah'-sah*] What's the matter?
  ¿Para qué? [*pah'-rah keh*] What for?
quedarse *v.* [*keh-dahr'-seh*] remain, stay
queja [*keh'-hah*] complaint
quejarse *v.* [*keh-hahr'-seh*] complain
quemar *v.* [*keh-mahr'*] burn
  quemadura de sol [*keh-mah-doo'-rah deh sohl*] sunburn
querer *v.* [*keh-rehr'*] want, will, wish
querido [*keh-ree'-doh*] dear
queso [*keh'-soh*] cheese
quien *sing.*, **quienes** *pl.* [*kee-ehn'*, *kee-eh'-nehs*] who
  a quien *sing.*, **a quienes** *pl.* [*ah kee-ehn'*, *ah kee-eh'-nehs*]
    whom
  ¿de quién es? [*deh kee-ehn' ehs*] whose?

quienquiera [*kee-ehn-kee-eh'-rah*] whoever
quince [*keen'-theh*] fifteen
quinto [*keen'-toh*] fifth
quitamanchas *m. sing.* [*kee-tah-mahn'-chahs*] stain remover
quitar *v.* [*kee-tahr'*] take away, remove
quizás [*kee-thahs'*] perhaps, maybe

R

rábano [*rah'-bah-noh*] radish
rabia [*rah'-bee-ah*] rage
racimo [*rah-thee'-moh*] bunch
radiador *m.* [*rah-dee-ah-dohr'*] radiator
radio *f.* [*rah'-dee-oh*] radio
   emisora de radio [*eh-mee-soh'-rah deh rah-'dee-oh*]
     radio station
raíz *f.* [*rah-eeth'*] root
raja [*rah'-hah*] slice, split
rajar *v.* [*rah-hahr'*] split
rama [*rah'-mah*] branch
rana [*rah'-nah*] frog
rápido [*rah'-pee-doh*] fast, quick, rapid
rápidamente [*rah-pee-dah-mehn'-teh*] fast, quickly, rapidly
raqueta [*rah-keh'-tah*] racket
raramente [*rah-rah-mehn'-teh*] seldom, rarely
raro [*rah'-roh*] rare, strange
rascacielos *m. sing. & pl.* [*rahs-kah-thee-eh'-lohs*] skyscraper
rascar *v.* [*rahs-kahr'*] scratch
rasgar *v.* [*rahs-gahr'*] tear, rip
rasgo [*rahs'-goh*] trait, feature
raso *m.* [*rah'-soh*] satin
rastro [*rahs'-troh*] trace
rata [*rah'-tah*] rat
rato [*rah'-toh*] short time, while
raya [*rah'-yah*] stripe

rayo [*rah'-yoh*] ray, lightning
rayón *m.* [*rah-yohn'*] rayon
raza [*rah'-thah*] race
razón *f.* [*rah-thohn'*] reason, right, ratio
razonable [*rah-thoh-nah'-bleh*] reasonable
razonar *v.* [*rah-thoh-nahr'*] reason
reacción *f.* [*reh-ahk-thee-ohn'*] reaction
reacio [*reh-ah'-thee-oh*] unwilling
real [*reh-ahl'*] real, royal, actual
realidad *f.* [*reh-ah-lee-dahd'*] reality, truth
   en realidad [*ehn reh-ah-lee-dahd'*] in fact
realización *f.* [*reh-ah-lee-thah-thee-ohn'*] accomplishment
realizar *v.* [*reh-ah-lee-thahr'*] carry out, accomplish
realmente [*reh-ahl-mehn'-teh*] actually
reanudar *v.* [*reh-ah-noo-dahr'*] resume
rebanada [*reh-bah-nah'-dah*] slice
rebelde [*reh-behl'-deh*] rebel
rebosar *v.* [*reh-boh-sahr'*] overflow
recado *m.* [*reh-kah'-doh*] errand, message
recalcar *v.* [*reh-kahl-kahr'*] emphasize
recepción *f.* [*reh-thehp-thee-ohn'*] reception
receta [*reh-theh'-tah*] prescription, recipe
recibir *v.* [*reh-thee-beer'*] receive
recibo [*reh-thee'-boh*] receipt
reciente [*reh-thee-ehn'-teh*] recent
recientemente [*reh-thee-ehn-teh-mehn'-teh*] recently
recipiente *m.* [*reh-thee-pee-ehn'-teh*] container
reclamar *v.* [*reh-klah-mahr'*] claim, demand
reclamo [*reh-klah'-moh*] claim
recobrar *v.* [*reh-koh-brahr'*] regain
recoger *v.* [*reh-koh-hehr'*] pick up
recomendación *f.* [*reh-koh-mehn-dah-thee-ohn'*]
   recommendation
recomendar *v. irreg.* [*reh-koh-mehn-dahr'*] recommend
recompensa [*reh-kohm-pehn'-sah*] reward
recompensar *v.* [*reh-kohm-pehn-sahr'*] reward
reconocer *v. irreg.* [*reh-koh-noh-thehr'*] acknowledge,
   recognize

recordar *v. irreg.* [*reh-kohr-dahr'*] remember, remind
recorrer *v.* [*reh-koh-rrehr'*] go over, travel over
recorrido [*reh-koh-rree'-doh*] route, course
recortar *v.* [*reh-kohr-tahr'*] trim
recreo [*reh-kreh'-oh*] recreation
recto [*rehk'-toh*] straight
recuerdo [*reh-koo-ehr'-doh*] souvenir
recuerdos [*reh-koo-ehr'-dohs*] regards
recuperación *f.* [*reh-koo-peh-rah-thee-ohn'*] recovery
recuperar *v.* [*reh-koo-peh-rahr'*] recover
recurrir *v.* [*reh-koo-rreer'*] resort
rechinar *v.* [*reh-chee-nahr'*] creak, squeak
red *f.* [*rehd*] net
redecilla [*reh-deh-thee'-yah*] hairnet
redondo [*reh-dohn'-doh*] round
reducción *f.* [*reh-dook-thee-ohn'*] reduction
reducir *v. irreg.* [*reh-doo-theer'*] reduce
reembolsar *v.* [*reh-ehm-bohl-sahr'*] refund
reemplazar *v.* [*reh-ehm-plah-thahr'*] replace
referencia [*reh-feh-rehn'-thee-ah*] reference
referir *v. irreg.* [*reh-feh-reer'*] refer
refinado [*reh-fee-nah'-doh*] refined
reflejar *v.* [*reh-fleh-hahr'*] reflect
reflejo [*reh-fleh'-hoh*] reflection, reflex
reformar *v.* [*reh-fohr-mahr'*] reform
refrescante [*reh-frehs-kahn'-teh*] refreshing
refrescar *v.* [*reh-frehs-kahr'*] refresh
refresco [*reh-frehs'-koh*] refreshment
refrigerador *m.* [*reh-free-heh-rah-dohr'*] refrigerator
refugiado [*reh-foo-hee-ah'-doh*] refugee
refugio [*reh-foo'-hee-oh*] shelter, refuge
regalo [*reh-gah'-loh*] gift, present
regañar *v.* [*reh-gah-nyahr'*] growl
regatear *v.* [*reh-gah-teh-ahr'*] bargain
régimen *m.* [*reh'-hee-mehn*] regime
regimiento [*reh-hee-mee-ehn'-toh*] regiment
región *f.* [*reh-hee-ohn'*] region
registrar *v.* [*reh-hees-trahr'*] register

registro [*reh-hees'-troh*] register, search
regla [*reh'-glah*] rule, ruler
reglamento [*reh-glah-mehn'-toh*] regulation
regresar *v.* [*reh-greh-sahr'*] return, get back, go back
regular *v.* [*reh-goo-lahr'*] regulate
regular *adj.* [*reh-goo-lahr'*] regular, fair
rehusar *v.* [*reh-oo-sahr'*] refuse
reina [*reh'-ee-nah*] queen
reino [*reh'-ee-noh*] kingdom
reír *v. irreg.* [*reh-eer'*] laugh
relación *f.* [*reh-lah-thee-ohn'*] relation
relacionado [*reh-lah-thee-oh-nah'-doh*] related
relajado [*reh-lah-hah'-doh*] lax
relámpago [*reh-lahm'-pah-goh*] lightning, flash
relativamente [*reh-lah-tee-vah-mehn'-teh*] relatively
relativo [*reh-lah-tee'-voh*] relative
  relativo a [*reh-lah-tee'-voh ah*] pertaining to
religión *f.* [*reh-lee-hee-ohn'*] religion
religioso [*reh-lee-hee-oh'-soh*] religious
reloj *m.* [*reh-lohh'*] watch, clock
  poner *v. irreg.* **un reloj en hora** [*poh-nehr' oon reh-lohh' ehn oh'-rah*] set a watch
relojero [*reh-loh-heh'-roh*] watch maker
rellenar *v.* [*reh-yeh-nahr'*] refill
remar *v.* [*reh-mahr'*] row
remendar *v. irreg.* [*reh-mehn-dahr'*] mend, patch
remiendo [*reh-mee-ehn'-doh*] patch
remitir *v.* [*reh-mee-teer'*] remit
remo [*reh'-moh*] oar
remolcador *m.* [*reh-mohl-kah-dohr'*] tugboat
remolcar *v.* [*reh-mohl-kahr'*] tow
rendir *v. irreg.* [*rehn-deer'*] surrender
renovar *v. irreg.* [*reh-noh-vahr'*] renew
renunciar *v.* [*reh-noon-thee-ahr'*] resign
reñir *v. irreg.* [*reh-nyeer'*] quarrel, scold
reparación *f.* [*reh-pah-rah-thee-ohn'*] repair
reparar *v.* [*reh-pah-rahr'*] repair
reparto [*reh-pahr'-toh*] distribution

repasar *v.* [*reh-pah-sahr'*] review
repeler *v.* [*reh-peh-lehr'*] repel
repentinamente [*reh-pehn-tee-nah-mehn'-teh*] suddenly
repentino [*reh-pehn-tee'-noh*] sudden
repetir *v. irreg.* [*reh-peh-teer'*] repeat
  Repita por favor [*reh-pee'-tah pohr fah-vohr'*] Please
    repeat
repique *m.* [*reh-pee'-keh*] chime
repisa [*reh-pee'-sah*] shelf
repollo [*reh-poh'-yoh*] cabbage
reportar *v.* [*reh-pohr-tahr'*] report
reportero [*reh-pohr-teh'-roh*] reporter
representante *m., f.* [*reh-preh-sehn-tahn'-teh*] representative
representar *v.* [*reh-preh-sehn-tahr'*] represent
reproducción *f.* [*reh-proh-dook-thee-ohn'*] reproduction
república [*reh-poo'-blee-kah*] republic
República Dominicana [*reh-poo'-blee-kah doh-mee-nee-kah'-
    nah*] Dominican Republic
reputación *f.* [*reh-poo-tah-thee-ohn'*] reputation
requerir *v. irreg.* [*reh-keh-reer'*] require
requisito [*reh-kee-see'-toh*] requirement
resbaladizo [*rehs-bah-lah-dee'-thoh*] slippery
resbalar *v.* [*rehs-bah-lahr'*] slide, slip
resbalón *m.* [*rehs-bah-lohn'*] slip
rescatar *v.* [*rehs-kah-tahr'*] rescue
resentimiento [*reh-sehn-tee-mee-ehn'-toh*] resentment
reserva [*reh-sehr'-vah*] reserve, reservation [at hotel]
resfriarse *v.* [*rehs-free-ahr'-seh*] catch a cold
resguardo [*rehs-goo-ahr'-doh*] guarantee
residencia [*reh-see-dehn'-thee-ah*] residence
residente *m., f.* [*reh-see-dehn'-teh*] resident
residir *v.* [*reh-see-deer'*] dwell
resistir *v.* [*reh-sees-teer'*] resist
resolución *f.* [*reh-soh-loo-thee-ohn'*] resolution
resolver *v. irreg.* [*reh-sohl-vehr'*] resolve
resorte *m.* [*reh-sohr'-teh*] spring [mech.], resort [means]
respetable [*rehs-peh-tah'-bleh*] respectable
respeto [*rehs-peh'-toh*] respect

respiración *f.* [*rehs-pee-rah-thee-ohn'*] breath
respirar *v.* [*rehs-pee-rahr'*] breathe
resplandor *m.* [*rehs-plahn-dohr'*] glare
responder *v.* [*rehs-pohn-dehr'*] answer
  responder de [*rehs-pohn-dehr' deh*] account for
responsabilidad *f.* [*rehs-pohn-sah-bee-lee-dahd'*] responsibility, liability
responsable [*rehs-pohn-sah'-bleh*] responsible
respuesta [*rehs-poo-ehs'-tah*] answer
restaurante *m.* [*rehs-tah-oo-rahn'-teh*] restaurant
restaurar *v.* [*rehs-tah-oo-rahr'*] restore
resto [*rehs'-toh*] remainder
restricción *f.* [*rehs-treek-thee-ohn'*] restraint
resultado [*reh-sool-tah'-doh*] result
resumen *m.* [*reh-soo'-mehn*] outline, abstract
resumir *v.* [*reh-soo-meer'*] outline
retener *v. irreg.* [*reh-teh-nehr'*] retain, withhold
retirar *v.* [*reh-tee-rahr'*] withdraw
reto [*reh'-toh*] dare, challenge
retorno [*reh-tohr'-noh*] return
retrasarse *v.* [*reh-trah-sahr'-seh*] be late
retraso [*reh-trah'-soh*] delay
retrato [*reh-trah'-toh*] portrait
retrete *m.* [*reh-treh'-teh*] toilet, rest room
retroceder *v.* [*reh-troh-theh-dehr'*] fall back
retroceso [*reh-troh-theh'-soh*] recession
reumatismo [*reh-oo-mah-thees'-moh*] rheumatism
reunión *f.* [*reh-oo-nee-ohn'*] meeting
reunir *v.* [*reh-oo-neer'*] gather, bring together
reunirse *v.* [*reh-oo-neer'-seh*] meet, rejoin
revancha [*reh-vahn'-chah*] revenge
revelar *v.* [*reh-veh-lahr'*] reveal, develop [a photo]
reventar *v. irreg.* [*reh-vehn-tahr'*] burst
reverencia [*reh-veh-rehn'-thee-ah*] reverence; bow, curtsy
revés *m.* [*reh-vehs'*] reverse, back
  al revés [*ahl reh-vehs'*] inside out
revista [*reh-vees'-tah*] magazine
revolución *f.* [*reh-voh-loo-thee-ohn'*] revolution

revolver *v. irreg.* [*reh-vohl-vehr'*] stir
revólver *m.* [*reh-vohl'-vehr*] revolver
rey *m.* [*reh'-ee*] king
rezar *v.* [*reh-thahr'*] pray
ribera [*ree-beh'-rah*] shore, bank
rico [*ree'-koh*] rich, wealthy
ridículo [*ree-dee'-koo-loh*] ridiculous
riesgo *m.* [*ree-ehs'-goh*] risk
rincón *m.* [*reen-kohn'*] corner
riña [*ree'-nyah*] quarrel, argument
riñón *m.* [*ree-nyohn'*] kidney
río [*ree'-oh*] river
riqueza [*ree-keh'-thah*] wealth
risa [*ree'-sah*] laugh, laughter
ritmo [*reet'-moh*] rhythm
ritual *m.* [*ree-too-ahl'*] ritual
rival *m., f.* [*ree-vahl'*] rival
rizar *v.* [*ree-thahr'*] curl
rizo [*ree'-thoh*] curl
robado [*roh-bah'-doh*] stolen
robar *v.* [*roh-bahr'*] rob, steal
roble *m.* [*roh'-bleh*] oak
robo [*roh'-boh*] robbery
roca [*roh'-kah*] rock
rociar *v.* [*roh-thee-ahr'*] spray
rocío [*roh-thee'-oh*] dew
rodar *v. irreg.* [*roh-dahr'*] roll, revolve
rodear *v.* [*roh-deh-ahr'*] surround, go around
rodilla [*roh-dee'-yah*] knee
rogar *v. irreg.* [*roh-gahr'*] beg
rojo [*roh'-hoh*] red
romano [*roh-mah'-noh*] Roman
romántico [*roh-mahn'-tee-koh*] romantic
rompecabezas *m.* [*rohm-peh-kah-beh'-thahs*] puzzle
romper *v.* [*rohm-pehr'*] break
roncar *v.* [*rohn-kahr'*] snore
ropa [*roh'-pah*] clothes
   ropa blanca [*roh'-pah blahn'-kah*] linen

ropa interior [*roh'-pah een-teh-ree-ohr'*] lingerie, underwear
ropero [*roh-peh'-roh*] wardrobe
rosa [*roh'-sah*] pink [color], rose [flower]
roto [*roh'-toh*] broken
rubí *m.* [*roo-bee'*] ruby
rubio [*roo'-bee-oh*] blond
ruborizar *v.* [*roo-boh-ree-thahr'*] blush
rudo [*roo'-doh*] rude
rueda [*roo-eh'-dah*] wheel
ruedo [*roo-eh'-doh*] circuit, arena
rugir *v.* [*roo-heer'*] roar
ruido [*roo-ee'-doh*] noise
ruidoso [*roo-ee-doh'-soh*] noisy, loud
ruin [*roo-een'*] mean, wretched
ruina [*roo-ee'-nah*] ruin, downfall
rumor *m.* [*roo-mohr'*] rumor
rural [*roo-ruhl'*] rural
Rusia [*roo'-see-ah*] Russia
ruso [*roo'-soh*] Russian
rústico [*roos'-tee-koh*] rustic
ruta [*roo'-tah*] route
rutina [*roo-tee'-nah*] routine

S

sábado [*sah'-bah-doh*] Saturday
sábana [*sah'-bah-nah*] sheet
saber *v. irreg.* [*sah-behr'*] know, taste
   Esto sabe bien [*ehs'-toh sah'-beh bee-ehn'*] This tastes
    good
sabiduría [*sah-bee-doo-ree'-ah*] wisdom
sabio [*sah'-bee-oh*] wise
sabor *m.* [*sah-bohr'*] flavor, taste
sabotaje *m.* [*sah-boh-tah'-heh*] sabotage
sabroso [*sah-broh'-soh*] tasty

sacacorchos *m. sing. & pl.* [*sah-kah-kohr'-chohs*] corkscrew
sacar *v.* [*sah-kahr'*] pull out, draw
sacerdote *m.* [*sah-thehr-doh'-teh*] priest
saco [*sah'-koh*] sack
sacudir *v.* [*sah-koo-deer'*] shake
sagrado [*sah-grah'-doh*] sacred
sal *f.* [*sahl*] salt
sala [*sah'-lah*] parlor, hall, large room
salado [*sah-lah'-doh*] salty
salario [*sah-lah'-ree-oh*] salary, wages
salchicha [*sahl-chee'-chah*] sausage
salida [*sah-lee'-dah*] exit, departure
salir *v. irreg.* [*sah-leer'*] leave, go out
salmón *m.* [*sahl-mohn'*] salmon
salón *m.* [*sah-lohn'*] hall, parlor
   salón de belleza [*sah-lohn' deh beh-yeh'-thah*] beauty
     parlor
salsa [*sahl'-sah*] sauce
saltar *v.* [*sahl-tahr'*] jump, leap
salto [*sahl'-toh*] jump
salud *f.* [*sah-lood'*] health
   a su salud [*ah soo sah-lood'*] to your health
saludar *v.* [*sah-loo-dahr'*] say hello, salute
saludo [*sah-loo'-doh*] greeting
salvadoreño [*sahl-vah-doh-reh'-nyoh*] Salvadorian
salvaje [*sahl-vah'-heh*] wild, savage
salvar *v.* [*sahl-vahr'*] save
salvo [*sahl'-voh*] safe
sancionar *v.* [*sahn-thee-oh-nahr'*] sanction
sandía [*sahn-dee'-ah*] watermelon
sangrar *v.* [*sahn-grahr'*] bleed
sangre *f.* [*sahn'-greh*] blood
sanitario [*sah-nee-tah'-ree-oh*] sanitary
sano [*sah'-noh*] healthy
santo *n.* [*sahn'-toh*] saint
santo *adj.* [*sahn'-toh*] holy
sarampión *m.* [*sah-rahm-pee-ohn'*] measles
sarcástico [*sahr-kahs'-tee-koh*] sarcastic

sartén *f.* [*sahr-tehn'*] frying pan
sastre *m.* [*sahs'-treh*] tailor
sastrería [*sahs-treh-ree'-ah*] tailor shop
satírico [*sah-tee'-ree-koh*] satirical
satisfacción *f.* [*sah-tees-fahk-thee-ohn'*] satisfaction
satisfacer *v. irreg.* [*sah-tees-fah-thehr'*] satisfy
satisfactorio [*sah-tees-fahk-toh'-ree-oh*] satisfactory
satisfecho [*sah-tees-feh'-choh*] satisfied
sazonar *v.* [*sah-thoh-nahr'*] season
secar *v.* [*seh-kahr'*] dry
sección *f.* [*sehk-thee-ohn'*] section
seco [*seh'-koh*] dry
secretario [*seh-kreh-tah'-ree-oh*] secretary
secreto *n. & adj.* [*seh-kreh'-toh*] secret
secuestrar *v.* [*seh-koo-ehs-trahr'*] kidnap
sed *f.* [*sehd*] thirst
   tener *v. irreg.* **sed** [*teh-nehr'-sehd*] be thirsty
seda [*seh'-dah*] silk
sediento [*seh-dee-ehn'-toh*] thirsty
seducir *v. irreg.* [*seh-doo-theer'*] seduce
seguir *v. irreg.* [*seh-gheer'*] follow
   en seguida [*ehn seh-ghee'-dah*] at once
   ¡Siga! [*see'-gah*] Go on!
según [*seh-goon'*] according to
segundo [*seh-goon'-doh*] second
seguramente [*seh-goo-rah-mehn'-teh*] surely
seguridad *f.* [*seh-goo-ree-dahd'*] security, safety
seguro *n.* [*seh-goo'-roh*] insurance
seguro *adj.* [*seh-goo'-roh*] secure, safe, sure
seis [*seh'-ees*] six
seleccionar *v.* [*seh-lehk-thee-oh-nahr'*] select
selva [*sehl'-vah*] jungle, forest
sellar *v.* [*seh-yahr'*] seal
sello [*seh'-yoh*] (postage) stamp, seal
semana [*seh-mah'-nah*] week
   la semana pasada [*lah seh-mah'-nah pah-sah'-dah*]
     last week
   fin *m.* **de semana** [*feen deh seh-mah'-nah*] weekend

semanal [*seh-mah-nahl'*] weekly
semejante [*seh-meh-hahn'-teh*] similar, alike
semilla [*seh-mee'-yah*] seed
senado [*seh-nah'-doh*] senate
senador *m.* [*seh-nah-dohr'*] senator
sencillo [*sehn-thee'-yoh*] plain, simple
senda [*sehn'-dah*] path
sendero [*sehn-deh'-roh*] trail, path
sensacional [*sehn-sah-thee-oh-nahl'*] sensational
sensato [*sehn-sah'-toh*] sensible
sensible [*sehn-see'-bleh*] sensitive
sensual [*sehn-soo-ahl'*] sensual
sentado [*sehn-tah'-doh*] seated
sentar *v. irreg.* [*sehn-tahr'*] seat
sentarse *v. irreg.* [*sehn-tahr'-seh*] sit down
sentido [*sehn-tee'-doh*] sense
  sentido común [*sehn-tee'-doh koh-moon'*] common sense
sentimental [*sehn-tee-mehn-tahl'*] sentimental
sentimiento [*sehn-tee-mee-ehn'-toh*] feeling
sentir *v. irreg.* [*sehn-teer'*] feel, regret
seña [*seh'-nyah*] sign
señas [*seh'-nyahs*] address
señor [*seh-nyohr'*] mister, sir, lord
señora [*seh-nyoh'-rah*] lady, madam, Mrs.
señorita [*seh-nyoh-ree'-tah*] Miss
separación *f.* [*seh-pah-rah-thee-ohn'*] separation
separado [*seh-pah-rah'-doh*] separate
  por separado [*pohr seh-pah-rah'-doh*] separately
separar *v.* [*seh-pah-rahr'*] separate
septiembre [*sehp-tee-ehm'-breh*] September
séptimo [*sehp'-tee-moh*] seventh
sepultura [*seh-pool-too'-rah*] grave
ser *v. irreg.* [*sehr*] be
ser *m.* [*sehr*] being
sereno *m.* [*seh-reh'-noh*] night watchman
sereno *adj.* [*seh-reh'-noh*] serene
seriamente [*seh-ree-ah-mehn'-teh*] seriously
serie *f.* [*seh'-ree-eh*] series

serio [*seh'-ree-oh*] serious
serpiente *f.* [*sehr-pee-ehn'-teh*] snake
servicio [*sehr-vee'-thee-oh*] service
  de servicio [*deh sehr-vee'-thee-oh*] on duty
servicios [*sehr-vee'-thee-ohs*] men's/ladies' room
servilleta [*sehr-vee-yeh'-tah*] napkin
servir *v. irreg.* [*sehr-veer'*] serve, be of use
  ¿En qué puedo servirle? [*ehn keh poo-eh'-doh sehr-veer'-leh*] What can I do for you?
sesenta [*seh-sehn'-tah*] sixty
sesión *f.* [*seh-see-ohn'*] session
seta [*seh'-tah*] mushroom
setenta [*seh-tehn'-tah*] seventy
severo [*seh-veh'-roh*] severe
sexo [*sehk'-soh*] sex
sexto [*sehks'-toh*] sixth
si [*see*] if, whether
sí [*see*] yes
sidra [*see'-drah*] cider
siempre [*see-ehm'-preh*] always
  como siempre [*koh'-moh see-ehm'-preh*] as ever
  para siempre [*pah'-rah see-ehm'-preh*] forever
sierra [*see-eh'-rrah*] mountain range
siesta [*see-ehs'-tah*] nap
siete [*see-eh'-teh*] seven
siglo [*see'-gloh*] century
significar *v.* [*seeg-nee-fee-kahr'*] mean, signify
signo [*seeg'-noh*] sign
  signo de interrogación [*seeg'-noh deh een-teh-rroh-gah-thee-ohn'*] question mark
siguiente [*see-ghee-ehn'-teh*] following
silbido [*seel-bee'-doh*] whistle
silencio [*see-lehn'-thee-oh*] silence
silenciosamente [*see-lehn-thee-oh-sah-mehn'-teh*] silently
silencioso [*see-lehn-thee-oh'-soh*] silent
silla [*see'-yah*] chair
  silla de montar [*see'-yah deh mohn-tahr'*] saddle
sillón *m.* [*see-yohn'*] large chair

similar [*see-mee-lahr'*] similar
simpatía [*seem-pah-tee'-ah*] liking
simpático [*seem-pah'-tee-koh*] likable, nice
simple [*seem'-pleh*] simple
simplemente [*seem-pleh-mehn'-teh*] simply
simultáneo [*see-mool-tah'-neh-oh*] simultaneous
sin [*seen*] without
   sin embargo [*seen ehm-bahr'-goh*] however, nevertheless
   sin importancia [*seen eem-pohr-tahn'-thee-ah*] unimportant
sinceramente [*seen-theh-rah-mehn'-teh*] sincerely
sinceridad *f.* [*seen-theh-ree-dahd'*] sincerity
sincero [*seen-theh'-roh*] sincere
sinfonía [*seen-foh-nee'-ah*] symphony
sino [*see'-noh*] but
sintético [*seen-teh'-tee-koh*] synthetic
sirviente *m.* [*seer-vee-ehn'-teh*] servant
sistema *m.* [*sees-teh'-mah*] system
   sistema métrico [*sees-teh'-mah meh'-tree-koh*] metric
    system
sistemático [*sees-teh-mah'-tee-koh*] systematic
sitio [*see'-tee-oh*] location
situación *f.* [*see-too-ah-thee-ohn'*] situation
situado [*see-too-ah'-doh*] situated, located
situar *v.* [*see-too-ahr'*] locate
soberbio [*soh-behr'-bee-oh*] superb
sobornar *v.* [*soh-bohr-nahr'*] bribe
sobre *m.* [*soh'-breh*] envelope
sobre [*soh'-breh*] above, upon, concerning
   sobre todo [*soh'-breh toh'-doh*] above all
sobrecarga [*soh-breh-kahr'-gah*] overload
sobrar *v.* [*soh-brahr'*] be left over
sobras *f. pl.* [*soh'-brahs*] leftovers
sobresaliente [*soh-breh-sah-lee-ehn'-teh*] outstanding
sobrevivir *v.* [*soh-breh-vee-veer'*] survive
sobrina [*soh-bree'-nah*] niece
sobrino [*soh-bree'-noh*] nephew
sobrio [*soh'-bree-oh*] sober
social [*soh-thee-ahl'*] social

socialista *m.*, *f.* [*soh-thee-ah-lees'-tah*] socialist
sociedad *f.* [*soh-thee-eh-dahd'*] society
socio *m.*, *f.* [*soh'-thee-oh*] member, partner
socorrer *v.* [*soh-koh-rrehr'*] help, aid
sofá *m.* [*soh-fah'*] sofa, couch
soga [*soh'-gah*] rope
sol *m.* [*sohl*] sun
  puesta del sol [*poo-ehs'-tah dehl sohl*] sunset
  salida del sol [*sah-lee'-dah dehl sohl*] sunrise
solamente [*soh-lah-mehn'-teh*] only
soldado [*sohl-dah'-doh*] soldier
soledad *f.* [*soh-leh-dahd'*] solitude, loneliness
solicitante *m.*, *f.* [*soh-lee-thee-tahn'-teh*] applicant
solicitar *v.* [*soh-lee-thee-tahr'*] request, apply for
solicitud *f.* [*soh-lee-thee-tood'*] application
sólido [*soh'-lee-doh*] solid
solitario [*soh-lee-tah'-ree-oh*] lonely
solo *adj.* [*soh'-loh*] alone
sólo *adv.* [*soh'-loh*] only
solomillo [*soh-loh-mee'-yoh*] sirloin
soltar *v. irreg.* [*sohl-tahr'*] release
solución *f.* [*soh-loo-thee-ohn'*] solution
soltera [*sohl-teh'-rah*] unmarried woman
soltero [*sohl-teh'-roh*] bachelor
sombra [*sohm'-brah*] shade, shadow
sombrero [*sohm-breh'-roh*] hat
someter *v.* [*soh-meh-tehr'*] submit
sonar *v. irreg.* [*soh-nahr'*] ring, sound
sonido [*soh-nee'-doh*] sound
sonreír *v. irreg.* [*sohn-reh-eer'*] smile
sonrisa [*sohn-ree'-sah*] smile
  sonrisa maliciosa [*sohn-ree'-sah mah-lee-thee-oh'-sah*]
    grin
soñar *v. irreg.* [*soh-nyahr'*] dream
  soñar con [*soh-nyahr' kohn*] dream of
sopa [*soh'-pah*] soup
soplar *v.* [*soh-plahr'*] blow
soplido [*soh-plee'-doh*] blowing, puffing

soportar v. [*soh-pohr-tahr'*] support
sordo [*sohr'-doh*] deaf
sorprendente [*sohr-prehn-dehn'-teh*] surprising
sorprender v. [*sohr-prehn-dehr'*] surprise
sorpresa [*sohr-preh'-sah*] surprise
sortija [*sohr-tee'-hah*] ring [finger]
soso [*soh'-soh*] tasteless
sospecha [*sohs-peh'-chah*] suspicion
sospechar v. [*sohs-peh-chahr'*] suspect
sospechoso [*sohs-peh-choh'-soh*] suspicious
sostener v. irreg. [*sohs-teh-nehr'*] hold, support
sótano [*soh'-tah-noh*] basement
su (de él) [*soo (deh ehl)*] his, her, its
su, sus (de usted) [*soo, soos (deh oo-stehd)*] your
su, sus (de ello) [*soo, soos (deh eh'-yoh)*] its
su, sus (de ellos) [*soo, soos (deh eh'-yohs)*] their
suave [*soo-ah'-veh*] soft, gentle, mild
suavidad f. [*soo-ah-vee-dahd'*] softness
subasta [*soo-bahs'-tah*] auction
subida [*soo-bee'-dah*] ascent, rise
subir v. [*soo-beer'*] go up, rise, climb
submarino [*soob-mah-ree'-noh*] submarine
subterráneo [*soob-teh-rrah'-neh-oh*] underground
suceder v. [*soo-theh-dehr'*] happen, follow
sucesivo [*soo-theh-see'-voh*] successive
suceso [*soo-theh'-soh*] event
suciedad f. [*soo-thee-eh-dahd'*] dirt
sucio [*soo'-thee-oh*] dirty
sudamericano [*sood-ah-meh-ree-kah'-noh*] South American
sudar v. [*soo-dahr'*] perspire
sudor m. [*soo-dohr'*] perspiration
Suecia [*soo-eh'-thee-ah*] Sweden
suegra [*soo-eh'-grah*] mother-in-law
suegro [*soo-eh'-groh*] father-in-law
suela [*soo-eh'-lah*] (shoe) sole
sueldo [*soo-ehl'-doh*] wages, salary
suelo [*soo-eh'-loh*] floor, ground
suelto [*soo-ehl'-toh*] loose

sueño [*soo-eh'-nyoh*] dream
suerte *f.* [*soo-ehr'-teh*] luck
   tener *v. irreg.* **suerte** [*teh-nehr' soo-ehr'-teh*] be lucky
suficiente [*soo-fee-thee-ehn'-teh*] sufficient
sufrir *v.* [*soo-freer'*] suffer
sugerencia [*soo-heh-rehn'-thee-ah*] suggestion
sugerir *v. irreg.* [*soo-heh-reer'*] suggest
suicidio [*soo-ee-thee'-dee-oh*] suicide
Suiza [*soo-ee'-thah*] Switzerland
suma [*soo'-mah*] addition
sumar *v.* [*soo-mahr'*] add
sumario [*soo-mah'-ree-oh*] summary
sumergirse *v.* [*soo-mehr-heer'-seh*] dive
suministrar *v.* [*soo-mee-nees-trahr'*] supply, furnish
suntuoso [*soon-too-oh'-soh*] gorgeous
superficial [*soo-pehr-fee-thee-ahl'*] superficial
superficie *f.* [*soo-pehr-fee'-thee-eh*] surface
superior [*soo-peh-ree-ohr'*] superior, upper
supersticioso [*soo-pehrs-tee-thee-oh'-soh*] superstitious
superviviente [*soo-pehr-vee-vee-ehn'-teh*] survivor
suplicar *v.* [*soo-plee-kahr'*] beg
suponer *v. irreg.* [*soo-poh-nehr'*] suppose
   por supuesto [*pohr soo-poo-ehs'-toh*] of course
suposición *f.* [*soo-poh-see-thee-ohn'*] supposition, assumption,
   guess
supremo [*soo-preh'-moh*] supreme
suprimir *v.* [*soo-pree-meer'*] abolish
sur *m.* [*soor*] south
suramericano [*soo-rah-meh-ree-kah'-noh*] South American
surtido *n.* [*soor-tee'-doh*] assortment
surtido *adj.* [*soor-tee'-doh*] assorted
susceptible [*soos-thehp-tee'-bleh*] touchy
suspender *v.* [*soos-pehn-dehr'*] fail, hang
suspiro [*soos-pee'-roh*] sigh
sustancia [*soos-tahn'-thee-ah*] substance
sustantivo [*soos-tahn-tee'-voh*] noun
sustitución *f.* [*soos-tee-too-thee-ohn'*] substitution
sustituir *v. irreg.* [*soos-tee-too-eer'*] substitute

susurrar *v.* [*soo-soo-rrahr'*] whisper
suyo, suya (de el, ella) [*soo'-yoh, soo'-yah (deh ehl, eh'-ya)*] his, her
suyo, suya (de usted, de ustedes) [*soo'-yoh, soo'-yah (deh oo-stehd', deh oo-stehd'-ehs)*] your
suyo, suya (de ellos, de ellas) [*soo'-yoh, soo'-yah (deh eh'-yohs, deh eh'-yahs)*] their

T

tabaco [*tah-bah'-koh*] tobacco
taberna [*tah-behr'-nah*] tavern
tabla [*tah'-blah*] board. table
tablero [*tah-bleh'-roh*] board
tableta [*tah-bleh'-tah*] tablet
tacón *m.* [*tah-kohn'*] heel [shoe]
tacto [*tahk'-toh*] tact
tajada [*tah-hah'-dah*] slice
tal [*tahl*] such, such a
  con tal que [*kohn tahl keh*] provided that
taladrar *v.* [*tah-lah-drahr'*] bore, drill
taladro [*tah-lah'-droh*] drill
talento [*tah-lehn'-toh*] talent
talón *m.* [*tah-lohn'*] heel [foot]
talonario [*tah-loh-nah'-ree-oh*] receipt, check book
talla [*tah'-yah*] size
tamaño [*tah-mah'-nyoh*] size
también [*tahm-bee-ehn'*] also, too, as well
tambor *m.* [*tahm-bohr'*] drum
tampoco [*tahm-poh'-koh*] either
tan [*tahn*] so, as, such a
  tan pronto como [*tahn prohn'-toh koh'-moh*] as soon as
tanto [*tahn'-toh*] so much
  tanto como [*tahn'-toh koh'-moh*] as much as
tapadera [*tah-pah-deh'-rah*] cover, lid

tapia [*tah'-pee-ah*] fence
tapiz *m.* [*tah-peeth'*] tapestry
taquígrafo [*tah-kee'-grah-foh*] stenographer
taquilla [*tah-kee'-yah*] ticket window, box office
tardar *v.* [*tahr-dahr'*] be late
tarde *f.* [*tahr'-deh*] evening, afternoon
tarde *adv.* [*tahr'-deh*] late
  más tarde [*mahs tahr'-deh*] later
  tarde o temprano [*tahr'-deh oh tehm-prah'-noh*] sooner
    or later
tarifa [*tah-ree'-fah*] fare, tariff
tarjeta [*tahr-heh'-tah*] card
  tarjeta postal [*tahr-heh'-tah pohs-tahl'*] postcard
  tarjeta de visita [*tahr-heh'-tah deh vee-see'-tah*] calling
    card
taxi *m.* [*tahk'-see*] taxi, cab
taza [*tah'-thah*] cup
te [*teh*] you
té *m.* [*teh*] tea
  té con hielo [*teh kohn ee-eh'-loh*] iced tea
teatro [*teh-ah'-troh*] theater
técnico *n.* [*tehk'-nee-koh*] technician
técnico *adj.* [*tehk'-nee-koh*] technical
techo [*teh'-choh*] ceiling
teja [*teh'-hah*] tile
tejado [*teh-hah'-doh*] roof
tejido [*teh-hee'-doh*] textile
tela [*teh'-lah*] cloth, fabric
telaraña [*teh-lah-rah'-nyah*] web
telefonear *v.* [*teh-leh-foh-neh-ahr'*] telephone
telefonista *m., f.* [*teh-leh-foh-nees'-tah*] telephone operator
teléfono [*teh-leh'-foh-noh*] telephone
  llamada telefónica [*yah-mah'-dah teh-leh-foh'-nee-kah*]
    phone call
  por teléfono [*pohr teh-leh'-foh-noh*] by phone
telegrafiar *v.* [*teh-leh-grah-fee-ahr'*] telegraph
telegrama *m.* [*teh-leh-grah'-mah*] telegram
televisión *f.* [*teh-leh-vee-see-ohn'*] television

televisor *m.* [*teh-leh-vee-sohr'*] television set
tema *m.* [*teh'-mah*] theme, topic
temblar *v. irreg.* [*tehm-blahr'*] tremble, shake
temer *v.* [*teh-mehr'*] fear
temeroso [*teh-meh-roh'-soh*] fearful
temor *m.* [*teh-mohr'*] dread
temperatura [*tehm-peh-rah-too'-rah*] temperature
tempestad *f.* [*tehm-pehs-tahd'*] storm
templado [*tehm-plah'-doh*] warm
templo [*tehm'-ploh*] temple, sanctuary
temporada [*tehm-poh-rah'-dah*] season, period of time
tempora. [*tehm-poh-rahl'*] storm
temporal *adj.* [*tehm-poh-rahl'*] temporary
temprano [*tehm-prah'-noh*] early
tendencia [*tehn-dehn'-thee-ah*] tendency
tenderse *v. irreg.* [*tehn-dehr'-seh*] lie down
tenedor *m.* [*teh-neh-dohr'*] fork
tener *v. irreg.* [*teh-nehr'*] have
  tener que [*teh-nehr' keh*] must, have to
  Tengo que ir [*tehn'-goh keh eer'*] I must go
  tener sueño [*teh-nehr' soo-eh'-nyoh*] be sleepy
tentación *f.* [*tehn-tah-thee-ohn'*] temptation
teñir *v. irreg.* [*teh-nyeer'*] dye
teoría [*teh-oh-ree'-ah*] theory
tercero [*tehr-theh'-roh*] third
terciopelo [*tehr-thee-oh-peh'-loh*] velvet
terco [*tehr'-koh*] stubborn
terminado [*tehr-mee-nah'-doh*] ended, done, through
terminal *f.* [*tehr-mee-nahl'*] terminal
terminar *v.* [*tehr-mee-nahr'*] end, finish
termómetro [*tehr-moh'-meh-troh*] thermometer
ternera [*tehr-neh'-rah*] veal
terraza [*teh-rrah'-thah*] terrace
terremoto [*teh-rreh-moh'-toh*] earthquake
terreno [*teh-rreh'-noh*] land, ground
terrible [*teh-rree'-bleh*] terrible
terriblemente [*teh-rree-bleh-mehn'-teh*] terribly
territorio [*teh-rree-toh'-ree-oh*] territory

terror *m.* [*teh-rrohr'*] terror
terso [*tehr'-soh*] smooth
tesoro [*teh-soh'-roh*] treasure
tesorero [*teh-soh-reh'-roh*] treasurer
tesorería [*teh-soh-reh-ree'-ah*] treasury
testamento [*tehs-tah-mehn'-toh*] will, testament
testigo [*tehs-tee'-goh*] witness
   testigo ocular [*tehs-tee'-goh oh-koo-lahr'*] eyewitness
tetera [*teh-teh'-rah*] teapot
texto [*tehks'-toh*] text
tía [*tee'-ah*] aunt
tiempo [*tee-ehm'-poh*] weather, time
   a tiempo [*ah tee-ehm'-poh*] on time
   ¿Cuánto tiempo? [*koo-ahn'-toh tee-ehm'-poh*] How long?
   más tiempo [*mahs tee-ehm'-poh*] longer
   mucho tiempo [*moo'-choh tee-ehm'-poh*] a long time
   hace mucho tiempo [*ah'-theh moo'-choh tee-ehm'-poh*]
     long ago
tienda [*tee-ehn'-dah*] shop
   tienda de comestibles [*tee-ehn'-dah deh koh-mehs-tee'-*
     blehs] grocery
tierno [*tee-ehr'-noh*] tender
tierra [*tee-eh'-rrah*] land, earth
   en tierra [*ehn tee-eh'-rrah*] ashore
   tierra adentro [*tee-eh'-rrah ah-dehn'-troh*] inland
tijeras *f. pl.* [*tee-heh'-rahs*] scissors
timbre *m.* [*teem'-breh*] bell, seal
tímido [*tee'-mee-doh*] shy, timid
tinta [*teen'-tah*] ink
tinte *m.* [*teen'-teh*] dye
tinto [*teen'-toh*] red (wine)
tintorería [*teen-toh-reh-ree'-ah*] cleaner's shop
tío [*tee'-oh*] uncle
típico [*tee'-pee-koh*] typical
tipo [*tee'-poh*] type
tiranía [*tee-rah-nee'-ah*] tyranny
tirano [*tee-rah'-noh*] tyrant
tirar *v.* [*tee-rahr'*] throw away

tirar de [*tee-rahr' deh*] pull
tiritar v. [*tee-ree-tahr'*] shiver
tiro [*tee'-roh*] shot
título [*tee'-too-loh*] title
tiza [*tee'-thah*] chalk
toalla [*toh-ah'-yah*] towel
tobillo [*toh-bee'-yoh*] ankle
tocador m. [*toh-kah-dohr'*] dressing table
tocar v. [*toh-kahr'*] touch, play an instrument
todavía [*toh-dah-vee'-ah*] still, yet
todo [*toh'-doh*] all, everything, whole
  por todas partes [*pohr toh'-dahs pahr'-tehs*] everywhere
  todo el mundo [*toh'-doh ehl moon'-doh*] everybody
  todos los días [*toh'-dohs lohs dee'-ahs*] every day
tolerar v. [*toh-leh-rahr'*] tolerate
tomar v. [*toh-mahr'*] take
  !Tómelo con calma! [*toh'-meh-loh kohn kahl'-mah*] Take it
    easy!
tomate m. [*toh-mah'-teh*] tomato
  jugo de tomate [*hoo'-goh deh toh-mah'-teh*] tomato juice
tonada [*toh-nah'-dah*] tune
tonel m. [*toh-nehl'*] keg
tonelada [*toh-neh-lah'-dah*] ton
tono [*toh'-noh*] tone
tonto [*tohn'-toh*] foolish, silly
tópico [*toh'-pee-koh*] topic
toque m. [*toh'-keh*] touch
torcer v. irreg. [*tohr-thehr'*] twist
torcido [*tohr-thee'-doh*] crooked
torero [*toh-reh'-roh*] toreador, bullfighter
tormenta [*tohr-mehn'-tah*] storm, thunderstorm
tornado [*tohr-nah'-doh*] tornado
tornillo [*tohr-nee'-yoh*] screw
toro [*toh'-roh*] bull
  corrida de toros [*koh-rree'-dah deh toh'-rohs*] bullfight
toronja [*toh-rohn'-hah*] grapefruit
torpe [*tohr'-peh*] awkward
torre f. [*toh'-rreh*] tower

torta [*tohr'-tah*] cake
   tortita de harina [*tohr-tee'-tah deh ah-ree'-nah*] pancake
tortilla de huevos [*tohr-tee'-yah deh oo-eh'-vohs*] omelet
tortura [*tohr-too'-rah*] torture
tos *f.* [*tohs*] cough
toser *v.* [*toh-sehr'*] cough
tostada [*tohs-tah'-dah*] toast
tostado [*tohs-tah'-doh*] sunburned, toasted
tostador *m.* [*tohs-tah-dohr'*] toaster
tostar *v. irreg.* [*tohs-tahr'*] toast
total *m.* [*toh-tahl'*] total
trabajador *m.* [*trah-bah-hah-dohr'*] worker
trabajar *v.* [*trah-bah-hahr'*] work
trabajo [*trah-bah'-hoh*] work, labor, job
tradición *f.* [*trah-dee-thee-ohn'*] tradition
tradicional [*trah-dee-thee-oh-nahl'*] traditional
traducción *f.* [*trah-dook-thee-ohn'*] translation
traducir *v. irreg.* [*trah-doo-theer'*] translate
traductor *m.* [*trah-dook-tohr'*] translator
traer *v. irreg.* [*trah-ehr'*] bring
tráfico [*trah'-fee-koh*] traffic
tragar *v.* [*trah-gahr'*] swallow
tragedia [*trah-heh'-dee-ah*] tragedy
trágico [*trah'-hee-koh*] tragic
traidor *m.* [*trah-ee-dohr'*] traitor
traje *m.* [*trah'-heh*] suit, dress
   traje de baño [*trah'-heh deh bah'-nyoh*] bathing suit
trampa [*trahm'-pah*] trap, fraud
tranquilo [*trahn-kee'-loh*] tranquil, quiet, calm
transeúnte *m.* [*trahn-seh-oon'-teh*] pedestrian, transient
transformar *v.* [*trahns-fohr-mahr'*] transform
transigir *v.* [*trahn-see-heer'*] compromise
transmisión *f.* [*trahns-mee-see-ohn'*] transmission, broadcast
transmitir *v.* [*trahns-mee-teer'*] transmit
transparente [*trahns-pah-rehn'-teh*] transparent
transpiración *f.* [*trahns-pee-rah-thee-ohn'*] perspiration
transporte *m.* [*trahns-pohr'-teh*] transportation
tranvía *m.* [*trahn-vee'-ah*] streetcar

trapo [*trah'-poh*] cloth, rag
tras [*trahs*] after, behind
trasero [*trah-seh'-roh*] back, rear
trasladar *v.* [*trahs-lah-dahr'*] transfer
trastornar *v.* [*trahs-tohr-nahr'*] upset
tratado [*trah-tah'-doh*] treaty
tratamiento [*trah-tah-mee-ehn'-toh*] treatment
tratar *v.* [*trah-tahr'*] treat, try, deal
   tratar de [*trah-tahr' deh*] deal with
trato [*trah'-toh*] deal
través: a través de [*ah trah-vehs' deh*] across
travesía [*trah-veh-see'-ah*] cruise
travesura [*trah-veh-soo'-rah*] mischief
travieso [*trah-vee-eh'-soh*] naughty
trece [*treh'-theh*] thirteen
treinta [*treh'-een-tah*] thirty
tremendo [*treh-mehn'-doh*] tremendous
tren *m.* [*trehn*] train
trenza [*trehn'-thah*] braid, tress
trepar *v.* [*treh-pahr'*] climb
tres [*trehs*] three
treta [*treh'-tah*] trick
triángulo [*tree-ahn'-goo-loh*] triangle
tribu *f.* [*tree'-boo*] tribe
tribunal *m.* [*tree-boo-nahl'*] court
trigo [*tree'-goh*] wheat
tripúlación *f.* [*tree-poo-lah-thee-ohn'*] crew
triste [*trees'-teh*] sad
tristeza [*trees-teh'-thah*] sadness
triunfante [*tree-oon-fahn'-teh*] triumphant
trivial [*tree-vee-ahl'*] trivial
trofeo [*troh-feh'-oh*] trophy
trono [*troh'-noh*] throne
tropa [*troh'-pah*] troop
tropezar *v. irreg.* [*troh-peh-thahr'*] stumble
tropical [*troh-pee-kahl'*] tropical
trozo [*troh'-thoh*] piece, bit
trucha [*troo'-chah*] trout

trueno [*troo-eh'-noh*] thunder
tu [*too*] your
tú [*too'*] you [*sing. familiar*]
   tú mismo [*too' mees'-moh*] yourself
tuberculosis *f.* [*too-behr-koo-loh'-sees*] tuberculosis
tubería [*too-beh-ree'-ah*] pipeline
tubo [*too'-boh*] tube
tuerca [*too-ehr'-kah*] nut [mech.]
tumba [*toom'-bah*] tomb
túnel *m.* [*too'-nehl*] tunnel
turista *m., f.* [*too-rees'-tah*] tourist
turno [*toor'-noh*] turn
Turquía [*toor-kee'-ah*] Turkey
tuyo [*too'-yoh*] yours

U

ubicado [*oo-bee-kah'-doh*] located
últimamente [*ool-tee-mah-mehn'-teh*] lately
último [*ool'-tee-moh*] last, latest, ultimate
un [*oon*] a, an
   un poco [*oon poh'-koh*] a little
   un tanto [*oon tahn'-toh*] somewhat
un, uno, una [*oon, oo'-noh, oo'-nah*] one
unánime [*oo-nah'-nee-meh*] unanimous
único [*oo'-nee-koh*] unique, distinct
unidad *f.* [*oo-nee-dahd'*] unit, unity
uniforme *m.* [*oo-nee-fohr'-meh*] uniform.
unión *f.* [*oo-nee-ohn'*] union
unir *v.* [*oo-neer'*] unite
universal [*oo-nee-vehr-sahl'*] universal
universidad *f.* [*oo-nee-vehr-see-dahd'*] university, college
universo [*oo-nee-vehr'-soh*] universe
uña [*oo'-nyah*] finger nail
urgente [*oor-hehn'-teh*] urgent

Uruguay [*oo-roo-goo-ah'-ee*] Uruguay
uruguayo [*oo-roo-goo-ah'-yoh*] Uruguayan
usado [*oo-sah'-doh*] used
usar *v.* [*oo-sahr'*] use, wear
uso [*oo'-soh*] use
usted [*oos-tehd'*] you [*sing. formal*]
útil [*oo'-teel*] useful
utilidad *f.* [*oo-tee-lee-dahd'*] utility
uva [*oo'-vah*] grape

V

vaca [*vah'-kah*] cow
vacaciones *f. pl.* [*vah-kah-thee-oh'-nehs*] vacation
vacante *f.* [*vah-kahn'-teh*] vacancy
vacilar *v.* [*vah-thee-lahr'*] hesitate
vacio [*vah-thee'-oh*] empty
vacuna [*vah-koo'-nah*] vaccination
vagabundo [*vah-gah-boon'-doh*] vagabond
vagar *v.* [*vah-gahr'*] wander
vago [*vah'-goh*] vague
vagón *m.* [*vah-gohn'*] railroad car
vainilla [*vah-ee-nee'-yah*] vanilla
vajilla [*vah-hee'-yah*] tableware
   vajilla de porcelana [*vah-hee'-yah deh pohr-theh-lah'-nah*]
   chinaware
valer *v. irreg.* [*vah-lehr'*] cost, be worth
válido [*vah'-lee-doh*] valid
valiente [*vah-lee-ehn'-teh*] valiant, courageous
valioso [*vah-lee-oh'-soh*] valuable, worthy
valor *m.* [*vah-lohr'*] courage, value, worth
valorar *v.* [*vah-loh-rahr'*] value
válvula [*vahl'-voo-lah*] valve
valla [*vah'-yah*] fence
valle *m.* [*vah'-yeh*] valley

vanidad *f.* [*vah-nee-dahd'*] vanity
vanidoso [*vah-nee-doh'-soh*] conceited, vain
vapor *m.* [*vah-pohr'*] steam
variable [*vah-ree-ah'-bleh*] variable
variar *v.* [*vah-ree-ahr'*] vary
variedad *f.* [*vah-ree-eh-dahd'*] variety
varios [*vah'-ree-ohs*] several, various
vaso [*vah'-soh*] glass [container]
vasto [*vahs'-toh*] vast
Vaticano [*vah-tee-kah'-noh*] Vatican
vecindad *f.* [*veh-theen-dahd'*] vicinity, neighborhood
vecindario [*veh-theen-dah'-ree-oh*] neighborhood
vecino [*veh-thee'-noh*] neighbor
vegetal *m.* [*veh-heh-tahl'*] vegetable
vehiculo [*veh-ee'-koo-loh*] vehicle
veinte [*veh'-een-teh*] twenty
vela [*veh'-lah*] candle, sail
velero [*veh-leh'-roh*] sailboat
velo [*veh'-loh*] veil
velocidad *f.* [*veh-loh-thee-dahd'*] speed
veloz [*veh-lohth'*] speedy
vena [*veh'-nah*] vein
venado [*veh-nah'-doh*] deer
vencedor *m.* [*vehn-theh-dohr'*] winner
vencer *v.* [*vehn-thehr'*] win
vencido [*vehn-thee'-doh*] defeated
   darse *v.* **irreg. por vencido** [*dahr'-seh pohr vehn-thee'-doh*]
    give up
venda [*vehn'-dah*] bandage
vendar *v.* [*vehn-dahr'*] bandage
vendedor *m.* [*vehn-deh-dohr'*] seller
   vendedor ambulante [*vehn-deh-dohr' ahm-boo-lahn'-teh*]
    peddler
vender *v.* [*vehn-dehr'*] sell
veneno [*veh-neh'-noh*] poison
venenoso [*veh-neh-noh'-soh*] poisonous
venezolano [*veh-neh-thoh-lah'-noh*] Venezuelan
Venezuela [*veh-neh-thoo-eh'-lah*] Venezuela

vengar *v.* [*vehn-gahr'*] avenge

venir *v. irreg.* [*veh-neer'*] come

  ¡Venga aquí! [*vehn'-gah ah-kee'*] Come here!

  venir por [*veh-neer' pohr*] come for

venta [*vehn'-tah*] sale

  en venta [*ehn vehn'-tah*] for sale

  venta de liquidación [*vehn'-tah deh lee-kee-dah-thee-ohn'*] clearance sale

ventaja [*vehn-tah'-hah*] advantage

ventana [*vehn-tah'-nah*] window

ventilador *m.* [*vehn-tee-lah-dohr'*] ventilator, fan

ver *v. irreg.* [*vehr*] see

verano [*veh-rah'-noh*] summer

verbo [*vehr'-boh*] verb

verdad *f.* [*vehr-dahd'*] truth

verdaderamente [*vehr-dah-deh-rah-mehn'-teh*] indeed, really

verdadero [*vehr-dah-deh'-roh*] true, real

verde [*vehr'-deh*] green

vergonzoso [*vehr-gohn-thoh'-soh*] shameful

vergüenza [*vehr-goo-ehn'-ıhah*] shame

verificar *v.* [*veh-ree-fee-kahr'*] verify, check

verja [*vehr'-hah*] grate

verso [*vehr'-soh*] verse

verter *v. irreg.* [*vehr-tehr'*] pour

vertical [*vehr-tee-kahl'*] vertical

vestíbulo [*vehs-tee'-boo-loh*] lobby, hall

vestido [*vehs-tee'-doh*] dress

  vestido de noche [*vehs-tee'-doh deh noh'-cheh*] evening dress

vestir *v. irreg.* [*vehs-teer'*] dress

vestirse *v. irreg.* [*vehs-teer'-seh*] get dressed

veterinario [*veh-teh-ree-nah'-ree-oh*] veterinary

vez *f.* [*vehth*] time

  de vez en cuando [*deh vehth ehn koo-ahn'-doh*] now and then

  dos veces [*dohs veh'-thehs*] twice

  una vez [*oo'-nah vehth*] once

  una vez más [*oo'-nah vehth mahs*] once again, once more

vía [*vee'-ah*] way, road, street, railroad track
viajar v. [*vee-ah-hahr'*] travel
viaje m. [*vee-ah'-heh*] travel, trip, voyage
   agencia de viajes [*ah-hehn'-thee-ah deh vee-ah'-hehs*] travel agency
   viaje de ida y vuelta [*vee-ah'-heh deh ee'-dah ee voo-ehl'-tah*] round trip
   viaje de placer [*vee-ah'-heh deh plah-thehr'*] pleasure trip
viajero [*vee-ah-heh'-roh*] traveler
vibrar v. [*vee-brahr'*] vibrate
vicio [*vee'-thee-oh*] vice
vicioso [*vee-thee-oh'-soh*] vicious
víctima [*veek'-tee-mah*] victim
victoria [*veek-toh'-ree-ah*] victory
vid f. [*veed*] vine
vida [*vee'-dah*] life
   seguro de vida [*seh-goo'-roh deh vee'-dah*] life insurance
   bote salvavidas [*boh'-teh sahl-vah-vee'-dahs*] life boat
   chaleco salvavidas [*chah-leh'-koh sahl-vah-vee'-dahs*] life jacket
vidriera [*vee-dree-eh'-rah*] glass window
vidrio [*vee'-dree-oh*] glass [material]
viejo n. [*vee-eh'-hoh*] old man
viejo adj. [*vee-eh'-hoh*] old
viento [*vee-ehn'-toh*] wind
vientre m. [*vee-ehn'-treh*] belly, abdomen
viernes m. [*vee-ehr'-nehs*] Friday
vigilante m. [*vee-hee-lahn'-teh*] watchman
vigoroso [*vee-goh-roh'-soh*] vigorous
vinagre m. [*vee-nah'-greh*] vinegar
vínculo [*veen'-koo-loh*] bond
vino [*vee'-noh*] wine
   vino blanco [*vee'-noh blahn'-koh*] white wine
   vino tinto [*vee'-noh teen'-toh*] red wine
viña [*vee'-nyah*] vineyard
violar v. [*vee-oh-lahr'*] violate, trespass, rape
violencia [*vee-oh-lehn'-thee-ah*] violence
violín m. [*vee-oh-leen'*] violin

viraje *m.* [*vee-rah'-heh*] turn
virar *v.* [*vee-rahr'*] turn
virgen *f.* [*veer'-hehn*] virgin
virtud *f.* [*veer-tood'*] virtue
virtuoso [*veer-too-oh'-soh*] virtuous
viruela [*vee-roo-eh'-lah*] smallpox
visado [*vee-sah'-doh*] visa
visible [*vee-see'-bleh*] visible
visita [*vee-see'-tah*] visit
visitante *m.*, *f.* [*vee-see-tahn'-teh*] visitor
visitar *v.* [*vee-see-tahr'*] visit, call on
vislumbrar *v.* [*vees-loom-brahr'*] glimpse, glance
víspera [*vees'-peh-rah*] eve
vista [*vees'-tah*] eyesight, sight, view
   punto de vista [*poon'-toh deh vees'-tah*] viewpoint, stand-
    point
visto [*vees'-toh*] seen
vistoso [*vees-toh'-soh*] gaudy
vital [*vee-tahl'*] vital
viuda [*vee-oo'-dah*] widow
viudo [*vee-oo'-doh*] widower
vivaz [*vee-vahth'*] lively
vivir *v.* [*vee-veer'*] live
vivo [*vee'-voh*] alive
vocabulario [*voh-kah-boo-lah'-ree-oh*] vocabulary
vocación *f.* [*voh-kah-thee-ohn'*] vocation
vocal *f.* [*voh-kahl'*] vowel
vocalista *m.*, *f.* [*voh-kah-lees'-tah*] vocalist
volante *m.* [*voh-lahn'-teh*] steering wheel
volar *v. irreg.* [*voh-lahr'*] fly, blow
volcán *m.* [*vohl-kahn'*] volcano
volcar *v. irreg.* [*vohl-kahr'*] overturn; turn over
volumen *m.* [*voh-loo'-mehn*] volume
voluntad *f.* [*voh-loon-tahd'*] will
voluntario [*voh-loon-tah'-ree-oh*] voluntary
volver *v. irreg.* [*vohl-vehr'*] return, be back
vomitar *v.* [*voh-mee-tahr'*] vomit
vosotros [*voh-soh'-trohs*] you

   vosotros mismos [*voh-soh'-trohs mees'-mohs*] yourselves
votar *v.* [*voh-tahr'*] vote
voto [*voh'-toh*] vote
voz *f.* [*vohth*] voice
   en voz alta [*ehn vohth ahl'-tah*] aloud
vuelo [*voo-eh'-loh*] flight
vuelta [*voo-ehl'-tah*] turn, return
   dar *v. irreg.* **la vuelta** [*dahr lah voo-ehl'-tah*] turn around
vuestro [*voo-ehs'-troh*] your
vulgar [*vool-gahr'*] vulgar

Y

y [*ee*] and
ya [*yah*] already
yate *m.* [*yah'-teh*] yacht
yema [*yeh'-mah*] egg yolk
yerno [*yehr'-noh*] son-in-law
yeso [*yeh'-soh*] plaster
yo [*yoh*] I
   yo mismo [*yoh mees'-moh*] myself
yodo [*yoh'-doh*] iodine

Z

zafarse *v.* [*thah-fahr'-seh*] slip away
zafiro [*thah-fee'-roh*] sapphire
zaguán *m.* [*thah-goo-ahn'*] vestibule
zambullirse *v.* [*thahm-boo-yeer'-seh*] dive
zanahoria [*thah-nah-oh'-ree-ah*] carrot
zanja [*thahn'-hah*] ditch
zapatería [*thah-pah-teh-ree'-ah*] shoe store

zapatero [*thah-pah-teh'-roh*] shoemaker
zapatillas [*thah-pah-tee'-yahs*] slippers
zapato [*thah-pah'-toh*] shoe
  cordón *m.* **de zapato** [*kohr-dohn' deh thah-pah'-toh*]
    shoelace
zarza [*thahr'-thah*] bush
zona [*thoh'-nah*] zone
zorro [*thoh'-rroh*] fox
zumbar *v.* [*thoom-bahr'*] buzz
zumo [*thoo'-moh*] juice
zurdo [*thoor'-doh*] left-handed

Phrases for Use Abroad

Helpful Expressions

Good morning.
Buenos días.
Boo-eh'-nohs dee'-ahs.

Good afternoon.
Buenas tardes.
Boo-eh'-nahs tahr'-dehs.

Good evening.
Buenas noches.
Boo-eh'-nahs noh'-chehs.

Hello. How do you do?
Hola. ¿Cómo está usted?
Oh'-lah. Koh'-moh ehs-tah' oos-tehd'?

Goodbye. See you later.
Adiós. Hasta luego.
Ah-dee-ohs'. Ahs'-tah loo-eh'-goh.

Thank you.
Gracias.
Grah'-thee-ahs.

You're welcome.
De nada.
Deh nah'-däh.

Excuse me.
Perdón.
Pehr-dohn'.

309

This is Mr./Mrs./Miss . . . .
Le presento/al señor/a la señora/a la señorita . . . .
Leh preh-sehn'-toh/ahl seh-nyohr'/ah lah seh-nyoh'-rah/ah lah seh-nyoh-ree'-tah . . . .

My name is . . . .
Me llamo . . . .
Meh yah'-moh . . . .

What is your name?
¿Cómo se llama usted?
Koh'-moh seh yah'-mah oos-tehd'?

I am pleased to meet you.
Mucho gusto en conocerle.
Moo'-choh goos'-toh ehn koh-noh-thehr'-leh.

I don't understand.
No entiendo.
Noh ehn-tee-ehn'-doh.

Could you speak more slowly, please?
¿Puede hablar más despacio, por favor?
Poo-eh'-deh ah-blahr' mahs dehs-pah'-thee-oh, pohr fah-vohr'?

Do you speak English?
¿Habla usted inglés?
Ah'-blah oos-tehd' een-glehs'?

How much?
¿Cuánto?
Koo-ahn'-toh?

Where?
¿Dónde?
Dohn'-deh?

When?
¿Cuándo?
Koo-ahn'-doh?

Can you help me, please?
¿Puede usted ayudarme, por favor?
Poo-eh'-deh oos-tehd' ah-yoo-dahr'-meh, pohr fah-vohr'?

How do you say . . . in Spanish?
¿Cómo se dice . . . en español?
Koh'-moh seh dee'-theh . . . ehn ehs-pah-nyohl'?

What does . . . mean?
¿Qué significa . . . ?
Keh seeg-nee-fee'-kah . . . ?

Time and Weather

What time is it?
¿Qué hora es?
Keh oh'-rah ehs?

It is nine A.M.
Son las nueve de la mañana.
Sohn lahs noo-eh'-veh deh lah mah-nyah'-nah.

I will meet you at half past two P.M.
Le veré a las dos y media de la tarde.
Leh veh-reh' ah lahs dohs ee meh'-dee-ah deh lah tahr'-deh.

How old are you?
¿Cuántos años tiene usted?
Koo-ahn'-tohs ah'-nyohs tee-eh'-neh oos-tehd'?

I am twenty-five years old.
Tengo veinticinco años.
Tehn'-goh veh-een-tee-theen'-koh ah'-nyohs.

How is the weather today?
¿Qué tal tiempo hace hoy?
Keh tahl tee-ehm'-poh ah'-theh oh'-ee?

It is a beautiful day.
Hace un día magnífico.
Ah'-theh oon dee'-ah mahg-nee'-fee-koh.

There will be rain tomorrow.
Mañana lloverá.
Mah-nyah'-nah yoh-veh-rah'.

Customs

May I see your passport, please?
¿Puedo ver su pasaporte, por favor?
Poo-eh'-doh vehr soo pah-sah-pohr'-teh, pohr fah-vohr'?

May I see your visa, please?
¿Puedo ver su visado, por favor?
Poo-eh'-doh vehr soo vee-sah'-doh, pohr fah-vohr'?

Open your suitcase.
Abra su maleta.
Ah'-brah soo mah-leh'-tah.

Do you have anything to declare?
¿Tiene algo que declarar?
Tee-eh'-neh ahl'-goh keh deh-klah-rahr'?

How long are you staying?
¿Cuánto tiempo piensa quedarse?
Koo-ahn'-toh tee-ehm'-poh pee-ehn'-sah keh-dahr'-seh?

I will be here for . . . days/weeks/months.
Estaré aquí . . . días/semanas/meses.
Ehs-tah-reh' ah-kee' . . . dee'-ahs/seh-mah'-nahs/meh'-sehs.

Money

Where can I cash this traveler's check?
¿Dónde puedo cambiar este cheque?
Dohn'-deh poo-eh'-doh kahm-bee-ahr' ehs'-teh cheh'-keh?

When does the bank open?
¿Cuándo abre el banco?
Koo-ahn'-doh ah'-breh ehl bahn'-koh?

When does the bank close?
¿Cuándo cierra el banco?
Koo-ahn'-doh thee-eh'-rrah ehl bahn'-koh?

Please give me some small change.
Por favor, deme algún dinero suelto.
Pohr fah-vohr', deh'-meh ahl-goon' dee-neh'-roh soo-ehl'-toh.

At the Hotel

I reserved a single/double room by mail/telephone.
Reservé una habitación sencilla/doble/por carta/por teléfono.
*Reh-sehr-veh' oo'-nah ah-bee-tah-thee-ohn' sehn-thee'-yah/
doh'-bleh/pohr kahr'-tah/pohr teh-leh'-foh-noh.*

I want a room with/without bath.
Quiero una habitación con baño/sin baño.
*Kee-eh'-roh oo'-nah ah-bee-tah-thee-ohn' kohn bah'-nyoh/
seen bah'-nyoh.*

What is the check-out time?
¿A qué hora hay que desocupar la habitación?
*Ah keh oh'-rah ah'-ee keh deh-soh-koo-pahr' lah ah-bee-tah-
thee-ohn'?*

How much is this room?
¿Cuál es el precio de esta habitación?
*Koo-ahl' ehs ehl preh'-thee-oh deh ehs'-tah ah-bee-tah-thee-
ohn'?*

Are the meals included?
¿Están las comidas incluídas?
Ehs-tahn' lahs koh-mee'-dahs een-kloo-ee'-dahs?

I would like something cheaper.
Quisiera algo más barato.
Kee-see-eh'-rah ahl'-goh mahs bah-rah'-toh.

There is no hot water.
No hay agua caliente.
Noh ah'-ee ah'-goo-ah kah-lee-ehn'-teh.

Where is the manager?
¿Dónde está el gerente?
Dohn'-deh ehs-tah' ehl heh-rehn'-teh?

Please give me the key to my room.
Por favor, deme la llave de mi habitación.
Pohr fah-vohr', deh'-meh lah yah'-veh deh mee ah-bee-tah-thee-ohn'.

Are there any messages for me?
¿Hay algún recado para mí?
Ah'-ee ahl-goon' reh-kah'-doh pah'-rah mee?

Please send me a boy for my luggage.
Por favor, envíeme un botones para recoger mi equipaje.
Pohr fah-vohr', ehn-vee'-eh-meh oon boh-toh'-nehs pah'-rah reh-koh-hehr' mee eh-kee-pah'-heh.

Communications

Where is the post office/telegraph office?
¿Dónde está el edificio de correos/telégrafos?
Dohn'-deh ehs-tah' ehl eh-dee-fee'-thee-oh deh koh-rreh'-ohs/ teh-leh'-grah-fohs?

When does it open/close?
¿A qué hora se abre/cierra?
Ah keh oh'-rah seh ah'-breh/thee-eh'-rrah?

Where is the nearest telephone?
¿Dónde hay un teléfono público cerca de aquí?
Dohn'-deh ah'-ee oon teh-leh'-foh-noh poo'-blee-koh thehr'-kah deh ah-kee'?

I want to make a long-distance call.
Deseo hablar a larga distancia.
Deh-seh'-oh ah-blar' ah lahr'-gah dees-tahn'-thee-ah.

I want to call . . . .
Deseo hablar con . . . .
Deh-seh'-oh ah-blahr' kohn . . . .

Please call station-to-station/collect/person-to-person.
Por favor, una conferencia teléfono a teléfono/ con cobro
al destinatario/persona a persona.
*Pohr fah-vohr', oo'-nah kohn-feh-rehn'-thee-ah/teh-leh'-foh-
noh ah teh-leh'-foh-noh/kohn koh'-broh ahl dehs-tee-nah-
tah'-ree-oh/pehr-soh'-nah ah pehr-soh'-nah.*

Where can I buy some stamps?
¿Dónde puedo comprar sellos?
Dohn'-deh poo-eh'-doh kohm-prahr' seh'-yohs?

Where is the nearest mail box?
¿Dónde está el buzón de correos más próximo?
*Dohn'-deh ehs-tah' ehl boo-thohn' deh koh-rreh'-ohs mahs
prohk'-see-moh?*

I want to send this letter/package via airmail/special delivery.
Deseo enviar esta carta/paquete por avión/urgente.
*Deh-seh'-oh ehn-vee-ahr' ehs'-tah kahr'-tah/pah-keh'-teh
pohr ah-vee-ohn'/oor-hehn'-teh.*

How much postage do I need on this letter/package?
¿Cuánto franqueo necesito para esta carta/paquete?
*Koo-ahn'-toh frahn-keh'-oh neh-theh-see'-toh pah'-rah ehs'-tah
kahr'-tah/pah-keh'-teh?*

I want to insure this package.
Deseo asegurar este paquete.
Deh-seh'-oh ah-seh-goo-rahr' ehs'-teh pah-keh'-teh.

Please forward my mail to . . . .
Por favor, envíe mi correspondencia a la siguiente dirección . . . .
*Pohr fah-vohr' ehn-vee'-eh mee koh-rrehs-pohn-dehn'-thee-ah
ah lah see-ghee-ehn'-teh dee-rehk-thee-ohn' . . . .*

Laundry/Dry Cleaning

Where is a laundry/dry cleaner?
¿Dónde hay una lavandería/limpieza en seco?
Dohn'-deh ah'-ee oo'-nah lah-vahn-deh-ree'-ah/leem-pee-eh'-thah ehn seh'-koh?

I want these clothes dry cleaned.
Deseo una limpieza en seco de esta ropa.
Deh-seh'-oh oo'-nah leem-pee-eh'-thah ehn seh'-koh deh ehs'-tah roh'-pah.

Please wash these clothes.
Por favor, lave esta ropa.
Pohr fah-vohr', lah'-veh ehs'-tah roh'-pah.

When will my clothes be ready?
¿Cuándo estará lista mi ropa?
Koo-ahn'-doh ehs-tah-rah' lees'-tah mee roh'-pah?

I must have these clothes tomorrow.
Necesito esa ropa para mañana.
Neh-theh-see'-toh eh'-sah roh'-pah pah'-rah mah-nyah'-nah.

Please press these trousers.
Por favor, planche estos pantalones.
Pohr fah-vohr', plahn'-cheh ehs'-tohs pahn-tah-loh'-nehs.

Can you mend this tear?
¿Puede coser este rasgón?
Poo-eh'-deh koh-sehr' ehs'-teh rahs'-gohn?

Hairdresser/Barber

I would like a haircut.
Desearía un corte de pelo.
Deh-seh-ah-ree'-ah oon kohr'-teh deh peh'-loh.

Make it shorter, please.
Más corto, por favor.
Mahs kohr'-toh, pohr fah-vohr'.

Don't take too much off the top.
No me corte demasiado por arriba.
Noh meh kohr'-teh deh-mah-see-ah'-doh pohr ah-rree'-bah.

I would like a shampoo and set.
Desearía un lavado y marcado de pelo.
Deh-seh-ah-ree'-ah oon lah-vah'-doh ee mahr-kah'-doh deh peh'-loh.

Getting Around

Where is stateroom 36?
¿Dónde está el camarote número treinta y seis?
Dohn'-deh ehs-tah' ehl cah-mah-roh'-teh noo'-meh-roh treh'-een-tah ee seh'-ees?

Take my bags to my cabin, please.
Lleve mi equipaje a mi camarote, por favor.
Yeh'-veh mee eh-kee-pah'-heh ah mee kah-mah-roh'-teh, pohr fah-vohr'.

What time is breakfast/lunch/dinner?
¿A qué hora se sirve el desayuno/el almuerzo/la cena?
Ah keh oh'-rah seh seer'-veh ehl deh-sah-yoo'-noh/ehl ahl-moo-ehr'-thoh/lah theh'-nah?

At what time does the boat dock?
¿A qué hora llega el barco?
Ah keh oh'-rah yeh'-gah ehl bahr'-koh?

I want a ticket to . . . , please.
Quiero un billete para . . . , por favor.
Kee-eh'-roh oon bee-yeh'-teh pah'-rah . . . , pohr fah-vohr'.

When is the next flight to . . . ?
¿A qué hora sale el próximo avión para . . . ?
Ah keh oh'-rah sah'-leh ehl prohk'-see-moh ah-vee-ohn' pah'-rah . . . ?

How much is the fare?
¿Cuánto cuesta el billete?
Koo-ahn'-toh koo-ehs'-tah ehl bee-yeh'-teh?

Is lunch served on this flight?
¿Sirven almuerzo en este vuelo?
Seer'-vehn ahl-moo-ehr'-thoh ehn ehs'-teh voo-eh'-loh?

Is dinner served on this flight?
¿Sirven cena en este vuelo?
Seer'-vehn theh'-nah ehn ehs'-teh voo-eh'-loh?

Where is the bus station?
¿Dónde está la estación de autobuses?
Dohn'-deh ehs-tah' lah ehs-tah-thee-ohn' deh ah-oo-toh-boo'-sehs?

When is the next bus to . . . ?
¿Cuándo sale el próximo autobús para . . . ?
Koo-ahn'-doh sah'-leh ehl prohk'-see-moh ah-oo-toh-boos' pah'-rah . . . ?

How long is the trip?
¿Cuánto dura el viaje?
Koo-ahn'-toh doo'-rah ehl vee-ah'-heh?

Take me to . . . .
Lléveme a . . . .
Yeh'-veh-meh ah . . . .

I am in a hurry to catch a bus/train/plane.
Tengo mucha prisa por tomar un autobus/un tren/un avión.
Tehn'-goh moo'-chah pree'-sah pohr toh-mahr' oon ah-oo-toh-boos'/oon trehn/oon ah-vee-ohn'.

Where can I rent a car?
¿Dónde puedo arrendar un coche?
Dohn'-deh poo-eh'-doh ah-rrehn-dahr' oon koh'-cheh?

Do you charge by the day or by the kilometer?
¿Cobran por día o por kilómetro?
Koh'-brahn pohr dee'-ah oh pohr kee-loh'-meh-troh?

Where is the nearest gas station?
¿Dónde está la estación de gasolina más cercana?
Dohn'-deh ehs-tah' lah ehs-tah-thee-ohn' deh gah-soh-lee'-nah mahs thehr-kah'-nah?

Fill it up with regular/premium.
Llene el depósito con gasolina ordinaria/superior.
Yeh'-neh ehl deh-poh'-see-toh kohn gah-soh-lee'-nah ohr-dee-nah'-ree-ah/soo-peh-ree-ohr'.

Please check the oil/the tires.
Por favor, revise el aceite/el aire de las ruedas.
Pohr fah-vohr', reh-vee'-seh ehl ah-theh-ee'-teh/ehl ah-ee'-reh deh lahs roo-eh'-dahs.

What is the best road to . . . ?
¿Cuál es la mejor carretera para . . . ?
Koo-ahl' ehs lah meh-hohr' kah-rreh-teh'-rah pah'-rah . . . ?

Is there a mechanic here?
¿Hay un mecánico aquí?
Ah'-ee oon meh-kah'-nee-koh ah-kee'?

I am having trouble with the . . . .
Parece que el . . . está fallando.
Pah-reh'-theh keh ehl . . . ehs-tah' fah-yahn'-doh.

When will my car be ready?
¿Cuándo estará mi coche listo?
Koo-ahn'-doh ehs-tah-rah' mee koh'-cheh lees'-toh?

Where is the ticket window?
¿Dónde está la ventanilla de billetes?
Dohn'-deh ehs-tah' lah vehn-tah-nee'-yah deh bee-yeh'-tehs?

May I have a timetable?
¿Puede darme un horario de trenes?
Poo-eh'-deh dahr'-meh oon oh-rah'-ree-oh deh treh'-nehs?

How much is a one-way/round-trip first-class/second-class ticket to . . . ?
¿Cuánto vale un billete sencillo/de ida y vuelta/de primera clase/de segunda clase a . . . ?
Koo-ahn'-toh vah'-leh oon bee-yeh'-teh sehn-thee'-yoh/deh ee'-dah ee voo-ehl'-tah/deh pree-meh'-rah klah'-seh/deh seh-goon'-dah klah'-seh ah . . . ?

From which track does the train for . . . leave?
¿De qué andén sale el tren para . . . ?
Deh keh ahn-dehn' sah'-leh ehl trehn pah'-rah . . . ?

What time does this train leave?
¿A qué hora sale este tren?
Ah keh oh'-rah sah'-leh ehs'-teh trehn?

Is this train an express or a local?
¿Es este tren expreso o para en todas las estaciones?
Ehs ehs'-teh trehn ehks-preh'-soh oh pah'-rah ehn toh'-dahs lahs ehs-tah-thee-oh'-nehs?

Is this seat taken?
¿Está este asiento ocupado?
Ehs-tah' ehs'-teh ah-see-ehn'-toh oh-koo-pah'-doh?

When is the dining car open?
¿Cuándo se abre el coche restaurante?
Koo-ahn'-doh seh ah'-breh ehl koh'-cheh rehs-tah-oo-rahn'-teh?

Which way to the lavatory, please?
¿Por dónde se va al lavabo, por favor?
Pohr dohn'-deh seh vah ahl lah-vah'-boh, pohr fah-vohr'?

Shopping

Where is there a bookstore?
¿Dónde hay una librería?
Dohn'-deh ah'-ee oo'-nah lee-breh-ree'-ah?

Where is there a department store?
¿Dónde hay unos almacenes?
Dohn'-deh ah'-ee oo'-nohs ahl-mah-theh'-nehs?

Where is there a pharmacy?
¿Dónde hay una farmacia?
Dohn'-deh ah'-ee oo'-nah fahr-mah'-thee-ah?

Where is there a florist?
¿Dónde hay una florería?
Dohn'-deh ah'-ee oo'-nah floh-reh-ree'-ah?

Where is there a grocery?
¿Dónde hay una tienda de comestibles?
Dohn'-deh ah'-ee oo'-nah tee-ehn'-dah deh koh-mehs-tee'-blehs?

Where is there a jewelry store?
¿Dónde hay una joyería?
Dohn'-deh ah'-ee oo'-nah hoh-yeh-ree'-ah?

On what floor are the clothes/leather goods?
¿En qué planta está la ropa/artículos de piel?
Ehn keh plahn'-tah ehs-tah' lah roh'-pah/ahr-tee'-koo-lohs deh pee-ehl'?

How much does this cost?
¿Cuánto cuesta esto?
Koo-ahn'-toh koo-ehs'-tah ehs'-toh?

Have you anything better/cheaper?
¿Tiene algo mejor/más barato?
Tee-eh'-neh ahl'-goh meh-hohr'/mahs bah-rah'-toh?

Is this handmade?
¿Esto está hecho a mano?
Ehs'-toh ehs-tah' eh'-choh ah mah'-noh?

Does this come in any other color?
¿Tienen el mismo artículo en otro color?
Tee-eh'-nehn ehl mees'-moh ahr-tee'-koo-loh ehn oh'-troh koh-lohr'?

This is too large/small.
Esto es demasiado grande/pequeño.
Ehs'-toh ehs deh-mah-see-ah'-doh grahn'-deh/peh-keh'-nyoh.

Please give me a sales slip for this purchase.
Por favor, deme el recibo de esta compra.
Pohr fah-vohr', deh'-meh ehl reh-thee'-boh deh ehs'-tah kohm'-prah.

Do you accept checks/traveler's checks?
¿Aceptan ustedes cheques/cheques de viajero?
Ah-thehp'-tahn oos-teh'-dehs cheh'-kehs'/cheh'-kehs deh vee-ah'-heh'-roh?

Sightseeing

I would like a tour of the city.
Me gustaría hacer una excursión por la ciudad.
Meh goos-tah-ree'-ah ah-thehr' oo'-nah ehks-koor-see-ohn' pohr lah thee-oo-dahd'.

How long will the tour last?
¿Cuánto tiempo durará la excursión?
Koo-ahn'-toh tee-ehm'-poh doo-rah-rah' lah ehks-koor-see-ohn'?

Where is the museum/zoo?
¿Dónde está el museo/el zoológico?
Dohn'-deh ehs-tah' ehl moo-seh'-oh/ehl thoh-oh-loh'-hee-koh?

What hours are the museums open?
¿A qué hora se abren los museos?
Ah keh oh'-rah seh ah'-brehn lohs moo-seh'-ohs?

What is the name of that building/monument?
¿Cómo se llama ese edificio/monumento?
Koh'-moh seh yah'-mah eh'-seh eh-dee-fee'-thee-oh/moh-noo-mehn'-toh?

Entertainment

I would like to see an opera/bullfight.
Me gustaría ver una opera/corrida de toros.
Meh goos-tah-ree'-ah vehr oo'-nah oh'-peh-rah/koh-rree'-dah deh toh'-rohs.

Where can I get theater/movie/opera tickets?
¿Dónde puedo comprar billetes para el teatro/el cine/la ópera?
Dohn'-deh poo-eh'-doh kohm-prahr' bee-yeh'-tehs pah'-rah ehl teh-ah'-troh/ehl thee'-neh/lah oh'-peh-rah?

When does the performance begin?
¿A qué hora empieza la representación?
Ah keh oh'-rah ehm-pee-eh'-thah lah reh-preh-sehn-tah-thee-ohn'?

I want to eat breakfast/lunch/dinner.
Quiero tomar el desayuno/el almuerzo/la cena.
Kee-eh'-roh toh-mahr' ehl deh-say-yoo'-noh/ehl ahl-moo-ehr'-thoh/lah theh'-nah.

We would like a table for two, please.
Nos gustaría una mesa para dos, por favor.
Nohs goos-tah-ree'-ah oo'-nah meh'-sah pah'-rah dohs, pohr fah-vohr'.

May we have a menu/wine list, please?
¿Nos da el menú/la lista de vinos, por favor?
Nohs dah ehl meh-noo'/lah lees'-tah deh vee'-nohs, pohr fah-vohr'?

What do you recommend?
¿Qué nos recomienda?
Keh nohs reh-koh-mee-ehn'-dah?

I didn't order this.
No he pedido esto.
Noh eh peh-dee'-doh ehs'-toh.

Please bring me the check.
Tráigame la cuenta, por favor.
Trah'-ee-gah-meh lah koo-ehn'-tah, pohr fah-vohr'.

How much do I owe you?
¿Cuánto le debo?
Koo-ahn'-toh leh deh'-boh?

Is the tip included?
¿Está incluída la propina?
Ehs-tah' een-kloo-ee'-dah lah proh-pee'-nah?

Where do I pay?
¿Dónde se paga?
Dohn'-deh seh pah'-gah?

There is a mistake in the bill.
Hay un error en la cuenta.
Ah'-ee oon eh-rrohr' ehn lah koo-ehn'-tah.

Health

I don't feel well.
No me siento bien.
Noh meh see-ehn'-toh bee-ehn'.

I need a doctor/dentist.
Necesito un médico/dentista.
Neh-theh-see'-toh oon meh'-dee-koh/dehn-tees'-tah.

I have a headache/stomachache/toothache.
Me duele la cabeza/el estómago/los dientes.
Meh doo-eh'-leh lah kah-beh'-thah/ehl ehs-toh'-mah-goh/lohs dee-ehn'-tehs.

I have a bad cold/fever.
Tengo un fuerte catarro/fiebre.
tehn'-goh oon foo-ehr'-teh kah-tah'-rroh/fee-eh'-breh.

My . . . is burned/hurt/bleeding.
Tengo el . . . quemado/dolorido/sangrante.
Tehn'-goh ehl . . . keh-mah'-doh/doh-loh-ree'-doh/sahn-grahn'-teh.

Please make up this prescription.
Deme esta medicina.
Deh'-meh ehs'-tah meh-dee-thee'-nah.

Emergencies

Help!
¡Socorro!
Soh-koh'-rroh!

Fire!
¡Fuego!
Foo-eh'-goh!

Police!
¡Policía!
Poh-lee-thee'-ah!

Please call a policeman/an ambulance.
Por favor llame a un policía/una ambulancia.
Pohr fah-vohr' yah'-meh ah oon poh-lee-thee'-ah/ah oo'-nah ahm-boo-lahn'-thee-ah.

I need a lawyer.
Necesito un abogado.
Neh-theh-see'-toh oon ah-boh-gah'-doh.

I want to call the American embassy.
Deseo llamar a la embajada americana.
Deh-seh'-oh yah-mahr' ah lah ehm-bah-hah'-dah ah-meh-ree-kah'-nah.

I've been robbed.
Me han robado.
Meh ahn roh-bah'-doh.

Is there anyone here who speaks English?
¿Hay aquí alguien que hable inglés?
Ah'-ee ah-kee' ahl'-ghee-ehn keh ah'-bleh een-glehs'?

I am lost.
Me he perdido.
Meh eh pehr-dee'-doh.

I have lost a suitcase/my purse.
He perdido una maleta/mi bolso.
Eh pehr-dee'-doh oo'-nah mah-leh'-tah/mee bohl'-soh.

There has been an accident.
Ha habido un accidente.
Ah ah-bee'-doh oon ahk-thee-dehn'-teh.

Someone is injured.
Ha habido algún herido.
Ah ah-bee'-doh ahl-goon' eh-ree'-doh.

MENU READER

Beverages

agua [*ah'-goo-ah*] water
anís [*ah-nees'*] aniseed liquor
anís seco [*ah-nees' seh'-koh*] aniseed brandy
batido [*bah-tee'-doh*] milk shake
bebidas [*beh-bee'-dahs*] drinks
botella [*boh-teh'-yah*] bottle
café [*kah-feh'*] coffee
   granizado [*grah-nee-thah'-doh*] iced (white) coffee
   solo [*soh'-loh*] black
cerveza [*thehr-veh'-thah*] beer
   de barril [*deh bah-rreel'*] draught
coñac [*koh-nyahk'*] Spanish brandy
Champán [*chahm-pahn'*] champagne
chocolate [*choh-koh-lah'-teh*] chocolate
   con leche [*kohn leh'-cheh*] hot chocolate
gaseosa [*gah-seh-oh'-sah*] soda water
hielo [*ee-eh'-loh*] ice
jerez [*heh-rehz'*] sherry wine
jugo [*hoo'-goh*] juice
   de naranja [*deh nah-rahn'-hah*] orange juice
   de tomate [*deh toh-mah'-teh*] tomato juice
leche [*leh'-cheh*] milk
limonada [*lee-moh-nah'-dah*] lemonade
mate [*mah'-teh*] Argentinian drink similar to tea
naranjada [*nah-rahn-hah'-dah*] orange drink
pulque [*pool'-keh*] a strong, fermented drink from the Mexican
    maguey plant
refresco [*reh-frehs'-koh*] cold drink

sangría [*sahn-gree'-ah*] punch made of red wine, soda, apples, lemon, orange, and sugar

seco [*seh'-koh*] dry

sidra [*see'-drah*] cider

té [*teh*] tea

té con limón [*teh kohn lee-mohn'*] tea with lemon

ron [*rohn*] rum

vino [*vee'-noh*] wine

   blanco [*blahn'-koh*] white wine

   rosado [*roh-sah'-doh*] rosé wine

   tinto [*teen'-toh*] red wine

zumo [*thoo'-moh*] juice

The Menu

aceite [*ah-theh'-ee-teh*] oil

aceitunas [*ah-theh-ee-too'-nahs*] olives

ajo [*ah'-hoh*] garlic

a la carta [*ah lah kahr'-tah*] a la carte

al ajillo [*ahl ah-hee'-yoh*] cooked in oil, garlic, and red pepper

a la española [*ah lah ehs-pah-nyoh'-lah*] spanish style

a la francesa [*ah lah frahn-theh'-sah*] French style

a la inglesa [*ah lah een-gleh'-sah*] English style

a la italiana [*ah lah ee-tah-lee-ah'-nah*] Italian style

al jerez [*ahl heh-rehth'*] braised in sherry

albóndigas [*ahl-bohn'-dee-gahs*] meatballs

alcachofas [*ahl-kah-choh'-fahs*] artichokes

almejas [*ahl-meh'-hahs*] clams

almendras [*ahl-mehn'-drahs*] almonds

almíbar [*ahl-mee'-bahr*] syrup

alubias [*ah-loo'-bee-ahs*] beans

anchoas [*ahn-choh'-ahs*] anchovies

anguila [*ahn-ghee'-lah*] eel

angulas [*ahn-goo'-lahs*] baby eels

arenque [*ah-rehn'-keh*] herring

arroz [*ah-rrohth'*] rice

arroz con pollo [*ah-rrohth' kohn poh'-yoh*] chicken with rice

asado [*ah-sah'-doh*] roast
atún [*ah-toon'*] tuna
azúcar [*ah-thoo'-kahr*] sugar

bacalao [*bah-kah-lah'-oh*] cod fish
batatas [*bah-tah'-tahs*] sweet potatoes
berrazas [*beh-rrah'-thahs*] parsnips
besugo [*beh-soo'-goh*] sea bream
biftec/bistec [*beef-tehk'/bees-tehk'*] steak
   muy hecho [*moo'-ee eh'-choh*] well done
   poco hecho [*poh'-koh eh'-choh*] rare
bizcocho [*beeth-koh'-choh*] sponge cake
bocadillo [*boh-kah-dee'-yoh*] sandwich
bollo, bollito [*boh'-yoh', boh-yee'-toh*] roll, bun
buñuelos [*boo-nyoo-eh'-lohs*] fritters
butifarra [*boo-tee-fah'-rrah*] Catalonian sausage

caballa [*kah-bah'-yah*] fish of the mackerel family
cacahuetes [*kah-kah-oo-eh'-tehs*] peanuts
calamares en su tinta [*kah-lah-mah'-rehs ehn soo teen'-tah*]
   fresh squid in red wine sauce and its own "ink"
caldo gallego [*kahl'-doh gah-yeh'-goh*] thick stew with meat
   and vegetables
camarones [*kah-mah-roh'-nehs*] shrimp
cangrejo [*kahn-greh'-hoh*] crab
caracoles [*kah-rah-koh'-lehs*] snails
caramelos [*kah-rah-meh'-lohs*] sweets, confectionary
carne [*kahr'-neh*] meat
carne de vaca [*kahr'-neh deh vah'-kah*] beef
carne de ternera [*kahr'-neh deh tehr-neh'-rah*] veal
casero [*kah-seh'-roh*] homemade
cebolla [*theh-boh'-yah*] onion
cerezas [*theh-reh'-thahs*] cherries
cerdo [*thehr'-doh*] pork
ceviche [*theh-vee'-cheh*] fish marinated in lemon and other
   juices
ciruela [*thee-roo-eh'-lah*] plum

ciruela seca [*thee-roo-eh'-lah seh'-kah*] prune
cocido [*koh-thee'-doh*] cooked, stewed
cocido [*koh-thee'-doh*] boiled dinner: meat, chicken, salt pork,
    ham, sausage, pigs feet, chick-peas, cabbage, potatoes
col [*kohl*] cabbage
coliflor [*koh-lee-flohr'*] cauliflower
conejo [*koh-neh'-hoh*] rabbit
confitura [*kohn-fee-too'-rah*] jam
consomé [*kohn-soh-meh'*] consommé
cordero [*kohr-deh'-roh*] lamb
    pierna de cordero [*pee-ehr'-nah deh kohr-deh'-roh*] leg of
    lamb
costilla [*kohs-tee'-yah*] cutlet
crema [*kreh'-mah*] cream, mousse
croquetas [*kroh-keh'-tahs*] croquettes
crudo [*kroo'-doh*] raw
cubierto [*koo-bee-ehr'-toh*] cover charge
champiñones [*chahm-pee-nyoh'-nehs*] mushrooms
chili [*chee'-lee*] chili peppers
chipirones [*chee-pee-roh'-nehs*] small squids
chorizo [*choh-ree'-thoh*] pork sausage
chuleta [*choo-leh'-tah*] chop, cutlet
churros [*choo'-rrohs*] breakfast fritters made of flour

damasco [*dah-mahs'-koh*] apricot
dátiles [*dah'-tee-lehs*] dates
de la casa [*deh lah kah'-sah*] specialty of the chef
dulces [*dool'-thehs*] sweets
durazno [*doo-rahth'-noh*] peach

embuchado [*ehm-boo-chah'-doh*] stuffed with meat
empanada [*ehm-pah-nah'-dah*] meat pie
empanado [*ehm-pah-nah'-doh*] breaded
encurtidos [*ehn-koor-tee'-dohs*] pickles
enchiladas [*ehn-chee-lah'-dahs*] corn cake stuffed with meat,
    cheese, chili
ensalada [*ehn-sah-lah'-dah*] salad

ensaladilla rusa [*ehn-sah-lah-dee'-yah roo'-sah*] potato salad
entrecot [*ehn-treh-koht'*] steak
entremeses [*ehn-treh-meh'-sehs*] hors d'oeuvres
escabeche [*ehs-kah-beh'-cheh*] marinated, pickled
escalfado [*ehs-kahl-fah'-doh*] poached
escalope [*ehs-kah-loh'-peh*] scallop
escalope de ternera [*ehs-kah-loh'-peh deh tehr-neh'-rah*]
    fried breaded veal fillet
escarola [*ehs-kah-roh'-lah*] endive
espárragos [*ehs-pah'-rrah-gohs*] asparagus
espinacas [*ehs-pee-nah'-kahs*] spinach
estofado [*ehs-toh-fah'-doh*] stew

favas/habas [*fah'-vahs/ah'-bahs*] lima beans
fiambres [*fee-ahm'-brehs*] cold cuts
fideos [*fee-deh'-ohs*] noodles
filete [*fee-leh'-teh*] steak
flan [*flahn*] caramel custard
frambuesas [*frahm-boo-eh'-sahs*] raspberries
fresas [*freh'-sahs*] strawberries
frijoles [*free-hoh'-lehs*] beans
frito [*free'-toh*] fried
fruta [*froo'-tah*] fruit

galletas [*gah-yeh'-tahs*] salted or sweet biscuits
gallina [*gah-yee'-nah*] hen
gambas [*gahm'-bahs*] shrimp
ganso [*gahn'-soh*] goose
garbanzos [*gahr-bahn'-thohs*] chick-peas
gazpacho [*gahth-pah'-choh*] chilled, seasoned vegetable soup
guacamole [*goo-ah-kah-moh'-leh*] mashed, seasoned avocado
guisantes [*ghee-sahn'-tehs*] green peas
guisado español [*ghee-sah'-doh ehs-pah-nyohl'*] beef stew
    with onions in olive oil
guisado de riñones de ternera [*ghee-sah'-doh deh ree-nyoh'-*
    nehs deh tehr-neh'-rah] stew of veal kidney with wine
    sauce

habichuelas [*ah-bee-choo-eh'-lahs*] green beans
helado [*eh-lah'-doh*] ice cream
hervido [*ehr-vee'-doh*] boiled
hígado [*ee'-gah-doh*] liver
higos [*ee'-gohs*] figs
    pasos [*pah'-sohs*] dried figs
hongos [*ohn'-gohs*] mushrooms
huevo(s) [*oo-eh'-voh(s)*] egg(s)
    cocidos [*koh-thee'-dohs*] hard-boiled eggs
    pasados por agua [*pah-sah'-dohs pohr ah'-goo-ah*] soft-
      boiled eggs
    revueltos [*reh-voo-ehl'-tohs*] scrambled eggs
humitas [*oo-mee'-tahs*] boiled corn with onions, green
    pepper, cheese

jamón [*hah-mohn'*] ham
judías [*hoo-dee'-ahs*] beans
    pintas [*peen'-tahs*] kidney beans

lacón [*lah-kohn'*] shoulder of pork
langosta [*lahn-gohs'-tah*] lobster
langostino [*lahn-gohs-tee'-noh*] prawn
lechuga [*leh-choo'-gah*] lettuce
lengua guisada en pepitoria [*lehn'-goo-ah ghee-sah'-dah ehn
    peh-pee-toh'-ree-ah*] sliced tongue or pieces of chicken in
    sauce of white wine, egg yolks, almonds and olives
lenguado [*lehn-goo-ah'-doh*] sole, flounder
lentejas [*lehn-teh'-hahs*] lentils
lista de platos [*lees'-tah deh plah'-tohs*] menu
lombarda [*lohm-bahr'-dah*] red cabbage
lomo [*loh'-moh*] loin

mayonesa [*mah-yoh-neh'-sah*] mayonnaise
maíz [*mah-eeth'*] corn
maní [*mah-nee'*] peanuts
mantequilla [*mahn-teh-kee'-yah*] butter
manzana [*mahn-thah'-nah*] apple
matambre [*mah-tahm'-breh*] rolled beef stuffed with

vegetables
melocotón [*meh-loh-koh-tohn'*] peach
melón [*meh-lohn'*] melon
menú del día [*meh-noo' dehl dee'-ah*] menu of the day
menú turístico [*meh-noo' too-rees'-tee-koh*] tourist menu
merengue [*meh-rehn'-gheh*] dessert of whipped cream with
    beaten egg whites
mermelada [*mehr-meh-lah'-dah*] jam, marmalade
miel [*mee-ehl'*] honey
moros y cristianos [*moh'-rohs ee krees-tee-ah'-nohs*] rice and
    black beans
mostaza [*mohs-tah'-thah*] mustard

nabo [*nah'-boh*] turnip
naranja [*nah-rahn'-hah*] orange
natillas [*nah-tee'-yahs*] custard, boiled
nuez [*noo-ehth'*] walnut

ostras [*ohs'-trahs*] oysters

paella [*pah-eh'-yah*] assorted seafood and meat and yellow
    rice
pan [*pahn*] bread
    moreno [*moh-reh'-noh*] brown bread
panecillo [*pah-neh-thee'-yoh*] roll
papas/patatas [*pah'-pahs/pah-tah'-tahs*] potatoes
    asadas [*ah-sah'-dahs*] baked potatoes
    puré de papas [*poo-reh' deh pah'-pahs*] mashed potatoes
a la parrilla [*ah lah pah-rree'-yah*] charcoal-grilled
pasas [*pah'-sahs*] raisins
pastel [*pahs-tehl'*] cake, pie
    de hojaldre [*deh oh-hahl'-dreh*] puff pastry
patata/papa [*pah-tah'-tah/pah'-pah*] potato
pato [*pah'-toh*] duck
pavo [*pah'-voh*] turkey
pechuga [*peh-choo'-gah*] breast (of fowl)
pepinillos [*peh-pee-nee'-yohs*] pickles
pepino [*peh-pee'-noh*] cucumber

pera [*peh'-rah*] pear
perca [*pehr'-kah*] perch
pescado en escabeche [*pehs-kah'-doh ehn ehs-kah-beh'-cheh*]
    fried or boiled fish marinated in oil-vinegar sauce and
    served cold
pescado en salsa verde [*pehs-kah'-doh ehn sahl'-sah vehr'-deh*]
    baked fish in sauce made with parsley
pescado relleno [*pehs-kah'-doh reh-yeh'-noh*] fish (as red
    snapper), boned and stuffed with vegetables and served
    in sauce
pez espada [*pehth ehs-pah'-dah*] swordfish
picadillo de carne [*pee-kah-dee'-yoh deh kahr'-neh*] highly
    seasoned chopped beef and pork cooked in sauce (olive
    oil)
picatostes [*pee-kah-tohs'-tehs*] deep-fried slices of bread
pimienta [*pee-mee-ehn'-tah*] black pepper
pimiento [*pee-mee-ehn'-toh*] green pepper
piña [*pee'-nyah*] pineapple
plátano [*plah'-tah-noh*] banana
pollo [*poh'-yoh*] chicken
polvorón [*pohl-voh-rohn'*] small, flaky cake (cookie)
pomelo [*poh-meh'-loh*] grapefruit
pudín [*poo-deen'*] pudding

queso [*keh'-soh*] cheese

rábanos picantes [*rah'-bah-nohs pee-kahn'-tehs*] horseradish
repollo [*reh-poh'-yoh*] cabbage
róbalo [*roh'-bah-loh*] haddock

sal [*sahl*] salt
salado [*sah-lah'-doh*] salted
salchichas [*sahl-chee'-chahs*] veal and pork sausage
salchichón [*sahl-chee-chohn'*] salami
salmón ahumado [*sahl-mohn' ah-oo-mah'-doh*] smoked salmon
sandía [*sahn-dee'-ah*] watermelon
solomillo asado a la parrilla [*soh-loh-mee'-yoh ah-sah'-doh ah
    lah pah-rree'-yah*] grilled tenderloin
sopa [*soh'-pah*] soup

tallarines [*tah-yah-ree'-nehs*] noodles
tamal [*tah-mahl'*] seasoned ground meat in cornmeal dough
tarta [*tahr'-tah*] tart, pie
tocino [*toh-thee'-noh*] bacon
tomate [*toh-mah'-teh*] tomato
toronja [*toh-rohn'-hah*] grapefruit
torta [*tohr'-tah*] cake
tortilla [*tohr-tee'-yah*] thin, unleavened corn cake (Mexico); omelet (Spain)
tortitas [*tohr-tee'-tahs*] waffles
tortuga [*tohr-too'-gah*] turtle
tostada [*tohs-tah'-dah*] toast
trucha [*troo'-chah*] trout

uvas [*oo'-vahs*] grapes

vaca [*vah'-kah*] beef
  estofada [*ehs-toh-fah'-dah*] beef stew
  salada [*sah-lah'-dah*] corned beef
vinagre [*vee-nah'-greh*] vinegar
vinagreta [*vee-nah-greh'-tah*] vinegar dressing (for salad)
venado [*veh-nah'-doh*] venison

yemas [*yeh'-mahs*] dessert of whipped egg yolk and sugar

zarzamoras [*thahr-thah-moh'-rahs*] blackberries
zarzuela [*thahr-thoo-eh'-lah*] stew of assorted fish and shellfish

A Concise Spanish Grammar

Articles

1. Both definite and indefinite articles agree in gender and number with the noun they modify.

    el hombre   the man   **un hombre** a man
    la mujer   the woman   **una mujer** a woman

2. The forms of the definite article *the* are:

    el *m. sing.*   **los** *m. pl.*
    la *f. sing.*   **las** *f. pl.*
    lo *neuter sing.*

3. There are two usual contractions of *el*, after *de* and *a*:

    del (de el)   of the   **al (a el)**   to the

4. The definite article is used:

(*a*) Before nouns employed in a general sense, but not before nouns with a particular sense.

Me gustan las patatas fritas.   I like fried potatoes.
Quiero patatas fritas.   I want some fried potatoes.

(*b*) Instead of *my*, *your*, etc., referring to parts of the body and personal belongings or clothing.

    Me lavo las manos.   I wash my hands.
    Me pongo el sombrero.   I put on my hat.

(*c*) Before seasons and days of the week, except after *ser*; and always before hours.

    Iré el lunes próximo.   I will go next Monday.
    Hoy es martes.   Today is Tuesday.
    Son las dos.   It is two o'clock.

(*d*) Before titles (except *don*) when talking about the person, but not when talking to the person.

El señor García es cubano. Mr. Garcia is Cuban.
Hola, señor García. Hello, Mr. Garcia.
Don Antonio está enfermo. Don Antonio is sick.

(*e*) Before names of languages except after *hablar, de, en.*

El español es fácil. Spanish is easy.
Hablo español. I speak Spanish.
Curso de español Spanish course

(*f*) With some names of countries or cities.

La Habana, La Argentina

Or when referring to a special time or situation of a country.

España   La España de Felipe II

5. *Lo* is used with participles and adjectives in the abstract sense:

lo bueno that which is good
lo leído that which has been read

6. The forms of the indefinite articles are:

un *m. sing.*, a, an	**unos** *m. pl.*, some
una *f. sing.*, a, an	**unas** *f. pl.*, some

7. Indefinite articles are used as in English, but should be omitted in the following cases:

(*a*) After *ser* to indicate a particular class of people (profession, religion, nationality).

Antonio es americano. Anthony is an American.
Pedro es médico. Peter is a doctor.

NOTE: Do not omit the indefinite article if the noun is modified by an adjective.

Pedro es un buen médico. Peter is a good doctor.

(*b*) Before *cien(to), mil.*

cien años one hundred years

(*c*) WARNING: Do not translate *a certain, another,* and *what a* by *un cierto, un otro,* and *que un* but by *cierto, otro,* and *que.*

Nouns

1. All nouns in Spanish are either masculine or feminine.

2. Nouns ending in -*o* are masculine.

    el libro the book   **el perro** the dog

EXCEPTION: **la mano** the hand

3. Nouns ending in -*a* are feminine.

    la casa the house   **la comida** the meal
    la acera the sidewalk

EXCEPTIONS: **el día,** the day; **el tema,** the subject; **el mapa,** the map; **el problema,** the problem; and some others which are marked *m.* in the dictionary.

4. Nouns ending in -*dad*, -*tad*, -*tud*, -*ión*, -*umbre*, -*ez*, -*ie* are feminine (their English counterparts are nouns ending in -*ship*, -*ness*, -*ty*, -*ion*). These nouns are marked *f.* in the dictionary.

    la nación the nation   **la bondad** the kindness

5. Nouns referring to male or female beings follow natural gender.

    el hombre the man   **la mujer** the woman

6. Nouns ending in -*or* are masculine. They are marked *m.* in the dictionary.

                el motor the engine

7. The remaining nouns do not follow any pattern for gender. They are marked for gender in the dictionary.

    la fuente *f.* the fountain   **el juguete** *m.* the toy

8. Noun plurals are formed as follows:
    (*a*) Nouns ending in a vowel add -*s*.

    libro book   **libros** books
    casa house   **casas** houses
    fuente fountain   **fuentes** fountains

EXCEPTION: A few nouns ending in -*i* add -*es*:

    alhelí flower   **alhelíes** flowers

(b) Nouns ending in -z change to -ces.

el lápiz pencil   **las lápices** pencils

(c) Nouns ending in -s do not change unless the accent is on the last syllable.

la crisis the crisis   **las crisis** the crises
el compás the compass   **los compases** the compasses

(d) All others ending in a consonant add -es.

el mar the sea   **los mares** the seas
el capitán the captain   **los capitanes** the captains

9. Present participles and infinitives are used as nouns in English. In Spanish only the infinitive is used as a noun:

(El) fumar es malo para ti.
To smoke/smoking is not good for you.

The Adjectives

1. Adjectives agree in gender and number with the noun or pronoun they modify. Usually they are placed after the noun, with the exception of limiting or emphasizing adjectives (demonstratives and interrogatives):

la casa grande the big house
la blanca nieve (emphatic) the white snow
esta casa this house

2. Feminine forms of masculine adjectives are formed as follows:

(a) If the masculine form ends in -o, the -o changes to -a for the feminine.

bueno m. good   **buena** f. good

(b) If the masculine form ends in a consonant or a vowel other than -o, the masculine singular and the feminine singular have the same form.

horno caliente hot oven   **agua caliente** hot water

EXCEPTIONS: (1) Adjectives of nationality ending in a consonant add -a for the feminine.

español m. Spanish **española** f.

(2) Adjectives ending in *-or*, *-an*, *-in* add *-a* for the feminine.

encantador *m.* enchanting **encantadora** *f.*

3. Adjectives follow the same rules as nouns for the formation of plurals:

bueno *m. sing.*; **buenos** *m. pl.*; **buena** *f. sing.*; **buenas** *f. pl.* good

feliz *m., f. sing.*; **felices** *m., f. pl.* happy

gris *m., f. sing.*; **grises** *m., f. pl.* grey

caliente *m., f. sing.*; **calientes** *m., f. pl.* warm, hot

español *m. sing.*; **españoles** *m. pl.*; **española** *f. sing.*; **españolas** *f. pl.* Spanish

4. An adjective that modifies two or more nouns is used in the plural masculine form if at least one noun is masculine:

El marido y la mujer son altos.

The husband and wife are tall.

5. Some adjectives drop the final *-o* when they precede a noun in the masculine singular form. They are:

bueno good **malo** bad **alguno** some **ninguno** no **uno** one **primero** first **tercero** third

hombre bueno, buen hombre good man

The adjective "grande" changes to "gran" when it precedes a noun:

hombre grande big man **gran hombre** great man

NOTE: In this, and other cases, the position of the adjectives influences meaning.

6. Comparatives are formed as follows:

(*a*) Place *más*, more, or *menos*, less, before the adjective.

más bonito prettier **menos hermoso** less beautiful

(*b*) Four adjectives have irregular comparatives in form. They are:

bueno	good	**mejor**	better
malo	bad	**peor**	worse
grande	big	**mayor**	larger
pequeño	little	**menor**	smaller

NOTE: *Grande* and *pequeño* can be also used in regular form:

> **más grande, menos grande**
> **más pequeño, menos pequeño**

7. Superlatives are formed by placing a definite article before the comparative form:

el mejor the best   **el más grande** the greatest

8. Other important comparatives are:

> **más ... que** more ... than
> **menos ... que** less ... than
> **cuanto más ... más** the more ... the more
> **cuanto menos ... menos** the less ... the less

Possessives

1. The forms of the possessive pronouns are:

BEFORE A NOUN

Singular	Plural	
mi	mis	my, of mine
tu	tus	yours, of yours
su	sus	his, her, its, your
nuestro, -a	nuestros, -as	our, of ours
vuestro, -a	vuestros, -as	your, of yours
su	sus	their, its, your

AFTER A NOUN

mío, -a	míos, -as	my, of mine
tuyo, -a	tuyos, -as	yours, of yours
suyo, -a	suyos, -as	his, her, its, your
nuestro, -a	nuestros, -as	our, of ours
vuestro, -a	vuestros, -as	your, of yours
suyo, -a	suyos, -as	their, its, your

> **mi libro** my book
> **tu casa** your house
> **su casa** his (her, your, their) house
> **amigo mío** friend of mine

Note that *su* and *sus* sometimes need clarification:

> **su casa de usted** your house

2. Possessive pronouns agree in gender and number with the thing(s) possessed, not with the possessor:

mis libros my books

3. When a possessive pronoun replaces a noun, the second form ("after a noun" form) of the possessive pronoun is used, but it is preceded by *el, la, los,* or *las:*

el mío mine	**la mía** mine
el tuyo yours	**el suyo** his

Mi casa es grande pero la tuya es mayor.
My house is large but yours is larger.

4. The relative possessive pronoun *whose* is *cuyo (-a, -os, -as)* and *de quien (-es).*

el libro cuyo autor es . . . the book whose author is . . .

NOTE: *Cuyo, cuya, cuyos, cuyas* agree in gender and number with the noun that follows.

5. The English possessive forms ' and 's are equal to *el . . . de, la . . . de,* etc., in Spanish.

la madre de Pedro Peter's mother

Interrogatives

1. Common interrogatives are:

qué what	**de quién** whose
cuál *sing.,* **cuáles** *pl.* which	**a quién** to whom
quién *sing.,* **quiénes** *pl.* who	

¿Qué es esto? What is this?
¿Qué libro lees? What book are you reading?
¿De quién es este libro? Whose is this book?

2. Other interrogatives are:

cómo how	**cuánto** how much
dónde where	**cuántos** how many
por qué why	**para qué** what for

¿Cómo esta usted? How are you?
¿Cuánto cuesta esto?
How much does this cost?
¿Para qué vienes? What are you coming for?

Indefinites and Negatives

1. The indefinite adjectives are:

    algun(o), -a, -os, -as some, any, a few
    ningun(o), -a, -os, -as no, not any, any
    mucho, -a, -os, -as much, many
    poco, -a, -os, -as little, few
    otro, -a, -os, -as another, other(s)
    tanto, -a, -os, -as as much, as many
    todo, -a, -os, -as all, every
    ambos, -as both
    cualquiera, cualesquiera any one
    cada each (only one form)
    tanto . . . como as much . . . as

2. The indefinite pronouns are:

    alguien (persons) someone, somebody, anyone
    algun(o), -a, -os, -as someone, anyone
    algo something
    nadie (persons) no one, nobody, none, no
    ningun(o), -a, -os, -as no one, nobody, none, no
    cualquier(a) (persons) any one
    otro, -a, -os, -as other, others

3. Important negatives are:

    nada nothing   **nunca** never   **no** no

4. Double negation is common in Spanish.

    No quiero nada.

      I want nothing. / I do not want anything.

Relative Pronouns

1. Relative pronouns are similar to the interrogatives, but are written without accent.

2. The relative pronouns are:

    (*a*) **que** that, which, who, whom

        El coche que compré está estropeado.
          The car that I bought does not work.

(b) **quien (quienes)** who, whom   Used usually instead of **que** after prepositions in secondary clauses, **quien** refers to persons only.

La persona de quien hablas ha muerto.
The person of whom you are talking is dead.

(c) **el (la, los, las) que / el (la) cual / los (las) cuales**   the one (s) who   Used instead of **que** or **quien** to avoid ambiguity or to emphasize:

Las personas de las cuales te hablo son muy extrañas.
The persons of whom I am talking are very strange.

(d) **lo que**   that, what   Used when referring to abstract objects or facts:

Viajar es lo que mas me gusta.
To travel is (that) what I like most.

Demonstratives

1. The demonstrative adjectives are:

este, -a	this	**estos, -as**	these
ese, -a	that	**esos, -as**	those
aquel, aquella	that (over there)		
aquellos, -as	those (over there)		

They precede the noun they modify:

este niño   this boy   **aquellos libros**   those books

2. The demonstrative pronouns are:

éste, -a	this one	**éstos, -as**	these ones
ése, -a	that one	**ésos, -as**	those ones
aquél, -lla	that one (over there)		

Note that these pronouns have a written accent and the adjectives do not.

The pronouns do not modify any noun.

Mira, éste es mi hijo.   Look, this is my son.

When referring to some abstract or general noun, the neuter form of the pronoun should be used:

esto, eso, aquello

Notice that these forms do not have a written accent.

Esto es impossible.   This is impossible.

Personal Pronouns

1. The forms of the personal pronouns are:

	SUBJECT		
I	yo	we	nosotros, -as
you	tú	you	vosotros, -sa*
you	usted	you	ustedes*
he	él	they	ellos
she	ella	they	ellas
it	ello		

	INDIRECT OBJECT	DIRECT OBJECT	AFTER PREPOSITION
me	me	me	mi
you	te	te	ti
you	le	le, lo *m.,** la *f.*	usted
him	le	le, lo	el
her	le	la	ella
it	le	lo *m.,* la *f.*	el, elle, ello
us	nos	nos	nosotros, -as
you	os	os	vosotros, -as
you	les	los	ustedes
them	les	las	ellos
them	les	los *m.,* las *f.*	ellas

*The second person of the plural is rarely used in Latin American Spanish. **Ustedes** is the form used.

The form **le is used in Castilian Spanish, **lo** in Latin American Spanish.

2. Indirect and direct objects precede the verb.
EXCEPTIONS: If the verb is in the imperative form, the object(s) follows and is attached to the verb.

dame   give me

If the verb phrase has an infinitive or gerund, the object(s) either follows and is attached to the infinitive or gerund form or precedes the auxiliary verb.

> **Estoy haciéndolo.** I am doing it.
> **Lo estoy haciendo.** I am doing it.

3. If both direct and indirect objects are present, the indirect precedes the direct object. If the preposition is present, it follows the verb.

> **Te lo digo.** I tell it to you.
> **Te lo digo a ti.** I tell it to you.

(The prepositional phrase is added for emphasis.)

4. *Lo* and *les* change to *se* before *la*, *le*, and *lo*.

> **Se lo digo.** I tell it to him.   (Not: Le lo digo.)

Adverbs

1. Most adverbs of manner are formed by adding *-mente* to the singular feminine form of the corresponding adjective.

> **verdadero** true   **verdaderamente** truly

2. When two or more of these adverbs come in a series, the *-mente* suffix is omitted from all but the last.

> **Habla clara y distintamente.**
> He speaks clearly and distinctly.

3. The comparative and the superlative are formed by placing before the adverb *más* and *lo más*, respectively.

> **más claramente** more clearly
> **lo más claramente** most clearly

4. Some irregular comparatives are:

bien	well	**mejor**	better
mal	badly	**peor**	worse
mucho	much	**más**	more
poco	little	**menos**	less

Conjunctions

The more important conjunctions are *y*, and; *o*, or; *pero*, but.

1. *Y* changes to *e* if the following word begins with *i*.

costoso e inútil   expensive and useless

2. *O* changes to *u* if the following word begins with *o*.

uno u otro   one or the other (one of the two)

3. *Pero* can be replaced by *mas* and should be replaced by *sino* in a contradictory statement that follows a negative sentence.

No quiero morir, sino vivir.
I do not want to die, but to live.

Prepositions

Most of the Spanish prepositions are used in the same sense as their English counterparts in ordinary speech. Others, however, have some important differences from their English correspondents. They are: *a*, *de*, *para*, *por*.

1. *A* expresses direction or motion toward a place (to) and is used after all verbs of motion.

Voy a casa.   I am going home.

A is used also to express purpose and after other verbs of beginning, teaching, or learning.

Empiezo a comer.   I am starting to eat.

A is always used before a direct object referring to a definite person (or personified animal or thing).

Amo a mis padres.   I love my parents.

A is omitted if the object is an indefinite person or when it follows *tener*.

Este hombre necesita un médico.
This man needs a doctor.
Tiene padre y madre.   He has father and mother.

2. *De* expresses possession, origin, or intended use of a thing.

> **el libro de Pedro**   Peter's book
> **¿De dónde es usted?**   Where are you from?
> **casa de campo**   country house

When referring to the result of an action, *in* and *with* should be translated by *de*, instead of by *con*, which is used to refer to the means that lead to such a result. *De* is also used to denote a characteristic of the noun involved in the description.

El coche está pintado de rojo.   The car is painted (in) red.
El hombre del abrigo gris   the man with the gray coat

3. Prepositions *por and para*.

Para indicates finality (destination, purpose, use, future time).

Lo dejo para mañana.   I am leaving it for tomorrow.
Voy para allá.   I am going up there.

Para is used for "to be about to."

El tren está para salir.   The train is about to leave.

Por expresses (1) motivation (for, out of, because of, in behalf of); (2) the agent or means of an action; (3) time (during).

(1) **El soldado muere por su patria.**
     The soldier dies for his country.
(2) **hablar por teléfono**   communicate by phone
(3) **La tienda está abierta por la mañana.**
     The store is open in (during) the morning.

In exchange for, *through*, *along*, *around*, are sometimes translated by *por*.

Saltó por la ventana.   He jumped through the window.

Use *por* after *ir*, *venir*, *mandar*, *preguntar* to mean *in search of*, *for*.

> **Preguntan por ti.**   They ask for you.

Sometimes purpose and motivation are not distinguishable, and either *por* or *para* can be used.

> **¿Por qué vienes? ¿Para qué vienes?**
> What are you coming for?

Verbs

1. Regular verbs. There are three conjugations in Spanish: verbs whose infinitive ends in *-ar;* verbs whose infinitive ends in *-er;* and verbs whose infinitive ends in *-ir.* Each tense is formed by adding the appropriate endings for person, tense, and mood to the common stem of the verb.

	FIRST CONJUGATION	SECOND CONJUGATION	THIRD CONJUGATION
INF.	am-ar	tem-er	viv-ir
	to love	to fear	to live
PRES. PART.	am-ando	tem-iendo	viv-iendo
	loving	fearing	living
PAST PART.	am-ado	tem-ido	viv-ido
	loved	feared	lived

INDICATIVE MOOD

PRESENT: I love, etc. I fear, etc. I live, etc.

am-o	tem-o	viv-o
-as	-es	-es
-a	-e	-e
-amos	-emos	-imos
-áis	-éis	-ís
-an	-en	-en

(NOTE: The pronouns *yo, tú,* etc., may be omitted in Spanish because the verb endings indicate person.)

IMPERFECT: I loved, I was loving, I used to love, etc.

am-aba	tem-ía	viv-ía
-abas	-ías	-ías
-aba	-ía	-ía
-ábamos	-íamos	-íamos
-abais	-íais	-íais
-aban	-ían	-ían

PRETERIT: I loved, etc.

am-é	tem-í	viv-í
-aste	-iste	-iste
-ó	-ió	-ió

	-amos	-imos	-imos
	-asteis	-isteis	-isteis
	-aron	-ieron	-ieron

FUTURE: I shall or will love, etc.

am-aré	tem-eré	viv-iré
-arás	-erás	-irás
-ará	-erá	-irá
-aremos	-eremos	-iremos
-aréis	-eréis	-iréis
-arán	-erán	-irán

CONDITIONAL: I should or would love, etc.

am-aría	tem-ería	viv-iría
-arías	-erías	-irías
-aría	-ería	-iría
-aríamos	-eríamos	-iríamos
-aríais	-eríais	-iríais
-arían	-erían	-irían

Compound tenses are formed by adding the past participle of the verb being conjugated to the proper tense of the auxiliary verb *haber*. (WARNING: *Haber* is of the second conjugation, but is an irregular verb.)

PERFECT INF.: haber amado, temido, vivido
             to have loved, feared, lived

PERFECT PART.: habiendo amado, temido, vivido
             having loved, feared, lived

PRESENT PERFECT: I have loved, feared, lived, etc.
             he amado, temido, vivido
             has amado, temido, vivido
             ha amado, temido, vivido
             hemos amado, temido, vivido
             habéis amado, temido, vivido
             han amado, temido, vivido

PLUPERFECT: I had loved, feared, lived, etc.
             había amado, temido, vivido
             habías amado, temido, vivido
             había amado, temido, vivido
             habíamos amado, temido, vivido

                habíais amado, temido, vivido
                habían amado, temido, vivido

FUTURE PERFECT: I will have loved, feared, lived, etc.
                habré amado, temido, vivido
                habrás amado, temido, vivido
                habrá amado, temido, vivido
                habremos amado, temido, vivido
                habréis amado, temido, vivido
                habrán amado, temido, vivido

CONDITIONAL PERFECT: I would have loved, feared, lived, etc.
                habría amado, temido, vivido
                habrías amado, temido, vivido
                habría amado, temido, vivido
                habríamos amado, temido, vivido
                habríais amado, temido, vivido
                habrían amado, temido, vivido

SUBJUNCTIVE MOOD

PRESENT:	am-e	tem-a	viv-a
	-es	-as	-as
	-e	-a	-a
	-emos	-amos	-amos
	-éis	-áis	-áis
	-en	-an	-an

IMPERFECT: This tense has two forms: the -se form and the -ra form.

-RA FORM	am-ara	tem-iera	viv-iera
	-aras	-ieras	-ieras
	-ara	-iera	-iera
	-áramos	-iéramos	-iéramos
	-arais	-ierais	-ierais
	-aran	-ieran	-ieran
-SE FORM	am-ase	tem-iese	viv-iese
	-ases	-ieses	-ieses
	-ase	-iese	-iese
	-ásemos	-iésemos	-iésemos
	-aseis	-ieseis	-ieseis
	-asen	-iesen	-iesen

The -ra form indicates possibility:

> **Yo amara las riquezas.**
> I would love riches.

The -se form conveys condition:

> **. . . se me diesen la salud.**
> . . . if they would give me health.

The future subjunctive is used very seldom.

The present perfect subjunctive and pluperfect subjunctive are formed by adding the past participle of the main verb to the present and imperfect subjunctives of *haber*.

PRESENT PERFECT:

> haya amado, temido, vivido
> hayas amado, temido, vivido
> haya amado, temido, vivido
> hayamos, amado, temido, vivido
> hayáis amado, temido, vivido
> hayan amado, temido, vivido

PLUPERFECT:

> hubiera (hubiese) amado, temido, vivido
> hubieras (hubieses) amado, temido, vivido
> hubiera (hubiese) amado, temido, vivido
> hubiéramos (hubiésemos)
>   amado, temido, vivido
> hubierais (hubieseis) amado, temido, vivido
> hubieran (hubiesen) amado, temido, vivido

The subjunctive mood is used in Spanish in dependent clauses in which a possibility or a subjective attitude or a contrary-to-fact statement is presented. Most often it occurs in a dependent clause that begins with *que*.

> **Dudo que venga.**
> I doubt that he is coming (he will come).
> **Siento que vivas así.**
> I regret you live in such a manner.

BUT: **Estoy seguro que viene.** (indicative)

> I am sure he is coming (he will come).

Sometimes in a dependent clause the infinitive replaces the

subjunctive. This construction occurs, as it also does in English, when the subject of the main clause is the same as that of the dependent clause.

> **No me gusta que hables así.** (subjunctive)
> I do not like you to talk in that way.
> **No me gusta hablar así.** (infinitive)
> I do not like to talk in that way. (same subject)

Other verbs that may take either the infinitive or subjunctive construction in the dependent clause are:

aconsejar advise   **mandar** command   **permitir** permit

Most impersonal expressions use the subjunctive form:

> **Es posible que muera.**   It is possible that he may die.
> **Puede ser que venga.**   Maybe he will come.

Notice that the present subjunctive sometimes expresses a future action. If the verb of the main clause has the past form, the corresponding subjunctive of the dependent clause must, however, be in the past form also.

> **No esperaba que (usted) viniera** (or **viniese**).
> I did not expect that you would come. / I did not expect you to come.

IMPERATIVE MOOD

ama (tú)	teme (tú)	vive (tú)
amad (vosotros)	temed (vosotros)	vivid (vosotros)

The imperative is used for informal positive commands. Formal commands take the subjunctive.

ame (usted)	tema (used)	viva (usted)
amen (ustedes)	teman (ustedes)	vivan (ustedes)

Formal and informal negative commands take the subjunctive mood.

no ames (tú)	no temas (tú)	no vivas (tú)
no ame (usted)	no tema (usted)	no viva (usted)
no améis (vosotros)	no temáis (vosotros)	no viváis (vosotros)
no amen (ustedes)	no teman (ustedes)	no vivan (ustedes)

NOTE: In Latin American Spanish, the imperative form is used less than the subjunctive form.

2. Irregular verbs. The following list contains the most important irregular Spanish verbs. Since none of the verbs is irregular throughout all of the basic tenses and moods, only those tenses having irregular forms are given.

andar walk
PRESENT PARTICIPLE andando
PAST PARTICIPLE andado
PRETERIT anduve, anduviste, anduvo, anduvimos, anduvisteis, aduvieron
IMPERFECT SUBJUNCTIVE *1* anduviese, anduvieses, anduviese, anduviésemos, anduvieseis, anduviesen
IMPERFECT SUBJUNCTIVE *2* anduviera, anduvieras, anduviera, anduviéramos, anduvierais, anduvieran

caber fit into
PRESENT PARTICIPLE cabiendo
PAST PARTICIPLE cabido
PRESENT quepo, cabes, cabe, cabemos, cabéis, caben
PRETERIT cupe, cupiste, cupo, cupimos, cupisteis, cupieron
FUTURE cabré, cabrás, cabrá, cabremos, cabréis, cabrán
CONDITIONAL cabría, cabrías, cabríamos, cabríais, cabrían
PRESENT SUBJUNCTIVE quepa, quepas, quepa, quepamos, quepáis, quepan
IMPERFECT SUBJUNCTIVE *1* cupiese, cupieses, cupiese, cupiésemos, cupieseis, cupiesen
IMPERFECT SUBJUNCTIVE *2* cupiera, cupieras, cupiera, cupiéramos, cupierais, cupieran

dar give
PRESENT PARTICIPLE dando
PAST PARTICIPLE dado
PRESENT doy, das, da, damos, dais, dan
PRETERIT di, diste, dio, dimos, disteis, dieron
PRESENT SUBJUNCTIVE dé, des, dé, demos, deis, den
IMPERFECT SUBJUNCTIVE *1* diese, dieses, diese, diésemos, dieseis, diesen

IMPERFECT SUBJUNCTIVE 2 diera, dieras, diera, diéramos, dierais, dieran

decir   say, tell
PRESENT PARTICIPLE diciendo
PAST PARTICIPLE dicho
PRESENT digo, dices, dice, decimos, decís, dicen
PRETERIT dije, dijiste, dijo, dijimos, dijisteis, dijeron
FUTURE diré, dirás, dirá, diremos, diréis, dirán
CONDITIONAL diría, dirías, diría, diríamos, diríais, dirían
IMPERATIVE di, decid
PRESENT SUBJUNCTIVE diga, digas, diga, digamos, digáis, digan
IMPERFECT SUBJUNCTIVE 1 dijese, dijeses, dijese, dijésemos, dijeseis, dijesen
IMPERFECT SUBJUNCTIVE 2 dijera, dijeras, dijera, dijéramos, dijerais, dijeran

estar   be
PRESENT PARTICIPLE estando
PAST PARTICIPLE estado
PRESENT estoy, estás, está, estamos, estáis, están
PRETERIT estuve, estuviste, estuvo, estuvimos, estuvisteis, estuvieron
IMPERATIVE está, estad
PRESENT SUBJUNCTIVE esté, estés, esté, estemos, estéis, estén
IMPERFECT SUBJUNCTIVE 1 estuviese, estuvieses, estuviese, estuviésemos, estuvieseis, estuviesen
IMPERFECT SUBJUNCTIVE 2 estuviera, estuvieras, estuviera, estuviéramos, estuvierais, estuvieran

haber   have
PRESENT PARTICIPLE habiendo
PAST PARTICIPLE habido
PRESENT he, has, ha, hemos, habéis, han
PRETERIT hube, hubiste, hubo, hubimos, hubisteis, hubieron
FUTURE habré, habrás, habrá, habremos, habréis, habrán
CONDITIONAL habría, habrías, habría, habríamos, habríais,

habrían
IMPERATIVE he, habed
PRESENT SUBJUNCTIVE haya, hayas, haya, hayamos, hayáis, hayan
IMPERFECT SUBJUNCTIVE *1* hubiese, hubieses, hubiese, hubiésemos, hubieseis, hubiesen
IMPERFECT SUBJUNCTIVE *2* hubiera, hubieras, hubiera, hubiéramos, hubierais, hubieran

hacer make, do
PRESENT PARTICIPLE haciendo
PAST PARTICIPLE hecho
PRESENT hago, haces, hace, hacemos, hacéis, hacen
PRETERIT hice, hiciste, hizo, hicimos, hicisteis, hicieron
FUTURE haré, harás, hará, haremos, haréis, harán
CONDITIONAL haría, harías, haría, haríamos, haríais, harían
IMPERATIVE haz, haced
PRESENT SUBJUNCTIVE haga, hagas, haga, hagamos, hagáis, hagan
IMPERFECT SUBJUNCTIVE *1* hiciese, hicieses, hiciese, hiciésemos, hicieseis, hiciesen
IMPERFECT SUBJUNCTIVE *2* hiciera, hicieras, hiciera, hiciéramos, hicierais, hicieran

ir go
PRESENT PARTICIPLE yendo
PAST PARTICIPLE ido
PRESENT voy, vas, va, vamos, vais, van
IMPERFECT iba, ibas, iba, íbamos, ibais, iban
PRETERIT fuí, fuiste, fué, fuimos, fuisteis, fueron
IMPERATIVE ve, id
PRESENT SUBJUNCTIVE vaya, vayas, vaya, vayamos, vayáis, vayan
IMPERFECT SUBJUNCTIVE *1* fuese, fueses, fuese, fuésemos, fueseis, fuesen
IMPERFECT SUBJUNCTIVE *2* fuera, fueras, fuera, fuéramos, fuerais, fueran

oír hear

PRESENT PARTICIPLE oyendo
PAST PARTICIPLE oído
PRESENT oigo, oyes, oye, oímos, oís, oyen
PRETERIT oí, oíste, oyó, oímos, oísteis, oyeron
IMPERATIVE oye, oíd
PRESENT SUBJUNCTIVE oiga, oigas, oiga, oigamos, oigáis,
  oigan
IMPERFECT SUBJUNCTIVE *1* oyese, oyeses, oyese, oyésemos,
  oyeseis, oyesen
IMPERFECT SUBJUNCTIVE *2* oyera, oyeras, oyera, oyéramos,
  oyerais, oyeran

poder be able

PRESENT PARTICIPLE pudiendo
PAST PARTICIPLE podido
PRESENT puedo, puedes, puede, podemos, podéis, pueden
PRETERIT pude, pudiste, pudo, pudimos, pudisteis, pudieron
FUTURE podré, podrás, podrá, podremos, podréis, podrán
PRESENT SUBJUNCTIVE pueda, puedas, pueda, podamos,
  podáis, puedan
IMPERFECT SUBJUNCTIVE *1* pudiese, pudieses, pudiese,
  pudiésemos, pudieseis, pudiesen
IMPERFECT SUBJUNCTIVE *2* pudiera, pudieras, pudiera,
  pudiéramos, pudierais, pudieran

poner put

PRESENT PARTICIPLE poniendo
PAST PARTICIPLE puesto
PRESENT pongo, pones, pone, ponemos, ponéis, ponen
PRETERIT puse, pusiste, puso, pusimos, pusisteis, pusieron
FUTURE pondré, pondrás, pondrá, pondremos, pondréis,
  pondrán
IMPERATIVE pon, poned
PRESENT SUBJUNCTIVE ponga, pongas, pongamos, pongáis,
  pongan
IMPERFECT SUBJUNCTIVE *1* pusiese, pusieses, pusiésemos,
  pusieseis, pusiesen

IMPERFECT SUBJUNCTIVE 2 pusiera, pusieras, pusiera,
  pusiéramos, pusierais, pusieran

querer want
PRESENT PARTICIPLE queriendo
PAST PARTICIPLE querido
PRESENT quiero, quieres, quiere, queremos, queréis, quieren
PRETERIT quise, quisiste, quiso, quisimos, quisisteis, quisieron
FUTURE querré, querrás, querrá, querremos, querréis, querrán
IMPERATIVE quiere, quered
PRESENT SUBJUNCTIVE quiera, quieras, quiera, queramos,
  queráis, quieran
IMPERFECT SUBJUNCTIVE 1 quisiese, quisieses, quisiese,
  quisiésemos, quisieseis, quisiesen
IMPERFECT SUBJUNCTIVE 2 quisiera, quisieras, quisiera,
  quisiéramos, quisierais, quisieran

saber know
PRESENT PARTICIPLE sabiendo
PAST PARTICIPLE sabido
PRESENT sé, sabes, sabe, sabemos, sabéis, saben
PRETERIT supe, supiste, supo, supimos, supisteis, supieron
FUTURE sabré, sabrás, sabrá, sabremos, sabréis, sabrán
PRESENT SUBJUNCTIVE sepa, sepas, sepa, sepamos, sepáis,
  sepan
IMPERFECT SUBJUNCTIVE 1 supiese, supieses, supiese,
  supiésemos, supieseis, supiesen
IMPERFECT SUBJUNCTIVE 2 supiera, supieras, supiera,
  supiéramos, supierais, supieran

salir go out
PRESENT PARTICIPLE saliendo
PAST PARTICIPLE salido
PRESENT salgo, sales, sale, salimos, salís, salen
FUTURE saldré, saldrás, saldrá, saldremos, saldréis, saldrán
CONDITIONAL saldría, saldrías, saldría, saldríamos, saldríais,
  saldrían
IMPERATIVE sal, salid

PRESENT SUBJUNCTIVE salga, salgas, salga, salgamos, salgáis, salgan

ser be
PRESENT PARTICIPLE siendo
PAST PARTICIPLE sido
PRESENT soy, eres, es, somos, sois, son
IMPERFECT era, eras, era, éramos, erais, eran
PRETERIT fui, fuiste, fue, fuimos, fuisteis, fueron
IMPERATIVE sé, sed
PRESENT SUBJUNCTIVE sea, seas, sea, seamos, seáis, sean
IMPERFECT SUBJUNCTIVE *1* fuese, fueses, fuese, fuésemos, fueseis, fuesen
IMPERFECT SUBJUNCTIVE *2* fuera, fueras, fuera, fuéramos, fuerais, fueran

tener have
PRESENT PARTICIPLE teniendo
PAST PARTICIPLE tenido
PRESENT tengo, tienes, tiene, tenemos, tenéis, tienen
PRETERIT tuve, tuviste, tuvo, tuvimos, tuvisteis, tuvieron
FUTURE tendré, tendrás, tendrá, tendremos, tendréis, tendrán
CONDITIONAL tendría, tendrías, tendría, tendríamos, tendríais, tendrían
IMPERATIVE ten, tened
PRESENT SUBJUNCTIVE tenga, tengas, tenga, tengamos, tengáis, tengan
IMPERFECT SUBJUNCTIVE *1* tuviese, tuvieses, tuviese, tuviésemos, tuvieseis, tuviesen
IMPERFECT SUBJUNCTIVE *2* tuviera, tuvieras, tuviera, tuviéramos, tuvierais, tuvieran

traducir translate
PRESENT PARTICIPLE traduciendo
PAST PARTICIPLE traducido
PRESENT traduzco, traduces, traduce, traducimos, traducís, traducen
PRETERIT traduje, tradujiste, tradujo, tradujimos, tradujisteis,

tradujeron

PRESENT SUBJUNCTIVE traduzca, traduzcas, traduzca,
traduzcamos, traduzcáis, traduzcan

IMPERFECT SUBJUNCTIVE *1* tradujese, tradujeses, tradujese,
tradujésemos, tradujeseis, tradujesen

IMPERFECT SUBJUNCTIVE *2* tradujera, tradujeras, tradujera,
tradujéramos, tradujerais, tradujeran

traer bring

PRESENT PARTICIPLE trayendo

PAST PARTICIPLE traído

PRESENT traigo, traes, trae, traemos, traéis, traen

PRETERIT traje, trajiste, trajo, trajimos, trajisteis, trajeron

PRESENT SUBJUNCTIVE traiga, traigas, traiga, traigamos,
traigáis, traigan

IMPERFECT SUBJUNCTIVE *1* trajese, trajeses, trajésemos,
trajeseis, trajesen

IMPERFECT SUBJUNCTIVE *2* trajera, trajeras, trajera, trajéramos,
trajerais, trajeran

valer be worth

PRESENT PARTICIPLE valiendo

PAST PARTICIPLE valido

PRESENT valgo, vales, vale, valemos, valéis, valen

FUTURE valdré, valdrás, valdrá, valdremos, valdréis, valdrán

CONDITIONAL valdría, valdrías, valdría, valdríamos, valdríais,
valdrían

IMPERATIVE val(e), valed

PRESENT SUBJUNCTIVE valga, valgas, valga, valgamos, valgáis,
valgan

venir come

PRESENT PARTICIPLE viniendo

PAST PARTICIPLE venido

PRESENT vengo, venes, viene, venimos, venís, vienen

PRETERIT vine, viniste, vino, vinimos, vinisteis, vinieron

FUTURE vendré, vendrás, vendrá, vendremos, vendréis,
vendrán

CONDITIONAL vendría, vendrías, vendría, vendríamos,
   vendríais, vendrían
IMPERATIVE ven, venid
PRESENT SUBJUNCTIVE venga, vengas, venga, vengamos,
   vengáis, vengan
IMPERFECT SUBJUNCTIVE *1* viniese, vinieses, viniese,
   viniésemos, vinieseis, viniesen
IMPERFECT SUBJUNCTIVE *2* viniera, vinieras, viniera,
   viniéramos, vinierais, vinieran

ver see
PRESENT PARTICIPLE viendo
PAST PARTICIPLE visto
PRESENT veo, ves, ve, vemos, veis, ven
IMPERFECT veía, veías, veía, veíamos, veíais, veían
PRETERIT vi, viste, vio, vimos, visteis, vieron
PRESENT SUBJUNCTIVE vea, veas, vea, veamos, veáis, vean
IMPERFECT SUBJUNCTIVE *1* viese, vieses, viese, viésemos,
   vieseis, viesen
IMPERFECT SUBJUNCTIVE *2* viera, vieras, viera, viéramos.
   vierais, vieran

   3. Stem-changing verbs. There are three groups or classes.
   (*a*) The first class verbs belong to the first and second
conjugations (see Section 1). These verbs change the stem
vowel *e* to *ie* and *o* to *ue* in the first and second persons of the
singular and in the third of the singular and plural. The first
and second persons of the plural are regular.
   NOTE: With all of the examples following, only the tenses
with irregular forms are given and the irregular forms are
italicized.

pensar to think
PRESENT INDICATIVE *pienso, piensas, piensa,* pensamos,
   pensáis, *piensan*
PRESENT SUBJUNCTIVE *piense, pienses, piense,* pensemos,
   penséis, *piensen*
IMPERATIVE *piensa,* pensad

Other verbs that change *e* to *ie* are:

cerrar to close	**entender** to understand
empezar to begin	**negar** to deny
nevar to snow	**perder** to lose

volver to return

PRESENT INDICATIVE *vuelvo, vuelves, vuelve*, volvemos, volvéis, *vuelven*

PRESENT SUBJUNCTIVE *vuelva, vuelvas, vuelva*, volvamos, volváis, *vuelvan*

IMPERATIVE *vuelve*, volved

Other verbs that change *o* to *ue* are:

accordarse to remember	**mostrar** to show
acostar to go to bed	**mover** to move
costar to cost	**recordar** to remember
encontrar to find	

(*b*) The second class verbs belong to the third conjugation (see Section 1). These verbs have the same changes as those of the first class plus a change from *e* to *i* or from *o* to *u* in the following cases:

The first and second persons of the plural in the present subjunctive.

The third person of the singular and plural in the preterit.

All persons in the imperfect subjunctive.

sentir to feel

PRESENT SUBJUNCTIVE *sienta, sientas, sienta, sintamos, sintáis, sientan*

PRETERIT sentí, sentiste, *sintió*, sentimos, sentisteis, *sintieron*

IMPERFECT SUBJUNCTIVE *sintiera, sintieras*, etc.

PRESENT PARTICIPLE *sintiendo*

Other verbs that follow the same pattern as sentir are:

consentir to consent	**convertir** to convert
divertir to amuse	**sugerir** to suggest

dormir to sleep

PRESENT SUBJUNCTIVE duerma, duermas, duerma, *durmamos*, *durmáis*, duerman

PRETERIT dormí, dormiste, *durmió*, dormimos, dormisteis, *durmieron*

IMPERFECT SUBJUNCTIVE *durmiera*, *durmieras*, etc.

PRESENT PARTICIPLE durmiendo

Morir, to die, follows the same pattern as *dormir*.

(*c*) The third class verbs belong to the third conjugation (see Section 1). In these verbs, the *e* changes to *i* in each place where any change occurs in verbs of the second class.

pedir to ask

PRESENT INDICATIVE *pido*, *pides*, *pide*, etc.

PRETERIT pedí, pediste, *pidió*, pedimos, pedisteis, *pidieron*, etc.

4. Verbs with spelling changes. In some verbs, there is a change in spelling in order to preserve the sound of the infinitive. For example, the verb *acercar*, to approach: *c* before *a*, *o*, *u* has the sound of *k*, but before *e* and *i*, *c* has the sound of *th*. In order to preserve the *k* sound in *acercar*, the preterit is *acerqué*, *acercaste*, *acercó*, etc. There are many verbs like this. The most common are changes from *c* to *qu*, from *g* to *gu*, from *z* to *c*, and vice versa. These verbs are listed as regular verbs.

5. Some common irregular past participles are the following:

abrir open **abierto**
componer repair, compose **compuesto**
cubrir cover **cubierto**
decir say, tell **dicho**
describir describe **descrito**
deshacer get rid of **deshecho**
envolver wrap **envuelto**
escribir write **escrito**
freir fry **frito**

hacer do, make **hecho**
imprimir print **impreso**
morir die **muerto**
proveer provide **provisto**
resolver decide **resuelto**
satisfacer satisfy **satisfecho**
ver see **visto**
volver return **vuelto**

6. The reflexive verb. Many Spanish verbs are reflexive. Some of them are:

acostarse to go to bed
acordarse to remember
fijarse to notice

Ordinary verbs become reflexive when used with reflexive pronouns to stress that the subject is acting upon itself.

lavar to wash
me lavo I wash myself
te lavas you wash yourself
se lava he washes himself
nos lavamos we wash ourselves
os laváis you wash yourselves
se lavan they wash themselves

The meaning of some verbs changes when they are in the reflexive form.

ir to go **irse** to go away, to leave
volver to return **volverse** to turn around

The reflexive form usually replaces the passive voice in those cases when the agent is not expressed.

Se abrirán las puertas mañana.
The doors will be open tomorrow.

7. *Ser* and *Estar*. Both verbs mean "to be." As in English, they link something to the subject of the sentence, but in different ways: *ser* links to the subject something that tells *what* the subject is, in other words, something that is intrinsic to the nature of the subject; *estar* links to the subject things that *do not really "belong"* to it, something that is added from the

outside. Examples:

Ser is used to link with the subject:

Adjectives that express a quality that belongs intrinsically to the subject:

> **Juan es simpático.**   John is friendly.

Nouns and pronouns:

> **Antonio es el menor de los hermanos.**
> Anthony is the youngest of the brothers.
> **Ellos son amigos.**   They are friends.

Expressions of possession or origin preceded by the preposition *de:*

Luis es de España.   Louis is from Spain.
Ese libro es de Antonio.   That book belongs to Anthony.

Estar is used:

To express location:

> **Carlos está aquí.**   Charles is here.

To link with the subject adjectives that express a transient condition of the subject or a quality that does not intrinsically belong to the subject:

> **La habitación está sucia.**   The room is dirty.

NOTE: In expressions of time of day, *ser* is always used:

> **¿Qué hora es? Son las tres y media.**
> What time is it? It is three-thirty.

Impersonal Expressions

1. *There is* and *there are* are both translated by *hay.*

   Hay muchas personas.   There are many persons.
   Hay una persona fuera.   There is a person outside.

2. *Hace* is used in expressions such as:

   > **Hace frío.**   It is cold.
   > **Hace una hora que vine.**
   > It has been an hour since I came.

Why We Make This Generous Offer

As a bonus to buyers of this book, Cortina Academy has arranged this special offer of a FREE Language Record and Lesson. Cortina Academy, the world-famous originator of the phonograph method of language learning, develops and publishes the most thorough and effective complete language courses available today. You have a special opportunity for introduction to these outstanding language materials—and there are several important reasons why you should take advantage of this opportunity *now*:

- Cortina's "learn-by-listening" Method is the *natural* way to learn;

- you learn almost without effort—at your own convenience;

- your rewards will be great—including the many business and travel opportunities available to speakers of foreign languages.

So take advantage of this unusual introductory offer. There is no obligation. Just mail the coupon today for your Free Language Record and Lesson.

Cortina Institute of Languages, Dept. GD-D 17 Riverside Ave., Westport, CT 06880

- -

(COUPON)

CORTINA INSTITUTE OF LANGUAGES

Dept. GD-D, **17 Riverside Avenue, Westport, CT 06880**

Please send me by mail—free of charge—the FREE Language Record and Lesson in the one language checked below; also a free booklet which describes fully the complete Course and Method.

(Please check language record you wish)

☐ Spanish ☐ French ☐ German ☐ Italian ☐ Brazilian-Portuguese
☐ Russian ☐ Japanese ☐ Modern Greek ☐ English (for Spanish- or Portuguese-speaking people)

Name ....

Address ....

City .... State .... Zip Code........
Offer good only in the U.S.A. and Canada.